# CLINICAL AND THERAPEUTIC NUTRITION PRACTICAL MANUAL 1

---For---
Semester III
M.Sc. Food Science and Nutrition

--- Author ---

Dr. Prajakta J. Nande

**BLUEROSE PUBLISHERS**
India | U.K.

Copyright © Dr. Prajakta J. Nande 2024

All rights reserved by author. No part of this publication may be reproduced, stored in a retrieval system or transmitted in any form or by any means, electronic, mechanical, photocopying, recording or otherwise, without the prior permission of the author. Although every precaution has been taken to verify the accuracy of the information contained herein, the publisher assumes no responsibility for any errors or omissions. No liability is assumed for damages that may result from the use of information contained within.

BlueRose Publishers takes no responsibility for any damages, losses, or liabilities that may arise from the use or misuse of the information, products, or services provided in this publication.

For permissions requests or inquiries regarding this publication, please contact:

BLUEROSE PUBLISHERS
www.BlueRoseONE.com
info@bluerosepublishers.com
+91 8882 898 898
+4407342408967

ISBN: 978-93-6452-634-0

First Edition: September 2024

# About the Author.......

**Dr. Prajakta J. Nande** is Senior Assistant Professor in Food Science and Nutrition in Department of Home Science, Rashtrasant Tukadoji Maharaj Nagpur University, Nagpur, Maharashtra. She has been involved in teaching and research at PG level in the field of Food Science and Nutrition since 25 years. She has extensive experience of research in the areas of sports nutrition, clinical and therapeutic nutrition, community nutrition and product development. She received her Ph.D. in sports nutrition. She is recipient of gold medals, awards and prizes for obtaining highest percentage of marks and for securing first position in merit list in B.Sc. and M.Sc. She has co-authored two books entitled *"Fitness Evaluation Tests for Competitive Sports"* and *"Diabetes Management: A Journey to Wellness through Nutrition and Lifestyle Choices"*. She has co-authored two practical manuals namely *"Advanced Food Science Practical Manual 1"* and *"Advanced Food Science Practical Manual 2"* written for M.Sc. Food Science and Nutrition students. More than 75 research papers are published in various esteemed National and International journals. Research papers and posters have been presented by many students under her guidance in National and International conferences. She is recognized Ph.D. Supervisor in Food Science and Nutrition. Six students have been awarded Ph.D. under her guidance and currently three students are working under her guidance for their doctoral research work. She has guided 115 M.Sc. students for their dissertation and research projects. She has completed one research project funded by Rashtrasant Tukadoji Maharaj Nagpur University. She worked as co-ordinator and secretary for national conferences, workshops, diet and health exhibitions. She has attended and participated in many national and international conferences, seminars, webinars, workshops and diet exhibitions. She is life member of Nutrition Society of India, Indian Dietetic Association and Home Science Association of India.

# Preface

Welcome to the *Clinical and Therapeutic Nutrition Practical Manual 1* specifically designed for M.Sc. students in Food Science and Nutrition for the subject Clinical and Therapeutic Nutrition. This manual is intended to serve as a vital tool for translating theoretical knowledge into practical expertise, preparing the students for the complexities and challenges of clinical nutrition practice.

In the field of Food Science and Nutrition, understanding the intricate relationship between diet, health, and disease is paramount. This manual provides a structured approach to mastering the application of nutritional principles in clinical settings. It is tailored to address the specific needs of students who are not only seeking academic excellence but also striving to make a tangible impact in the field of therapeutic nutrition.

In the pages that follow, students will find a series of hands-on exercises, case studies, and practical exercises that enhance the skills of the students in assessing nutritional needs and planning dietary interventions. Each section has been meticulously developed to enhance the student's ability to assess, plan, and implement nutritional interventions tailored to diverse patient needs.

The author's goal is to foster a learning environment where theory and practice seamlessly intersect. By engaging with the material, students will gain valuable experience in conducting nutritional assessments and developing therapeutic diet plans. This hands-on approach is crucial for developing the critical thinking and problem-solving skills required for success in clinical settings.

As students embark on this practical journey, the author encourages them to approach each exercise with curiosity and an open mind. The author trusts that this manual will serve as a valuable companion throughout their academic and professional endeavors, and wish them success in their exploration of clinical and therapeutic nutrition.

**Dr. Prajakta J. Nande**

# === CERTIFICATE ===

This is to certify that this practical record contains the bonafide practical work of Ms./Mrs.----------------------------------------- ----------------------------------- during the academic year---------------- for the class of M.Sc. Semester-III of Food Science and Nutrition for the subject Clinical and Therapeutic Nutrition-I.

Date:------------------------------------------------------------------------

| |
|---|
| **Overall Performance:** <br> **Practicals:** <br> **Attendance:** <br> **Record:** |

**Grades:**
$A^+$     : Outstanding
A       : Excellent
$B^+$    : Very Good
B       : Good
C       : Fair
D       : Poor

Signature with Stamp

**HEAD OF THE DEPARTMENT**

Signature with Stamp

**SUBJECT TEACHER**

# INDEX

| Sr. No. | Name of Practical | Page No. | Dates | Signature of Teacher |
|---|---|---|---|---|
| 1 | CALCULATION OF IDEAL BODY WEIGHT, BODY MASS INDEX, ENERGY REQUIREMENT AND DIVISION OF ENERGY INTO MACRONUTRIENTS | 1-6 | | |
| i | Aim [A]: To calculate the ideal body weight (IBW) | 2 | | |
| ii | Aim [B]: To calculate the body mass index (BMI) | 3 | | |
| iii | Aim [C]: To calculate the energy requirement | 4 | | |
| iv | Aim [D]: To calculate the percentage of energy derived from macronutrients (protein, fat and carbohydrate) | 5 | | |
| v | Results and Conclusion | 6 | | |
| 2 | STANDARDS FOR HOSPITAL DIETS: FORMULATION OF FOOD EXCHANGE LIST AND DETERMINATION OF COOKED MEASURES OF RAW EXCHANGES OF FREQUENTLY USED FOODS | 7-48 | | |
| i | Introduction of Food Exchange List | 8 | | |
| ii | Advantages of Food Exchange List | 9 | | |
| iii | Limitations of Food Exchange List | 9 | | |
| iv | Cereal and Millet Exchange | 10 | | |
| | Common Recipes using Cereal and Millet Exchange | 10-15 | | |
| v | Pulse and Legume Exchange | 16 | | |
| | Common Recipes using Pulse and Legume Exchange | 16-18 | | |
| vi | Vegetable Exchange: Vegetable Exchange A | 19-20 | | |
| vii | Vegetable Exchange: Vegetable Exchange B | 20-21 | | |
| | Common Recipes using Vegetable A and B Exchange | 21-24 | | |
| xiii | Fruit Exchange | 25-26 | | |
| | Common Recipes using Fruit Exchange | 27-29 | | |

| ivx | Milk Exchange | 30 | | |
|---|---|---|---|---|
| | Common Recipes using Milk Exchange | 30-38 | | |
| x | Nuts and Oil Seeds Exchange | 39 | | |
| xi | Dry Fruits Exchange | 39 | | |
| xii | Fat Exchange | 40 | | |
| xiii | Sugar and Starch Exchange | 40 | | |
| | Common Recipes using Sugar and Starch Exchange | 40-41 | | |
| xiv | Meat and Poultry Exchange | 42 | | |
| | Common Recipes using Egg | 42-45 | | |
| | Common Recipes using Chicken and Mutton | 46 | | |
| xv | Fish Exchange | 47 | | |
| | Common Recipes using Fish | 47-48 | | |
| 3 | **INVESTIGATIONS FOR DIAGNOSIS OF VARIOUS DISEASES - SYSTEM-WISE: PLANNING AND PREPARATION OF THERAPEUTIC DIETS** | **49-190** | | |
| I | **WEIGHT MANAGEMENT** | **51-85** | | |
| i | **NORMAL WEIGHT** AIM: To plan and prepare a day's diet for a normal weight person using a case study approach | 52-62 | | |
| ii | **UNDERWEIGHT** AIM: To plan and prepare a day's diet for a underweight person using a case study approach | 63-73 | | |
| iii | **OBESITY** AIM: To plan and prepare a day's diet for an obese person using a case study approach | 74-85 | | |
| II | **GASTROINTESTINAL TRACT DISORDERS** | **86-110** | | |
| i | **GASTRITIS** AIM: To plan and prepare a day's diet for an individual suffering from gastritis using a case study approach | 87-98 | | |
| ii | **PEPTIC ULCER** AIM: To plan and prepare a day's diet for an individual suffering from peptic ulcer using a case study approach | 99-110 | | |

| III | LIVER DISEASES | 111-163 | | |
|---|---|---|---|---|
| i | **HEPATITIS**<br>AIM: To plan and prepare a day's diet for an individual suffering from hepatitis using a case study approach | 112-123 | | |
| ii | **ALCOHOLIC CIRRHOSIS**<br>AIM: To plan and prepare a day's diet for an individual suffering from alcoholic cirrhosis using a case study approach | 124-135 | | |
| iii | **CIRRHOSIS OF LIVER WITH PORTAL HYPERTENSION AND ASCITES**<br>AIM: To plan and prepare a day's diet for an individual suffering from cirrhosis of liver with portal hypertension and ascites using a case study approach | 136-149 | | |
| iv | **HEPATIC COMA**<br>AIM: To plan and prepare a day's tube feeds for an individual suffering from hepatic coma using a case study approach | 150-163 | | |
| IV | CARDIOVASCULAR DISEASES | 164-190 | | |
| i | **HYPERTENSION**<br>AIM: To plan and prepare a day's diet for an individual suffering from hypertension using a case study approach | 165-177 | | |
| ii | **CORONARY HEART DISEASE**<br>AIM: To plan and prepare a day's diet for an individual suffering from coronary heart disease using a case study approach | 178-190 | | |
| V | ANNEXURES | 191-329 | | |
| 1 | Energy Content of Foods | 191-195 | | |
| 2 | Carbohydrate Content of Foods | 195-198 | | |
| 3 | Protein Content of Foods | 198-202 | | |
| 4 | Total Fat Content of Foods | 203-207 | | |
| 5 | Fiber Content of Foods | 207-217 | | |
| i | Soluble Dietary Fiber (SDF) | 207-210 | | |
| ii | Insoluble Dietary Fiber (IDF) | 210-214 | | |
| iii | Total Dietary Fiber (TDF) | 214-217 | | |

| 6 | Branched Chain Amino Acid Content of Foods | 217-230 | | |
|---|---|---|---|---|
| i | Isoleucine | 217-221 | | |
| ii | Leucine | 222-226 | | |
| iii | Valine | 226-230 | | |
| 7 | Aromatic Amino Acid Content of Foods | 231-244 | | |
| i | Phenylalanine | 231-235 | | |
| ii | Tryptophan | 235-240 | | |
| iii | Tyrosine | 240-244 | | |
| 8 | Fatty Acid and Cholesterol Content of Foods | 244-265 | | |
| i | Total Saturated Fatty Acid (TSFA) | 244-248 | | |
| ii | Total Monounsaturated Fatty Acid (TMUFA) | 248-252 | | |
| iii | Total Polyunsaturated Fatty Acid (TPUFA) | 252-256 | | |
| iv | Linoleic Acid (LA) (n6 Fatty Acid) | 257-260 | | |
| v | Alpha Linoleic Acid (ALA) (n3 Fatty Acid) | 261-264 | | |
| vi | Cholesterol | 264-265 | | |
| 9 | Sodium (Na) Content of Foods | 265-269 | | |
| 10 | Potassium (K) Content of Foods | 269-273 | | |
| 11 | Calcium (Ca) Content of Foods | 274-278 | | |
| 12 | Magnesium (Mg) Content of Foods | 278-282 | | |
| 13 | Iron (Fe) Content of Foods | 282-286 | | |
| 14 | Zinc (Zn) Content of Foods | 286-290 | | |
| 15 | Selenium (Se) Content of Foods | 290-293 | | |
| 16 | Thiamine (Vitamin B1) Content of Foods | 294-298 | | |
| 17 | Riboflavin (Vitamin B2) Content of Foods | 298-302 | | |
| 18 | Niacin (Vitamin B3) Content of Foods | 302-306 | | |
| 19 | Pyridoxine (Vitamin B6) Content of Foods | 306-310 | | |
| 20 | Total Folate (Vitamin B9) Content of Foods | 310-314 | | |
| 21 | Total Ascorbic Acid (Vitamin C) Content of Foods | 314-317 | | |
| 22 | Laboratory Reference Values: Blood, Plasma and Serum | 318-329 | | |

**Clinical and Therapeutic Nutrition Practical Manual 1**
For M.Sc. Food Science and Nutrition (Semester-III)

# PRACTICAL 1

## CALCULATION OF IDEAL BODY WEIGHT, BODY MASS INDEX, ENERGY REQUIREMENT AND DIVISION OF ENERGY INTO MACRONUTRIENTS

--- **Author** ---
Dr. Prajakta J. Nande

# Clinical and Therapeutic Nutrition Practical Manual 1
For M.Sc. Food Science and Nutrition (Semester-III)

## PRACTICAL: 1

Date:

## AIM [A]: To calculate the ideal body weight (IBW)

**Clinical and Therapeutic Nutrition Practical Manual 1**
For M.Sc. Food Science and Nutrition (Semester-III)

# AIM [B]: To calculate the body mass index (BMI)

## TABLE 1: BMI CLASSIFICATION

| Sr. No. | Classification | BMI (kg/m$^2$) |
|---------|----------------|----------------|
| 1 | **UNDERWEIGHT** | **<18.5** |
| i | Severe Thinness | <16.00 |
| ii | Moderate Thinness | 16.00-16.99 |
| iii | Mild Thinness | 17.00-18.49 |
| 2 | **NORMAL** | **18.50-22.99** |
| i | Pre-Obese | 23.00-24.99 |
| 3 | **OVERWEIGHT** | **25.00-29.99** |
| 4 | **OBESE** | **≥30.00** |
| i | Obese Class I | 30.00-34.99 |
| ii | Obese Class II | 35.00-39.99 |
| iii | Obese Class III | ≥40.00 |

--- **Author** ---
Dr. Prajakta J. Nande

# Clinical and Therapeutic Nutrition Practical Manual 1
For M.Sc. Food Science and Nutrition (Semester-III)

## AIM [C]: To calculate the energy requirement

# AIM [D]: To calculate the percentage of energy derived from macronutrients (protein, fat and carbohydrate)

**Protein:**

**Total Fat:**

**Carbohydrates:**

# Clinical and Therapeutic Nutrition Practical Manual 1
For M.Sc. Food Science and Nutrition (Semester-III)

**Results:**

**Conclusion:**

# PRACTICAL 2

## :STANDARDS FOR HOSPITAL DIETS:

## FORMULATION OF FOOD EXCHANGE LIST ANDDETERMINATION OF COOKED MEASURES OF RAW EXCHANGES OF FREQUENTLY USED FOODS

# PRACTICAL: 2

**Dates:**

## Introduction of Food Exchange List:

# Clinical and Therapeutic Nutrition Practical Manual 1
For M.Sc. Food Science and Nutrition (Semester-III)

## Advantages of Food Exchange List:

## Limitations of Food Exchange List:

**Clinical and Therapeutic Nutrition Practical Manual 1**
For M.Sc. Food Science and Nutrition (Semester-III)

# CEREAL AND MILLET EXCHANGE

One Exchange of Cereal and Millet = 30 g

One Exchange provides: Energy-100 kcal; Carbohydrate-21 g; Protein-3 g and Fat-0.5 g

| Food Stuffs | |
|---|---|
| Bajra | Rice Puffed |
| Barley | Wheat Flour Whole |
| Jowar | Wheat Flour, Refined |
| Maize, Dry | Wheat Semolina |
| Ragi | Wheat Bread (Brown) |
| Rice, Raw Milled | Wheat Bread (White) |
| Rice Flakes | Vermicelli |

# COMMON RECIPES USING CEREAL AND MILLET EXCHANGE

### 1. Recipe Card for Chapati

| S. No. | Ingredients | Quantity (g) | No. of Exchanges |
|---|---|---|---|
| 1. | Wheat flour | 30 | 1 |
| 2. | Oil | 5.5 | ½ |
| 3. | Water | As needed | - |
| Yield:1 Chapati **(Weight of Chapati:     g)** | | | |

### 1. Nutritive Value Chart for Chapati

| S. No. | Nutrients | Values |
|---|---|---|
| 1. | Energy (kcal) | 150 |
| 2. | Carbohydrates (g) | 21 |
| 3. | Protein (g) | 3 |
| 4. | Fat (g) | 6 |

--- Author ---
Dr. Prajakta J. Nande

# Clinical and Therapeutic Nutrition Practical Manual 1
For M.Sc. Food Science and Nutrition (Semester-III)

## 2. Recipe Card for Phulka

| S. No. | Ingredients | Quantity (g) | No. of Exchanges |
|--------|-------------|--------------|------------------|
| 1. | Wheat flour | 30 | 1 |
| 2. | Water | As needed | - |
| **Yield:** 2 Phulkas (**Weight per Phulka:** g) | | | |

## 2. Nutritive Value Chart for Phulka

| S. No. | Nutrients | Values |
|--------|-----------|--------|
| 1. | Energy (kcal) | 100 |
| 2. | Carbohydrates (g) | 21 |
| 3. | Protein (g) | 3 |
| 4. | Fat (g) | 0.5 |

## 3. Recipe Card for Bhakri

| S. No. | Ingredients | Quantity (g) | No. of Exchanges |
|--------|-------------|--------------|------------------|
| 1. | Jowar/Bajra/Ragi flour | 30 | 1 |
| 2. | Water | As needed | - |
| **Yield:** 1 Small Bhakri (**Weight of Bhakri:** g) | | | |

## 3. Nutritive Value Chart for Bhakri

| S. No. | Nutrients | Values |
|--------|-----------|--------|
| 1. | Energy (kcal) | 100 |
| 2. | Carbohydrates (g) | 21 |
| 3. | Protein (g) | 3 |
| 4. | Fat (g) | 0.5 |

## 4. Recipe Card forSpinach/Fenugreek Leaves Paratha

| S. No. | Ingredients | Quantity (g) | No. of Exchanges |
|--------|-------------|--------------|------------------|
| 1. | Wheat flour | 30 | 1 |
| 2. | Spinach/Fenugreek Leaves | 34 | ½ |
| 3. | Oil | 11 | 1 |
| 4. | Water | As needed | - |
| 5. | Salt | To taste | - |
| **Yield:** 2 Small Parathas (**Weight per Paratha:** g) | | | |

# Clinical and Therapeutic Nutrition Practical Manual 1
For M.Sc. Food Science and Nutrition (Semester-III)

### 4. Nutritive Value Chart for Spinach/Fenugreek Leaves Paratha

| S. No. | Nutrients | Values |
|--------|-----------|--------|
| 1. | Energy (kcal) | 212.5 |
| 2. | Carbohydrates (g) | 22.2 |
| 3. | Protein (g) | 4.0 |
| 4. | Fat (g) | 11.7 |

### 5. Recipe Card for Semolina Upma

| S. No. | Ingredients | Quantity (g) | No. of Exchanges |
|--------|-------------|--------------|------------------|
| 1. | Semolina | 30 | 1 |
| 2. | Onion | 27 | ¼ |
| 3. | Green Chillies | 5 | - |
| 4. | Oil | 5.5 | ½ |
| 5. | Salt | To taste | - |
| 6. | Water | As needed | - |
| **Yield:** 1 Medium Bowl **(Cooked Weight:     g)** | | | |

### 5. Nutritive Value Chart for Semolina Upma

| S. No. | Nutrients | Values |
|--------|-----------|--------|
| 1. | Energy (kcal) | 159 |
| 2. | Carbohydrates (g) | 22.05 |
| 3. | Protein (g) | 3.18 |
| 4. | Fat (g) | 6.01 |

### 6. Recipe Card for Poha

| S. No. | Ingredients | Quantity (g) | No. of Exchanges |
|--------|-------------|--------------|------------------|
| 1. | Rice Flakes | 30 | 1 |
| 2. | Onion | 27 | ¼ |
| 3. | Potato | 23 | ½ |
| 4. | Groundnut | 9 | 1 |
| 5. | Oil | 5.5 | ½ |
| 6. | Salt | To taste | - |
| **Yield:** 1 Quarter Plate **(Cooked Weight:     g)** | | | |

--- **Author** ---
Dr. Prajakta J. Nande

# Clinical and Therapeutic Nutrition Practical Manual 1
### For M.Sc. Food Science and Nutrition (Semester-III)

### 6. Nutritive Value Chart for Poha

| S. No. | Nutrients | Values |
|---|---|---|
| 1. | Energy (kcal) | 250 |
| 2. | Carbohydrates (g) | 33.34 |
| 3. | Protein (g) | 6.12 |
| 4. | Fat (g) | 10.1 g |

### 7. Recipe Card for Puffed Rice Mix

| S. No. | Ingredients | Quantity (g) | No. of Exchanges |
|---|---|---|---|
| 1. | Puffed Rice | 30 | 1 |
| 2. | Bengal Gram Roasted (Dalia) | 15 | ½ |
| 3. | Onion | 27 | ¼ |
| 4. | Oil | 11 | 1 |
| 5. | Salt | To taste | - |
| **Yield:** 1 Full Plate **(Prepared Weight:    g)** | | | |

### 7. Nutritive Value Chart for Puffed Rice Mix

| S. No. | Nutrients | Values |
|---|---|---|
| 1. | Energy (kcal) | 263 |
| 2. | Carbohydrates (g) | 32.25 |
| 3. | Protein (g) | 6.75 |
| 4. | Fat (g) | 11.78 |

### 8. Recipe Card for Broken Wheat Upma

| S. No. | Ingredients | Quantity (g) | No. of Exchanges |
|---|---|---|---|
| 1. | Broken Wheat/Daliya | 30 | 1 |
| 2. | Onion | 27 | ¼ |
| 3. | Green Chillies | 5 | - |
| 4. | Oil | 5.5 | ½ |
| 5. | Salt | To taste | - |
| 6. | Water | As needed | - |
| **Yield:** 1 Big Bowl **(Cooked Weight:    g)** | | | |

### 8. Nutritive Value Chart for Broken Wheat Upma

| S. No. | Nutrients | Values |
|---|---|---|
| 1. | Energy (kcal) | 159 |
| 2. | Carbohydrates (g) | 22.05 |
| 3. | Protein (g) | 3.18 |
| 4. | Fat (g) | 6.01 |

**--- Author ---**
Dr. Prajakta J. Nande

# Clinical and Therapeutic Nutrition Practical Manual 1
## For M.Sc. Food Science and Nutrition (Semester-III)

### 9. Recipe Card for Plain Rice

| S. No. | Ingredients | Quantity (g) | No. of Exchanges |
|---|---|---|---|
| 1. | Rice | 30 | 1 |
| 2. | Water | As needed | - |
| **Yield:** 1 Medium Bowl **(Cooked Weight:    g)** | | | |

### 9. Nutritive Value Chart for Plain Rice

| S. No. | Nutrients | Values |
|---|---|---|
| 1. | Energy (kcal) | 100 |
| 2. | Carbohydrates (g) | 21 |
| 3. | Protein (g) | 3 |
| 4. | Fat (g) | 0.5 |

### 10. Recipe Card for Khichdi

| S. No. | Ingredients | Quantity (g) | No. of Exchanges |
|---|---|---|---|
| 1. | Rice | 30 | 1 |
| 2. | Lentil/Green Gram Dal/ Green Gram Dal with Husk | 15 | ½ |
| 3. | Salt | To taste | - |
| 4. | Water | As needed | - |
| **Yield:** 1 Big Bowl **(Cooked Weight:    g)** | | | |

### 10. Nutritive Value Chart for Khichdi

| S. No. | Nutrients | Values |
|---|---|---|
| 1. | Energy (kcal) | 150 |
| 2. | Carbohydrates (g) | 29.3 |
| 3. | Protein (g) | 6.5 |
| 4. | Fat (g) | 0.75 |

### 11. Recipe Card for Idli

| S. No. | Ingredients | Quantity (g) | No. of Exchanges |
|---|---|---|---|
| 1. | Rice | 30 | 1 |
| 2. | Black Gram Dal | 15 | ½ |
| 3. | Salt | To taste | - |
| 4. | Water | As needed | - |
| **Yield:** 4 Small Idlis **(Weight per Idli:    g)** | | | |

--- Author ---
Dr. Prajakta J. Nande

# Clinical and Therapeutic Nutrition Practical Manual 1
## For M.Sc. Food Science and Nutrition (Semester-III)

### 11. Nutritive Value Chart for Idli

| S. No. | Nutrients | Values |
|--------|-----------|--------|
| 1. | Energy (kcal) | 150 |
| 2. | Carbohydrates (g) | 29.3 |
| 3. | Protein (g) | 6.5 |
| 4. | Fat (g) | 0.75 |

### 12. Recipe Card for Dosa

| S. No. | Ingredients | Quantity (g) | No. of Exchanges |
|--------|-------------|--------------|------------------|
| 1. | Rice | 30 | 1 |
| 2. | Black Gram Dal | 15 | ½ |
| 3. | Oil | 5.5 | ½ |
| 4. | Salt | To taste | - |
| 5. | Water | As needed | - |

**Yield:** 1 Medium Dosa **(Weight of Dosa:    g)**

### 12. Nutritive Value Chart for Dosa

| S. No. | Nutrients | Values |
|--------|-----------|--------|
| 1. | Energy (kcal) | 200 |
| 2. | Carbohydrates (g) | 29.3 |
| 3. | Protein (g) | 6.5 |
| 4. | Fat (g) | 6.25 |

--- **Author** ---
Dr. Prajakta J. Nande

**Clinical and Therapeutic Nutrition Practical Manual 1**
For M.Sc. Food Science and Nutrition (Semester-III)

# PULSE AND LEGUME EXCHANGE

One Exchange of Pulse and Legume = 30 g

One Exchange provides: Energy-100 kcal; Carbohydrate-17 g; Protein-6 g and Fat-0.5 g

| Food Stuffs | |
|---|---|
| Bengal Gram Dal | Bengal Gram Whole |
| Black Gram Dal | Cow Peas |
| Black Gram Dal with Husk | Green Gram Whole |
| Green Gram Dal | Moth Beans |
| Green Gram Dal with Husk | Peas (Dried) |
| Lentil | Rajmah |
| Red Gram Dal | Soybean* |

*23 g provides Energy-100 kcal; Carbohydrate- 4.8 g; Protein- 10 g & Fat- 4.5 g

# COMMON RECIPES USING PULSE AND LEGUME EXCHANGE

### 1. Recipe Card for Plain Dal

| S. No. | Ingredients | Quantity (g) | No. of Exchanges |
|---|---|---|---|
| 1. | Red Gram Dal/Lentil/Green Gram Dal | 30 | 1 |
| 2. | Salt | To taste | - |
| 3. | Water | As needed | - |
| **Yield:** 1 Medium Bowl **(Cooked Weight:     g)** | | | |

### 1. Nutritive Value Chart for Plain Dal

| S. No. | Nutrients | Values |
|---|---|---|
| 1. | Energy (kcal) | 100 |
| 2. | Carbohydrates (g) | 17 |
| 3. | Protein (g) | 6 |
| 4. | Fat (g) | 0.5 |

--- **Author** ---
Dr. Prajakta J. Nande

# Clinical and Therapeutic Nutrition Practical Manual 1
For M.Sc. Food Science and Nutrition (Semester-III)

## 2. Recipe Card for Dal Fry

| S. No. | Ingredients | Quantity (g) | No. of Exchanges |
|---|---|---|---|
| 1. | Red Gram Dal/Lentil/Green Gram Dal | 30 | 1 |
| 2. | Oil | 5.5 | ½ |
| 3. | Onion | 27 | ¼ |
| 4. | Salt | To taste | - |
| 5. | Water | As needed | - |
| **Yield:** 1 Medium Bowl **(Cooked Weight:  g)** | | | |

## 2. Nutritive Value Chart for Dal Fry

| S. No. | Nutrients | Values |
|---|---|---|
| 1. | Energy (kcal) | 163 |
| 2. | Carbohydrates (g) | 19.75 |
| 3. | Protein (g) | 6.25 |
| 4. | Fat (g) | 6.03 |

## 3. Recipe Card for Mixed Dal

| S. No. | Ingredients | Quantity (g) | No. of Exchanges |
|---|---|---|---|
| 1. | Green Gram Dal | 10 | 1/3 |
| 2. | Lentil | 10 | 1/3 |
| 3. | Red Gram Dal | 10 | 1/3 |
| 4. | Onion | 27 | ¼ |
| 5. | Oil | 5.5 | ½ |
| 6. | Salt | To taste | - |
| 7. | Water | As needed | - |
| **Yield:** 1 Medium Bowl **(Cooked Weight:  g)** | | | |

## 3. Nutritive Value Chart for Mixed Dal

| S. No. | Nutrients | Values |
|---|---|---|
| 1. | Energy (kcal) | 163 |
| 2. | Carbohydrates (g) | 19.75 |
| 3. | Protein (g) | 6.25 |
| 4. | Fat (g) | 6.03 |

--- Author ---
Dr. Prajakta J. Nande

# Clinical and Therapeutic Nutrition Practical Manual 1
## For M.Sc. Food Science and Nutrition (Semester-III)

### 4. Recipe Card for Fenugreek Leaves/SpinachDal

| S. No. | Ingredients | Quantity (g) | No. of Exchanges |
|--------|-------------|--------------|------------------|
| 1. | Red Gram Dal | 30 | 1 |
| 2. | Fenugreek Leaves/Spinach | 17 | ¼ |
| 3. | Oil | 5.5 | ½ |
| 4. | Salt | To taste | - |
| 5. | Water | As needed | - |
| **Yield:** 1 Medium Bowl **(Cooked Weight:      g)** | | | |

### 4. Nutritive Value Chart for Fenugreek Leaves/Spinach Dal

| S. No. | Nutrients | Values |
|--------|-----------|--------|
| 1. | Energy (kcal) | 156 |
| 2. | Carbohydrates (g) | 17.75 |
| 3. | Protein (g) | 6.25 |
| 4. | Fat (g) | 6.1 |

### 5. Recipe Card for Sambar

| S. No. | Ingredients | Quantity (g) | No. of Exchanges |
|--------|-------------|--------------|------------------|
| 1. | Red Gram Dal | 30 | 1 |
| 2. | Onion | 27 | ¼ |
| 3. | Bottle Gourd | 35 | ¼ |
| 4. | Oil | 5.5 | ½ |
| 5. | Salt | To taste | - |
| 6. | Water | As needed | - |
| **Yield:** 1 Big Bowl **(Cooked Weight:      g)** | | | |

### 5. Nutritive Value Chart for Sambar

| S. No. | Nutrients | Values |
|--------|-----------|--------|
| 1. | Energy (kcal) | 169 |
| 2. | Carbohydrates (g) | 20.75 |
| 3. | Protein (g) | 7.5 |
| 4. | Fat (g) | 6.1 |

--- **Author** ---
Dr. Prajakta J. Nande

# Clinical and Therapeutic Nutrition Practical Manual 1
## For M.Sc. Food Science and Nutrition (Semester-III)

---

# VEGETABLE EXCHANGE

## VEGETABLE EXCHANGE A

One Exchange of Vegetables in Group I (Green Leafy Vegetables) = 68 g

One Exchange provides: Energy-25 kcal; Carbohydrate-3 g; Protein-2 g and Fat-0.4 g

| Food Stuffs |
| --- |
| Amaranth |
| Cabbage |
| Cauliflower Leaves |
| Fenugreek Leaves |
| Mint |
| Radish Leaves |
| Spinach |

One Exchange of Vegetables in Group II (Other Vegetables) = 95 g

One Exchange provides: Energy-25 kcal; Carbohydrate-4 g; Protein-1.5 g and Fat-0.2 g

| Food Stuffs |
| --- |
| Ladies Finger |
| Cauliflower |
| French Beans |
| Brinjal |
| Bitter Gourd |
| Pumpkin |
| Capsicum |

--- **Author** ---
Dr. Prajakta J. Nande

| One Exchange of Vegetables in Group III (Other Vegetables) = 145 g |
|---|

| One Exchange provides: Energy-25 kcal; Carbohydrate-4 g; Protein-1 g and Fat-0.2 g |
|---|

| Food Stuffs |
|---|
| Tinda |
| Knol Khol |
| Parwar |
| Tomato |
| Ghosala |
| Snake Gourd |
| Ridge Gourd |
| Cucumber |
| Bottle Gourd |

# VEGETABLE EXCHANGE B

| One Exchange of Vegetables in Group I (Roots and Tubers) = 47 g |
|---|

| One Exchange provides: Energy-50 kcal; Carbohydrate-11.5 g; Protein-0.8 g & Fat-0.1 g |
|---|

| Food Stuffs |
|---|
| Potato |
| Sweet Potato |
| Yam |
| Colocasia |

# Clinical and Therapeutic Nutrition Practical Manual 1
For M.Sc. Food Science and Nutrition (Semester-III)

---

> One Exchange of Vegetables in Group II (Roots and Tubers) = 107 g

> One Exchange provides: Energy-50 kcal; Carbohydrate-11 g; Protein-1 g and Fat-0.1 g

| Food Stuffs |
| --- |
| Beetroot |
| Carrot |
| Onion |

> One Exchange of Vegetables in Group III (Other Vegetables) = 87 g

> One Exchange provides: Energy-50 kcal; Carbohydrate-10 g; Protein-2 g and Fat-0.2 g

| Food Stuffs |
| --- |
| Cluster Beans |
| Green Plantain |
| Jackfruit, tender |

# COMMON RECIPES USING VEGETABLE A AND BEXCHANGE

### 1. Recipe Card for Brinjal Sabji

| S. No. | Ingredients | Quantity (g) | No. of Exchanges |
| --- | --- | --- | --- |
| 1. | Brinjal | 95 | 1 |
| 2. | Tomato | 36 | ¼ |
| 3. | Onion | 27 | ¼ |
| 4. | Oil | 5.5 | ½ |
| 5. | Salt | To taste | - |
| 6. | Water | As needed | - |
| **Yield:** 1 Medium Bowl **(Cooked Weight:      g)** | | | |

--- **Author** ---
Dr. Prajakta J. Nande

# Clinical and Therapeutic Nutrition Practical Manual 1
### For M.Sc. Food Science and Nutrition (Semester-III)

### 1. Nutritive Value Chart for Brinjal Sabji

| S. No. | Nutrients | Values |
|--------|-----------|--------|
| 1. | Energy (kcal) | 94 |
| 2. | Carbohydrates (g) | 7.75 |
| 3. | Protein (g) | 2.0 |
| 4. | Fat (g) | 11.28 |

### 2. Recipe Card for Bitter Gourd Sabji

| S. No. | Ingredients | Quantity (g) | No. of Exchanges |
|--------|-------------|--------------|------------------|
| 1. | Bitter Gourd | 95 | 1 |
| 2. | Oil | 5.5 | ½ |
| 3. | Salt | To taste | - |
| **Yield:** 1 Medium Bowl **(Cooked Weight:     g)** | | | |

### 2. Nutritive Value Chart for Bitter Gourd Sabji

| S. No. | Nutrients | Values |
|--------|-----------|--------|
| 1. | Energy (kcal) | 75 |
| 2. | Carbohydrates (g) | 5 |
| 3. | Protein (g) | 1 |
| 4. | Fat (g) | 11.2 |

### 3. Recipe Card for Parwar Sabji

| S. No. | Ingredients | Quantity (g) | No. of Exchanges |
|--------|-------------|--------------|------------------|
| 1. | Parwar | 145 | 1 |
| 2. | Oil | 5.5 | ½ |
| 3. | Onion | 27 | ¼ |
| 4. | Salt | To taste | - |
| 5. | Water | As needed | - |
| **Yield:** 1 Medium Bowl **(Cooked Weight:     g)** | | | |

### 3. Nutritive Value Chart for Parwar Sabji

| S. No. | Nutrients | Values |
|--------|-----------|--------|
| 1. | Energy (kcal) | 88 |
| 2. | Carbohydrates (g) | 6.75 |
| 3. | Protein (g) | 1.25 |
| 4. | Fat (g) | 11.23 |

--- **Author** ---
Dr. Prajakta J. Nande

# Clinical and Therapeutic Nutrition Practical Manual 1
## For M.Sc. Food Science and Nutrition (Semester-III)

### 4. Recipe Card for Fenugreek-Potato Sabji

| S. No. | Ingredients | Quantity (g) | No. of Exchanges |
|---|---|---|---|
| 1. | Fenugreek Leaves | 70 | 1 |
| 2. | Potato | 23 | ½ |
| 3. | Onion | 27 | ¼ |
| 4. | Oil | 5.5 | ½ |
| 5. | Salt | To taste | - |
| 6. | Water | As needed | - |
| **Yield:** 1 Medium Bowl (**Cooked Weight:**      g) | | | |

### 4. Nutritive Value Chart for Fenugreek-Potato Sabji

| S. No. | Nutrients | Values |
|---|---|---|
| 1. | Energy (kcal) | 113 |
| 2. | Carbohydrates (g) | 11.75 |
| 3. | Protein (g) | 2.6 |
| 4. | Fat (g) | 5.98 |

### 5. Recipe Card for Lady's Finger Sabji

| S. No. | Ingredients | Quantity (g) | No. of Exchanges |
|---|---|---|---|
| 1. | Lady's Finger | 95 | 1 |
| 2. | Onion | 27 | ¼ |
| 3. | Oil | 5.5 | ½ |
| 4. | Salt | To taste | - |
| **Yield:** 1 Medium Bowl (**Cooked Weight:**      g) | | | |

### 5. Nutritive Value Chart for Lady's Finger Sabji

| S. No. | Nutrients | Values |
|---|---|---|
| 1. | Energy (kcal) | 88 |
| 2. | Carbohydrates (g) | 6.75 |
| 3. | Protein (g) | 1.75 |
| 4. | Fat (g) | 5.73 |

### 6. Recipe Card for Cabbage Sabji

| S. No. | Ingredients | Quantity (g) | No. of Exchanges |
|---|---|---|---|
| 1. | Cabbage | 70 | 1 |
| 2. | Onion | 27 | ¼ |
| 3. | Oil | 5.5 | ½ |
| 4. | Salt | To taste | - |
| **Yield:** 1 Medium Bowl (**Cooked Weight:**      g) | | | |

--- **Author** ---
Dr. Prajakta J. Nande

# Clinical and Therapeutic Nutrition Practical Manual 1
For M.Sc. Food Science and Nutrition (Semester-III)

### 6. Nutritive Value Chart for Cabbage Sabji

| S. No. | Nutrients | Values |
|--------|-----------|--------|
| 1. | Energy (kcal) | 88 |
| 2. | Carbohydrates (g) | 5.75 |
| 3. | Protein (g) | 2.25 |
| 4. | Fat (g) | 5.93 |

### 7. Recipe Card for Bottle Gourd Sabji

| S. No. | Ingredients | Quantity (g) | No. of Exchanges |
|--------|-------------|--------------|------------------|
| 1. | Bottle Gourd | 145 | 1 |
| 2. | Oil | 5.5 | ½ |
| 3. | Salt | To taste | - |
| **Yield:** 1 Medium Bowl **(Cooked Weight:       g)** | | | |

### 7. Nutritive Value Chart for Bottle Gourd Sabji

| S. No. | Nutrients | Values |
|--------|-----------|--------|
| 1. | Energy (kcal) | 75 |
| 2. | Carbohydrates (g) | 5 |
| 3. | Protein (g) | 1 |
| 4. | Fat (g) | 5.7 |

--- Author ---
Dr. Prajakta J. Nande

# FRUIT EXCHANGE

**One Exchange of Fruits in Group I = 300 g**

**One Exchange provides: Energy-50 kcal; Carbohydrate-10 g; Protein-0.8 g and Fat-0.6 g**

| Food Stuffs |
| --- |
| Musk Melon |
| Water Melon |

**One Exchange of Fruits in Group II = 146 g**

**One Exchange provides: Energy-50 kcal; Carbohydrate-11 g; Protein-1 g and Fat-0.2 g**

| Food Stuffs |
| --- |
| Figs, Fresh |
| Papaya |

**One Exchange of Fruits in Group III = 104 g**

**One Exchange provides: Energy-50 kcal; Carbohydrate-11 g; Protein-0.8 g and Fat-0.3 g**

| Food Stuffs |
| --- |
| Guava |
| Orange |
| Peach |
| Pear |
| Pineapple |
| Plum |
| Sweet Lime |
| Strawberry |

# Clinical and Therapeutic Nutrition Practical Manual 1
For M.Sc. Food Science and Nutrition (Semester-III)

---

**One Exchange of Fruits in Group IV = 80 g**

**One Exchange provides: Energy-50 kcal; Carbohydrate-11 g; Protein-0.6 g and Fat-0.3 g**

| Food Stuffs |
|---|
| Apple |
| Cherries |
| Litchi |
| Pomegranate |
| Grapes (green) |
| Grapes (blue) |
| Jamun |
| Lemon |
| Mango |

**One Exchange of Fruits in Group IV = 44 g**

**One Exchange provides: Energy-50 kcal; Carbohydrate-11 g; Protein-0.5 g and Fat-0.3 g**

| Food Stuffs |
|---|
| Sapota |
| Banana |
| Custard Apple |
| Dates, Fresh |

**Clinical and Therapeutic Nutrition Practical Manual 1**
For M.Sc. Food Science and Nutrition (Semester-III)

---

# COMMON RECIPES USING FRUIT EXCHANGE

### 1. Recipe Card forFruit Juice (Concentrated)

| S. No. | Ingredients | Quantity (g) | No. of Exchanges |
|---|---|---|---|
| 1. | Orange/Pineapple/Sweet Lime /Pomegranate/Grapes/Lemon | 104/104/104/80/80/80 | 1 |
| Yield:   /  /  /  /  /   ml and  /  /  /  /  /  g and :  /  /  /  /  / teaspoons and  /  /  /  /  /  cup,  respectively) | | | |

### 1. Nutritive Value Chart for Fruit Juice (Concentrated)

| S. No. | Nutrients | Values |
|---|---|---|
| 1. | Energy (kcal) | 50 |
| 2. | Carbohydrates (g) | 11 |
| 3. | Protein (g) | 0.8 g for Orange/Pineapple/Sweet Lime and 0.6 g for Pomegranate/Grapes/ Lemon |
| 4. | Fat (g) | 0.3 |

### 2. Recipe Card for Fruit Juice (Diluted)

| S. No. | Ingredients | Quantity (g) | No. of Exchanges |
|---|---|---|---|
| 1. | Orange/Pineapple/Sweet Lime /Pomegranate/Grapes/Lemon | 104/104/104/80/80/80 | 1 |
| 2. | Sugar | 14 | 1 |
| 3. | Water | As needed | - |
| Yield:  /  /  /  /  /  ml and  /  /  /  /  /  g and :  /  /  /  /  / glass and  /  /  /  /  /  cup,  respectively) | | | |

### 2. Nutritive Value Chart for Fruit Juice (Diluted)

| S. No. | Nutrients | Values |
|---|---|---|
| 1. | Energy (kcal) | 100 |
| 2. | Carbohydrates (g) | 24.5 g for Orange/Pineapple/Sweet Lime; 22.5 g for Pomegranate/Grapes/Lemon |
| 3. | Protein (g) | 0.8 g for Orange/Pineapple/Sweet Lime; 0.6 g for Pomegranate/Grapes/Lemon |
| 4. | Fat (g) | 0.3 |

--- **Author** ---
Dr. Prajakta J. Nande

# Clinical and Therapeutic Nutrition Practical Manual 1

For M.Sc. Food Science and Nutrition (Semester-III)

## 3. Recipe Card for Stewed Apple

| S. No. | Ingredients | Quantity (g) | No. of Exchanges |
|--------|-------------|--------------|------------------|
| 1. | Apple | 80 | 1 |
| 2. | Sugar | 15 | 1 |
| 3. | Water | As needed | - |
| **Yield:** 1 Medium Bowl **(Cooked Weight:     g)** |||

## 3. Nutritive Value Chart for Stewed Apple

| S. No. | Nutrients | Values |
|--------|-----------|--------|
| 1. | Energy (kcal) | 100 |
| 2. | Carbohydrates (g) | 22 .4 |
| 3. | Protein (g) | 0.6 |
| 4. | Fat (g) | 0.3 |

## 4. Recipe Card for Stewed Pineapple

| S. No. | Ingredients | Quantity (g) | No. of Exchanges |
|--------|-------------|--------------|------------------|
| 1. | Pineapple | 100 | 1 |
| 2. | Sugar | 15 | 1 |
| 3. | Water | As needed | - |
| **Yield:** 1 Medium Bowl **(Cooked Weight:     g)** |||

## 4. Nutritive Value Chart for Stewed Pineapple

| S. No. | Nutrients | Values |
|--------|-----------|--------|
| 1. | Energy (kcal) | 104 |
| 2. | Carbohydrates (g) | 24.4 |
| 3. | Protein (g) | 0.8 |
| 4. | Fat (g) | 0.3 |

## 5. Recipe Card for Apple Delight

| S. No. | Ingredients | Quantity (g) | No. of Exchanges |
|--------|-------------|--------------|------------------|
| 1. | Milk (Cow's) | 150 | 1 |
| 2. | Apple | 40 | ½ |
| 3. | Bread | 15 | ½ |
| 4. | Sugar | 15 | 1 |
| 5. | Custard Powder | 5 | - |
| 6. | Walnut | 9 | 1 |
| **Yield:** 2 Medium Bowls **(Cooked Weight per Bowl:     g)** |||

--- Author ---

Dr. Prajakta J. Nande

### 5. Nutritive Value Chart for Apple Delight

| S. No. | Nutrients | Values |
|---|---|---|
| 1. | Energy (kcal) | 275 |
| 2. | Carbohydrates (g) | 37.8 |
| 3. | Protein (g) | 8.1 |
| 4. | Fat (g) | 10.3 |

### 6. Recipe Card for Fruit Salad

| S. No. | Ingredients | Quantity (g) | No. of Exchanges |
|---|---|---|---|
| 1. | Papaya | 35 | ¼ |
| 2. | Sweet Lime | 25 | ¼ |
| 3. | Apple | 20 | ¼ |
| 4. | Pomegranate | 20 | ¼ |
| **Yield:** 1 Medium Bowl **(Prepared Weight:        g)** | | | |

### 6. Nutritive Value Chart for Fruit Salad

| S. No. | Nutrients | Values |
|---|---|---|
| 1. | Energy (kcal) | 50 |
| 2. | Carbohydrates (g) | 11 |
| 3. | Protein (g) | 0.75 |
| 4. | Fat (g) | 0.29 |

**Clinical and Therapeutic Nutrition Practical Manual 1**
For M.Sc. Food Science and Nutrition (Semester-III)

# MILK EXCHANGE

**One Exchange provides: Energy-100 kcal; Carbohydrate-4 g; Protein-5 g and Fat-7 g**

| Food Stuffs | Quantity (g) |
|---|---|
| Milk (Buffalo's) | 85 |
| Milk (Cow's) | 149 |
| Skimmed Milk* | 345 |
| Curd (Cow's Milk) | 167 |
| Channa (Cow's Milk) | 38 |
| Channa (Buffalo's Milk) | 34 |
| Cheese | 29 |
| Skim Milk Powder* | 28 |
| Whole Milk Powder | 20 |
| Khoa (Whole Buffalo's Milk ) | 24 |
| Khoa (Skimmed Buffalo's Milk )* | 49 |
| Khoa (Whole Cow's Milk ) | 24 |

* provides 14 g carbohydrate; 10 g protein and negligible amount of fat

# COMMON RECIPES USING MILK EXCHANGE

### 1. Recipe Card for Lassi

| S. No. | Ingredients | Quantity (g) | No. of Exchanges |
|---|---|---|---|
| 1. | Curd | 167 | 1 |
| 2. | Sugar | 42 | 3 |
| **Yield:** 1 Glass **(Prepared Weight:** g) | | | |

### 1. Nutritive Value Chart for Lassi

| S. No. | Nutrients | Values |
|---|---|---|
| 1. | Energy (kcal) | 250 |
| 2. | Carbohydrates (g) | 42.2 |
| 3. | Protein (g) | 5 |
| 4. | Fat (g) | 7 |

**--- Author ---**
Dr. Prajakta J. Nande

# Clinical and Therapeutic Nutrition Practical Manual 1
## For M.Sc. Food Science and Nutrition (Semester-III)

### 2. Recipe Card for Butter Milk

| S. No. | Ingredients | Quantity (g) | No. of Exchanges |
|--------|-------------|--------------|------------------|
| 1. | Curd | 84 | ½ |
| 2. | Water | As needed | - |
| **Yield: 1 Glass (Prepared Weight:      g)** | | | |

### 2. Nutritive Value Chart for Butter Milk

| S. No. | Nutrients | Values |
|--------|-----------|--------|
| 1. | Energy (kcal) | 50 |
| 2. | Carbohydrates (g) | 2.5 |
| 3. | Protein (g) | 2.5 |
| 4. | Fat (g) | 3.5 |

### 3. Recipe Card for Sapota/Banana/Custard Apple Shake (Cow's Milk)

| S. No. | Ingredients | Quantity (g) | No. of Exchanges |
|--------|-------------|--------------|------------------|
| 1. | Sapota/Banana/Custard Apple | 44 | 1 |
| 2. | Milk (Cow's) | 149 | 1 |
| 3. | Sugar | 7 | ½ |
| **Yield: 1 Glass (Prepared Weight:      g)** | | | |

### 3. Nutritive Value Chart for Sapota/Banana/ Custard Apple Shake (Cow's Milk)

| S. No. | Nutrients | Values |
|--------|-----------|--------|
| 1. | Energy (kcal) | 175 |
| 2. | Carbohydrates (g) | 24.2 |
| 3. | Protein (g) | 5.5 |
| 4. | Fat (g) | 6.3 |

### 4. Recipe Card for Sapota/Banana/Custard Apple Shake (Buffalo's Milk)

| S. No. | Ingredients | Quantity (g) | No. of Exchanges |
|--------|-------------|--------------|------------------|
| 1. | Sapota/Banana/Custard Apple | 44 | 1 |
| 2. | Milk (Buffalo's) | 85 | 1 |
| 3. | Sugar | 7 | ½ |
| **Yield: 1 Glass (Prepared Weight:      g)** | | | |

--- **Author** ---
Dr. Prajakta J. Nande

# Clinical and Therapeutic Nutrition Practical Manual 1
For M.Sc. Food Science and Nutrition (Semester-III)

### 4. Nutritive Value Chart for Sapota/Banana/ Custard Apple Shake (Buffalo's Milk)

| S. No. | Nutrients | Values |
|---|---|---|
| 1. | Energy (kcal) | 175 |
| 2. | Carbohydrates (g) | 21.2 |
| 3. | Protein (g) | 4.5 |
| 4. | Fat (g) | 6.3 |

### 5. Recipe Card for Papaya Shake (Cow's Milk)

| S. No. | Ingredients | Quantity (g) | No. of Exchanges |
|---|---|---|---|
| 1. | Papaya | 73 | ½ |
| 2. | Milk (Cow's) | 149 | 1 |
| 3. | Sugar | 14 | 1 |
| **Yield:** 1 Glass **(Prepared Weight:    g)** | | | |

### 5. Nutritive Value Chart for Papaya Shake (Cow's Milk)

| S. No. | Nutrients | Values | |
|---|---|---|---|
| | | Buffalo Milk | Cow Milk |
| 1. | Energy (kcal) | 150 | 175 |
| 2. | Carbohydrates (g) | 15.7 | 24.9 |
| 3. | Protein (g) | 4.5 | 5.5 |
| 4. | Fat (g) | 6.2 | 6.2 |

### 6. Recipe Card for Papaya Shake (Buffalo's Milk)

| S. No. | Ingredients | Quantity (g) | No. of Exchanges |
|---|---|---|---|
| 1. | Papaya | 73 | ½ |
| 2. | Milk (Buffalo's) | 85 | 1 |
| 3. | Sugar | 7 | ½ |
| **Yield:** 1 Glass **(Prepared Weight:    g)** | | | |

### 6. Nutritive Value Chart for Papaya Shake (Buffalo's Milk)

| S. No. | Nutrients | Values | |
|---|---|---|---|
| | | Buffalo Milk | Cow Milk |
| 1. | Energy (kcal) | 150 | 175 |
| 2. | Carbohydrates (g) | 15.7 | 24.9 |
| 3. | Protein (g) | 4.5 | 5.5 |
| 4. | Fat (g) | 6.2 | 6.2 |

--- Author ---
Dr. Prajakta J. Nande

# Clinical and Therapeutic Nutrition Practical Manual 1
### For M.Sc. Food Science and Nutrition (Semester-III)

### 7. Recipe Card for Apple Shake (Cow's Milk)

| S. No. | Ingredients | Quantity (g) | No. of Exchanges |
|--------|-------------|--------------|------------------|
| 1. | Apple | 80 | 1 |
| 2. | Milk (Cow's) | 149 | 1 |
| 3. | Sugar | 14 | 1 |
| **Yield:** 1 Glass **(Prepared Weight:        g)** | | | |

### 7. Nutritive Value Chart for Apple Shake (Cow's Milk)

| S. No. | Nutrients | Values | |
|--------|-----------|--------------|----------|
| | | Buffalo Milk | Cow Milk |
| 1. | Energy (kcal) | 175 | 200 |
| 2. | Carbohydrates (g) | 21.2 | 30.4 |
| 3. | Protein (g) | 4.6 | 5.6 |
| 4. | Fat (g) | 6.3 | 6.3 |

### 8. Recipe Card for Apple Shake (Buffalo's Milk)

| S. No. | Ingredients | Quantity (g) | No. of Exchanges |
|--------|-------------|--------------|------------------|
| 1. | Apple | 80 | 1 |
| 2. | Milk (Buffalo's) | 85 | 1 |
| 3. | Sugar | 7 | ½ |
| **Yield:** 1 Glass **(Prepared Weight:        g)** | | | |

### 8. Nutritive Value Chart for Apple Shake (Buffalo's Milk)

| S. No. | Nutrients | Values | |
|--------|-----------|--------------|----------|
| | | Buffalo Milk | Cow Milk |
| 1. | Energy (kcal) | 175 | 200 |
| 2. | Carbohydrates (g) | 21.2 | 30.4 |
| 3. | Protein (g) | 4.6 | 5.6 |
| 4. | Fat (g) | 6.3 | 6.3 |

### 9. Recipe Card for Fruit Custard (Cow's Milk)

| S. No. | Ingredients | Quantity (g) | No. of Exchanges |
|--------|-------------|--------------|------------------|
| 1. | Milk (Cow's) | 149 | 1 |
| 2. | Apple | 20 | ¼ |
| 3. | Pomegranate | 20 | ¼ |
| 4. | Banana | 44 | 1 |
| 5. | Sugar | 14 | 1 |
| 6. | Custard Powder | 5 | - |
| **Yield:** 1 Big Bowl **(Prepared Weight:        g)** | | | |

--- **Author** ---
Dr. Prajakta J. Nande

# Clinical and Therapeutic Nutrition Practical Manual 1
For M.Sc. Food Science and Nutrition (Semester-III)

### 9. Nutritive Value Chart for Fruit Custard (Cow's Milk)

| S. No. | Nutrients | Values |
|--------|-----------|--------|
| 1. | Energy (kcal) | 225 |
| 2. | Carbohydrates (g) | 35.9 |
| 3. | Protein (g) | 5.8 |
| 4. | Fat (g) | 6.46 |

### 10. Recipe Card for Fruit Custard (Buffalo's Milk)

| S. No. | Ingredients | Quantity (g) | No. of Exchanges |
|--------|-------------|--------------|------------------|
| 1. | Milk (Buffalo's) | 85 | 1 |
| 2. | Apple | 20 | ¼ |
| 3. | Banana | 22 | ½ |
| 4. | Pomegranate | 20 | ¼ |
| 5. | Sugar | 14 | 1 |
| 6. | Custard Powder | 5 | - |
| **Yield:** 1 Medium Bowl **(Prepared Weight:      g)** | | | |

### 10. Nutritive Value Chart for Fruit Custard (Buffalo's Milk)

| S. No. | Nutrients | Values |
|--------|-----------|--------|
| 1. | Energy (kcal) | 200 |
| 2. | Carbohydrates (g) | 27.4 |
| 3. | Protein (g) | 4.55 |
| 4. | Fat (g) | 6.31 |

### 11. Recipe Card for Apple Delight

| S. No. | Ingredients | Quantity (g) | No. of Exchanges |
|--------|-------------|--------------|------------------|
| 1. | Milk (Cow's) | 149 | 1 |
| 2. | Apple | 40 | ½ |
| 3. | Bread | 15 | ½ |
| 4. | Sugar | 14 | 1 |
| 5. | Custard Powder | 5 | - |
| 6. | Walnut | 9 | 1 |
| **Yield:** 1 Big Bowl **(Prepared Weight:      g)** | | | |

### 11. Nutritive Value Chart for Apple Delight

| S. No. | Nutrients | Values |
|--------|-----------|--------|
| 1. | Energy (kcal) | 275 |
| 2. | Carbohydrates (g) | 37.8 |
| 3. | Protein (g) | 8.1 |
| 4. | Fat (g) | 10.3 |

--- **Author** ---
Dr. Prajakta J. Nande

# Clinical and Therapeutic Nutrition Practical Manual 1
For M.Sc. Food Science and Nutrition (Semester-III)

### 12. Recipe Card for Vermicelli Porridge (Cow's Milk)

| S. No. | Ingredients | Quantity (g) | No. of Exchanges |
|--------|-------------|--------------|------------------|
| 1. | Vermicelli | 7.5 | ¼ |
| 2. | Sugar | 14 | 1 |
| 3. | Ghee | 5.5 | ½ |
| 4. | Milk (Cow's milk) | 167 | 1 |
| 5. | Almond | 2.25 | ¼ |
| 6. | Cashew nut | 2.25 | ¼ |
| 7. | Raisins | 8 | ½ |
| **Yield:** 1 Big Bowl **(Prepared Weight:    g)** | | | |

### 12. Nutritive Value Chart for Vermicelli Porridge (Cow's Milk)

| S. No. | Nutrients | Values |
|--------|-----------|--------|
| 1. | Energy (kcal) | 300 |
| 2. | Carbohydrates (g) | 36.6 |
| 3. | Protein (g) | 7.51 |
| 4. | Fat (g) | 13.8 |

### 13. Recipe Card for Vermicelli Porridge (Buffalo's Milk)

| S. No. | Ingredients | Quantity (g) | No. of Exchanges |
|--------|-------------|--------------|------------------|
| 1. | Vermicelli | 15 | ½ |
| 2. | Sugar | 7 | ½ |
| 3. | Ghee | 5.5 | ½ |
| 4. | Milk (Buffalo's milk) | 128 | 1½ |
| 5. | Almond | 2.25 | ¼ |
| 6. | Cashew nut | 2.25 | ¼ |
| 7. | Raisins | 8 | ½ |
| **Yield:** 1 Big Bowl **(Prepared Weight:    g)** | | | |

### 13. Nutritive Value Chart for Vermicelli Porridge (Buffalo's Milk)

| S. No. | Nutrients | Values |
|--------|-----------|--------|
| 1. | Energy (kcal) | 258 |
| 2. | Carbohydrates (g) | 24.46 |
| 3. | Protein (g) | 6.41 |
| 4. | Fat (g) | 13.8 |

--- **Author** ---
Dr. Prajakta J. Nande

# Clinical and Therapeutic Nutrition Practical Manual 1
For M.Sc. Food Science and Nutrition (Semester-III)

## 14. Recipe Card for Ragi Porridge

| S. No. | Ingredients | Quantity (g) | No. of Exchanges |
|--------|-------------|--------------|------------------|
| 1. | Ragi Malt | 7.5 | ¼ |
| 2. | Milk (Cow's) | 149 | 1 |
| 3. | Sugar | 14 | 1 |
| 4. | Ghee | 5.5 | ½ |
| Yield: 1 Medium Bowl (Prepared Weight:     g) | | | |

## 14. Nutritive Value Chart for Ragi Porridge

| S. No. | Nutrients | Values |
|--------|-----------|--------|
| 1. | Energy (kcal) | 225 |
| 2. | Carbohydrates (g) | 24.65 |
| 3. | Protein (g) | 5.75 |
| 4. | Fat (g) | 11.63 |

## 15. Recipe Card for Rice Porridge

| S. No. | Ingredients | Quantity (g) | No. of Exchanges |
|--------|-------------|--------------|------------------|
| 1. | Rice, raw | 15 | ½ |
| 2. | Milk (Buffalo's) | 170 | 2 |
| 3. | Coconut, Dry | 9 | 1 |
| 4. | Almond | 2.25 | ¼ |
| 5. | Cashew nut | 2.25 | ¼ |
| 6. | Ghee | 5.5 | ½ |
| 7. | Sugar | 14 | 1 |
| Yield: 1 Medium Bowl (Prepared Weight:     g) | | | |

## 15. Nutritive Value Chart for Rice Porridge

| S. No. | Nutrients | Values |
|--------|-----------|--------|
| 1. | Energy (kcal) | 425 |
| 2. | Carbohydrates (g) | 33.3 |
| 3. | Protein (g) | 11.86 |
| 4. | Fat (g) | 23.75 |

## 16. Recipe Card for Bottle Gourd Raita

| S. No. | Ingredients | Quantity (g) | No. of Exchanges |
|--------|-------------|--------------|------------------|
| 1. | Bottle Gourd | 48 | 1/3 |
| 2. | Curd | 84 | ½ |
| Yield: 1 Medium Bowl (Prepared Weight:     g) | | | |

--- Author ---
Dr. Prajakta J. Nande

# Clinical and Therapeutic Nutrition Practical Manual 1
### For M.Sc. Food Science and Nutrition (Semester-III)

### 16. Nutritive Value Chart for Bottle Gourd Raita

| S. No. | Nutrients | Values |
|--------|-----------|--------|
| 1. | Energy (kcal) | 58 |
| 2. | Carbohydrates (g) | 3.83 |
| 3. | Protein (g) | 2.83 |
| 4. | Fat (g) | 3.83 |

### 17. Recipe Card for Mix Raita

| S. No. | Ingredients | Quantity (g) | No. of Exchanges |
|--------|-------------|--------------|------------------|
| 1. | Tomato | 36 | ¼ |
| 2. | Cucumber | 36 | ¼ |
| 3. | Onion | 27 | ¼ |
| 4. | Pomegranate | 20 | ¼ |
| 5. | Curd | 84 | ½ |

**Yield:** 1 Big Bowl **(Prepared Weight:       g)**

### 17. Nutritive Value Chart for Mix Raita

| S. No. | Nutrients | Values |
|--------|-----------|--------|
| 1. | Energy (kcal) | 87.5 |
| 2. | Carbohydrates (g) | 10 |
| 3. | Protein (g) | 3.4 |
| 4. | Fat (g) | 3.71 |

### 18. Recipe Card for Kadhi

| S. No. | Ingredients | Quantity (g) | No. of Exchanges |
|--------|-------------|--------------|------------------|
| 1. | Curd | 167 | 1 |
| 2. | Bengal Gram Dal | 10 | 1/3 |
| 3. | Oil | 5.5 | ½ |
| 4. | Curry Leaves | 5 leaves | - |
| 5. | Salt | 2-4 | - |
| 6. | Water | 200 ml | - |

**Yield:** 1 Big Bowl **(Prepared Weight:       g)**

### 18. Nutritive Value Chart for Kadhi

| S. No. | Nutrients | Values |
|--------|-----------|--------|
| 1. | Energy (kcal) | 183 kcal |
| 2. | Carbohydrates (g) | 10.7 g |
| 3. | Protein (g) | 7.43 g |
| 4. | Fat (g) | 12.27 g |

# Clinical and Therapeutic Nutrition Practical Manual 1
For M.Sc. Food Science and Nutrition (Semester-III)

### 19. Recipe Card for Paneer Bhurji

| S. No. | Ingredients | Quantity (g) | No. of Exchanges |
|--------|-------------|--------------|------------------|
| 1. | Paneer (Cow's Milk) | 38 | 1 |
| 2. | Onion | 27 | ¼ |
| 3. | Oil | 11 | 1 |
| **Yield:** 1 Small Bowl **(Prepared Weight:        g)** ||||

### 19. Nutritive Value Chart for Paneer Bhurji

| S. No. | Nutrients | Values |
|--------|-----------|--------|
| 1. | Energy (kcal) | 213 |
| 2. | Carbohydrates (g) | 2.75 |
| 3. | Protein (g) | 7.25 |
| 4. | Fat (g) | 19.03 |

**Clinical and Therapeutic Nutrition Practical Manual 1**
For M.Sc. Food Science and Nutrition (Semester-III)

# NUTS AND OIL SEEDS EXCHANGE

**One Exchange of Nuts and Oil Seeds Exchange = 9 g**

**One Exchange provides: Energy-50 kcal; Carbohydrate-1.7 g; Protein-1.5 g and Fat-1.7 g**

| Food Stuffs |
| --- |
| Almonds |
| Cashew Nuts |
| Coconut, Dry |
| Coconut, Fresh |
| Coconut Milk |
| Gingelly Seeds |
| Garden Cress Seeds |
| Ground Nuts |
| Linseed Seeds |
| Pistachio Nuts |
| Piyal Seeds |
| Walnuts |

# DRY FRUITS EXCHANGE

**One Exchange of Dry Fruits = 16 g**

**One Exchange provides: Energy-50 kcal; Carbohydrate-12 g; Protein-0.3 g and Fat-0.1 g**

| Food Stuffs |
| --- |
| Apricots |
| Black Currents |
| Dried Dates |
| Raisins |

--- **Author** ---
Dr. Prajakta J. Nande

**Clinical and Therapeutic Nutrition Practical Manual 1**
For M.Sc. Food Science and Nutrition (Semester-III)

---

# FAT EXCHANGE

### One Exchange of Fats = 11 g

### One Exchange provides: Energy-100 kcal and Fat-11 g

| Food Stuffs |
| --- |
| Butter |
| Ghee |
| Cooking Oil |

# SUGAR AND STARCH EXCHANGE

### One Exchange of Dry Fruits = 14 g

### One Exchange provides: Energy-50 kcal and Carbohydrate-12 g

| Food Stuffs |
| --- |
| Sugarcane Sugar |
| Honey |
| Jaggery |
| Sago |

# COMMON RECIPES USING SUGAR AND STARCH EXCHANGE

### 1. Recipe Card for Sago Porridge

| S. No. | Ingredients | Quantity (g) | No. of Exchanges |
| --- | --- | --- | --- |
| 1. | Sago | 15 | 1 |
| 2. | Sugar | 7.5 | ½ |
| 3. | Milk (Cow's) | 160 | 1 |
| **Yield:** 1 Big Bowl **(Prepared Weight:** g) | | | |

--- Author ---
Dr. Prajakta J. Nande

# Clinical and Therapeutic Nutrition Practical Manual 1
For M.Sc. Food Science and Nutrition (Semester-III)

### 1. Nutritive Value Chart for Sago Porridge

| S. No. | Nutrients | Values |
|---|---|---|
| 1. | Energy (kcal) | 175 |
| 2. | Carbohydrates (g) | 25.6 |
| 3. | Protein (g) | 5 |
| 4. | Fat (g) | 6 |

### 2. Recipe Card for Sago Khichdi

| S. No. | Ingredients | Quantity (g) | No. of Exchanges |
|---|---|---|---|
| 1. | Sago | 30 | 2 |
| 2. | Groundnuts | 9 | 1 |
| 3. | Potato | 23 | ½ |
| 4. | Green Chillies | 2-3 | - |
| 5. | Oil | 11 | 1 |
| | Salt | 2-3 | - |
| **Yield:** 1 Small Bowl **(Prepared Weight:     g)** | | | |

### 2. Nutritive Value Chart for Sago Khichdi

| S. No. | Nutrients | Values |
|---|---|---|
| 1. | Energy (kcal) | 275 |
| 2. | Carbohydrates (g) | 32.25 |
| 3. | Protein (g) | 1.9 |
| 4. | Fat (g) | 15.05 |

--- **Author** ---
Dr. Prajakta J. Nande

**Clinical and Therapeutic Nutrition Practical Manual 1**

For M.Sc. Food Science and Nutrition (Semester-III)

---

# MEAT AND POULTRY EXCHANGE

One Exchange of Meat and Poultry = 90 g

One Exchange provides: Energy-100 kcal; Protein-20 g and Fat-2.5 g

| Food Stuffs |
|:---:|
| Chicken |
| Liver |
| Meat (Lean) |
| Egg, Whole, Hen* |
| Egg, White, Hen** |
| Egg, Yolk, Hen*** |

*58 g provides 8 g protein and 8 g of fat
**33 g provides 15 kcal and 4 g protein
***17 g provides 60 kcal, 3 g protein and 5 g fat

# COMMON RECIPES USING EGG

### 1. Recipe Card for Full Boiled/Half Boiled Egg

| S. No. | Ingredients | Quantity (g) | No. of Exchanges |
|:---:|:---:|:---:|:---:|
| 1. | Egg | 58 | 1 |
| Yield: 1 Serving (Cooked Weight:    g) | | | |

### 1. Nutritive Value Chart for Full Boiled/Half Boiled Egg

| S. No. | Nutrients | Values |
|:---:|:---:|:---:|
| 1. | Energy (kcal) | 100 |
| 2. | Carbohydrates (g) | - |
| 3. | Protein (g) | 8 |
| 4. | Fat (g) | 8 |

---

**--- Author ---**
Dr. Prajakta J. Nande

# Clinical and Therapeutic Nutrition Practical Manual 1
For M.Sc. Food Science and Nutrition (Semester-III)

## 2. Recipe Card for Fried Egg

| S. No. | Ingredients | Quantity (g) | No. of Exchanges |
|--------|-------------|--------------|------------------|
| 1. | Egg | 58 | 1 |
| 2. | Oil | 5.5 | ½ |
| **Yield:** 1 Serving **(Cooked Weight:      g)** | | | |

## 2. Nutritive Value Chart for Fried Egg

| S. No. | Nutrients | Values |
|--------|-----------|--------|
| 1. | Energy (kcal) | 150 |
| 2. | Carbohydrates (g) | - |
| 3. | Protein (g) | 8 |
| 4. | Fat (g) | 13.5 |

## 3. Recipe Card for Egg Omlette

| S. No. | Ingredients | Quantity (g) | No. of Exchanges |
|--------|-------------|--------------|------------------|
| 1. | Egg | 58 | 1 |
| 2. | Oil | 5.5 | ½ |
| **Yield:** 1 Serving **(Cooked Weight:      g)** | | | |

## 3. Nutritive Value Chart for Egg Omlette

| S. No. | Nutrients | Values |
|--------|-----------|--------|
| 1. | Energy (kcal) | 150 |
| 2. | Carbohydrates (g) | - |
| 3. | Protein (g) | 8 |
| 4. | Fat (g) | 13.5 |

## 4. Recipe Card for Egg White Omlette

| S. No. | Ingredients | Quantity (g) | No. of Exchanges |
|--------|-------------|--------------|------------------|
| 1. | Egg White | 66 | 2 |
| 2. | Oil | 5.5 | ½ |
| 3. | Onion | 5 | - |
| 4. | Green Chillies | 2 | - |
| **Yield:** 1 Serving **(Cooked Weight:      g)** | | | |

## 4. Nutritive Value Chart for Egg White Omlette

| S. No. | Nutrients | Values |
|--------|-----------|--------|
| 1. | Energy (kcal) | 80 |
| 2. | Carbohydrates (g) | - |
| 3. | Protein (g) | 8 |
| 4. | Fat (g) | 5.5 |

--- **Author** ---
Dr. Prajakta J. Nande

# Clinical and Therapeutic Nutrition Practical Manual 1
For M.Sc. Food Science and Nutrition (Semester-III)

### 5. Recipe Card for Scrambled Egg

| S. No. | Ingredients | Quantity (g) | No. of Exchanges |
|---|---|---|---|
| 1. | Egg | 58 | 1 |
| 2. | Oil | 11 | 1 |
| **Yield:** 1 Medium Bowl **(Prepared Weight:      g)** | | | |

### 5. Nutritive Value Chart for Scrambled Egg

| S. No. | Nutrients | Values |
|---|---|---|
| 1. | Energy (kcal) | 130 |
| 2. | Carbohydrates (g) | - |
| 3. | Protein (g) | 8 |
| 4. | Fat (g) | 17 |

### 6. Recipe Card for Egg Curry

| S. No. | Ingredients | Quantity (g) | No. of Exchanges |
|---|---|---|---|
| 1. | Egg | 58 | 1 |
| 2. | Oil | 11 | 1 |
| 3. | Onion | 27 | ¼ |
| 4. | Tomato | 35 | ¼ |
| **Yield:** 1 Medium Bowl **(Prepared Weight:      g)** | | | |

### 6. Nutritive Value Chart for Egg Curry

| S. No. | Nutrients | Values |
|---|---|---|
| 1. | Energy (kcal) | 218 |
| 2. | Carbohydrates (g) | 3.53 |
| 3. | Protein (g) | 8.57 |
| 4. | Fat (g) | 19.04 |

### 7. Recipe Card for Egg Pudding (Steamed)

| S. No. | Ingredients | Quantity (g) | No. of Exchanges |
|---|---|---|---|
| 1. | Egg | 58 | 1 |
| 2. | Milk (Cow's) | 149 | 1 |
| 3. | Sugar | 21 | 1½ |
| 4. | Toast | 15 | ½ |
| **Yield:** 2 Servings **(Cooked Weight:      g)** | | | |

## Clinical and Therapeutic Nutrition Practical Manual 1
### For M.Sc. Food Science and Nutrition (Semester-III)

### 7. Nutritive Value Chart for Egg Pudding (Steamed)

| S. No. | Nutrients | Values |
|--------|-----------|--------|
| 1. | Energy (kcal) | 325 |
| 2. | Carbohydrates (g) | 36.1 |
| 3. | Protein (g) | 14.5 |
| 4. | Fat (g) | 14.25 |

### 8. Recipe Card for Caramel Pudding

| S. No. | Ingredients | Quantity (g) | No. of Exchanges |
|--------|-------------|--------------|------------------|
| 1. | Egg | 58 | 1 |
| 2. | Milk (Cow's) | 149 | 1 |
| 3. | Sugar | 21 | 1½ |

Yield: 2 Small Bowls (Prepared Weight:     g)

### 8. Nutritive Value Chart for Caramel Pudding

| S. No. | Nutrients | Values |
|--------|-----------|--------|
| 1. | Energy (kcal) | 275 |
| 2. | Carbohydrates (g) | 25.6 |
| 3. | Protein (g) | 13 |
| 4. | Fat (g) | 14 |

### 9. Recipe Card for French Toast

| S. No. | Ingredients | Quantity (g) | No. of Exchanges |
|--------|-------------|--------------|------------------|
| 1. | Egg | 58 | 1 |
| 2. | Bread | 15 | ½ |
| 3. | Butter | 5.5 | ½ |
| 4. | Sugar | 7.5 | ½ |

Yield: 2 Servings (Cooked Weight:     g)

### 9. Nutritive Value Chart for French Toast

| S. No. | Nutrients | Values |
|--------|-----------|--------|
| 1. | Energy (kcal) | 225 |
| 2. | Carbohydrates (g) | 16.7 |
| 3. | Protein (g) | 9.25 |
| 4. | Fat (g) | 13.75 |

--- Author ---
Dr. Prajakta J. Nande

# COMMON RECIPES USING CHICKEN AND MUTTON

### 1. Recipe Card for Chicken Curry

| S. No. | Ingredients | Quantity (g) | No. of Exchanges |
|--------|-------------|--------------|------------------|
| 1. | Chicken | 90 | 1 |
| 2. | Oil | 11 | 1 |
| 3. | Groundnuts | 4.5 | ½ |
| 4. | Coconut | 9 | 1 |
| 5. | Onion | 27 | ¼ |
| 6. | Tomato | 36 | ¼ |
| 7. | Water | As needed | - |
| **Yield:** 1 Medium Bowl (**Cooked Weight:**     g) | | | |

### 1. Nutritive Value Chart for Chicken Curry

| S. No. | Nutrients | Values |
|--------|-----------|--------|
| 1. | Energy (kcal) | 294 |
| 2. | Carbohydrates (g) | 6.3 |
| 3. | Protein (g) | 26.75 |
| 4. | Fat (g) | 18.08 |

### 2. Recipe Card for Plain Mutton Curry

| S. No. | Ingredients | Quantity (g) | No. of Exchanges |
|--------|-------------|--------------|------------------|
| 1. | Mutton | 128 | 1½ |
| 2. | Oil | 11 | 1 |
| 3. | Onion | 54 | ½ |
| 4. | Tomato | 36 | ¼ |
| 5. | Water | As needed | - |
| **Yield:** 1 Medium Bowl (**Cooked Weight:**     g) | | | |

### 2. Nutritive Value Chart for Plain Mutton Curry

| S. No. | Nutrients | Values |
|--------|-----------|--------|
| 1. | Energy (kcal) | 286 |
| 2. | Carbohydrates (g) | 7.4 |
| 3. | Protein (g) | 28.07 |
| 4. | Fat (g) | 15.61 |

# Clinical and Therapeutic Nutrition Practical Manual 1
For M.Sc. Food Science and Nutrition (Semester-III)

## FISH EXCHANGE

One Exchange of Fish = 100 g

One Exchange provides: Energy-100 kcal; Protein-18 g and Fat-1.6 g

| Food Stuffs |
|---|
| Rohu |
| Catla |
| Pomfret (White) |
| Pomfret (Black) |
| Fish (Fresh Water) |

# COMMON RECIPES USING FISH

### 1. Recipe Card for Fried Fish (Shallow Fry)

| S. No. | Ingredients | Quantity (g) | No. of Exchanges |
|---|---|---|---|
| 1. | Fish | 100 | 1 |
| 2. | Oil | 11 | 1 |
| 3. | Lemon juice | 5 g | 1 teaspoon |
| **Yield:** 2 Pieces (Cooked Weight:      g) | | | |

### 1. Nutritive Value Chart for Fried Fish (Shallow Fry)

| S. No. | Nutrients | Values |
|---|---|---|
| 1. | Energy (kcal) | 200 |
| 2. | Carbohydrates (g) | 5 |
| 3. | Protein (g) | 17 |
| 4. | Fat (g) | 12 |

--- **Author** ---
Dr. Prajakta J. Nande

# Clinical and Therapeutic Nutrition Practical Manual 1
For M.Sc. Food Science and Nutrition (Semester-III)

## 2. Recipe Card for Baked Fish

| S. No. | Ingredients | Quantity (g) | No. of Exchanges |
|--------|-------------|--------------|------------------|
| 1. | Fish | 100 | 1 |
| 2. | Oil | 11 | 1 |
| 3. | Lemon juice | 5 ml | 1 teaspoon |
| **Yield:** 2 Pieces (Cooked Weight:     g) | | | |

## 2. Nutritive Value Chart for Baked Fish

| S. No. | Nutrients | Values |
|--------|-----------|--------|
| 1. | Energy (kcal) | 200 |
| 2. | Carbohydrates (g) | 5 |
| 3. | Protein (g) | 17 |
| 4. | Fat (g) | 12 |

--- Author ---
Dr. Prajakta J. Nande

# PRACTICAL 3

## INVESTIGATIONS FOR DIAGNOSIS OF VARIOUS DISEASES - SYSTEM-WISE

## PLANNING AND PREPARATION OF THERAPEUTIC DIETS

**Clinical and Therapeutic Nutrition Practical Manual 1**
For M.Sc. Food Science and Nutrition (Semester-III)

# PRACTICAL: 3

**1. Interpretation of patient data and diagnostic tests and drawing up of patient diet prescription using a case study approach**

**2. Follow-Up: Acceptability of diet prescription, compliance and discharge diet plan**

## [A] WEIGHT MANAGEMENT

> Normal Weight
> Underweight
> Obesity

## [B] GASTROINTESTINAL TRACT DISORDERS

> Gastritis
> Peptic Ulcer

## [C] LIVER DISEASES

> Hepatitis
> Alcoholic Cirrhosis
> Cirrhosis with Portal Hypertension and Ascites
> Hepatic Coma

## [D] CARDIOVASCULAR DISEASES

> Hypertension
> Coronary Heart Disease

--- Author ---
Dr. Prajakta J. Nande

# WEIGHT MANAGEMENT

**Clinical and Therapeutic Nutrition Practical Manual 1**
For M.Sc. Food Science and Nutrition (Semester-III)
---------------------------------------------------------------------------------------------------------------

## NORMAL WEIGHT

## AIM: To plan and prepare a day's diet for a normal weight person using a case study approach

### Personal Information:                                           Dates:

**Name:**
**Sex:** Female/Male
**Age [Yrs]:**
**Height [cm]:**
**Actual Body Weight (ABW)/Present Body Weight [kg]:**
**Occupation:** Service/Business/Housewife/Any Other
**Monthly Family Income [Rs./-]:**
**Type of Work:** Sedentary/Moderate/Heavy
**Duration of Work [Hours]:**
**Any Other:**

### Clinical andBiochemical Investigations:
**Bowel Movements**                  : Regular/Irregular
**Blood, Urine and other Parameters:**

### Dietary Information:
| | |
|---|---|
| **Food Habits** | : Vegetarian/Non Vegetarian/Eggetarian |
| **Common Dietary Pattern** | : 2 meals/3 meals/4 meals/Any Other |
| **Meal Timings** | : Regular/Irregular |
| **Type of Oils used for Cooking** | : |
| **Salt used for Cooking** | : Iodized/Non Iodized |
| **Milk used** | : Cow's/Buffalo's [Wholesome/Skimmed] |
| **Approximate Water Intake** | :---------glasses/day |
| **Frequency of Non-Veg Intake** | : Weekly/Fortnightly/Monthly/Any Other |
| **Any Other** | : |

--- **Author** ---
Dr. Prajakta J. Nande

## Existing Meal Plan:

| Name of Meal with Timing | Meal Plan | No. of Servings |
|---|---|---|
|  |  |  |

# Clinical and Therapeutic Nutrition Practical Manual 1
For M.Sc. Food Science and Nutrition (Semester-III)

## Calculations for Requirements:
### 1. Ideal Body Weight [IBW]:

### 2. Body Mass Index [BMI]:

### 3. Energy Requirement:

## Division of Energy into Three Major Nutrients:
### 4. Protein Requirement:

### 5. Total Fat Requirement:

### 6. Carbohydrate Requirement:

# Clinical and Therapeutic Nutrition Practical Manual 1
For M.Sc. Food Science and Nutrition (Semester-III)

**7. Micro-Nutrient Requirement**:

| Sr. No. | Vitamins/Minerals | Values |
|---|---|---|
| 1 | | |
| 2 | | |
| 3 | | |
| 4 | | |
| 5 | | |
| 6 | | |
| 7 | | |
| 8 | | |
| 9 | | |
| 10 | | |

**8. Amount of Salt and Sodium from Salt**:

**9. Fluid Intake**:

**10. Amount of Fats and Oils**:

**11. Amount of Sugars**:

**12. Non Veg Food Intake**:

# Clinical and Therapeutic Nutrition Practical Manual 1
## For M.Sc. Food Science and Nutrition (Semester-III)

**Nutritional Goals:**

**Principles of Dietary Modifications:**

# Clinical and Therapeutic Nutrition Practical Manual 1
For M.Sc. Food Science and Nutrition (Semester-III)

## TABLE 1: FOOD EXCHANGE LIST

| Sr. No. | Name of Exchanges | | No. of Exchanges | Energy (kcal) | Carbohydrate (g) | Protein (g) | Fat (g) |
|---|---|---|---|---|---|---|---|
| 1 | Cereal Exchange | | | | | | |
| 2 | Pulse Exchange | | | | | | |
| 3 | Vegetable Exchange A | Group I | | | | | |
| | | Group II | | | | | |
| | | Group III | | | | | |
| 4 | Vegetable Exchange B | Group I | | | | | |
| | | Group II | | | | | |
| | | Group III | | | | | |
| 5 | Fruit Exchange | Group I | | | | | |
| | | Group II | | | | | |
| | | Group III | | | | | |
| | | Group IV | | | | | |
| | | Group V | | | | | |
| 6 | Milk Exchange | Whole Milk and Products | | | | | |
| | | Skimmed Milk and Products | | | | | |
| 7 | Nut and Oil Seed Exchange | | | | | | |
| 8 | Dry Fruit Exchange | | | | | | |
| 9 | Fat Exchange | | | | | | |
| 10 | Sugar and Starch Exchange | Sugar | | | | | |
| | | Jaggery | | | | | |
| | | Honey | | | | | |
| | | Sago | | | | | |
| 11 | Meat and Poultry Exchange | Egg | | | | | |
| | | Chicken | | | | | |
| | | Mutton | | | | | |
| 12 | Fish Exchange | | | | | | |
| 13 | Others | | | | | | |
| | Total | | | | | | |
| | Requirement | | | | | | |

--- **Author** ---
Dr. Prajakta J. Nande

# Clinical and Therapeutic Nutrition Practical Manual 1
For M.Sc. Food Science and Nutrition (Semester-III)

------------------------------------------------------------------------------------

## :MEAL PLAN:

Suggested Meal Plan for--------------------------------------------------------------------------------

| Meal/Time | Menu | No. of Servings/ Measures/ Quantity |
|---|---|---|
| **Early Morning** (----------am) | | |
| **Breakfast** (----------am) | | |
| **Mid Morning** (----------am) | | |
| **Lunch** (----------pm) | | |
| **Snacks** (----------pm) | | |
| **Evening** (----------pm) | | |
| **Dinner** (----------pm) | | |
| **Bed Time** (----------pm) | | |

--- **Author** ---
Dr. Prajakta J. Nande

# Clinical and Therapeutic Nutrition Practical Manual 1
For M.Sc. Food Science and Nutrition (Semester-III)

## TABLE 2: BREAK UP OF EXCHANGES

| Sr. No. | Name of Exchanges | | Early Morning (-----am) | Breakfast (-----am) | Mid Morning (-----am) | Lunch (-----pm) | Snacks (-----pm) | Evening (-----pm) | Dinner (-----pm) | Bed Time (-----pm) | Total |
|---|---|---|---|---|---|---|---|---|---|---|---|
| 1 | Cereal and Millet Exchange | | | | | | | | | | |
| 2 | Pulse and Legume Exchange | | | | | | | | | | |
| 3 | Vegetable Exchange A | Group I | | | | | | | | | |
| | | Group II | | | | | | | | | |
| | | Group III | | | | | | | | | |
| 4 | Vegetable Exchange B | Group I | | | | | | | | | |
| | | Group II | | | | | | | | | |
| | | Group III | | | | | | | | | |
| 5 | Fruit Exchange | Group I | | | | | | | | | |
| | | Group II | | | | | | | | | |
| | | Group III | | | | | | | | | |
| | | Group IV | | | | | | | | | |
| | | Group V | | | | | | | | | |
| 6 | Milk Exchange | Whole Milk and Products | | | | | | | | | |
| | | Skimmed Milk and Products | | | | | | | | | |
| 7 | Nutsand Oil Seed Exchange | | | | | | | | | | |
| 8 | Dry Fruit Exchange | | | | | | | | | | |
| 9 | Fat Exchange | | | | | | | | | | |
| 10 | Sugar and Starch Exchange | Sugar | | | | | | | | | |
| | | Jaggery | | | | | | | | | |
| | | Honey | | | | | | | | | |
| | | Sago | | | | | | | | | |
| 11 | Meat and Poultry Exchange | Egg | | | | | | | | | |
| | | Chicken | | | | | | | | | |
| | | Mutton | | | | | | | | | |
| 12 | Fish Exchange | | | | | | | | | | |
| 13 | Others | | | | | | | | | | |

--- Author ---
Dr. Prajakta J. Nande

# Clinical and Therapeutic Nutrition Practical Manual 1
For M.Sc. Food Science and Nutrition (Semester-III)

## LIST OF FOODS TO BE INCLUDED AND AVOIDED

| Name of Exchanges | Foods to be Included | Foods to be Restricted | Foods to be Avoided |
|---|---|---|---|
| Cereals and Millets | | | |
| Pulses and Legumes | | | |
| Vegetables | | | |
| Fruits | | | |
| Milk and It's Products | | | |
| Nuts and Oil Seeds | | | |
| Dry Fruits | | | |
| Fats and Oils | | | |
| Sugars and Starch | | | |
| Meat, Fish and Poultry | | | |
| Others | | | |

--- **Author** ---
Dr. Prajakta J. Nande

# Clinical and Therapeutic Nutrition Practical Manual 1
For M.Sc. Food Science and Nutrition (Semester-III)

## TABLE 3: NUTRITIVE VALUE OF THE PRESCRIBED DIET (VITAMINS AND MINERALS)

| Sr. No. | Food Stuffs | Weight (g) | B1 (mg) | B2 (mg) | Niacin (mg) | Carotene (µg) | Vitamin C (mg) | Ca (mg) | P (mg) | Fe (mg) | Na (mg) | K (mg) |
|---------|-------------|------------|---------|---------|-------------|---------------|----------------|---------|--------|---------|---------|--------|
|  |  |  |  |  |  |  |  |  |  |  |  |  |
|  |  |  |  |  |  |  |  |  |  |  |  |  |
|  |  |  |  |  |  |  |  |  |  |  |  |  |
|  |  |  |  |  |  |  |  |  |  |  |  |  |
|  |  |  |  |  |  |  |  |  |  |  |  |  |
|  |  |  |  |  |  |  |  |  |  |  |  |  |
|  |  |  |  |  |  |  |  |  |  |  |  |  |
|  |  |  |  |  |  |  |  |  |  |  |  |  |
|  |  |  |  |  |  |  |  |  |  |  |  |  |
|  |  |  |  |  |  |  |  |  |  |  |  |  |
|  |  |  |  |  |  |  |  |  |  |  |  |  |
|  |  |  |  |  |  |  |  |  |  |  |  |  |
|  |  |  |  |  |  |  |  |  |  |  |  |  |
|  |  |  |  |  |  |  |  |  |  |  |  |  |
|  |  |  |  |  |  |  |  |  |  |  |  |  |
|  |  |  |  |  |  |  |  |  |  |  |  |  |
|  |  |  |  |  |  |  |  |  |  |  |  |  |
|  |  |  |  |  |  |  |  |  |  |  |  |  |
|  |  |  |  |  |  |  |  |  |  |  |  |  |
|  |  |  |  |  |  |  |  |  |  |  |  |  |
|  |  |  |  |  |  |  |  |  |  |  |  |  |
|  |  |  |  |  |  |  |  |  |  |  |  |  |
|  |  |  |  |  |  |  |  |  |  |  |  |  |
|  |  |  |  |  |  |  |  |  |  |  |  |  |
|  |  |  |  |  |  |  |  |  |  |  |  |  |
|  |  |  |  |  |  |  |  |  |  |  |  |  |
|  |  |  |  |  |  |  |  |  |  |  |  |  |
|  |  |  |  |  |  |  |  |  |  |  |  |  |
|  |  |  |  |  |  |  |  |  |  |  |  |  |
|  |  |  |  |  |  |  |  |  |  |  |  |  |
|  |  |  |  |  |  |  |  |  |  |  |  |  |
|  |  |  |  |  |  |  |  |  |  |  |  |  |
|  |  |  |  |  |  |  |  |  |  |  |  |  |
|  | **Total** |  |  |  |  |  |  |  |  |  |  |  |
|  | **Required** |  |  |  |  |  |  |  |  |  |  |  |

--- Author ---
Dr. Prajakta J. Nande

# Clinical and Therapeutic Nutrition Practical Manual 1
For M.Sc. Food Science and Nutrition (Semester-III)

## Comments:

## References:

**Clinical and Therapeutic Nutrition Practical Manual 1**
For M.Sc. Food Science and Nutrition (Semester-III)

---

| **UNDERWEIGHT** |
|---|

## AIM: To plan and prepare a day's diet for an underweight person using a case study approach

### Personal Information:                                    Dates:

**Name:**
**Sex:** Female/Male
**Age [Yrs]:**
**Height [cm]:**
**Actual Body Weight (ABW)/Present Body Weight [kg]:**
**Occupation:** Service/Business/Housewife/Any Other
**Monthly Family Income [Rs./-]:**
**Type of Work:** Sedentary/Moderate/Heavy
**Duration of Work [Hours]:**
**Any Other:**

### Clinical and Biochemical Investigations:

**Bowel Movements**                    : Regular/Irregular
**Blood, Urine and other Parameters:**

### Dietary Information:

| | |
|---|---|
| **Food Habits** | : Vegetarian/Non Vegetarian/Eggetarian |
| **Common Dietary Pattern** | : 2 meals/3 meals/4 meals/Any Other |
| **Meal Timings** | : Regular/Irregular |
| **Type of Oils used for Cooking** | : |
| **Salt used for Cooking** | : Iodized/Non Iodized |
| **Milk used** | : Cow's/Buffalo's [Wholesome/Skimmed] |
| **Approximate Water Intake** | :---------glasses/day |
| **Frequency of Non-Veg Intake** | : Weekly/Fortnightly/Monthly/Any Other |
| **Any Other** | : |

--- **Author** ---
Dr. Prajakta J. Nande

## Existing Meal Plan:

| Name of Meal with Timing | Meal Plan | No. of Servings |
|---|---|---|
| | | |

# Calculations for Requirements:

## 1. Ideal Body Weight [IBW]:

## 2. Body Mass Index [BMI]:

## 3. Energy Requirement:

# Division of Energy into Three Major Nutrients:

## 4. Protein Requirement:

## 5. Total Fat Requirement:

## 6. Carbohydrate Requirement:

# 7. Micro-Nutrient Requirement:

| Sr. No. | Vitamins/Minerals | Values |
|---------|-------------------|--------|
| 1 | | |
| 2 | | |
| 3 | | |
| 4 | | |
| 5 | | |
| 6 | | |
| 7 | | |
| 8 | | |
| 9 | | |
| 10 | | |

# 8. Amount of Salt and Sodium from Salt:

# 9. Fluid Intake:

# 10. Amount of Fats and Oils:

# 11. Amount of Sugars:

# 12. Non Veg Food Intake:

# Nutritional Goals:

# Principles of Dietary Modifications:

# Clinical and Therapeutic Nutrition Practical Manual 1
For M.Sc. Food Science and Nutrition (Semester-III)

------------------------------------------------------------------------------------------

## TABLE 1: FOOD EXCHANGE LIST

| Sr. No. | Name of Exchanges | | No. of Exchanges | Energy (kcal) | Carbohydrate (g) | Protein (g) | Fat (g) |
|---|---|---|---|---|---|---|---|
| 1 | Cereal Exchange | | | | | | |
| 2 | Pulse Exchange | | | | | | |
| 3 | Vegetable Exchange A | Group I | | | | | |
| | | Group II | | | | | |
| | | Group III | | | | | |
| 4 | Vegetable Exchange B | Group I | | | | | |
| | | Group II | | | | | |
| | | Group III | | | | | |
| 5 | Fruit Exchange | Group I | | | | | |
| | | Group II | | | | | |
| | | Group III | | | | | |
| | | Group IV | | | | | |
| | | Group V | | | | | |
| 6 | Milk Exchange | Whole Milk and Products | | | | | |
| | | Skimmed Milk and Products | | | | | |
| 7 | Nut and Oil Seed Exchange | | | | | | |
| 8 | Dry Fruit Exchange | | | | | | |
| 9 | Fat Exchange | | | | | | |
| 10 | Sugar and Starch Exchange | Sugar | | | | | |
| | | Jaggery | | | | | |
| | | Honey | | | | | |
| | | Sago | | | | | |
| 11 | Meat and Poultry Exchange | Egg | | | | | |
| | | Chicken | | | | | |
| | | Mutton | | | | | |
| 12 | Fish Exchange | | | | | | |
| 13 | Others | | | | | | |
| | Total | | | | | | |
| | Requirement | | | | | | |

------------------------------------------------------------------------------------------

--- **Author** ---
Dr. Prajakta J. Nande

# Clinical and Therapeutic Nutrition Practical Manual 1
For M.Sc. Food Science and Nutrition (Semester-III)

-----------------------------------------------------------------------------------------------------------

## :MEAL PLAN:

Suggested Meal Plan for----------------------------------------------------------------------------------------------

| Meal/Time | Menu | No. of Servings/ Measures/ Quantity |
|---|---|---|
| Early Morning (----------am) | | |
| Breakfast (----------am) | | |
| Mid Morning (----------am) | | |
| Lunch (----------pm) | | |
| Snacks (----------pm) | | |
| Evening (----------pm) | | |
| Dinner (----------pm) | | |
| Bed Time (----------pm) | | |

--------------------------------------------------------------------------------------------
--- **Author** ---
Dr. Prajakta J. Nande

# Clinical and Therapeutic Nutrition Practical Manual 1
For M.Sc. Food Science and Nutrition (Semester-III)

## TABLE 2: BREAK UP OF EXCHANGES

| Sr. No. | Name of Exchanges | | Early Morning (----am) | Breakfast (----am) | Mid Morning (----am) | Lunch (----pm) | Snacks (----pm) | Evening (----pm) | Dinner (----pm) | Bed Time (----pm) | Total |
|---|---|---|---|---|---|---|---|---|---|---|---|
| 1 | Cereal and Millet Exchange | | | | | | | | | | |
| 2 | Pulse and Legume Exchange | | | | | | | | | | |
| 3 | Vegetable Exchange A | Group I | | | | | | | | | |
| | | Group II | | | | | | | | | |
| | | Group III | | | | | | | | | |
| 4 | Vegetable Exchange B | Group I | | | | | | | | | |
| | | Group II | | | | | | | | | |
| | | Group III | | | | | | | | | |
| 5 | Fruit Exchange | Group I | | | | | | | | | |
| | | Group II | | | | | | | | | |
| | | Group III | | | | | | | | | |
| | | Group IV | | | | | | | | | |
| | | Group V | | | | | | | | | |
| 6 | Milk Exchange | Whole Milk and Products | | | | | | | | | |
| | | Skimmed Milk and Products | | | | | | | | | |
| 7 | Nuts and Oil Seed Exchange | | | | | | | | | | |
| 8 | Dry Fruit Exchange | | | | | | | | | | |
| 9 | Fat Exchange | | | | | | | | | | |
| 10 | Sugar and Starch Exchange | Sugar | | | | | | | | | |
| | | Jaggery | | | | | | | | | |
| | | Honey | | | | | | | | | |
| | | Sago | | | | | | | | | |
| 11 | Meat and Poultry Exchange | Egg | | | | | | | | | |
| | | Chicken | | | | | | | | | |
| | | Mutton | | | | | | | | | |
| 12 | Fish Exchange | | | | | | | | | | |
| 13 | Others | | | | | | | | | | |

--- Author ---
Dr. Prajakta J. Nande

# Clinical and Therapeutic Nutrition Practical Manual 1
For M.Sc. Food Science and Nutrition (Semester-III)

## LIST OF FOODS TO BE INCLUDED AND AVOIDED

| Name of Exchanges | Foods to be Included | Foods to be Restricted | Foods to be Avoided |
|---|---|---|---|
| Cereals and Millets | | | |
| Pulses and Legumes | | | |
| Vegetables | | | |
| Fruits | | | |
| Milk and It's Products | | | |
| Nuts and Oil Seeds | | | |
| Dry Fruits | | | |
| Fats and Oils | | | |
| Sugars and Starch | | | |
| Meat, Fish and Poultry | | | |
| Others | | | |

--- Author ---
Dr. Prajakta J. Nande

# Clinical and Therapeutic Nutrition Practical Manual 1
For M.Sc. Food Science and Nutrition (Semester-III)

## TABLE 3: NUTRITIVE VALUE OF THE PRESCRIBED DIET
## (VITAMINS AND MINERALS)

| Sr. No. | Food Stuffs | Weight (g) | B1 (mg) | B2 (mg) | Niacin (mg) | Carotene (µg) | Vitamin C (mg) | Ca (mg) | P (mg) | Fe (mg) | Na (mg) | K (mg) |
|---|---|---|---|---|---|---|---|---|---|---|---|---|
| | | | | | | | | | | | | |
| | | | | | | | | | | | | |
| | | | | | | | | | | | | |
| | | | | | | | | | | | | |
| | | | | | | | | | | | | |
| | | | | | | | | | | | | |
| | | | | | | | | | | | | |
| | | | | | | | | | | | | |
| | | | | | | | | | | | | |
| | | | | | | | | | | | | |
| | | | | | | | | | | | | |
| | | | | | | | | | | | | |
| | | | | | | | | | | | | |
| | | | | | | | | | | | | |
| | | | | | | | | | | | | |
| | | | | | | | | | | | | |
| | | | | | | | | | | | | |
| | | | | | | | | | | | | |
| | | | | | | | | | | | | |
| | | | | | | | | | | | | |
| | | | | | | | | | | | | |
| | | | | | | | | | | | | |
| | | | | | | | | | | | | |
| | | | | | | | | | | | | |
| | | | | | | | | | | | | |
| | | | | | | | | | | | | |
| | | | | | | | | | | | | |
| | | | | | | | | | | | | |
| | **Total** | | | | | | | | | | | |
| | **Required** | | | | | | | | | | | |

--- **Author** ---
Dr. Prajakta J. Nande

# Clinical and Therapeutic Nutrition Practical Manual 1

For M.Sc. Food Science and Nutrition (Semester-III)

## Comments:

## References:

**Clinical and Therapeutic Nutrition Practical Manual 1**
For M.Sc. Food Science and Nutrition (Semester-III)

---

## OBESITY

# AIM: To plan and prepare a day's diet for an obese person using a case study approach

## Personal Information:                                          Dates:

**Name:**
**Sex:** Female/Male
**Age [Yrs]:**
**Height [cm]:**
**Actual Body Weight (ABW)/Present Body Weight [kg]:**
**Occupation:** Service/Business/Housewife/Any Other
**Monthly Family Income [Rs./-]:**
**Type of Work:** Sedentary/Moderate/Heavy
**Duration of Work [Hours]:**
**Any Other:**

## Clinical and Biochemical Investigations:

**Bowel Movements**                        : Regular/Irregular
**Blood, Urine and other Parameters:**

## Dietary Information:

| | |
|---|---|
| **Food Habits** | : Vegetarian/Non Vegetarian/Eggetarian |
| **Common Dietary Pattern** | : 2 meals/3 meals/4 meals/Any Other |
| **Meal Timings** | : Regular/Irregular |
| **Type of Oils used for Cooking** | : |
| **Salt used for Cooking** | : Iodized/Non Iodized |
| **Milk used** | : Cow's/Buffalo's [Wholesome/Skimmed] |
| **Approximate Water Intake** | :---------glasses/day |
| **Frequency of Non-Veg Intake** | : Weekly/Fortnightly/Monthly/Any Other |
| **Any Other** | : |

---

--- **Author** ---
Dr. Prajakta J. Nande

# Clinical and Therapeutic Nutrition Practical Manual 1
For M.Sc. Food Science and Nutrition (Semester-III)

## Existing Meal Plan:

| Name of Meal with Timing | Meal Plan | No. of Servings |
|---|---|---|
| | | |

## Calculations for Requirements:

**1. Ideal Body Weight [IBW]:**

**2. Body Mass Index [BMI]:**

**3. Energy Requirement:**

## Division of Energy into Three Major Nutrients:

**4. Protein Requirement:**

**5. Total Fat Requirement:**

**6. Carbohydrate Requirement:**

# Clinical and Therapeutic Nutrition Practical Manual 1
For M.Sc. Food Science and Nutrition (Semester-III)

**7. Micro-Nutrient Requirement**:

| Sr. No. | Vitamins/Minerals | Values |
|---|---|---|
| 1 | | |
| 2 | | |
| 3 | | |
| 4 | | |
| 5 | | |
| 6 | | |
| 7 | | |
| 8 | | |
| 9 | | |
| 10 | | |

**8. Amount of Salt and Sodium from Salt**:

**9. Fluid Intake**:

**10. Amount of Fats and Oils**:

**11. Amount of Sugars**:

**12. Non Veg Food Intake**:

--- **Author** ---
Dr. Prajakta J. Nande

# Clinical and Therapeutic Nutrition Practical Manual 1

For M.Sc. Food Science and Nutrition (Semester-III)

**Nutritional Goals:**

**Principles of Dietary Modifications:**

# Clinical and Therapeutic Nutrition Practical Manual 1
For M.Sc. Food Science and Nutrition (Semester-III)

## TABLE 1: FOOD EXCHANGE LIST

| Sr. No. | Name of Exchanges | | No. of Exchanges | Energy (kcal) | Carbohydrate (g) | Protein (g) | Fat (g) |
|---|---|---|---|---|---|---|---|
| 1 | Cereal Exchange | | | | | | |
| 2 | Pulse Exchange | | | | | | |
| 3 | Vegetable Exchange A | Group I | | | | | |
| | | Group II | | | | | |
| | | Group III | | | | | |
| 4 | Vegetable Exchange B | Group I | | | | | |
| | | Group II | | | | | |
| | | Group III | | | | | |
| 5 | Fruit Exchange | Group I | | | | | |
| | | Group II | | | | | |
| | | Group III | | | | | |
| | | Group IV | | | | | |
| | | Group V | | | | | |
| 6 | Milk Exchange | Whole Milk and Products | | | | | |
| | | Skimmed Milk and Products | | | | | |
| 7 | Nut and Oil Seed Exchange | | | | | | |
| 8 | Dry Fruit Exchange | | | | | | |
| 9 | Fat Exchange | | | | | | |
| 10 | Sugar and Starch Exchange | Sugar | | | | | |
| | | Jaggery | | | | | |
| | | Honey | | | | | |
| | | Sago | | | | | |
| 11 | Meat and Poultry Exchange | Egg | | | | | |
| | | Chicken | | | | | |
| | | Mutton | | | | | |
| 12 | Fish Exchange | | | | | | |
| 13 | Others | | | | | | |
| | Total | | | | | | |
| | Requirement | | | | | | |

--- **Author** ---
Dr. Prajakta J. Nande

# Clinical and Therapeutic Nutrition Practical Manual 1
For M.Sc. Food Science and Nutrition (Semester-III)

## :MEAL PLAN:

Suggested Meal Plan for---------------------------------------------------------------------------------------

| Meal/Time | Menu | No. of Servings/ Measures/ Quantity |
|---|---|---|
| Early Morning (----------am) | | |
| Breakfast (----------am) | | |
| Mid Morning (----------am) | | |
| Lunch (----------pm) | | |
| Snacks (----------pm) | | |
| Evening (----------pm) | | |
| Dinner (----------pm) | | |
| Bed Time (----------pm) | | |

--- Author ---
Dr. Prajakta J. Nande

# Clinical and Therapeutic Nutrition Practical Manual 1
For M.Sc. Food Science and Nutrition (Semester-III)

## TABLE 2: BREAK UP OF EXCHANGES

| Sr. No. | Name of Exchanges | | Early Morning (-----am) | Breakfast (-----am) | Mid Morning (-----am) | Lunch (-----pm) | Snacks (-----pm) | Evening (-----pm) | Dinner (-----pm) | Bed Time (-----pm) | Total |
|---|---|---|---|---|---|---|---|---|---|---|---|
| 1 | Cereal and Millet Exchange | | | | | | | | | | |
| 2 | Pulse and Legume Exchange | | | | | | | | | | |
| 3 | Vegetable Exchange A | Group I | | | | | | | | | |
| | | Group II | | | | | | | | | |
| | | Group III | | | | | | | | | |
| 4 | Vegetable Exchange B | Group I | | | | | | | | | |
| | | Group II | | | | | | | | | |
| | | Group III | | | | | | | | | |
| 5 | Fruit Exchange | Group I | | | | | | | | | |
| | | Group II | | | | | | | | | |
| | | Group III | | | | | | | | | |
| | | Group IV | | | | | | | | | |
| | | Group V | | | | | | | | | |
| 6 | Milk Exchange | Whole Milk and Products | | | | | | | | | |
| | | Skimmed Milk and Products | | | | | | | | | |
| 7 | Nuts and Oil Seed Exchange | | | | | | | | | | |
| 8 | Dry Fruit Exchange | | | | | | | | | | |
| 9 | Fat Exchange | | | | | | | | | | |
| 10 | Sugar and Starch Exchange | Sugar | | | | | | | | | |
| | | Jaggery | | | | | | | | | |
| | | Honey | | | | | | | | | |
| | | Sago | | | | | | | | | |
| 11 | Meat and Poultry Exchange | Egg | | | | | | | | | |
| | | Chicken | | | | | | | | | |
| | | Mutton | | | | | | | | | |
| 12 | Fish Exchange | | | | | | | | | | |
| 13 | Others | | | | | | | | | | |

--- **Author** ---
Dr. Prajakta J. Nande

# LIST OF FOODS TO BE INCLUDED AND AVOIDED

| Name of Exchanges | Foods to be Included | Foods to be Restricted | Foods to be Avoided |
|---|---|---|---|
| Cereals and Millets | | | |
| Pulses and Legumes | | | |
| Vegetables | | | |
| Fruits | | | |
| Milk and It's Products | | | |
| Nuts and Oil Seeds | | | |
| Dry Fruits | | | |
| Fats and Oils | | | |
| Sugars and Starch | | | |
| Meat, Fish and Poultry | | | |
| Others | | | |

# Clinical and Therapeutic Nutrition Practical Manual 1
For M.Sc. Food Science and Nutrition (Semester-III)

## TABLE 3: NUTRITIVE VALUE OF THE PRESCRIBED DIET
### (VITAMINS AND MINERALS)

| Sr. No. | Food Stuffs | Weight (g) | B1 (mg) | B2 (mg) | Niacin (mg) | Carotene (µg) | Vitamin C (mg) | Ca (mg) | P (mg) | Fe (mg) | Na (mg) | K (mg) |
|---------|-------------|------------|---------|---------|-------------|---------------|----------------|---------|--------|---------|---------|--------|
|  |  |  |  |  |  |  |  |  |  |  |  |  |
|  |  |  |  |  |  |  |  |  |  |  |  |  |
|  |  |  |  |  |  |  |  |  |  |  |  |  |
|  |  |  |  |  |  |  |  |  |  |  |  |  |
|  |  |  |  |  |  |  |  |  |  |  |  |  |
|  |  |  |  |  |  |  |  |  |  |  |  |  |
|  |  |  |  |  |  |  |  |  |  |  |  |  |
|  |  |  |  |  |  |  |  |  |  |  |  |  |
|  |  |  |  |  |  |  |  |  |  |  |  |  |
|  |  |  |  |  |  |  |  |  |  |  |  |  |
|  |  |  |  |  |  |  |  |  |  |  |  |  |
|  |  |  |  |  |  |  |  |  |  |  |  |  |
|  |  |  |  |  |  |  |  |  |  |  |  |  |
|  |  |  |  |  |  |  |  |  |  |  |  |  |
|  |  |  |  |  |  |  |  |  |  |  |  |  |
|  |  |  |  |  |  |  |  |  |  |  |  |  |
|  |  |  |  |  |  |  |  |  |  |  |  |  |
|  |  |  |  |  |  |  |  |  |  |  |  |  |
|  |  |  |  |  |  |  |  |  |  |  |  |  |
|  |  |  |  |  |  |  |  |  |  |  |  |  |
|  |  |  |  |  |  |  |  |  |  |  |  |  |
|  |  |  |  |  |  |  |  |  |  |  |  |  |
|  |  |  |  |  |  |  |  |  |  |  |  |  |
|  |  |  |  |  |  |  |  |  |  |  |  |  |
|  |  |  |  |  |  |  |  |  |  |  |  |  |
|  |  |  |  |  |  |  |  |  |  |  |  |  |
|  |  |  |  |  |  |  |  |  |  |  |  |  |
|  |  |  |  |  |  |  |  |  |  |  |  |  |
|  |  |  |  |  |  |  |  |  |  |  |  |  |
|  | **Total** |  |  |  |  |  |  |  |  |  |  |  |
|  | **Required** |  |  |  |  |  |  |  |  |  |  |  |

--- **Author** ---
Dr. Prajakta J. Nande

# Clinical and Therapeutic Nutrition Practical Manual 1
For M.Sc. Food Science and Nutrition (Semester-III)

## TABLE 4: FIBER CONTENT OF THE PRESCRIBED DIET

| Sr. No. | Food Stuffs | Weight (g) | Soluble Dietary Fiber (g) | Insoluble Dietary Fiber (g) | Total Dietary Fiber (g) |
|---|---|---|---|---|---|
| | | | | | |
| | | | | | |
| | | | | | |
| | | | | | |
| | | | | | |
| | | | | | |
| | | | | | |
| | | | | | |
| | | | | | |
| | | | | | |
| | | | | | |
| | | | | | |
| | | | | | |
| | | | | | |
| | | | | | |
| | | | | | |
| | | | | | |
| | | | | | |
| | | | | | |
| | | | | | |
| | | | | | |
| | | | | | |
| | | | | | |
| | | | | | |
| | | | | | |
| | | | | | |
| | | | | | |
| | | | | | |
| | | | | | |
| | | | | | |
| | | | | | |
| | | | | | |
| | | | | | |
| | | | | | |
| | | | | | |
| | | | | | |
| | Total | | | | |
| | Required | | | | |

--- Author ---
Dr. Prajakta J. Nande

## Comments:

## References:

# Clinical and Therapeutic Nutrition Practical Manual 1
For M.Sc. Food Science and Nutrition (Semester-III)

# GASTROINTESTINAL TRACT DISORDERS

**Clinical and Therapeutic Nutrition Practical Manual 1**
For M.Sc. Food Science and Nutrition (Semester-III)

----------------------------------------------------------------------

## GASTRITIS

## AIM: To plan and prepare a day's diet for an individual suffering from gastritis using a case study approach

## Personal Information:                                    Dates:
**Name:**
**Sex:** Female/Male
**Age [Yrs]:**
**Height [cm]:**
**Actual Body Weight (ABW)/Present Body Weight [kg]:**
**Occupation:** Service/Business/Housewife/Any Other
**Monthly Family Income [Rs./-]:**
**Type of Work:** Sedentary/Moderate/Heavy
**Duration of Work [Hours]:**
**Any Other:**

## Clinical and Biochemical Investigations:
**Bowel Movements**                  : Regular/Irregular
**Blood, Urine and other Parameters:**

## Dietary Information:
| | |
|---|---|
| **Food Habits** | : Vegetarian/Non Vegetarian/Eggetarian |
| **Common Dietary Pattern** | : 2 meals/3 meals/4 meals/Any Other |
| **Meal Timings** | : Regular/Irregular |
| **Type of Oils used for Cooking** | : |
| **Salt used for Cooking** | : Iodized/Non Iodized |
| **Milk used** | : Cow's/Buffalo's [Wholesome/Skimmed] |
| **Approximate Water Intake** | :---------glasses/day |
| **Frequency of Non-Veg Intake** | : Weekly/Fortnightly/Monthly/Any Other |
| **Any Other** | : |

--- **Author** ---
Dr. Prajakta J. Nande

# Clinical and Therapeutic Nutrition Practical Manual 1
For M.Sc. Food Science and Nutrition (Semester-III)

## Existing Meal Plan:

| Name of Meal with Timing | Meal Plan | No. of Servings |
|---|---|---|
| | | |

## Calculations for Requirements:

**1. Ideal Body Weight [IBW]:**

**2. Body Mass Index [BMI]:**

**3. Energy Requirement:**

## Division of Energy into Three Major Nutrients:

**4. Protein Requirement:**

**5. Total Fat Requirement:**

**6. Carbohydrate Requirement:**

# Clinical and Therapeutic Nutrition Practical Manual 1
For M.Sc. Food Science and Nutrition (Semester-III)

**7. Micro-Nutrient Requirement:**

| Sr. No. | Vitamins/Minerals | Values |
|---------|-------------------|--------|
| 1 | | |
| 2 | | |
| 3 | | |
| 4 | | |
| 5 | | |
| 6 | | |
| 7 | | |
| 8 | | |
| 9 | | |
| 10 | | |

**8. Amount of Salt and Sodium from Salt:**

**9. Fluid Intake:**

**10. Amount of Fats and Oils:**

**11. Amount of Sugars:**

**12. Non Veg Food Intake:**

# Nutritional Goals:

# Principles of Dietary Modifications:

# Clinical and Therapeutic Nutrition Practical Manual 1
For M.Sc. Food Science and Nutrition (Semester-III)

## TABLE 1: FOOD EXCHANGE LIST

| Sr. No. | Name of Exchanges | | No. of Exchanges | Energy (kcal) | Carbohydrate (g) | Protein (g) | Fat (g) |
|---|---|---|---|---|---|---|---|
| 1 | Cereal Exchange | | | | | | |
| 2 | Pulse Exchange | | | | | | |
| 3 | Vegetable Exchange A | Group I | | | | | |
| | | Group II | | | | | |
| | | Group III | | | | | |
| 4 | Vegetable Exchange B | Group I | | | | | |
| | | Group II | | | | | |
| | | Group III | | | | | |
| 5 | Fruit Exchange | Group I | | | | | |
| | | Group II | | | | | |
| | | Group III | | | | | |
| | | Group IV | | | | | |
| | | Group V | | | | | |
| 6 | Milk Exchange | Whole Milk and Products | | | | | |
| | | Skimmed Milk and Products | | | | | |
| 7 | Nut and Oil Seed Exchange | | | | | | |
| 8 | Dry Fruit Exchange | | | | | | |
| 9 | Fat Exchange | | | | | | |
| 10 | Sugar and Starch Exchange | Sugar | | | | | |
| | | Jaggery | | | | | |
| | | Honey | | | | | |
| | | Sago | | | | | |
| 11 | Meat and Poultry Exchange | Egg | | | | | |
| | | Chicken | | | | | |
| | | Mutton | | | | | |
| 12 | Fish Exchange | | | | | | |
| 13 | Others | | | | | | |
| | Total | | | | | | |
| | Requirement | | | | | | |

--- Author ---
Dr. Prajakta J. Nande

# Clinical and Therapeutic Nutrition Practical Manual 1
For M.Sc. Food Science and Nutrition (Semester-III)

-----------------------------------------------------------------------------------------------------
## :MEAL PLAN:

Suggested Meal Plan for---------------------------------------------------------------------------------------

| Meal/Time | Menu | No. of Servings/ Measures/ Quantity |
|---|---|---|
| Early Morning (----------am) | | |
| Breakfast (----------am) | | |
| Mid Morning (----------am) | | |
| Lunch (----------pm) | | |
| Snacks (----------pm) | | |
| Evening (----------pm) | | |
| Dinner (----------pm) | | |
| Bed Time (----------pm) | | |

--- Author ---
Dr. Prajakta J. Nande

# Clinical and Therapeutic Nutrition Practical Manual 1
For M.Sc. Food Science and Nutrition (Semester-III)

## TABLE 2: BREAK UP OF EXCHANGES

| Sr. No. | Name of Exchanges | | Early Morning (-----am) | Breakfast (-----am) | Mid Morning (-----am) | Lunch (-----pm) | Snacks (-----pm) | Evening (-----pm) | Dinner (-----pm) | Bed Time (-----pm) | Total |
|---|---|---|---|---|---|---|---|---|---|---|---|
| 1 | Cereal and Millet Exchange | | | | | | | | | | |
| 2 | Pulse and Legume Exchange | | | | | | | | | | |
| 3 | Vegetable Exchange A | Group I | | | | | | | | | |
| | | Group II | | | | | | | | | |
| | | Group III | | | | | | | | | |
| 4 | Vegetable Exchange B | Group I | | | | | | | | | |
| | | Group II | | | | | | | | | |
| | | Group III | | | | | | | | | |
| 5 | Fruit Exchange | Group I | | | | | | | | | |
| | | Group II | | | | | | | | | |
| | | Group III | | | | | | | | | |
| | | Group IV | | | | | | | | | |
| | | Group V | | | | | | | | | |
| 6 | Milk Exchange | Whole Milk and Products | | | | | | | | | |
| | | Skimmed Milk and Products | | | | | | | | | |
| 7 | Nuts and Oil Seed Exchange | | | | | | | | | | |
| 8 | Dry Fruit Exchange | | | | | | | | | | |
| 9 | Fat Exchange | | | | | | | | | | |
| 10 | Sugar and Starch Exchange | Sugar | | | | | | | | | |
| | | Jaggery | | | | | | | | | |
| | | Honey | | | | | | | | | |
| | | Sago | | | | | | | | | |
| 11 | Meat and Poultry Exchange | Egg | | | | | | | | | |
| | | Chicken | | | | | | | | | |
| | | Mutton | | | | | | | | | |
| 12 | Fish Exchange | | | | | | | | | | |
| 13 | Others | | | | | | | | | | |

--- Author ---
Dr. Prajakta J. Nande

# Clinical and Therapeutic Nutrition Practical Manual 1
For M.Sc. Food Science and Nutrition (Semester-III)

## LIST OF FOODS TO BE INCLUDED AND AVOIDED

| Name of Exchanges | Foods to be Included | Foods to be Restricted | Foods to be Avoided |
|---|---|---|---|
| Cereals and Millets | | | |
| Pulses and Legumes | | | |
| Vegetables | | | |
| Fruits | | | |
| Milk and It's Products | | | |
| Nuts and Oil Seeds | | | |
| Dry Fruits | | | |
| Fats and Oils | | | |
| Sugars and Starch | | | |
| Meat, Fish and Poultry | | | |
| Others | | | |

--- Author ---
Dr. Prajakta J. Nande

# Clinical and Therapeutic Nutrition Practical Manual 1
For M.Sc. Food Science and Nutrition (Semester-III)

## TABLE 3: NUTRITIVE VALUE OF THE PRESCRIBED DIET (VITAMINS AND MINERALS)

| Sr. No. | Food Stuffs | Weight (g) | B1 (mg) | B2 (mg) | Niacin (mg) | Carotene (µg) | Vitamin C (mg) | Ca (mg) | P (mg) | Fe (mg) | Na (mg) | K (mg) |
|---------|-------------|------------|---------|---------|-------------|---------------|----------------|---------|--------|---------|---------|--------|
|         |             |            |         |         |             |               |                |         |        |         |         |        |
|         |             |            |         |         |             |               |                |         |        |         |         |        |
|         |             |            |         |         |             |               |                |         |        |         |         |        |
|         |             |            |         |         |             |               |                |         |        |         |         |        |
|         |             |            |         |         |             |               |                |         |        |         |         |        |
|         |             |            |         |         |             |               |                |         |        |         |         |        |
|         |             |            |         |         |             |               |                |         |        |         |         |        |
|         |             |            |         |         |             |               |                |         |        |         |         |        |
|         |             |            |         |         |             |               |                |         |        |         |         |        |
|         |             |            |         |         |             |               |                |         |        |         |         |        |
|         |             |            |         |         |             |               |                |         |        |         |         |        |
|         |             |            |         |         |             |               |                |         |        |         |         |        |
|         |             |            |         |         |             |               |                |         |        |         |         |        |
| **Total** |           |            |         |         |             |               |                |         |        |         |         |        |
| **Required** |        |            |         |         |             |               |                |         |        |         |         |        |

# Clinical and Therapeutic Nutrition Practical Manual 1
For M.Sc. Food Science and Nutrition (Semester-III)

## TABLE 4: FIBER CONTENT OF THE PRESCRIBED DIET

| Sr. No. | Food Stuffs | Weight (g) | Soluble Dietary Fiber (g) | Insoluble Dietary Fiber (g) | Total Dietary Fiber (g) |
|---|---|---|---|---|---|
| | | | | | |
| | | | | | |
| | | | | | |
| | | | | | |
| | | | | | |
| | | | | | |
| | | | | | |
| | | | | | |
| | | | | | |
| | | | | | |
| | | | | | |
| | | | | | |
| | | | | | |
| | | | | | |
| | | | | | |
| | | | | | |
| | | | | | |
| | | | | | |
| | | | | | |
| | | | | | |
| | | | | | |
| | | | | | |
| | | | | | |
| | | | | | |
| | | | | | |
| | | | | | |
| | | | | | |
| | | | | | |
| | | | | | |
| | | | | | |
| | | | | | |
| | | | | | |
| | | | | | |
| | | | | | |
| | | | | | |
| | | | | | |
| | Total | | | | |
| | Required | | | | |

--- **Author** ---
Dr. Prajakta J. Nande

# Clinical and Therapeutic Nutrition Practical Manual 1
For M.Sc. Food Science and Nutrition (Semester-III)

## Comments:

## References:

**Clinical and Therapeutic Nutrition Practical Manual 1**
For M.Sc. Food Science and Nutrition (Semester-III)

---

## PEPTIC ULCER

## AIM: To plan and prepare a day's diet for an individual suffering from peptic ulcer using a case study approach

### Personal Information:                          Dates:

**Name:**
**Sex:** Female/Male
**Age [Yrs]:**
**Height [cm]:**
**Actual Body Weight (ABW)/Present Body Weight [kg]:**
**Occupation:** Service/Business/Housewife/Any Other
**Monthly Family Income [Rs./-]:**
**Type of Work:** Sedentary/Moderate/Heavy
**Duration of Work [Hours]:**
**Any Other:**

### Clinical and Biochemical Investigations:
**Bowel Movements**                  : Regular/Irregular
**Blood, Urine and other Parameters:**

### Dietary Information:
**Food Habits**                       : Vegetarian/Non Vegetarian/Eggetarian
**Common Dietary Pattern**            : 2 meals/3 meals/4 meals/Any Other
**Meal Timings**                      : Regular/Irregular
**Type of Oils used for Cooking**     :
**Salt used for Cooking**             : Iodized/Non Iodized
**Milk used**                         : Cow's/Buffalo's [Wholesome/Skimmed]
**Approximate Water Intake**          :---------glasses/day
**Frequency of Non-Veg Intake**       : Weekly/Fortnightly/Monthly/Any Other
**Any Other**                         :

---

--- **Author** ---
Dr. Prajakta J. Nande

## Existing Meal Plan:

| Name of Meal with Timing | Meal Plan | No. of Servings |
|---|---|---|
|  |  |  |

## Calculations for Requirements:
**1. Ideal Body Weight [IBW]:**

**2. Body Mass Index [BMI]:**

**3. Energy Requirement:**

## Division of Energy into Three Major Nutrients:
**4. Protein Requirement:**

**5. Total Fat Requirement:**

**6. Carbohydrate Requirement:**

# Clinical and Therapeutic Nutrition Practical Manual 1
For M.Sc. Food Science and Nutrition (Semester-III)

## 7. Micro-Nutrient Requirement:

| Sr. No. | Vitamins/Minerals | Values |
|---------|-------------------|--------|
| 1 | | |
| 2 | | |
| 3 | | |
| 4 | | |
| 5 | | |
| 6 | | |
| 7 | | |
| 8 | | |
| 9 | | |
| 10 | | |

## 8. Amount of Salt and Sodium from Salt:

## 9. Fluid Intake:

## 10. Amount of Fats and Oils:

## 11. Amount of Sugars:

## 12. Non Veg Food Intake:

# Clinical and Therapeutic Nutrition Practical Manual 1
For M.Sc. Food Science and Nutrition (Semester-III)

**Nutritional Goals:**

**Principles of Dietary Modifications:**

# Clinical and Therapeutic Nutrition Practical Manual 1
For M.Sc. Food Science and Nutrition (Semester-III)

## TABLE 1: FOOD EXCHANGE LIST

| Sr. No. | Name of Exchanges | | No. of Exchanges | Energy (kcal) | Carbohydrate (g) | Protein (g) | Fat (g) |
|---|---|---|---|---|---|---|---|
| 1 | Cereal Exchange | | | | | | |
| 2 | Pulse Exchange | | | | | | |
| 3 | Vegetable Exchange A | Group I | | | | | |
| | | Group II | | | | | |
| | | Group III | | | | | |
| 4 | Vegetable Exchange B | Group I | | | | | |
| | | Group II | | | | | |
| | | Group III | | | | | |
| 5 | Fruit Exchange | Group I | | | | | |
| | | Group II | | | | | |
| | | Group III | | | | | |
| | | Group IV | | | | | |
| | | Group V | | | | | |
| 6 | Milk Exchange | Whole Milk and Products | | | | | |
| | | Skimmed Milk and Products | | | | | |
| 7 | Nut and Oil Seed Exchange | | | | | | |
| 8 | Dry Fruit Exchange | | | | | | |
| 9 | Fat Exchange | | | | | | |
| 10 | Sugar and Starch Exchange | Sugar | | | | | |
| | | Jaggery | | | | | |
| | | Honey | | | | | |
| | | Sago | | | | | |
| 11 | Meat and Poultry Exchange | Egg | | | | | |
| | | Chicken | | | | | |
| | | Mutton | | | | | |
| 12 | Fish Exchange | | | | | | |
| 13 | Others | | | | | | |
| | Total | | | | | | |
| | Requirement | | | | | | |

--- Author ---
Dr. Prajakta J. Nande

# Clinical and Therapeutic Nutrition Practical Manual 1
For M.Sc. Food Science and Nutrition (Semester-III)

------------------------------------------------------------------------------------------

## :MEAL PLAN:

Suggested Meal Plan for------------------------------------------------------------------------------

| Meal/Time | Menu | No. of Servings/ Measures/ Quantity |
|---|---|---|
| Early Morning (----------am) | | |
| Breakfast (----------am) | | |
| Mid Morning (----------am) | | |
| Lunch (----------pm) | | |
| Snacks (----------pm) | | |
| Evening (----------pm) | | |
| Dinner (----------pm) | | |
| Bed Time (----------pm) | | |

--- Author ---
Dr. Prajakta J. Nande

# Clinical and Therapeutic Nutrition Practical Manual 1
For M.Sc. Food Science and Nutrition (Semester-III)

## TABLE 2: BREAK UP OF EXCHANGES

| Sr. No. | Name of Exchanges | | Early Morning (----am) | Breakfast (----am) | Mid Morning (----am) | Lunch (----pm) | Snacks (----pm) | Evening (----pm) | Dinner (----pm) | Bed Time (----pm) | Total |
|---|---|---|---|---|---|---|---|---|---|---|---|
| 1 | Cereal and Millet Exchange | | | | | | | | | | |
| 2 | Pulse and Legume Exchange | | | | | | | | | | |
| 3 | Vegetable Exchange A | Group I | | | | | | | | | |
| | | Group II | | | | | | | | | |
| | | Group III | | | | | | | | | |
| 4 | Vegetable Exchange B | Group I | | | | | | | | | |
| | | Group II | | | | | | | | | |
| | | Group III | | | | | | | | | |
| 5 | Fruit Exchange | Group I | | | | | | | | | |
| | | Group II | | | | | | | | | |
| | | Group III | | | | | | | | | |
| | | Group IV | | | | | | | | | |
| | | Group V | | | | | | | | | |
| 6 | Milk Exchange | Whole Milk and Products | | | | | | | | | |
| | | Skimmed Milk and Products | | | | | | | | | |
| 7 | Nuts and Oil Seed Exchange | | | | | | | | | | |
| 8 | Dry Fruit Exchange | | | | | | | | | | |
| 9 | Fat Exchange | | | | | | | | | | |
| 10 | Sugar and Starch Exchange | Sugar | | | | | | | | | |
| | | Jaggery | | | | | | | | | |
| | | Honey | | | | | | | | | |
| | | Sago | | | | | | | | | |
| 11 | Meat and Poultry Exchange | Egg | | | | | | | | | |
| | | Chicken | | | | | | | | | |
| | | Mutton | | | | | | | | | |
| 12 | Fish Exchange | | | | | | | | | | |
| 13 | Others | | | | | | | | | | |

--- Author ---
Dr. Prajakta J. Nande

# Clinical and Therapeutic Nutrition Practical Manual 1
For M.Sc. Food Science and Nutrition (Semester-III)

## LIST OF FOODS TO BE INCLUDED AND AVOIDED

| Name of Exchanges | Foods to be Included | Foods to be Restricted | Foods to be Avoided |
|---|---|---|---|
| Cereals and Millets | | | |
| Pulses and Legumes | | | |
| Vegetables | | | |
| Fruits | | | |
| Milk and It's Products | | | |
| Nuts and Oil Seeds | | | |
| Dry Fruits | | | |
| Fats and Oils | | | |
| Sugars and Starch | | | |
| Meat, Fish and Poultry | | | |
| Others | | | |

--- Author ---
Dr. Prajakta J. Nande

# Clinical and Therapeutic Nutrition Practical Manual 1

For M.Sc. Food Science and Nutrition (Semester-III)

## TABLE 3: NUTRITIVE VALUE OF THE PRESCRIBED DIET
### (VITAMINS AND MINERALS)

| Sr. No. | Food Stuffs | Weight (g) | B1 (mg) | B2 (mg) | Niacin (mg) | Carotene (µg) | Vitamin C (mg) | Ca (mg) | P (mg) | Fe (mg) | Na (mg) | K (mg) |
|---------|-------------|------------|---------|---------|-------------|---------------|----------------|---------|--------|---------|---------|--------|
| | | | | | | | | | | | | |
| | | | | | | | | | | | | |
| | | | | | | | | | | | | |
| | | | | | | | | | | | | |
| | | | | | | | | | | | | |
| | | | | | | | | | | | | |
| | | | | | | | | | | | | |
| | | | | | | | | | | | | |
| | | | | | | | | | | | | |
| | | | | | | | | | | | | |
| | | | | | | | | | | | | |
| | | | | | | | | | | | | |
| | | | | | | | | | | | | |
| | | | | | | | | | | | | |
| | | | | | | | | | | | | |
| | | | | | | | | | | | | |
| | | | | | | | | | | | | |
| | | | | | | | | | | | | |
| | | | | | | | | | | | | |
| | | | | | | | | | | | | |
| | | | | | | | | | | | | |
| | | | | | | | | | | | | |
| | | | | | | | | | | | | |
| | | | | | | | | | | | | |
| | | | | | | | | | | | | |
| | | | | | | | | | | | | |
| | | | | | | | | | | | | |
| | | | | | | | | | | | | |
| | | | | | | | | | | | | |
| | **Total** | | | | | | | | | | | |
| | **Required** | | | | | | | | | | | |

--- **Author** ---

Dr. Prajakta J. Nande

# Clinical and Therapeutic Nutrition Practical Manual 1
For M.Sc. Food Science and Nutrition (Semester-III)

## TABLE 4: FIBER CONTENT OF THE PRESCRIBED DIET

| Sr. No. | Food Stuffs | Weight (g) | Soluble Dietary Fiber (g) | Insoluble Dietary Fiber (g) | Total Dietary Fiber (g) |
|---|---|---|---|---|---|
| | | | | | |
| | | | | | |
| | | | | | |
| | | | | | |
| | | | | | |
| | | | | | |
| | | | | | |
| | | | | | |
| | | | | | |
| | | | | | |
| | | | | | |
| | | | | | |
| | | | | | |
| | | | | | |
| | | | | | |
| | | | | | |
| | | | | | |
| | | | | | |
| | | | | | |
| | | | | | |
| | | | | | |
| | | | | | |
| | | | | | |
| | | | | | |
| | | | | | |
| | | | | | |
| | | | | | |
| | | | | | |
| | | | | | |
| | | | | | |
| | | | | | |
| | | | | | |
| | | | | | |
| | | | | | |
| | | | | | |
| | | | | | |
| | | | | | |
| | **Total** | | | | |
| | **Required** | | | | |

--- **Author** ---
Dr. Prajakta J. Nande

# Clinical and Therapeutic Nutrition Practical Manual 1
## For M.Sc. Food Science and Nutrition (Semester-III)

## Comments:

## References:

# LIVER DISEASES

## Clinical and Therapeutic Nutrition Practical Manual 1
For M.Sc. Food Science and Nutrition (Semester-III)

---

| HEPATITIS |
|:---:|

## AIM: To plan and prepare a day's diet for an individual suffering from hepatitis using a case study approach

### Personal Information:                                    Dates:

**Name:**
**Sex:** Female/Male
**Age [Yrs]:**
**Height [cm]:**
**Actual Body Weight (ABW)/Present Body Weight [kg]:**
**Occupation:** Service/Business/Housewife/Any Other
**Monthly Family Income [Rs./-]:**
**Type of Work:** Sedentary/Moderate/Heavy
**Duration of Work [Hours]:**
**Any Other:**


### Clinical and Biochemical Investigations:
**Bowel Movements**                  : Regular/Irregular
**Blood, Urine and other Parameters:**


### Dietary Information:

| | |
|---|---|
| **Food Habits** | : Vegetarian/Non Vegetarian/Eggetarian |
| **Common Dietary Pattern** | : 2 meals/3 meals/4 meals/Any Other |
| **Meal Timings** | : Regular/Irregular |
| **Type of Oils used for Cooking** | : |
| **Salt used for Cooking** | : Iodized/Non Iodized |
| **Milk used** | : Cow's/Buffalo's [Wholesome/Skimmed] |
| **Approximate Water Intake** | :---------glasses/day |
| **Frequency of Non-Veg Intake** | : Weekly/Fortnightly/Monthly/Any Other |
| **Any Other** | : |

# Clinical and Therapeutic Nutrition Practical Manual 1
For M.Sc. Food Science and Nutrition (Semester-III)

## Existing Meal Plan:

| Name of Meal with Timing | Meal Plan | No. of Servings |
|---|---|---|
| | | |

# Clinical and Therapeutic Nutrition Practical Manual 1
For M.Sc. Food Science and Nutrition (Semester-III)

## Calculations for Requirements:
### 1. Ideal Body Weight [IBW]:

### 2. Body Mass Index [BMI]:

### 3. Energy Requirement:

## Division of Energy into Three Major Nutrients:
### 4. Protein Requirement:

### 5. Total Fat Requirement:

### 6. Carbohydrate Requirement:

# Clinical and Therapeutic Nutrition Practical Manual 1

**7. Micro-Nutrient Requirement**:

| Sr. No. | Vitamins/Minerals | Values |
|---|---|---|
| 1 | | |
| 2 | | |
| 3 | | |
| 4 | | |
| 5 | | |
| 6 | | |
| 7 | | |
| 8 | | |
| 9 | | |
| 10 | | |

**8. Amount of Salt and Sodium from Salt:**

**9. Fluid Intake**:

**10. Amount of Fats and Oils:**

**11. Amount of Sugars:**

**12. Non Veg Food Intake:**

# Clinical and Therapeutic Nutrition Practical Manual 1
For M.Sc. Food Science and Nutrition (Semester-III)

**Nutritional Goals:**

**Principles of Dietary Modifications:**

# Clinical and Therapeutic Nutrition Practical Manual 1
For M.Sc. Food Science and Nutrition (Semester-III)

## TABLE 1: FOOD EXCHANGE LIST

| Sr. No. | Name of Exchanges | | No. of Exchanges | Energy (kcal) | Carbohydrate (g) | Protein (g) | Fat (g) |
|---|---|---|---|---|---|---|---|
| 1 | Cereal Exchange | | | | | | |
| 2 | Pulse Exchange | | | | | | |
| 3 | Vegetable Exchange A | Group I | | | | | |
| | | Group II | | | | | |
| | | Group III | | | | | |
| 4 | Vegetable Exchange B | Group I | | | | | |
| | | Group II | | | | | |
| | | Group III | | | | | |
| 5 | Fruit Exchange | Group I | | | | | |
| | | Group II | | | | | |
| | | Group III | | | | | |
| | | Group IV | | | | | |
| | | Group V | | | | | |
| 6 | Milk Exchange | Whole Milk and Products | | | | | |
| | | Skimmed Milk and Products | | | | | |
| 7 | Nut and Oil Seed Exchange | | | | | | |
| 8 | Dry Fruit Exchange | | | | | | |
| 9 | Fat Exchange | | | | | | |
| 10 | Sugar and Starch Exchange | Sugar | | | | | |
| | | Jaggery | | | | | |
| | | Honey | | | | | |
| | | Sago | | | | | |
| 11 | Meat and Poultry Exchange | Egg | | | | | |
| | | Chicken | | | | | |
| | | Mutton | | | | | |
| 12 | Fish Exchange | | | | | | |
| 13 | Others | | | | | | |
| | Total | | | | | | |
| | Requirement | | | | | | |

--- **Author** ---
Dr. Prajakta J. Nande

# Clinical and Therapeutic Nutrition Practical Manual 1
For M.Sc. Food Science and Nutrition (Semester-III)

----------------------------------------------------------------------------------------------------

## :MEAL PLAN:

**Suggested Meal Plan for**----------------------------------------------------------------------------------------------------

| Meal/Time | Menu | No. of Servings/ Measures/ Quantity |
|---|---|---|
| **Early Morning** (----------am) | | |
| **Breakfast** (----------am) | | |
| **Mid Morning** (----------am) | | |
| **Lunch** (----------pm) | | |
| **Snacks** (----------pm) | | |
| **Evening** (----------pm) | | |
| **Dinner** (----------pm) | | |
| **Bed Time** (----------pm) | | |

--- **Author** ---
Dr. Prajakta J. Nande

# Clinical and Therapeutic Nutrition Practical Manual 1
For M.Sc. Food Science and Nutrition (Semester-III)

## TABLE 2: BREAK UP OF EXCHANGES

| Sr. No. | Name of Exchanges | | Early Morning (----am) | Breakfast (----am) | Mid Morning (----am) | Lunch (----pm) | Snacks (----pm) | Evening (----pm) | Dinner (----pm) | Bed Time (----pm) | Total |
|---|---|---|---|---|---|---|---|---|---|---|---|
| 1 | Cereal and Millet Exchange | | | | | | | | | | |
| 2 | Pulse and Legume Exchange | | | | | | | | | | |
| 3 | Vegetable Exchange A | Group I | | | | | | | | | |
| | | Group II | | | | | | | | | |
| | | Group III | | | | | | | | | |
| 4 | Vegetable Exchange B | Group I | | | | | | | | | |
| | | Group II | | | | | | | | | |
| | | Group III | | | | | | | | | |
| 5 | Fruit Exchange | Group I | | | | | | | | | |
| | | Group II | | | | | | | | | |
| | | Group III | | | | | | | | | |
| | | Group IV | | | | | | | | | |
| | | Group V | | | | | | | | | |
| 6 | Milk Exchange | Whole Milk and Products | | | | | | | | | |
| | | Skimmed Milk and Products | | | | | | | | | |
| 7 | Nuts and Oil Seed Exchange | | | | | | | | | | |
| 8 | Dry Fruit Exchange | | | | | | | | | | |
| 9 | Fat Exchange | | | | | | | | | | |
| 10 | Sugar and Starch Exchange | Sugar | | | | | | | | | |
| | | Jaggery | | | | | | | | | |
| | | Honey | | | | | | | | | |
| | | Sago | | | | | | | | | |
| 11 | Meat and Poultry Exchange | Egg | | | | | | | | | |
| | | Chicken | | | | | | | | | |
| | | Mutton | | | | | | | | | |
| 12 | Fish Exchange | | | | | | | | | | |
| 13 | Others | | | | | | | | | | |

--- Author ---
Dr. Prajakta J. Nande

# Clinical and Therapeutic Nutrition Practical Manual 1
For M.Sc. Food Science and Nutrition (Semester-III)

## LIST OF FOODS TO BE INCLUDED AND AVOIDED

| Name of Exchanges | Foods to be Included | Foods to be Restricted | Foods to be Avoided |
|---|---|---|---|
| Cereals and Millets | | | |
| Pulses and Legumes | | | |
| Vegetables | | | |
| Fruits | | | |
| Milk and It's Products | | | |
| Nuts and Oil Seeds | | | |
| Dry Fruits | | | |
| Fats and Oils | | | |
| Sugars and Starch | | | |
| Meat, Fish and Poultry | | | |
| Others | | | |

--- Author ---
Dr. Prajakta J. Nande

# Clinical and Therapeutic Nutrition Practical Manual 1
For M.Sc. Food Science and Nutrition (Semester-III)

## TABLE 3: NUTRITIVE VALUE OF THE PRESCRIBED DIET
## (VITAMINS AND MINERALS)

| Sr. No. | Food Stuffs | Weight (g) | B1 (mg) | B2 (mg) | Niacin (mg) | Carotene (µg) | Vitamin C (mg) | Ca (mg) | P (mg) | Fe (mg) | Na (mg) | K (mg) |
|---|---|---|---|---|---|---|---|---|---|---|---|---|
| | | | | | | | | | | | | |
| | | | | | | | | | | | | |
| | | | | | | | | | | | | |
| | | | | | | | | | | | | |
| | | | | | | | | | | | | |
| | | | | | | | | | | | | |
| | | | | | | | | | | | | |
| | | | | | | | | | | | | |
| | | | | | | | | | | | | |
| | | | | | | | | | | | | |
| | | | | | | | | | | | | |
| | | | | | | | | | | | | |
| | | | | | | | | | | | | |
| | | | | | | | | | | | | |
| | | | | | | | | | | | | |
| | | | | | | | | | | | | |
| | | | | | | | | | | | | |
| | | | | | | | | | | | | |
| | | | | | | | | | | | | |
| | | | | | | | | | | | | |
| | | | | | | | | | | | | |
| | | | | | | | | | | | | |
| | | | | | | | | | | | | |
| | | | | | | | | | | | | |
| | | | | | | | | | | | | |
| | | | | | | | | | | | | |
| | | | | | | | | | | | | |
| | | | | | | | | | | | | |
| | | | | | | | | | | | | |
| | | | | | | | | | | | | |
| | | | | | | | | | | | | |
| | | | | | | | | | | | | |
| | | | | | | | | | | | | |
| | | | | | | | | | | | | |
| | | | | | | | | | | | | |
| | **Total** | | | | | | | | | | | |
| | **Required** | | | | | | | | | | | |

--- **Author** ---
Dr. Prajakta J. Nande

# Clinical and Therapeutic Nutrition Practical Manual 1
For M.Sc. Food Science and Nutrition (Semester-III)

## TABLE 4: FIBER CONTENT OF THE PRESCRIBED DIET

| Sr. No. | Food Stuffs | Weight (g) | Soluble Dietary Fiber (g) | Insoluble Dietary Fiber (g) | Total Dietary Fiber (g) |
|---------|-------------|------------|---------------------------|-----------------------------|-------------------------|
|         |             |            |                           |                             |                         |
|         |             |            |                           |                             |                         |
|         |             |            |                           |                             |                         |
|         |             |            |                           |                             |                         |
|         |             |            |                           |                             |                         |
|         |             |            |                           |                             |                         |
|         |             |            |                           |                             |                         |
|         |             |            |                           |                             |                         |
|         |             |            |                           |                             |                         |
|         |             |            |                           |                             |                         |
|         |             |            |                           |                             |                         |
|         |             |            |                           |                             |                         |
|         |             |            |                           |                             |                         |
|         |             |            |                           |                             |                         |
|         |             |            |                           |                             |                         |
|         |             |            |                           |                             |                         |
|         |             |            |                           |                             |                         |
|         |             |            |                           |                             |                         |
|         |             |            |                           |                             |                         |
|         |             |            |                           |                             |                         |
|         |             |            |                           |                             |                         |
|         |             |            |                           |                             |                         |
|         |             |            |                           |                             |                         |
|         |             |            |                           |                             |                         |
|         |             |            |                           |                             |                         |
|         |             |            |                           |                             |                         |
|         |             |            |                           |                             |                         |
|         |             |            |                           |                             |                         |
|         |             |            |                           |                             |                         |
|         |             |            |                           |                             |                         |
|         |             |            |                           |                             |                         |
|         |             |            |                           |                             |                         |
|         |             |            |                           |                             |                         |
|         | **Total**   |            |                           |                             |                         |
|         | **Required**|            |                           |                             |                         |

--- Author ---
Dr. Prajakta J. Nande

# Comments:

# References:

**Clinical and Therapeutic Nutrition Practical Manual 1**
For M.Sc. Food Science and Nutrition (Semester-III)

---

## ALCOHOLIC CIRRHOSIS

### AIM: To plan and prepare a day's diet for an individual suffering from alcoholic cirrhosis using a case study approach

## Personal Information:                                    Dates:

**Name:**
**Sex:** Female/Male
**Age [Yrs]:**
**Height [cm]:**
**Actual Body Weight (ABW)/Present Body Weight [kg]:**
**Occupation:** Service/Business/Housewife/Any Other
**Monthly Family Income [Rs./-]:**
**Type of Work:** Sedentary/Moderate/Heavy
**Duration of Work [Hours]:**
**Any Other:**


## Clinical and Biochemical Investigations:
**Bowel Movements**              : Regular/Irregular
**Blood, Urine and other Parameters:**


## Dietary Information:

| | |
|---|---|
| **Food Habits** | : Vegetarian/Non Vegetarian/Eggetarian |
| **Common Dietary Pattern** | : 2 meals/3 meals/4 meals/Any Other |
| **Meal Timings** | : Regular/Irregular |
| **Type of Oils used for Cooking** | : |
| **Salt used for Cooking** | : Iodized/Non Iodized |
| **Milk used** | : Cow's/Buffalo's [Wholesome/Skimmed] |
| **Approximate Water Intake** | :---------glasses/day |
| **Frequency of Non-Veg Intake** | : Weekly/Fortnightly/Monthly/Any Other |
| **Any Other** | : |

---
124

--- **Author** ---
Dr. Prajakta J. Nande

## Existing Meal Plan:

| Name of Meal with Timing | Meal Plan | No. of Servings |
|---|---|---|
|  |  |  |

# Calculations for Requirements:
## 1. Ideal Body Weight [IBW]:




## 2. Body Mass Index [BMI]:





## 3. Energy Requirement:




# Division of Energy into Three Major Nutrients:
## 4. Protein Requirement:




## 5. Total Fat Requirement:




## 6. Carbohydrate Requirement:

# Clinical and Therapeutic Nutrition Practical Manual 1
### For M.Sc. Food Science and Nutrition (Semester-III)

**7. Micro-Nutrient Requirement:**

| Sr. No. | Vitamins/Minerals | Values |
|---------|-------------------|--------|
| 1 | | |
| 2 | | |
| 3 | | |
| 4 | | |
| 5 | | |
| 6 | | |
| 7 | | |
| 8 | | |
| 9 | | |
| 10 | | |

**8. Amount of Salt and Sodium from Salt:**

**9. Fluid Intake:**

**10. Amount of Fats and Oils:**

**11. Amount of Sugars:**

**12. Non Veg Food Intake:**

# Clinical and Therapeutic Nutrition Practical Manual 1
For M.Sc. Food Science and Nutrition (Semester-III)

**Nutritional Goals:**

**Principles of Dietary Modifications:**

# Clinical and Therapeutic Nutrition Practical Manual 1
For M.Sc. Food Science and Nutrition (Semester-III)

## TABLE 1: FOOD EXCHANGE LIST

| Sr. No. | Name of Exchanges | | No. of Exchanges | Energy (kcal) | Carbohydrate (g) | Protein (g) | Fat (g) |
|---|---|---|---|---|---|---|---|
| 1 | Cereal Exchange | | | | | | |
| 2 | Pulse Exchange | | | | | | |
| 3 | Vegetable Exchange A | Group I | | | | | |
| | | Group II | | | | | |
| | | Group III | | | | | |
| 4 | Vegetable Exchange B | Group I | | | | | |
| | | Group II | | | | | |
| | | Group III | | | | | |
| 5 | Fruit Exchange | Group I | | | | | |
| | | Group II | | | | | |
| | | Group III | | | | | |
| | | Group IV | | | | | |
| | | Group V | | | | | |
| 6 | Milk Exchange | Whole Milk and Products | | | | | |
| | | Skimmed Milk and Products | | | | | |
| 7 | Nut and Oil Seed Exchange | | | | | | |
| 8 | Dry Fruit Exchange | | | | | | |
| 9 | Fat Exchange | | | | | | |
| 10 | Sugar and Starch Exchange | Sugar | | | | | |
| | | Jaggery | | | | | |
| | | Honey | | | | | |
| | | Sago | | | | | |
| 11 | Meat and Poultry Exchange | Egg | | | | | |
| | | Chicken | | | | | |
| | | Mutton | | | | | |
| 12 | Fish Exchange | | | | | | |
| 13 | Others | | | | | | |
| | Total | | | | | | |
| | Requirement | | | | | | |

--- **Author** ---
Dr. Prajakta J. Nande

# Clinical and Therapeutic Nutrition Practical Manual 1
For M.Sc. Food Science and Nutrition (Semester-III)

---

## :MEAL PLAN:

**Suggested Meal Plan for**--------------------------------------------------------------------------------

| Meal/Time | Menu | No. of Servings/ Measures/ Quantity |
|---|---|---|
| **Early Morning** (----------am) | | |
| **Breakfast** (----------am) | | |
| **Mid Morning** (----------am) | | |
| **Lunch** (----------pm) | | |
| **Snacks** (----------pm) | | |
| **Evening** (----------pm) | | |
| **Dinner** (----------pm) | | |
| **Bed Time** (----------pm) | | |

# Clinical and Therapeutic Nutrition Practical Manual 1
For M.Sc. Food Science and Nutrition (Semester-III)

## TABLE 2: BREAK UP OF EXCHANGES

| Sr. No. | Name of Exchanges | | Early Morning (-----am) | Breakfast (-----am) | Mid Morning (-----am) | Lunch (-----pm) | Snacks (-----pm) | Evening (-----pm) | Dinner (-----pm) | Bed Time (-----pm) | Total |
|---|---|---|---|---|---|---|---|---|---|---|---|
| 1 | Cereal and Millet Exchange | | | | | | | | | | |
| 2 | Pulse and Legume Exchange | | | | | | | | | | |
| 3 | Vegetable Exchange A | Group I | | | | | | | | | |
| | | Group II | | | | | | | | | |
| | | Group III | | | | | | | | | |
| 4 | Vegetable Exchange B | Group I | | | | | | | | | |
| | | Group II | | | | | | | | | |
| | | Group III | | | | | | | | | |
| 5 | Fruit Exchange | Group I | | | | | | | | | |
| | | Group II | | | | | | | | | |
| | | Group III | | | | | | | | | |
| | | Group IV | | | | | | | | | |
| | | Group V | | | | | | | | | |
| 6 | Milk Exchange | Whole Milk and Products | | | | | | | | | |
| | | Skimmed Milk and Products | | | | | | | | | |
| 7 | Nuts and Oil Seed Exchange | | | | | | | | | | |
| 8 | Dry Fruit Exchange | | | | | | | | | | |
| 9 | Fat Exchange | | | | | | | | | | |
| 10 | Sugar and Starch Exchange | Sugar | | | | | | | | | |
| | | Jaggery | | | | | | | | | |
| | | Honey | | | | | | | | | |
| | | Sago | | | | | | | | | |
| 11 | Meat and Poultry Exchange | Egg | | | | | | | | | |
| | | Chicken | | | | | | | | | |
| | | Mutton | | | | | | | | | |
| 12 | Fish Exchange | | | | | | | | | | |
| 13 | Others | | | | | | | | | | |

--- Author ---
Dr. Prajakta J. Nande

# Clinical and Therapeutic Nutrition Practical Manual 1

For M.Sc. Food Science and Nutrition (Semester-III)

## LIST OF FOODS TO BE INCLUDED AND AVOIDED

| Name of Exchanges | Foods to be Included | Foods to be Restricted | Foods to be Avoided |
|---|---|---|---|
| Cereals and Millets | | | |
| Pulses and Legumes | | | |
| Vegetables | | | |
| Fruits | | | |
| Milk and It's Products | | | |
| Nuts and Oil Seeds | | | |
| Dry Fruits | | | |
| Fats and Oils | | | |
| Sugars and Starch | | | |
| Meat, Fish and Poultry | | | |
| Others | | | |

# Clinical and Therapeutic Nutrition Practical Manual 1
For M.Sc. Food Science and Nutrition (Semester-III)

## TABLE 3: NUTRITIVE VALUE OF THE PRESCRIBED DIET
## (VITAMINS AND MINERALS)

| Sr. No. | Food Stuffs | Weight (g) | B1 (mg) | B2 (mg) | Niacin (mg) | Carotene (µg) | Vitamin C (mg) | Ca (mg) | P (mg) | Fe (mg) | Na (mg) | K (mg) |
|---------|-------------|------------|---------|---------|-------------|---------------|----------------|---------|--------|---------|---------|--------|
| | | | | | | | | | | | | |
| | | | | | | | | | | | | |
| | | | | | | | | | | | | |
| | | | | | | | | | | | | |
| | | | | | | | | | | | | |
| | | | | | | | | | | | | |
| | | | | | | | | | | | | |
| | | | | | | | | | | | | |
| | | | | | | | | | | | | |
| | | | | | | | | | | | | |
| | | | | | | | | | | | | |
| | | | | | | | | | | | | |
| | | | | | | | | | | | | |
| | | | | | | | | | | | | |
| | | | | | | | | | | | | |
| | | | | | | | | | | | | |
| | | | | | | | | | | | | |
| | | | | | | | | | | | | |
| | | | | | | | | | | | | |
| | | | | | | | | | | | | |
| | | | | | | | | | | | | |
| | | | | | | | | | | | | |
| | | | | | | | | | | | | |
| | | | | | | | | | | | | |
| | | | | | | | | | | | | |
| | | | | | | | | | | | | |
| | | | | | | | | | | | | |
| | | | | | | | | | | | | |
| | | | | | | | | | | | | |
| | | | | | | | | | | | | |
| | Total | | | | | | | | | | | |
| | Required | | | | | | | | | | | |

--- **Author** ---
Dr. Prajakta J. Nande

# Clinical and Therapeutic Nutrition Practical Manual 1
For M.Sc. Food Science and Nutrition (Semester-III)

## TABLE 4: FIBER CONTENT OF THE PRESCRIBED DIET

| Sr. No. | Food Stuffs | Weight (g) | Soluble Dietary Fiber (g) | Insoluble Dietary Fiber (g) | Total Dietary Fiber (g) |
|---------|-------------|------------|---------------------------|-----------------------------|-------------------------|
| | | | | | |
| | | | | | |
| | | | | | |
| | | | | | |
| | | | | | |
| | | | | | |
| | | | | | |
| | | | | | |
| | | | | | |
| | | | | | |
| | | | | | |
| | | | | | |
| | | | | | |
| | | | | | |
| | | | | | |
| | | | | | |
| | | | | | |
| | | | | | |
| | | | | | |
| | | | | | |
| | | | | | |
| | | | | | |
| | | | | | |
| | | | | | |
| | | | | | |
| | | | | | |
| | | | | | |
| | | | | | |
| | | | | | |
| | | | | | |
| | | | | | |
| | | | | | |
| | | | | | |
| | | | | | |
| | | | | | |
| | | | | | |
| | | | | | |
| | | | | | |
| | | | | | |
| | | | | | |
| **Total** | | | | | |
| **Required** | | | | | |

--- Author ---
Dr. Prajakta J. Nande

# Comments:

# References:

**Clinical and Therapeutic Nutrition Practical Manual 1**
For M.Sc. Food Science and Nutrition (Semester-III)

---

# CIRRHOSIS OF LIVER WITH PORTAL HYPERTENSION AND ASCITES

**AIM:** To plan and prepare a day's diet for an individual suffering from cirrhosis of liver with portal hypertension and ascites using a case study approach

## Personal Information:

Dates:

**Name:**
**Sex:** Female/Male
**Age [Yrs]:**
**Height [cm]:**
**Actual Body Weight (ABW)/Present Body Weight [kg]:**
**Occupation:** Service/Business/Housewife/Any Other
**Monthly Family Income [Rs./-]:**
**Type of Work:** Sedentary/Moderate/Heavy
**Duration of Work [Hours]:**
**Any Other:**

## Clinical and Biochemical Investigations:

**Bowel Movements** : Regular/Irregular
**Blood, Urine and other Parameters:**

## Dietary Information:

| | |
|---|---|
| **Food Habits** | : Vegetarian/Non Vegetarian/Eggetarian |
| **Common Dietary Pattern** | : 2 meals/3 meals/4 meals/Any Other |
| **Meal Timings** | : Regular/Irregular |
| **Type of Oils used for Cooking** | : |
| **Salt used for Cooking** | : Iodized/Non Iodized |
| **Milk used** | : Cow's/Buffalo's [Wholesome/Skimmed] |
| **Approximate Water Intake** | :---------glasses/day |
| **Frequency of Non-Veg Intake** | : Weekly/Fortnightly/Monthly/Any Other |
| **Any Other** | : |

--- **Author** ---
Dr. Prajakta J. Nande

# Clinical and Therapeutic Nutrition Practical Manual 1
For M.Sc. Food Science and Nutrition (Semester-III)

## Existing Meal Plan:

| Name of Meal with Timing | Meal Plan | No. of Servings |
|---|---|---|
| | | |

## Calculations for Requirements:

**1. Ideal Body Weight [IBW]:**

**2. Body Mass Index [BMI]:**

**3. Energy Requirement:**

## Division of Energy into Three Major Nutrients:

**4. Protein Requirement:**

**5. Total Fat Requirement:**

**6. Carbohydrate Requirement:**

# Clinical and Therapeutic Nutrition Practical Manual 1
For M.Sc. Food Science and Nutrition (Semester-III)

**7. Micro-Nutrient Requirement**:

| Sr. No. | Vitamins/Minerals | Values |
|---------|-------------------|--------|
| 1 | | |
| 2 | | |
| 3 | | |
| 4 | | |
| 5 | | |
| 6 | | |
| 7 | | |
| 8 | | |
| 9 | | |
| 10 | | |

**8. Amount of Salt and Sodium from Salt**:

**9. Fluid Intake**:

**10. Amount of Fats and Oils**:

**11. Amount of Sugars**:

**12. Non Veg Food Intake**:

# Clinical and Therapeutic Nutrition Practical Manual 1
## For M.Sc. Food Science and Nutrition (Semester-III)

**Nutritional Goals:**

**Principles of Dietary Modifications:**

# Clinical and Therapeutic Nutrition Practical Manual 1
For M.Sc. Food Science and Nutrition (Semester-III)

## TABLE 1: FOOD EXCHANGE LIST

| Sr. No. | Name of Exchanges | | No. of Exchanges | Energy (kcal) | Carbohydrate (g) | Protein (g) | Fat (g) |
|---|---|---|---|---|---|---|---|
| 1 | Cereal Exchange | | | | | | |
| 2 | Pulse Exchange | | | | | | |
| 3 | Vegetable Exchange A | Group I | | | | | |
| | | Group II | | | | | |
| | | Group III | | | | | |
| 4 | Vegetable Exchange B | Group I | | | | | |
| | | Group II | | | | | |
| | | Group III | | | | | |
| 5 | Fruit Exchange | Group I | | | | | |
| | | Group II | | | | | |
| | | Group III | | | | | |
| | | Group IV | | | | | |
| | | Group V | | | | | |
| 6 | Milk Exchange | Whole Milk and Products | | | | | |
| | | Skimmed Milk and Products | | | | | |
| 7 | Nut and Oil Seed Exchange | | | | | | |
| 8 | Dry Fruit Exchange | | | | | | |
| 9 | Fat Exchange | | | | | | |
| 10 | Sugar and Starch Exchange | Sugar | | | | | |
| | | Jaggery | | | | | |
| | | Honey | | | | | |
| | | Sago | | | | | |
| 11 | Meat and Poultry Exchange | Egg | | | | | |
| | | Chicken | | | | | |
| | | Mutton | | | | | |
| 12 | Fish Exchange | | | | | | |
| 13 | Others | | | | | | |
| | Total | | | | | | |
| | Requirement | | | | | | |

--- **Author** ---
Dr. Prajakta J. Nande

# Clinical and Therapeutic Nutrition Practical Manual 1
For M.Sc. Food Science and Nutrition (Semester-III)

-----------------------------------------------------------------------------------------------

## :MEAL PLAN:

Suggested Meal Plan for----------------------------------------------------------------------------------

| Meal/Time | Menu | No. of Servings/ Measures/ Quantity |
|---|---|---|
| **Early Morning** (----------am) | | |
| **Breakfast** (----------am) | | |
| **Mid Morning** (----------am) | | |
| **Lunch** (----------pm) | | |
| **Snacks** (----------pm) | | |
| **Evening** (----------pm) | | |
| **Dinner** (----------pm) | | |
| **Bed Time** (----------pm) | | |

--- **Author** ---
Dr. Prajakta J. Nande

# Clinical and Therapeutic Nutrition Practical Manual 1
For M.Sc. Food Science and Nutrition (Semester-III)

## TABLE 2: BREAK UP OF EXCHANGES

| Sr. No. | Name of Exchanges | | Early Morning (----am) | Breakfast (----am) | Mid Morning (----am) | Lunch (----pm) | Snacks (----pm) | Evening (----pm) | Dinner (----pm) | Bed Time (----pm) | Total |
|---|---|---|---|---|---|---|---|---|---|---|---|
| 1 | Cereal and Millet Exchange | | | | | | | | | | |
| 2 | Pulse and Legume Exchange | | | | | | | | | | |
| 3 | Vegetable Exchange A | Group I | | | | | | | | | |
| | | Group II | | | | | | | | | |
| | | Group III | | | | | | | | | |
| 4 | Vegetable Exchange B | Group I | | | | | | | | | |
| | | Group II | | | | | | | | | |
| | | Group III | | | | | | | | | |
| 5 | Fruit Exchange | Group I | | | | | | | | | |
| | | Group II | | | | | | | | | |
| | | Group III | | | | | | | | | |
| | | Group IV | | | | | | | | | |
| | | Group V | | | | | | | | | |
| 6 | Milk Exchange | Whole Milk and Products | | | | | | | | | |
| | | Skimmed Milk and Products | | | | | | | | | |
| 7 | Nuts and Oil Seed Exchange | | | | | | | | | | |
| 8 | Dry Fruit Exchange | | | | | | | | | | |
| 9 | Fat Exchange | | | | | | | | | | |
| 10 | Sugar and Starch Exchange | Sugar | | | | | | | | | |
| | | Jaggery | | | | | | | | | |
| | | Honey | | | | | | | | | |
| | | Sago | | | | | | | | | |
| 11 | Meat and Poultry Exchange | Egg | | | | | | | | | |
| | | Chicken | | | | | | | | | |
| | | Mutton | | | | | | | | | |
| 12 | Fish Exchange | | | | | | | | | | |
| 13 | Others | | | | | | | | | | |

--- **Author** ---
Dr. Prajakta J. Nande

# Clinical and Therapeutic Nutrition Practical Manual 1
For M.Sc. Food Science and Nutrition (Semester-III)

## LIST OF FOODS TO BE INCLUDED AND AVOIDED

| Name of Exchanges | Foods to be Included | Foods to be Restricted | Foods to be Avoided |
|---|---|---|---|
| Cereals and Millets | | | |
| Pulses and Legumes | | | |
| Vegetables | | | |
| Fruits | | | |
| Milk and It's Products | | | |
| Nuts and Oil Seeds | | | |
| Dry Fruits | | | |
| Fats and Oils | | | |
| Sugars and Starch | | | |
| Meat, Fish and Poultry | | | |
| Others | | | |

--- Author ---
Dr. Prajakta J. Nande

# Clinical and Therapeutic Nutrition Practical Manual 1
For M.Sc. Food Science and Nutrition (Semester-III)

## TABLE 3: NUTRITIVE VALUE OF THE PRESCRIBED DIET
## (VITAMINS AND MINERALS)

| Sr. No. | Food Stuffs | Weight (g) | B1 (mg) | B2 (mg) | Niacin (mg) | Carotene (µg) | Vitamin C (mg) | Ca (mg) | P (mg) | Fe (mg) | Na (mg) | K (mg) |
|---------|-------------|-----------|---------|---------|-------------|---------------|----------------|---------|--------|---------|---------|--------|
| | | | | | | | | | | | | |
| | | | | | | | | | | | | |
| | | | | | | | | | | | | |
| | | | | | | | | | | | | |
| | | | | | | | | | | | | |
| | | | | | | | | | | | | |
| | | | | | | | | | | | | |
| | | | | | | | | | | | | |
| | | | | | | | | | | | | |
| | | | | | | | | | | | | |
| | | | | | | | | | | | | |
| | | | | | | | | | | | | |
| | | | | | | | | | | | | |
| | | | | | | | | | | | | |
| | | | | | | | | | | | | |
| | | | | | | | | | | | | |
| | | | | | | | | | | | | |
| | | | | | | | | | | | | |
| | | | | | | | | | | | | |
| | | | | | | | | | | | | |
| | | | | | | | | | | | | |
| | | | | | | | | | | | | |
| | | | | | | | | | | | | |
| | | | | | | | | | | | | |
| | | | | | | | | | | | | |
| | | | | | | | | | | | | |
| | | | | | | | | | | | | |
| | | | | | | | | | | | | |
| | | | | | | | | | | | | |
| | | | | | | | | | | | | |
| | | | | | | | | | | | | |
| | **Total** | | | | | | | | | | | |
| | **Required** | | | | | | | | | | | |

--- Author ---
Dr. Prajakta J. Nande

# Clinical and Therapeutic Nutrition Practical Manual 1
For M.Sc. Food Science and Nutrition (Semester-III)

## TABLE 4: FIBER AND MOISTURE CONTENT OF THE PRESCRIBED DIET

| Sr. No. | Food Stuffs | Weight (g) | Soluble Dietary Fiber (g) | Insoluble Dietary Fiber (g) | Total Dietary Fiber (g) | Moisture (g) |
|---------|-------------|------------|---------------------------|-----------------------------|-------------------------|--------------|
|         |             |            |                           |                             |                         |              |
|         |             |            |                           |                             |                         |              |
|         |             |            |                           |                             |                         |              |
|         |             |            |                           |                             |                         |              |
|         |             |            |                           |                             |                         |              |
|         |             |            |                           |                             |                         |              |
|         |             |            |                           |                             |                         |              |
|         |             |            |                           |                             |                         |              |
|         |             |            |                           |                             |                         |              |
|         |             |            |                           |                             |                         |              |
|         |             |            |                           |                             |                         |              |
|         |             |            |                           |                             |                         |              |
|         |             |            |                           |                             |                         |              |
|         |             |            |                           |                             |                         |              |
|         |             |            |                           |                             |                         |              |
|         |             |            |                           |                             |                         |              |
|         |             |            |                           |                             |                         |              |
|         |             |            |                           |                             |                         |              |
|         |             |            |                           |                             |                         |              |
|         |             |            |                           |                             |                         |              |
|         |             |            |                           |                             |                         |              |
|         |             |            |                           |                             |                         |              |
|         |             |            |                           |                             |                         |              |
|         |             |            |                           |                             |                         |              |
|         |             |            |                           |                             |                         |              |
|         |             |            |                           |                             |                         |              |
|         |             |            |                           |                             |                         |              |
|         |             |            |                           |                             |                         |              |
|         |             |            |                           |                             |                         |              |
|         | **Total**   |            |                           |                             |                         |              |
|         | **Required**|            |                           |                             |                         |              |

--- **Author** ---
Dr. Prajakta J. Nande

# Clinical and Therapeutic Nutrition Practical Manual 1
For M.Sc. Food Science and Nutrition (Semester-III)

## TABLE 5: BRANCHED CHAIN AMINO ACID CONTENT OF THE PRESCRIBED DIET (g/100 g of Protein)

| Sr. No. | Food Stuffs | Weight (g) | Isoleucine (g) | Leucine (g) | Valine (g) |
|---|---|---|---|---|---|
| | | | | | |
| | | | | | |
| | | | | | |
| | | | | | |
| | | | | | |
| | | | | | |
| | | | | | |
| | | | | | |
| | | | | | |
| | | | | | |
| | | | | | |
| | | | | | |
| | | | | | |
| | | | | | |
| | | | | | |
| | | | | | |
| | | | | | |
| | | | | | |
| | | | | | |
| | | | | | |
| | | | | | |
| | | | | | |
| | | | | | |
| | | | | | |
| | | | | | |
| | | | | | |
| | | | | | |
| | | | | | |
| | | | | | |
| | | | | | |
| | | | | | |
| | | | | | |
| | | | | | |
| | | | | | |
| | | | | | |
| | | | | | |
| | | | | | |
| | | | | | |
| | Total | | | | |
| | Required | | | | |

# Clinical and Therapeutic Nutrition Practical Manual 1

For M.Sc. Food Science and Nutrition (Semester-III)

## TABLE 6: AROMATIC AMINO ACID CONTENT OF THE PRESCRIBED DIET
### (g/100 g of Protein)

| Sr. No. | Food Stuffs | Weight (g) | Phenylalanine (g) | Tyrosine (g) | Tryptophan (g) |
|---------|-------------|------------|-------------------|--------------|----------------|
|  |  |  |  |  |  |
|  |  |  |  |  |  |
|  |  |  |  |  |  |
|  |  |  |  |  |  |
|  |  |  |  |  |  |
|  |  |  |  |  |  |
|  |  |  |  |  |  |
|  |  |  |  |  |  |
|  |  |  |  |  |  |
|  |  |  |  |  |  |
|  |  |  |  |  |  |
|  |  |  |  |  |  |
|  |  |  |  |  |  |
|  |  |  |  |  |  |
|  |  |  |  |  |  |
|  |  |  |  |  |  |
|  |  |  |  |  |  |
|  |  |  |  |  |  |
|  |  |  |  |  |  |
|  |  |  |  |  |  |
|  |  |  |  |  |  |
|  |  |  |  |  |  |
|  |  |  |  |  |  |
|  |  |  |  |  |  |
|  |  |  |  |  |  |
|  |  |  |  |  |  |
|  |  |  |  |  |  |
|  |  |  |  |  |  |
|  |  |  |  |  |  |
|  | **Total** |  |  |  |  |
|  | **Required** |  |  |  |  |

# Comments:

# References:

**Clinical and Therapeutic Nutrition Practical Manual 1**
For M.Sc. Food Science and Nutrition (Semester-III)

---

## HEPATIC COMA

**AIM: To plan and prepare a day's tube feeds for an individual suffering from hepatic coma using a case study approach**

# Personal Information:
Dates:

**Name:**
**Sex:** Female/Male
**Age [Yrs]:**
**Height [cm]:**
**Actual Body Weight (ABW)/Present Body Weight [kg]:**
**Occupation:** Service/Business/Housewife/Any Other
**Monthly Family Income [Rs./-]:**
**Type of Work:** Sedentary/Moderate/Heavy
**Duration of Work [Hours]:**
**Any Other:**

# Clinical and Biochemical Investigations:
**Bowel Movements** : Regular/Irregular
**Blood, Urine and other Parameters:**

# Dietary Information:
**Food Habits** : Vegetarian/Non Vegetarian/Eggetarian
**Common Dietary Pattern** : 2 meals/3 meals/4 meals/Any Other
**Meal Timings** : Regular/Irregular
**Type of Oils used for Cooking** :
**Salt used for Cooking** : Iodized/Non Iodized
**Milk used** : Cow's/Buffalo's [Wholesome/Skimmed]
**Approximate Water Intake** :---------glasses/day
**Frequency of Non-Veg Intake** : Weekly/Fortnightly/Monthly/Any Other
**Any Other** :

---

150

--- **Author** ---
Dr. Prajakta J. Nande

# Clinical and Therapeutic Nutrition Practical Manual 1

For M.Sc. Food Science and Nutrition (Semester-III)

## Existing Meal Plan:

| Name of Meal with Timing | Meal Plan | No. of Servings |
|---|---|---|
| | | |

# Clinical and Therapeutic Nutrition Practical Manual 1
For M.Sc. Food Science and Nutrition (Semester-III)

## Calculations for Requirements:
### 1. Ideal Body Weight [IBW]:

### 2. Body Mass Index [BMI]:

### 3. Energy Requirement:

## Division of Energy into Three Major Nutrients:
### 4. Protein Requirement:

### 5. Total Fat Requirement:

### 6. Carbohydrate Requirement:

## Clinical and Therapeutic Nutrition Practical Manual 1
For M.Sc. Food Science and Nutrition (Semester-III)

**7. Micro-Nutrient Requirement:**

| Sr. No. | Vitamins/Minerals | Values |
|---------|-------------------|--------|
| 1 | | |
| 2 | | |
| 3 | | |
| 4 | | |
| 5 | | |
| 6 | | |
| 7 | | |
| 8 | | |
| 9 | | |
| 10 | | |

**8. Amount of Salt and Sodium from Salt:**

**9. Fluid Intake:**

**10. Amount of Fats and Oils:**

**11. Amount of Sugars:**

**12. Non Veg Food Intake:**

**Nutritional Goals:**

**Principles of Dietary Modifications:**

# Clinical and Therapeutic Nutrition Practical Manual 1

For M.Sc. Food Science and Nutrition (Semester-III)

## TABLE 1: FOOD EXCHANGE LIST

| Sr. No. | Name of Exchanges | | No. of Exchanges | Energy (kcal) | Carbohydrate (g) | Protein (g) | Fat (g) |
|---|---|---|---|---|---|---|---|
| 1 | Cereal Exchange | | | | | | |
| 2 | Pulse Exchange | | | | | | |
| 3 | Vegetable Exchange A | Group I | | | | | |
| | | Group II | | | | | |
| | | Group III | | | | | |
| 4 | Vegetable Exchange B | Group I | | | | | |
| | | Group II | | | | | |
| | | Group III | | | | | |
| 5 | Fruit Exchange | Group I | | | | | |
| | | Group II | | | | | |
| | | Group III | | | | | |
| | | Group IV | | | | | |
| | | Group V | | | | | |
| 6 | Milk Exchange | Whole Milk and Products | | | | | |
| | | Skimmed Milk and Products | | | | | |
| 7 | Nut and Oil Seed Exchange | | | | | | |
| 8 | Dry Fruit Exchange | | | | | | |
| 9 | Fat Exchange | | | | | | |
| 10 | Sugar and Starch Exchange | Sugar | | | | | |
| | | Jaggery | | | | | |
| | | Honey | | | | | |
| | | Sago | | | | | |
| 11 | Meat and Poultry Exchange | Egg | | | | | |
| | | Chicken | | | | | |
| | | Mutton | | | | | |
| 12 | Fish Exchange | | | | | | |
| 13 | Others | | | | | | |
| | Total | | | | | | |
| | Requirement | | | | | | |

--- Author ---
Dr. Prajakta J. Nande

# Clinical and Therapeutic Nutrition Practical Manual 1

For M.Sc. Food Science and Nutrition (Semester-III)

---

## :MEAL PLAN:

Suggested Tube Feeds for-----------------------------------------------------------------------------------

| Meal/Time | Menu | Measures/ Weight & Quantity of Prepared Feed/ | Quantity of Water Required (ml) |
|---|---|---|---|
| Early Morning (----------am) | | | |
| Morning (----------am) | | | |
| Breakfast (----------am) | | | |
| Mid Morning (----------am) | | | |
| Lunch (----------pm) | | | |
| Afternoon (----------pm) | | | |
| Evening (----------pm) | | | |
| Dinner (----------pm) | | | |
| Night (----------pm) | | | |
| Late Night (----------pm) | | | |

--- Author ---

Dr. Prajakta J. Nande

# Clinical and Therapeutic Nutrition Practical Manual 1
For M.Sc. Food Science and Nutrition (Semester-III)

## TABLE 2: BREAK UP OF EXCHANGES

| Sr. No. | Name of Exchanges | | Early Morning (----am) | Morning (----am) | Breakfast (----am) | Mid Morning (----am) | Lunch (----pm) | Afternoon (----pm) | Evening (----pm) | Dinner (----pm) | Night (----pm) | Late Night (----pm) | Total |
|---|---|---|---|---|---|---|---|---|---|---|---|---|---|
| 1 | Cereal and Millet Exchange | | | | | | | | | | | | |
| 2 | Pulse and Legume Exchange | | | | | | | | | | | | |
| 3 | Vegetable Exchange A | Group I | | | | | | | | | | | |
| | | Group II | | | | | | | | | | | |
| | | Group III | | | | | | | | | | | |
| 4 | Vegetable Exchange B | Group I | | | | | | | | | | | |
| | | Group II | | | | | | | | | | | |
| | | Group III | | | | | | | | | | | |
| 5 | Fruit Exchange | Group I | | | | | | | | | | | |
| | | Group II | | | | | | | | | | | |
| | | Group III | | | | | | | | | | | |
| | | Group IV | | | | | | | | | | | |
| | | Group V | | | | | | | | | | | |
| 6 | Milk Exchange | Whole Milk and Products | | | | | | | | | | | |
| | | Skimmed Milk and Products | | | | | | | | | | | |
| 7 | Nuts and Oil Seed Exchange | | | | | | | | | | | | |
| 8 | Dry Fruit Exchange | | | | | | | | | | | | |
| 9 | Fat Exchange | | | | | | | | | | | | |
| 10 | Sugar and Starch Exchange | Sugar | | | | | | | | | | | |
| | | Jaggery | | | | | | | | | | | |
| | | Honey | | | | | | | | | | | |
| | | Sago | | | | | | | | | | | |
| 11 | Meat and Poultry Exchange | Egg | | | | | | | | | | | |
| | | Chicken | | | | | | | | | | | |
| | | Mutton | | | | | | | | | | | |
| 12 | Fish Exchange | | | | | | | | | | | | |
| 13 | Others | | | | | | | | | | | | |

--- Author ---
Dr. Prajakta J. Nande

# Clinical and Therapeutic Nutrition Practical Manual 1
For M.Sc. Food Science and Nutrition (Semester-III)

## LIST OF FOODS TO BE INCLUDED AND AVOIDED

| Name of Exchanges | Foods to be Included | Foods to be Restricted | Foods to be Avoided |
|---|---|---|---|
| Cereals and Millets | | | |
| Pulses and Legumes | | | |
| Vegetables | | | |
| Fruits | | | |
| Milk and It's Products | | | |
| Nuts and Oil Seeds | | | |
| Dry Fruits | | | |
| Fats and Oils | | | |
| Sugars and Starch | | | |
| Meat, Fish and Poultry | | | |
| Others | | | |

--- Author ---
Dr. Prajakta J. Nande

# Clinical and Therapeutic Nutrition Practical Manual 1

For M.Sc. Food Science and Nutrition (Semester-III)

## TABLE 3: NUTRITIVE VALUE OF THE PRESCRIBED TUBE FEEDS (VITAMINS AND MINERALS)

| Sr. No. | Food Stuffs | Weight (g) | B1 (mg) | B2 (mg) | Niacin (mg) | Carotene (µg) | Vitamin C (mg) | Ca (mg) | P (mg) | Fe (mg) | Na (mg) | K (mg) |
|---------|-------------|------------|---------|---------|-------------|---------------|----------------|---------|--------|---------|---------|--------|
| | | | | | | | | | | | | |
| | | | | | | | | | | | | |
| | | | | | | | | | | | | |
| | | | | | | | | | | | | |
| | | | | | | | | | | | | |
| | | | | | | | | | | | | |
| | | | | | | | | | | | | |
| | | | | | | | | | | | | |
| | | | | | | | | | | | | |
| | | | | | | | | | | | | |
| | | | | | | | | | | | | |
| | | | | | | | | | | | | |
| | | | | | | | | | | | | |
| | | | | | | | | | | | | |
| | | | | | | | | | | | | |
| | | | | | | | | | | | | |
| | | | | | | | | | | | | |
| | | | | | | | | | | | | |
| | | | | | | | | | | | | |
| | | | | | | | | | | | | |
| | | | | | | | | | | | | |
| | | | | | | | | | | | | |
| | | | | | | | | | | | | |
| | | | | | | | | | | | | |
| | | | | | | | | | | | | |
| | | | | | | | | | | | | |
| | | | | | | | | | | | | |
| | | | | | | | | | | | | |
| | | | | | | | | | | | | |
| | | | | | | | | | | | | |
| | **Total** | | | | | | | | | | | |
| | **Required** | | | | | | | | | | | |

--- Author ---

Dr. Prajakta J. Nande

# Clinical and Therapeutic Nutrition Practical Manual 1
For M.Sc. Food Science and Nutrition (Semester-III)

## TABLE 4: FIBER AND MOISTURE CONTENT OF THE PRESCRIBED TUBE FEEDS

| Sr. No. | Food Stuffs | Weight (g) | Soluble Dietary Fiber (g) | Insoluble Dietary Fiber (g) | Total Dietary Fiber (g) | Moisture (g) |
|---------|-------------|------------|---------------------------|-----------------------------|-------------------------|--------------|
| | | | | | | |
| | | | | | | |
| | | | | | | |
| | | | | | | |
| | | | | | | |
| | | | | | | |
| | | | | | | |
| | | | | | | |
| | | | | | | |
| | | | | | | |
| | | | | | | |
| | | | | | | |
| | | | | | | |
| | | | | | | |
| | | | | | | |
| | | | | | | |
| | | | | | | |
| | | | | | | |
| | | | | | | |
| | | | | | | |
| | | | | | | |
| | | | | | | |
| | | | | | | |
| | | | | | | |
| | | | | | | |
| | | | | | | |
| | | | | | | |
| | | | | | | |
| | | | | | | |
| | | | | | | |
| | | | | | | |
| | | | | | | |
| | | | | | | |
| | | | | | | |
| | | | | | | |
| | | | | | | |
| | | | | | | |
| | | | | | | |
| | | | | | | |
| | | | | | | |
| | **Total** | | | | | |
| | **Required** | | | | | |

--- Author ---
Dr. Prajakta J. Nande

# Clinical and Therapeutic Nutrition Practical Manual 1
For M.Sc. Food Science and Nutrition (Semester-III)

## TABLE 5: BRANCHED CHAIN AMINO ACID CONTENT OF THE PRESCRIBED TUBE FEEDS (g/100 g of Protein)

| Sr. No. | Food Stuffs | Weight (g) | Isoleucine (g) | Leucine (g) | Valine (g) |
|---------|-------------|------------|----------------|-------------|------------|
|  |  |  |  |  |  |
|  |  |  |  |  |  |
|  |  |  |  |  |  |
|  |  |  |  |  |  |
|  |  |  |  |  |  |
|  |  |  |  |  |  |
|  |  |  |  |  |  |
|  |  |  |  |  |  |
|  |  |  |  |  |  |
|  |  |  |  |  |  |
|  |  |  |  |  |  |
|  |  |  |  |  |  |
|  |  |  |  |  |  |
|  |  |  |  |  |  |
|  |  |  |  |  |  |
|  |  |  |  |  |  |
|  |  |  |  |  |  |
|  |  |  |  |  |  |
|  |  |  |  |  |  |
|  |  |  |  |  |  |
|  |  |  |  |  |  |
|  |  |  |  |  |  |
|  |  |  |  |  |  |
|  |  |  |  |  |  |
|  |  |  |  |  |  |
|  |  |  |  |  |  |
|  |  |  |  |  |  |
|  |  |  |  |  |  |
|  |  |  |  |  |  |
|  |  |  |  |  |  |
|  |  |  |  |  |  |
|  |  |  |  |  |  |
|  |  |  |  |  |  |
|  |  |  |  |  |  |
|  |  |  |  |  |  |
|  |  |  |  |  |  |
|  |  |  |  |  |  |
|  | **Total** |  |  |  |  |
|  | **Required** |  |  |  |  |

--- **Author** ---
Dr. Prajakta J. Nande

# Clinical and Therapeutic Nutrition Practical Manual 1
For M.Sc. Food Science and Nutrition (Semester-III)

## TABLE 6: AROMATIC AMINO ACID CONTENT OF THE PRESCRIBED TUBE FEEDS (g/100 g of Protein)

| Sr. No. | Food Stuffs | Weight (g) | Phenylalanine (g) | Tyrosine (g) | Tryptophan (g) |
|---------|-------------|------------|-------------------|--------------|----------------|
|  |  |  |  |  |  |
|  |  |  |  |  |  |
|  |  |  |  |  |  |
|  |  |  |  |  |  |
|  |  |  |  |  |  |
|  |  |  |  |  |  |
|  |  |  |  |  |  |
|  |  |  |  |  |  |
|  |  |  |  |  |  |
|  |  |  |  |  |  |
|  |  |  |  |  |  |
|  |  |  |  |  |  |
|  |  |  |  |  |  |
|  |  |  |  |  |  |
|  |  |  |  |  |  |
|  |  |  |  |  |  |
|  |  |  |  |  |  |
|  |  |  |  |  |  |
|  |  |  |  |  |  |
|  |  |  |  |  |  |
|  |  |  |  |  |  |
|  |  |  |  |  |  |
|  |  |  |  |  |  |
|  |  |  |  |  |  |
|  |  |  |  |  |  |
|  |  |  |  |  |  |
|  |  |  |  |  |  |
|  |  |  |  |  |  |
|  |  |  |  |  |  |
|  |  |  |  |  |  |
|  |  |  |  |  |  |
|  |  |  |  |  |  |
|  | **Total** |  |  |  |  |
|  | **Required** |  |  |  |  |

--- **Author** ---
Dr. Prajakta J. Nande

# Comments:

# References:

# CARDIOVASCULAR DISEASES

**Clinical and Therapeutic Nutrition Practical Manual 1**
For M.Sc. Food Science and Nutrition (Semester-III)

---

# HYPERTENSION

## AIM: To plan and prepare a day's diet for an individual suffering from hypertension using a case study approach

### Personal Information:                                    Dates:
**Name:**
**Sex:** Female/Male
**Age [Yrs]:**
**Height [cm]:**
**Actual Body Weight (ABW)/Present Body Weight [kg]:**
**Occupation:** Service/Business/Housewife/Any Other
**Monthly Family Income [Rs./-]:**
**Type of Work:** Sedentary/Moderate/Heavy
**Duration of Work [Hours]:**
**Any Other:**

### Clinical and Biochemical Investigations:
**Bowel Movements**                    : Regular/Irregular
**Blood, Urine and other Parameters:**

### Dietary Information:
| | |
|---|---|
| **Food Habits** | : Vegetarian/Non Vegetarian/Eggetarian |
| **Common Dietary Pattern** | : 2 meals/3 meals/4 meals/Any Other |
| **Meal Timings** | : Regular/Irregular |
| **Type of Oils used for Cooking** | : |
| **Salt used for Cooking** | : Iodized/Non Iodized |
| **Milk used** | : Cow's/Buffalo's [Wholesome/Skimmed] |
| **Approximate Water Intake** | :---------glasses/day |
| **Frequency of Non-Veg Intake** | : Weekly/Fortnightly/Monthly/Any Other |
| **Any Other** | : |

--- **Author** ---
Dr. Prajakta J. Nande

## Existing Meal Plan:

| Name of Meal with Timing | Meal Plan | No. of Servings |
|---|---|---|
|  |  |  |

## Calculations for Requirements:

**1. Ideal Body Weight [IBW]:**

**2. Body Mass Index [BMI]:**

**3. Energy Requirement:**

## Division of Energy into Three Major Nutrients:

**4. Protein Requirement:**

**5. Total Fat Requirement:**

**Division of Total Fat into SFA, PUFA and MUFA:**

**(1) Saturated Fatty Acids (SFA):**

**(2) Poly Unsaturated Fatty Acids (PUFA):**

**(3) Mono Unsaturated Fatty Acids (MUFA):**

**(4) P: S Ratio:**

**Division of PUFA into n3 and n6:**

**(1) n3:**

**(2) n6:**

**(3) n6-n3 Ratio:**

# Clinical and Therapeutic Nutrition Practical Manual 1

For M.Sc. Food Science and Nutrition (Semester-III)

---

**6. Carbohydrate Requirement:**

**7. Micro-Nutrient Requirement:**

| Sr. No. | Vitamins/Minerals | Values |
|---------|-------------------|--------|
| 1 | | |
| 2 | | |
| 3 | | |
| 4 | | |
| 5 | | |
| 6 | | |
| 7 | | |
| 8 | | |
| 9 | | |
| 10 | | |

**8. Amount of Salt and Sodium from Salt:**

**9. Fluid Intake:**

**10. Amount of Fats and Oils:**

**11. Amount of Sugars:**

**12. Non Veg Food Intake:**

**Nutritional Goals:**

**Principles of Dietary Modifications:**

# Clinical and Therapeutic Nutrition Practical Manual 1
For M.Sc. Food Science and Nutrition (Semester-III)

## TABLE 1: FOOD EXCHANGE LIST

| Sr. No. | Name of Exchanges | | No. of Exchanges | Energy (kcal) | Carbohydrate (g) | Protein (g) | Fat (g) |
|---|---|---|---|---|---|---|---|
| 1 | Cereal Exchange | | | | | | |
| 2 | Pulse Exchange | | | | | | |
| 3 | Vegetable Exchange A | Group I | | | | | |
| | | Group II | | | | | |
| | | Group III | | | | | |
| 4 | Vegetable Exchange B | Group I | | | | | |
| | | Group II | | | | | |
| | | Group III | | | | | |
| 5 | Fruit Exchange | Group I | | | | | |
| | | Group II | | | | | |
| | | Group III | | | | | |
| | | Group IV | | | | | |
| | | Group V | | | | | |
| 6 | Milk Exchange | Whole Milk and Products | | | | | |
| | | Skimmed Milk and Products | | | | | |
| 7 | Nut and Oil Seed Exchange | | | | | | |
| 8 | Dry Fruit Exchange | | | | | | |
| 9 | Fat Exchange | | | | | | |
| 10 | Sugar and Starch Exchange | Sugar | | | | | |
| | | Jaggery | | | | | |
| | | Honey | | | | | |
| | | Sago | | | | | |
| 11 | Meat and Poultry Exchange | Egg | | | | | |
| | | Chicken | | | | | |
| | | Mutton | | | | | |
| 12 | Fish Exchange | | | | | | |
| 13 | Others | | | | | | |
| | Total | | | | | | |
| | Requirement | | | | | | |

--- Author ---
Dr. Prajakta J. Nande

# Clinical and Therapeutic Nutrition Practical Manual 1
For M.Sc. Food Science and Nutrition (Semester-III)

-----------------------------------------------------------------------------------------------------

## :MEAL PLAN:

Suggested Meal Plan for-------------------------------------------------------------------------------

| Meal/Time | Menu | No. of Servings/ Measures/ Quantity |
|---|---|---|
| Early Morning (----------am) | | |
| Breakfast (----------am) | | |
| Mid Morning (----------am) | | |
| Lunch (----------pm) | | |
| Snacks (----------pm) | | |
| Evening (----------pm) | | |
| Dinner (----------pm) | | |
| Bed Time (----------pm) | | |

--- **Author** ---
Dr. Prajakta J. Nande

# Clinical and Therapeutic Nutrition Practical Manual 1
For M.Sc. Food Science and Nutrition (Semester-III)

## TABLE 2: BREAK UP OF EXCHANGES

| Sr. No. | Name of Exchanges | | Early Morning (----am) | Breakfast (----am) | Mid Morning (----am) | Lunch (----pm) | Snacks (----pm) | Evening (----pm) | Dinner (----pm) | Bed Time (----pm) | Total |
|---|---|---|---|---|---|---|---|---|---|---|---|
| 1 | Cereal and Millet Exchange | | | | | | | | | | |
| 2 | Pulse and Legume Exchange | | | | | | | | | | |
| 3 | Vegetable Exchange A | Group I | | | | | | | | | |
| | | Group II | | | | | | | | | |
| | | Group III | | | | | | | | | |
| 4 | Vegetable Exchange B | Group I | | | | | | | | | |
| | | Group II | | | | | | | | | |
| | | Group III | | | | | | | | | |
| 5 | Fruit Exchange | Group I | | | | | | | | | |
| | | Group II | | | | | | | | | |
| | | Group III | | | | | | | | | |
| | | Group IV | | | | | | | | | |
| | | Group V | | | | | | | | | |
| 6 | Milk Exchange | Whole Milk and Products | | | | | | | | | |
| | | Skimmed Milk and Products | | | | | | | | | |
| 7 | Nuts and Oil Seed Exchange | | | | | | | | | | |
| 8 | Dry Fruit Exchange | | | | | | | | | | |
| 9 | Fat Exchange | | | | | | | | | | |
| 10 | Sugar and Starch Exchange | Sugar | | | | | | | | | |
| | | Jaggery | | | | | | | | | |
| | | Honey | | | | | | | | | |
| | | Sago | | | | | | | | | |
| 11 | Meat and Poultry Exchange | Egg | | | | | | | | | |
| | | Chicken | | | | | | | | | |
| | | Mutton | | | | | | | | | |
| 12 | Fish Exchange | | | | | | | | | | |
| 13 | Others | | | | | | | | | | |

--- Author ---
Dr. Prajakta J. Nande

# LIST OF FOODS TO BE INCLUDED AND AVOIDED

| Name of Exchanges | Foods to be Included | Foods to be Restricted | Foods to be Avoided |
|---|---|---|---|
| Cereals and Millets | | | |
| Pulses and Legumes | | | |
| Vegetables | | | |
| Fruits | | | |
| Milk and It's Products | | | |
| Nuts and Oil Seeds | | | |
| Dry Fruits | | | |
| Fats and Oils | | | |
| Sugars and Starch | | | |
| Meat, Fish and Poultry | | | |
| Others | | | |

# Clinical and Therapeutic Nutrition Practical Manual 1
For M.Sc. Food Science and Nutrition (Semester-III)

## TABLE 3: NUTRITIVE VALUE OF THE PRESCRIBED DIET (VITAMINS AND MINERALS)

| Sr. No. | Food Stuffs | Weight (g) | B1 (mg) | B2 (mg) | Niacin (mg) | Carotene (µg) | Vitamin C (mg) | Ca (mg) | P (mg) | Fe (mg) | Mg (mg) | Na (mg) | K (mg) |
|---------|-------------|-----------|---------|---------|-------------|----------------|-----------------|---------|--------|---------|---------|---------|--------|
|         |             |           |         |         |             |                |                 |         |        |         |         |         |        |
|         |             |           |         |         |             |                |                 |         |        |         |         |         |        |
|         |             |           |         |         |             |                |                 |         |        |         |         |         |        |
|         |             |           |         |         |             |                |                 |         |        |         |         |         |        |
|         |             |           |         |         |             |                |                 |         |        |         |         |         |        |
|         |             |           |         |         |             |                |                 |         |        |         |         |         |        |
|         |             |           |         |         |             |                |                 |         |        |         |         |         |        |
|         |             |           |         |         |             |                |                 |         |        |         |         |         |        |
|         |             |           |         |         |             |                |                 |         |        |         |         |         |        |
|         |             |           |         |         |             |                |                 |         |        |         |         |         |        |
|         |             |           |         |         |             |                |                 |         |        |         |         |         |        |
|         |             |           |         |         |             |                |                 |         |        |         |         |         |        |
|         |             |           |         |         |             |                |                 |         |        |         |         |         |        |
|         |             |           |         |         |             |                |                 |         |        |         |         |         |        |
|         |             |           |         |         |             |                |                 |         |        |         |         |         |        |
|         | **Total**   |           |         |         |             |                |                 |         |        |         |         |         |        |
|         | **Required**|           |         |         |             |                |                 |         |        |         |         |         |        |

--- **Author** ---
Dr. Prajakta J. Nande

# Clinical and Therapeutic Nutrition Practical Manual 1
For M.Sc. Food Science and Nutrition (Semester-III)

## TABLE 4: FIBER CONTENT OF THE PRESCRIBED DIET

| Sr. No. | Food Stuffs | Weight (g) | Soluble Dietary Fiber (g) | Insoluble Dietary Fiber (g) | Total Dietary Fiber (g) |
|---------|-------------|------------|---------------------------|-----------------------------|-------------------------|
|  |  |  |  |  |  |
|  |  |  |  |  |  |
|  |  |  |  |  |  |
|  |  |  |  |  |  |
|  |  |  |  |  |  |
|  |  |  |  |  |  |
|  |  |  |  |  |  |
|  |  |  |  |  |  |
|  |  |  |  |  |  |
|  |  |  |  |  |  |
|  |  |  |  |  |  |
|  |  |  |  |  |  |
|  |  |  |  |  |  |
|  |  |  |  |  |  |
|  |  |  |  |  |  |
|  |  |  |  |  |  |
|  |  |  |  |  |  |
|  |  |  |  |  |  |
|  |  |  |  |  |  |
|  |  |  |  |  |  |
|  |  |  |  |  |  |
|  |  |  |  |  |  |
|  |  |  |  |  |  |
|  |  |  |  |  |  |
|  |  |  |  |  |  |
|  |  |  |  |  |  |
|  |  |  |  |  |  |
|  |  |  |  |  |  |
|  |  |  |  |  |  |
|  |  |  |  |  |  |
|  |  |  |  |  |  |
|  |  |  |  |  |  |
|  |  |  |  |  |  |
|  |  |  |  |  |  |
|  |  |  |  |  |  |
|  |  |  |  |  |  |
|  | **Total** |  |  |  |  |
|  | **Required** |  |  |  |  |

--- **Author** ---
Dr. Prajakta J. Nande

# Clinical and Therapeutic Nutrition Practical Manual 1

For M.Sc. Food Science and Nutrition (Semester-III)

## TABLE 5: TOTAL SFA, PUFA, MUFA AND CHOLESTEROL CONTENT OF THE PRESCRIBED DIET

| Sr. No. | Food Stuffs | Weight (g) | Total SFA (mg) | PUFA (mg) | | | TotalMUFA (mg) | Cholesterol (mg) |
|---|---|---|---|---|---|---|---|---|
| | | | | n3 | n6 | Total | | |
| **I** | **Visible Fat** | | | | | | | |
| | | | | | | | | |
| | | | | | | | | |
| | | | | | | | | |
| | | | | | | | | |
| | Total (Visible) | | | | | | | |
| **II** | **Invisible Fat** | | | | | | | |
| | | | | | | | | |
| | | | | | | | | |
| | | | | | | | | |
| | | | | | | | | |
| | | | | | | | | |
| | | | | | | | | |
| | | | | | | | | |
| | | | | | | | | |
| | | | | | | | | |
| | | | | | | | | |
| | | | | | | | | |
| | | | | | | | | |
| | | | | | | | | |
| | | | | | | | | |
| | | | | | | | | |
| | | | | | | | | |
| | | | | | | | | |
| | | | | | | | | |
| | | | | | | | | |
| | | | | | | | | |
| | | | | | | | | |
| | | | | | | | | |
| | | | | | | | | |
| | | | | | | | | |
| | | | | | | | | |
| | | | | | | | | |
| | Total (Invisible) | | | | | | | |
| | **Total (Visible + Invisible)** | | | | | | | |
| | **Required (Visible + Invisible)** | | | | | | | |

--- **Author** ---

Dr. Prajakta J. Nande

## Comments:

## References:

**Clinical and Therapeutic Nutrition Practical Manual 1**
For M.Sc. Food Science and Nutrition (Semester-III)

---

## CORONARY HEART DISEASE

**AIM: To plan and prepare a day's diet for an individual suffering from coronary heart disease using a case study approach**

### Personal Information:                          Dates:

**Name:**
**Sex:** Female/Male
**Age [Yrs]:**
**Height [cm]:**
**Actual Body Weight (ABW)/Present Body Weight [kg]:**
**Occupation:** Service/Business/Housewife/Any Other
**Monthly Family Income [Rs./-]:**
**Type of Work:** Sedentary/Moderate/Heavy
**Duration of Work [Hours]:**
**Any Other:**


### Clinical and Biochemical Investigations:
**Bowel Movements**                  : Regular/Irregular
**Blood, Urine and other Parameters:**


### Dietary Information:

| | |
|---|---|
| **Food Habits** | : Vegetarian/Non Vegetarian/Eggetarian |
| **Common Dietary Pattern** | : 2 meals/3 meals/4 meals/Any Other |
| **Meal Timings** | : Regular/Irregular |
| **Type of Oils used for Cooking** | : |
| **Salt used for Cooking** | : Iodized/Non Iodized |
| **Milk used** | : Cow's/Buffalo's [Wholesome/Skimmed] |
| **Approximate Water Intake** | :---------glasses/day |
| **Frequency of Non-Veg Intake** | : Weekly/Fortnightly/Monthly/Any Other |
| **Any Other** | : |

---

--- **Author** ---
Dr. Prajakta J. Nande

# Clinical and Therapeutic Nutrition Practical Manual 1
For M.Sc. Food Science and Nutrition (Semester-III)

## Existing Meal Plan:

| Name of Meal with Timing | Meal Plan | No. of Servings |
|---|---|---|
| | | |

# Clinical and Therapeutic Nutrition Practical Manual 1
## For M.Sc. Food Science and Nutrition (Semester-III)

## Calculations for Requirements:
### 1. Ideal Body Weight [IBW]:

### 2. Body Mass Index [BMI]:

### 3. Energy Requirement:

## Division of Energy into Three Major Nutrients:
### 4. Protein Requirement:

### 5. Total Fat Requirement:

### Division of Total Fat into SFA, PUFA and MUFA:
**(1) Saturated Fatty Acids (SFA):**

**(2) Poly Unsaturated Fatty Acids (PUFA):**

**(3) Mono Unsaturated Fatty Acids (MUFA):**

**(4) P: S Ratio:**

### Division of PUFA into n3 and n6:
**(1) n3:**

**(2) n6:**

**(3) n6-n3 Ratio:**

--- Author ---
Dr. Prajakta J. Nande

# Clinical and Therapeutic Nutrition Practical Manual 1
For M.Sc. Food Science and Nutrition (Semester-III)

**6. Carbohydrate Requirement:**

**7. Micro-Nutrient Requirement:**

| Sr. No. | Vitamins/Minerals | Values |
|---------|-------------------|--------|
| 1 | | |
| 2 | | |
| 3 | | |
| 4 | | |
| 5 | | |
| 6 | | |
| 7 | | |
| 8 | | |
| 9 | | |
| 10 | | |

**8. Amount of Salt and Sodium from Salt:**

**9. Fluid Intake:**

**10. Amount of Fats and Oils:**

**11. Amount of Sugars:**

**12. Non Veg Food Intake:**

# Clinical and Therapeutic Nutrition Practical Manual 1
For M.Sc. Food Science and Nutrition (Semester-III)

**Nutritional Goals:**

**Principles of Dietary Modifications:**

# Clinical and Therapeutic Nutrition Practical Manual 1

For M.Sc. Food Science and Nutrition (Semester-III)

------------------------------------------------------------------------------------------------------

## TABLE 1: FOOD EXCHANGE LIST

| Sr. No. | Name of Exchanges | | No. of Exchanges | Energy (kcal) | Carbohydrate (g) | Protein (g) | Fat (g) |
|---|---|---|---|---|---|---|---|
| 1 | Cereal Exchange | | | | | | |
| 2 | Pulse Exchange | | | | | | |
| 3 | Vegetable Exchange A | Group I | | | | | |
| | | Group II | | | | | |
| | | Group III | | | | | |
| 4 | Vegetable Exchange B | Group I | | | | | |
| | | Group II | | | | | |
| | | Group III | | | | | |
| 5 | Fruit Exchange | Group I | | | | | |
| | | Group II | | | | | |
| | | Group III | | | | | |
| | | Group IV | | | | | |
| | | Group V | | | | | |
| 6 | Milk Exchange | Whole Milk and Products | | | | | |
| | | Skimmed Milk and Products | | | | | |
| 7 | Nut and Oil Seed Exchange | | | | | | |
| 8 | Dry Fruit Exchange | | | | | | |
| 9 | Fat Exchange | | | | | | |
| 10 | Sugar and Starch Exchange | Sugar | | | | | |
| | | Jaggery | | | | | |
| | | Honey | | | | | |
| | | Sago | | | | | |
| 11 | Meat and Poultry Exchange | Egg | | | | | |
| | | Chicken | | | | | |
| | | Mutton | | | | | |
| 12 | Fish Exchange | | | | | | |
| 13 | Others | | | | | | |
| | Total | | | | | | |
| | Requirement | | | | | | |

------------------------------------------------------------------------------------------------------

--- **Author** ---

Dr. Prajakta J. Nande

# Clinical and Therapeutic Nutrition Practical Manual 1
For M.Sc. Food Science and Nutrition (Semester-III)

---

## :MEAL PLAN:

Suggested Meal Plan for------------------------------------------------------------------------------------

| Meal/Time | Menu | No. of Servings/ Measures/ Quantity |
|---|---|---|
| Early Morning (----------am) | | |
| Breakfast (----------am) | | |
| Mid Morning (----------am) | | |
| Lunch (----------pm) | | |
| Snacks (----------pm) | | |
| Evening (----------pm) | | |
| Dinner (----------pm) | | |
| Bed Time (----------pm) | | |

--- Author ---
Dr. Prajakta J. Nande

# Clinical and Therapeutic Nutrition Practical Manual 1
For M.Sc. Food Science and Nutrition (Semester-III)

## TABLE 2: BREAK UP OF EXCHANGES

| Sr. No. | Name of Exchanges | | Early Morning (----am) | Breakfast (----am) | Mid Morning (----am) | Lunch (----pm) | Snacks (----pm) | Evening (----pm) | Dinner (----pm) | Bed Time (----pm) | Total |
|---|---|---|---|---|---|---|---|---|---|---|---|
| 1 | Cereal and Millet Exchange | | | | | | | | | | |
| 2 | Pulse and Legume Exchange | | | | | | | | | | |
| 3 | Vegetable Exchange A | Group I | | | | | | | | | |
| | | Group II | | | | | | | | | |
| | | Group III | | | | | | | | | |
| 4 | Vegetable Exchange B | Group I | | | | | | | | | |
| | | Group II | | | | | | | | | |
| | | Group III | | | | | | | | | |
| 5 | Fruit Exchange | Group I | | | | | | | | | |
| | | Group II | | | | | | | | | |
| | | Group III | | | | | | | | | |
| | | Group IV | | | | | | | | | |
| | | Group V | | | | | | | | | |
| 6 | Milk Exchange | Whole Milk and Products | | | | | | | | | |
| | | Skimmed Milk and Products | | | | | | | | | |
| 7 | Nuts and Oil Seed Exchange | | | | | | | | | | |
| 8 | Dry Fruit Exchange | | | | | | | | | | |
| 9 | Fat Exchange | | | | | | | | | | |
| 10 | Sugar and Starch Exchange | Sugar | | | | | | | | | |
| | | Jaggery | | | | | | | | | |
| | | Honey | | | | | | | | | |
| | | Sago | | | | | | | | | |
| 11 | Meat and Poultry Exchange | Egg | | | | | | | | | |
| | | Chicken | | | | | | | | | |
| | | Mutton | | | | | | | | | |
| 12 | Fish Exchange | | | | | | | | | | |
| 13 | Others | | | | | | | | | | |

--- **Author** ---
Dr. Prajakta J. Nande

# Clinical and Therapeutic Nutrition Practical Manual 1

For M.Sc. Food Science and Nutrition (Semester-III)

## LIST OF FOODS TO BE INCLUDED AND AVOIDED

| Name of Exchanges | Foods to be Included | Foods to be Restricted | Foods to be Avoided |
|---|---|---|---|
| Cereals and Millets | | | |
| Pulses and Legumes | | | |
| Vegetables | | | |
| Fruits | | | |
| Milk and It's Products | | | |
| Nuts and Oil Seeds | | | |
| Dry Fruits | | | |
| Fats and Oils | | | |
| Sugars and Starch | | | |
| Meat, Fish and Poultry | | | |
| Others | | | |

--- Author ---
Dr. Prajakta J. Nande

**Clinical and Therapeutic Nutrition Practical Manual 1**

For M.Sc. Food Science and Nutrition (Semester-III)

## TABLE 3: NUTRITIVE VALUE OF THE PRESCRIBED DIET
### (VITAMINS AND MINERALS)

| Sr. No. | Food Stuffs | Weight (g) | B1 (mg) | B2 (mg) | Niacin (mg) | Carotene (µg) | Vitamin C (mg) | Ca (mg) | P (mg) | Fe (mg) | Mg (mg) | Na (mg) | K (mg) |
|---------|-------------|------------|---------|---------|-------------|---------------|----------------|---------|--------|---------|---------|---------|--------|
|  |  |  |  |  |  |  |  |  |  |  |  |  |  |
|  |  |  |  |  |  |  |  |  |  |  |  |  |  |
|  |  |  |  |  |  |  |  |  |  |  |  |  |  |
|  |  |  |  |  |  |  |  |  |  |  |  |  |  |
|  |  |  |  |  |  |  |  |  |  |  |  |  |  |
|  |  |  |  |  |  |  |  |  |  |  |  |  |  |
|  |  |  |  |  |  |  |  |  |  |  |  |  |  |
|  |  |  |  |  |  |  |  |  |  |  |  |  |  |
|  |  |  |  |  |  |  |  |  |  |  |  |  |  |
|  |  |  |  |  |  |  |  |  |  |  |  |  |  |
|  |  |  |  |  |  |  |  |  |  |  |  |  |  |
|  |  |  |  |  |  |  |  |  |  |  |  |  |  |
|  |  |  |  |  |  |  |  |  |  |  |  |  |  |
|  |  |  |  |  |  |  |  |  |  |  |  |  |  |
|  |  |  |  |  |  |  |  |  |  |  |  |  |  |
|  |  |  |  |  |  |  |  |  |  |  |  |  |  |
|  |  |  |  |  |  |  |  |  |  |  |  |  |  |
|  |  |  |  |  |  |  |  |  |  |  |  |  |  |
|  |  |  |  |  |  |  |  |  |  |  |  |  |  |
|  |  |  |  |  |  |  |  |  |  |  |  |  |  |
|  |  |  |  |  |  |  |  |  |  |  |  |  |  |
|  |  |  |  |  |  |  |  |  |  |  |  |  |  |
|  |  |  |  |  |  |  |  |  |  |  |  |  |  |
|  |  |  |  |  |  |  |  |  |  |  |  |  |  |
|  |  |  |  |  |  |  |  |  |  |  |  |  |  |
|  |  |  |  |  |  |  |  |  |  |  |  |  |  |
| | **Total** |  |  |  |  |  |  |  |  |  |  |  |  |
| | **Required** |  |  |  |  |  |  |  |  |  |  |  |  |

--- **Author** ---

Dr. Prajakta J. Nande

# Clinical and Therapeutic Nutrition Practical Manual 1
For M.Sc. Food Science and Nutrition (Semester-III)

## TABLE 4: FIBER CONTENT OF THE PRESCRIBED DIET

| Sr. No. | Food Stuffs | Weight (g) | Soluble Dietary Fiber (g) | Insoluble Dietary Fiber (g) | Total Dietary Fiber (g) |
|---------|-------------|------------|---------------------------|-----------------------------|-------------------------|
|  |  |  |  |  |  |
|  |  |  |  |  |  |
|  |  |  |  |  |  |
|  |  |  |  |  |  |
|  |  |  |  |  |  |
|  |  |  |  |  |  |
|  |  |  |  |  |  |
|  |  |  |  |  |  |
|  |  |  |  |  |  |
|  |  |  |  |  |  |
|  |  |  |  |  |  |
|  |  |  |  |  |  |
|  |  |  |  |  |  |
|  |  |  |  |  |  |
|  |  |  |  |  |  |
|  |  |  |  |  |  |
|  |  |  |  |  |  |
|  |  |  |  |  |  |
|  |  |  |  |  |  |
|  |  |  |  |  |  |
|  |  |  |  |  |  |
|  |  |  |  |  |  |
|  |  |  |  |  |  |
|  |  |  |  |  |  |
|  |  |  |  |  |  |
|  |  |  |  |  |  |
|  |  |  |  |  |  |
|  |  |  |  |  |  |
|  |  |  |  |  |  |
|  |  |  |  |  |  |
|  |  |  |  |  |  |
|  |  |  |  |  |  |
|  |  |  |  |  |  |
|  |  |  |  |  |  |
|  |  |  |  |  |  |
|  |  |  |  |  |  |
|  |  |  |  |  |  |
|  | **Total** |  |  |  |  |
|  | **Required** |  |  |  |  |

--- Author ---
Dr. Prajakta J. Nande

# Clinical and Therapeutic Nutrition Practical Manual 1
For M.Sc. Food Science and Nutrition (Semester-III)

## TABLE 5: TOTAL SFA, PUFA, MUFA AND CHOLESTEROL CONTENT OF THE PRESCRIBED DIET

| Sr. No. | Food Stuffs | Weight (g) | Total SFA (mg) | PUFA (mg) | | | Total MUFA (mg) | Cholesterol (mg) |
|---|---|---|---|---|---|---|---|---|
| | | | | n3 | n6 | Total | | |
| I | Visible Fat | | | | | | | |
| | | | | | | | | |
| | | | | | | | | |
| | | | | | | | | |
| | | | | | | | | |
| | Total (Visible) | | | | | | | |
| II | Invisible Fat | | | | | | | |
| | | | | | | | | |
| | | | | | | | | |
| | | | | | | | | |
| | | | | | | | | |
| | | | | | | | | |
| | | | | | | | | |
| | | | | | | | | |
| | | | | | | | | |
| | | | | | | | | |
| | | | | | | | | |
| | | | | | | | | |
| | | | | | | | | |
| | | | | | | | | |
| | | | | | | | | |
| | | | | | | | | |
| | | | | | | | | |
| | | | | | | | | |
| | | | | | | | | |
| | | | | | | | | |
| | | | | | | | | |
| | | | | | | | | |
| | | | | | | | | |
| | | | | | | | | |
| | | | | | | | | |
| | Total (Invisible) | | | | | | | |
| | Total (Visible + Invisible) | | | | | | | |
| | Required (Visible + Invisible) | | | | | | | |

--- Author ---
Dr. Prajakta J. Nande

## Comments:

## References:

**Clinical and Therapeutic Nutrition Practical Manual 1**
For M.Sc. Food Science and Nutrition (Semester-III)

## ANNEXURE - 1

## ENERGY CONTENT OF FOODS

| FOOD STUFFS | Energy (kcal/ 100 g) |
|---|---|
| **CEREALS AND MILLETS** | |
| Maize tender, sweet | 96.80 |
| Maize, tender, local | 119.98 |
| Barley | 315.73 |
| Wheat flour | 320.27 |
| Ragi | 320.75 |
| Wheat, whole | 321.94 |
| Quinoa | 328.39 |
| Varagu | 331.74 |
| Wheat, vermicelli | 332.70 |
| Wheat, semolina | 333.65 |
| Jowar | 334.13 |
| Maize, dry | 334.13 |
| Wheat, vermicelli, roasted | 340.11 |
| Wheat, bulgur | 341.78 |
| Samai | 346.32 |
| Bajra | 347.99 |
| Rice, parboiled, milled | 351.58 |
| Wheat flour, refined | 351.82 |
| Rice flakes | 353.73 |
| Rice, raw, brown | 353.73 |
| Amaranth seeds, pale brown | 355.88 |
| Amaranth seeds, black | 356.12 |
| Rice, raw, milled | 356.36 |
| Rice puffed | 361.85 |
| **GRAIN LEGUMES** | |
| Red gram, whole | 273.90 |
| Field bean, black | 276.05 |
| Field bean, white | 280.35 |
| Field bean, brown | 282.98 |
| Bengal gram, whole | 287.05 |
| Black gram, whole | 291.35 |
| Green gram, whole | 293.74 |
| Rajmah, brown | 297.56 |
| Lentil whole, yellowish | 297.80 |
| Rajmah, black | 298.04 |
| Lentil whole, brown | 299.00 |
| Rajmah, red | 299.24 |

| | |
|---|---|
| Rice bean | 302.34 |
| Peas, dry | 303.30 |
| Moth bean | 308.56 |
| Cowpea, brown | 320.27 |
| Cowpea, white | 320.27 |
| Lentil dal | 322.42 |
| Black gram, dal | 324.09 |
| Green gram, dal | 325.76 |
| Bengal gram, dal | 329.11 |
| Horse gram, whole | 329.59 |
| Red gram, dal | 330.78 |
| Soya bean, white | 377.39 |
| Soya bean, brown | 381.45 |
| **GREEN LEAFY VEGETABLES** | |
| Pak choi leaves | 16.01 |
| Cabbage, Chinese | 17.93 |
| Basella leaves | 19.60 |
| Rumex leaves | 19.60 |
| Cabbage, green | 21.51 |
| Lettuce | 21.75 |
| Cabbage, violet | 23.18 |
| Amaranth spinosus, leaves, red and green mix | 23.66 |
| Spinach | 24.38 |
| Radish leaves | 26.05 |
| Amaranth spinosus, leaves, green | 26.29 |
| Bathua leaves | 27.72 |
| Cabbage, collard greens | 30.11 |
| Mustard leaves | 30.35 |
| Amaranth leaves, green | 30.59 |
| Amaranth leaves, red and green mix | 31.55 |
| Amaranth leaves, red | 33.46 |
| Fenugreek leaves | 34.42 |
| Beet greens | 34.66 |
| Cauliflower leaves | 35.37 |
| Gogu leaves, green | 36.33 |
| Gogu leaves, red | 36.57 |
| Knol-khol leaves | 42.54 |
| Colocasia leaves, green | 43.50 |
| Betel leaves, small | 43.74 |
| Brussels sprouts | 44.22 |

--- **Author** ---
Dr. Prajakta J. Nande

# Clinical and Therapeutic Nutrition Practical Manual 1
For M.Sc. Food Science and Nutrition (Semester-III)

| | | | |
|---|---|---|---|
| Pumpkin leaves, tender | 44.22 | Pumpkin, orange, round | 23.18 |
| Betel leaves, big (Kolkata) | 48.28 | Colocasia, stem, black | 23.90 |
| Garden cress | 49.71 | Papaya, raw | 23.90 |
| Ponnaganni | 50.91 | Parwar | 24.14 |
| Drumstick leaves | 67.40 | French beans, country | 24.38 |
| Agathi leaves | 70.51 | Pumpkin, green, cylindrical | 24.62 |
| Tamarind leaves, tender | 71.46 | Brinjal-all varieties | 25.33 |
| Parsley | 72.90 | Onion, stalk | 25.57 |
| **OTHER VEGETABLES** | | Jack fruit, raw | 26.29 |
| Bottle gourd, elongate, pale green | 10.99 | Ladies finger | 27.49 |
| Snake gourd, long, dark green | 11.95 | Broad beans | 29.40 |
| Snake gourd, long, pale green | 12.43 | Drumstick | 29.40 |
| Bottle gourd, elongate, dark green | 12.91 | Field beans, tender, broad | 30.83 |
| Ridge gourd | 13.15 | Field beans, tender, lean | 33.46 |
| Bottle gourd, round, pale green | 13.62 | Plantain, stem | 39.44 |
| Tinda, tender | 13.86 | Cluster beans | 40.15 |
| Snake gourd, short | 14.58 | Bean scarlet, tender | 42.78 |
| Ridge gourd, smooth skin | 15.30 | Mango, green, raw | 49.00 |
| Knol-khol | 16.01 | Corn, baby | 73.14 |
| Bamboo shoot, tender | 16.25 | Jack fruit, seed, mature | 76.96 |
| Capsicum, green | 16.25 | Plantain, green | 79.83 |
| Celery stalk | 16.49 | Peas, fresh | 81.26 |
| Ash gourd | 17.45 | Red gram, tender, fresh | 124.28 |
| Cucumber, green, short | 17.45 | **FRUITS** | |
| Kovai, big | 17.45 | Water melon, pale green | 16.73 |
| Capsicum, yellow | 18.64 | Water melon, dark green | 20.32 |
| Bitter gourd, jagged, teeth ridges, short | 18.88 | Musk melon, orange flesh | 23.18 |
| | | Gooseberry | 23.66 |
| Cho-cho-marrow | 18.88 | Papaya, ripe | 23.90 |
| Tomato, ripe, hybrid | 18.88 | Palm fruit, tender | 24.14 |
| Zucchini, yellow | 18.88 | Strawberry | 24.62 |
| Kovai, small | 19.12 | Star fruit | 26.29 |
| Bitter gourd, jagged, smooth ridges, elongate | 19.36 | Lime, sweet,pulp | 27.25 |
| | | Musk melon, yellow flesh | 27.72 |
| Colocasia, stem, green | 19.36 | Guava, white flesh | 32.27 |
| Cucumber, green, elongate | 19.60 | Karonda fruit | 33.70 |
| Cucumber, round | 19.60 | Lemon, juice | 36.57 |
| Tomato, ripe, local | 19.60 | Orange, pulp | 37.28 |
| Capsicum, red | 19.84 | Pear | 37.52 |
| Zucchini, green | 20.08 | Peach | 40.15 |
| Bitter gourd, jagged, teeth ridges, elongate | 20.79 | Mango, ripe, banganapalli | 41.83 |
| | | Mango, ripe, neelam | 42.54 |
| Tomato, green | 20.79 | Pineapple | 43.02 |
| Plantain, flower | 21.27 | Mango, ripe, himsagar | 44.69 |
| French beans, hybrid | 22.23 | Mango, ripe, paheri | 44.93 |
| Cauliflower | 22.94 | Guava, pink flesh | 46.61 |

--- **Author** ---
Dr. Prajakta J. Nande

# Clinical and Therapeutic Nutrition Practical Manual 1
For M.Sc. Food Science and Nutrition (Semester-III)

| | | | |
|---|---|---|---|
| Zizyphus | 48.76 | **ROOTS AND TUBERS** | |
| Mango, ripe, gulabkhas | 49.95 | Radish, round, white skin | 30.83 |
| Pummelo | 50.19 | Radish, round, red skin | 31.07 |
| Apple, green | 51.15 | Radish, elongate, red skin | 32.03 |
| Mangosteen | 52.34 | Radish, elongate, white skin | 32.27 |
| Grapes, seedless, round, green | 53.54 | Carrot, orange | 33.22 |
| Litchi | 53.78 | Beet root | 35.61 |
| Black berry | 54.25 | Carrot, red | 38.24 |
| Currants, black | 54.25 | Potato, brown skin, small | 60.95 |
| Pomegranate, maroon seeds | 54.73 | Potato, brown skin, big | 69.79 |
| Mango, ripe, kesar | 55.21 | Potato, red skin | 73.14 |
| Grapes, seeded, round, green | 56.17 | Lotus root | 79.35 |
| Jambu fruit, ripe | 56.17 | Tapioca | 79.83 |
| Apricot, processed | 56.41 | Yam, ordinary | 83.41 |
| Plum | 56.88 | Yam, elephant | 84.37 |
| Grapes, seeded, round, red | 58.32 | Colocasia | 88.91 |
| Mango, ripe, totapari | 59.27 | Water chestnut | 95.60 |
| Cherries, red | 59.75 | Yam, wild | 102.77 |
| Grapes, seeded, round, black | 60.71 | Sweet potato, pink skin | 108.03 |
| Soursop | 62.14 | Sweet potato, brown skin | 108.99 |
| Apple, big | 62.38 | **CONDIMENTS AND SPICES- FRESH** | |
| Apple, small | 63.81 | Coriander leaves | 31.07 |
| Apple, small, Kashmir | 64.29 | Mint leaves | 37.05 |
| Phalsa | 71.46 | Chillies, green all varieties | 42.30 |
| Jack fruit, ripe | 72.18 | Mango ginger | 42.30 |
| Rambutan | 73.14 | Onion, big | 48.04 |
| Sapota | 73.37 | Ginger, fresh | 54.97 |
| Wood apple | 78.15 | Onion, small | 56.64 |
| Fig | 81.50 | Curry leaves | 63.58 |
| Manila tamarind | 81.74 | Garlic, small clove | 122.85 |
| Grapes, seedless, round, black | 89.39 | Garlic, big clove | 123.80 |
| Grapes, seedless, oval, black | 94.41 | Garlic, single clove, Kashmir | 125.00 |
| Custard apple | 98.95 | **CONDIMENTS AND SPICES - DRY** | |
| Banana, ripe, robusta | 105.16 | Cloves | 186.66 |
| Banana, ripe, poovam | 106.36 | Pippali | 216.54 |
| Banana, ripe, montham | 110.66 | Pepper, black | 217.50 |
| Banana, ripe, red | 111.62 | Fenugreek seeds | 234.94 |
| Bael fruit | 135.99 | Chillies, red | 236.62 |
| Avocado fruit | 144.36 | Cardamom, green | 255.02 |
| Dates, processed | 286.09 | Coriander seeds | 268.88 |
| Tamarind, pulp | 288.48 | Cardamom, black | 270.55 |
| Raisins, dried, golden | 296.61 | Turmeric powder | 280.59 |
| Raisins, dried, black | 305.69 | Cumin seeds | 304.49 |
| Dates, dry, dark brown | 310.95 | Asafoetida | 331.50 |
| Apricot, dried | 315.73 | Mace | 355.64 |
| Dates, dry, pale brown | 320.27 | Omum | 357.31 |

--- **Author** ---
Dr. Prajakta J. Nande

# Clinical and Therapeutic Nutrition Practical Manual 1
For M.Sc. Food Science and Nutrition (Semester-III)

| | | | |
|---|---|---|---|
| Poppy seeds | 422.56 | Chicken, poultry, wing, skinless | 192.88 |
| Nutmeg | 463.67 | Chicken, poultry, thigh, skinless | 199.81 |
| **NUTS AND OIL SEEDS** | | Chicken, poultry, legs, skinless | 383.60 |
| Arecanut, fresh | 244.74 | **ANIMAL MEAT** | |
| Arecanut, dried, brown | 350.62 | Beef, lungs | 83.89 |
| Arecanut, dried, red color | 353.01 | Pork, spleen | 85.33 |
| Coconut kernel, fresh | 408.94 | Pork, lungs | 85.56 |
| Linseeds | 443.83 | Goat, kidneys | 89.39 |
| Garden cress, seeds | 445.27 | Beef, spleen | 90.34 |
| Safflower seeds | 473.47 | Pork, kidneys | 90.58 |
| Gingelly seeds, black | 507.65 | Goat, lungs | 95.84 |
| Niger seeds, gray | 508.60 | Goat, spleen | 95.84 |
| Mustard seeds | 509.56 | Beef, heart | 103.49 |
| Niger seeds, black | 512.43 | Beef, kidney | 104.92 |
| Gingelly seeds, brown | 516.49 | Pork, heart | 109.23 |
| Gingelly seeds, white | 519.60 | Goat, heart | 117.59 |
| Groundnut | 520.08 | Beef, liver | 119.26 |
| Pistachio nut | 539.44 | Beef, brain | 125.00 |
| Cashew nut | 582.70 | Goat, liver | 125.72 |
| Sunflower seeds | 586.28 | Goat, brain | 127.39 |
| Pine seeds | 594.17 | Pork, stomach | 131.45 |
| Almond | 609.23 | Goat, chops | 135.76 |
| Coconut kernel, dry | 624.04 | Beef, chops | 139.82 |
| Walnut | 671.37 | Beef, round (leg) | 157.27 |
| **SUGAR** | | Goat, legs | 159.89 |
| Sugarcane, juice | 57.84 | Pork, chops | 178.78 |
| Jaggery, cane | 353.73 | Goat, shoulder meat | 188.10 |
| **MUSHROOMS** | | Beef, shoulder | 212.48 |
| Chicken mushroom, fresh | 21.27 | Pork, shoulder | 222.99 |
| Button mushroom, fresh | 27.49 | **MARINE FISH** | |
| Shiitake mushroom, fresh | 58.08 | Bombay duck | 68.59 |
| **MISCELLANEOUS FOODS** | | Mural | 82.46 |
| Coconut water | 15.30 | Tuna | 112.33 |
| **MILK AND MILK PRODUCTS** | | Pomfret, white | 122.61 |
| Milk, whole, cow | 72.90 | Pomfret, black | 123.09 |
| Milk, whole, buffalo | 107.31 | Sardine | 152.25 |
| Paneer | 257.89 | Salmon | 172.32 |
| Khoa | 315.97 | **MARINE SHELLFISH** | |
| **EGG AND EGG PRODUCTS** | | Tiger prawns, orange | 64.53 |
| Eggs, poultry, white, raw | 44.69 | Crab, sea | 67.64 |
| Eggs, poultry, whole, raw | 134.80 | Lobster, brown | 69.79 |
| Egg, country hen, whole, raw | 168.26 | Crab | 81.98 |
| Egg, poultry, yolk, raw | 296.85 | Lobster, king size | 89.63 |
| **POULTRY** | | **FRESH WATER FISH AND SHELLFISH** | |
| Poultry, chicken, liver | 123.80 | Prawns, small | 70.98 |
| Chicken, poultry, breast, skinless | 168.26 | Crab | 78.15 |

**Clinical and Therapeutic Nutrition Practical Manual 1**
For M.Sc. Food Science and Nutrition (Semester-III)

| | | | |
|---|---|---|---|
| Prawns, big | 90.82 | **FATTY FISH** | |
| Catla | 94.17 | Hilsa | 258.84 |
| Rohu | 102.29 | | |

*(Source: T. Longvah, R. Ananthan, K. Bhaskaracharya, K. Venkaiah. Indian Food Composition Tables, National Institute of Nutrition (Indian Council of Medical Research), 3-30, 2017)*

## ANNEXURE - 2

## CARBOHYDRATE CONTENT OF FOODS

| FOOD STUFFS | Carboh-ydrate (g/100 g) | | |
|---|---|---|---|
| **CEREALS AND MILLETS** | | Field bean, black | 43.48 |
| Maize tender, sweet | 16.42 | Black gram, whole | 43.99 |
| Maize, tender, local | 22.69 | Field bean, white | 44.53 |
| Quinoa | 53.65 | Field bean, brown | 45.24 |
| Amaranth seeds, black | 59.98 | Green gram, whole | 46.13 |
| Barley | 61.29 | Bengal gram, dal | 46.72 |
| Amaranth seeds, pale brown | 61.46 | Lentil whole, yellowish | 47.91 |
| Bajra | 61.78 | Lentil whole, brown | 48.47 |
| Wheat flour | 64.17 | Rajmah, red | 48.61 |
| Wheat, whole | 64.72 | Rajmah, brown | 48.83 |
| Maize, dry | 64.77 | Peas, dry | 48.93 |
| Samai | 65.55 | Rajmah, black | 49.59 |
| Varagu | 66.19 | Black gram, dal | 51 |
| Ragi | 66.82 | Rice bean | 51.26 |
| Wheat, bulgur | 67.06 | Moth bean | 52.09 |
| Jowar | 67.68 | Lentil dal | 52.53 |
| Wheat, semolina | 68.43 | Green gram, dal | 52.59 |
| Wheat, vermicelli | 70.39 | Cowpea, white | 53.77 |
| Wheat, vermicelli, roasted | 71.42 | Cowpea, brown | 54.82 |
| Wheat flour, refined | 74.27 | Red gram, dal | 55.23 |
| Rice, raw, brown | 74.8 | Horse gram, whole | 57.24 |
| Rice flakes | 76.75 | **GREEN LEAFY VEGETABLES** | |
| Rice, parboiled, milled | 77.16 | Amaranth spinosus, leaves, red and green mix | 1.45 |
| Rice puffed | 77.68 | Amaranth spinosus, leaves, green | 1.61 |
| Rice, raw, milled | 78.24 | Pak choi leaves | 1.78 |
| **GRAIN LEGUMES** | | Basella leaves | 2.01 |
| Soya bean, white | 10.16 | Spinach | 2.05 |
| Soya bean, brown | 12.79 | Fenugreek leaves | 2.17 |
| Bengal gram, whole | 39.56 | Amaranth leaves, green | 2.28 |
| Red gram, whole | 42.48 | Rumex leaves | 2.33 |
| | | Cabbage, Chinese | 2.36 |
| | | Amaranth leaves, red | 2.37 |
| | | Mustard leaves | 2.41 |

--- **Author** ---
Dr. Prajakta J. Nande

# Clinical and Therapeutic Nutrition Practical Manual 1
For M.Sc. Food Science and Nutrition (Semester-III)

| | | | | |
|---|---|---|---|---|
| Bathua leaves | 2.56 | Zucchini, green | 2.33 |
| Radish leaves | 2.77 | Kovai, small | 2.41 |
| Cabbage, collard greens | 2.79 | Bitter gourd, jagged, teeth ridges, short | 2.53 |
| Amaranth leaves, red and green mix | 2.87 | Bottle gourd, round, pale green | 2.53 |
| Lettuce | 3.01 | French beans, hybrid | 2.63 |
| Cabbage, green | 3.25 | French beans, country | 2.68 |
| Cauliflower leaves | 3.39 | Tomato, ripe, local | 2.71 |
| Cabbage, violet | 3.54 | Field beans, tender, broad | 2.75 |
| Colocasia leaves, green | 3.69 | Bitter gourd, jagged, teeth ridges, elongate | 2.82 |
| Beet greens | 3.86 | Cucumber, green, short | 2.82 |
| Gogu leaves, green | 4.06 | Ash gourd | 2.84 |
| Gogu leaves, red | 4.24 | Field beans, tender, lean | 2.85 |
| Garden cress | 4.48 | Colocasia, stem, green | 2.86 |
| Pumpkin leaves, tender | 4.75 | Onion, stalk | 2.99 |
| Brussels sprouts | 5.09 | Cucumber, round | 3.01 |
| Ponnaganni | 5.17 | Tomato, green | 3.18 |
| Agathi leaves | 5.21 | Tomato, ripe, hybrid | 3.2 |
| Drumstick leaves | 5.62 | Cho-cho-marrow | 3.47 |
| Betel leaves, small | 6.16 | Cucumber, green, elongate | 3.48 |
| Knol-khol leaves | 6.16 | Jack fruit, raw | 3.48 |
| Betel leaves, big (Kolkata) | 7.37 | Brinjal-all varieties | 3.52 |
| Parsley | 7.43 | Parwar | 3.54 |
| Tamarind leaves, tender | 10.04 | Ladies finger | 3.62 |
| **OTHER VEGETABLES** | | Drumstick | 3.76 |
| Snake gourd, long, dark green | 1.23 | Colocasia, stem, black | 3.83 |
| Snake gourd, long, pale green | 1.27 | Pumpkin, orange, round | 4 |
| Knol-khol | 1.39 | Pumpkin, green, cylindrical | 4.22 |
| Bamboo shoot, tender | 1.67 | Papaya, raw | 4.4 |
| Bottle gourd, elongate, pale green | 1.68 | Cluster beans | 4.91 |
| Ridge gourd | 1.72 | Bean scarlet, tender | 5.16 |
| Capsicum, green | 1.84 | Plantain, stem | 8.64 |
| Tinda, tender | 1.9 | Mango, green, raw | 10.59 |
| Capsicum, yellow | 1.95 | Corn, baby | 11.66 |
| Kovai, big | 2.01 | Jack fruit, seed, mature | 11.81 |
| Cauliflower | 2.03 | Peas, fresh | 11.88 |
| Broad beans | 2.11 | Plantain, green | 17.58 |
| Capsicum, red | 2.14 | Red gram, tender, fresh | 19.46 |
| Plantain, flower | 2.15 | **FRUITS** | |
| Snake gourd, short | 2.15 | Avocado fruit | 1.75 |
| Zucchini, yellow | 2.2 | Karonda fruit | 2.89 |
| Ridge gourd, smooth skin | 2.24 | Water melon, pale green | 3.02 |
| Bottle gourd, elongate, dark green | 2.25 | Strawberry | 3.4 |
| Bitter gourd, jagged, smooth ridges, elongate | 2.29 | Water melon, dark green | 3.86 |
| Celery stalk | 2.33 | Musk melon, orange flesh | 4.24 |

--- **Author** ---
Dr. Prajakta J. Nande

# Clinical and Therapeutic Nutrition Practical Manual 1
## For M.Sc. Food Science and Nutrition (Semester-III)

| | | | | |
|---|---|---|---|---|
| Gooseberry | 4.39 | Guava, pink flesh | 19.14 |
| Star fruit | 4.51 | Grapes, seedless, round, black | 19.86 |
| Papaya, ripe | 4.61 | Custard apple | 20.38 |
| Palm fruit, tender | 4.92 | Grapes, seedless, oval, black | 20.48 |
| Guava, white flesh | 5.13 | Banana, ripe, poovam | 23.41 |
| Lime, sweet, pulp | 5.18 | Banana, ripe, robusta | 23.63 |
| Musk melon, yellow flesh | 5.4 | Banana, ripe, montham | 24.95 |
| Lemon, juice | 6.97 | Banana, ripe, red | 25.21 |
| Wood apple | 7.52 | Bael fruit | 28.21 |
| Peach | 7.82 | Tamarind, pulp | 67.75 |
| Orange, pulp | 7.92 | Dates, processed | 67.95 |
| Pear | 8.09 | Raisins, dried, golden | 68.79 |
| Mango, ripe, banganapalli | 8.18 | Raisins, dried, black | 71.29 |
| Mango, ripe, neelam | 8.21 | Apricot, dried | 72.63 |
| Mango, ripe, paheri | 8.67 | Dates, dry, dark brown | 72.67 |
| Mango, ripe, himsagar | 9.03 | Dates, dry, pale brown | 74.91 |
| Zizyphus | 9.4 | **ROOTS AND TUBERS** | |
| Pineapple | 9.42 | Carrot, orange | 5.55 |
| Currants, black | 9.93 | Radish, round, red skin | 6.07 |
| Mango, ripe, gulabkhas | 10.32 | Radish, round, white skin | 6.13 |
| Black berry | 10.64 | Beet root | 6.18 |
| Pummelo | 10.64 | Radish, elongate, white skin | 6.56 |
| Apple, green | 10.65 | Carrot, red | 6.71 |
| Apricot, processed | 10.93 | Radish, elongate, red skin | 6.71 |
| Litchi | 11.41 | Yam, ordinary | 7.65 |
| Mangosteen | 11.41 | Colocasia | 7.85 |
| Pomegranate, maroon seeds | 11.58 | Potato, brown skin, small | 12.9 |
| Mango, ripe, kesar | 11.69 | Lotus root | 14.67 |
| Grapes, seedless, round, green | 11.81 | Potato, brown skin, big | 14.89 |
| Cherries, red | 11.87 | Potato, red skin | 15.43 |
| Soursop | 11.94 | Yam, elephant | 17.46 |
| Plum | 12.1 | Tapioca | 17.81 |
| Grapes, seeded, round, green | 12.19 | Yam, wild | 20.95 |
| Jambu fruit, ripe | 12.3 | Water chestnut | 21.46 |
| Grapes, seeded, round, red | 12.55 | Sweet potato, pink skin | 23.93 |
| Mango, ripe, totapari | 12.75 | Sweet potato, brown skin | 24.25 |
| Apple, big | 13.11 | **CONDIMENTS AND SPICES - FRESH** | |
| Manila tamarind | 13.54 | Coriander leaves | 1.93 |
| Sapota | 13.9 | Mint leaves | 2.39 |
| Apple, small | 13.95 | Curry leaves | 4.51 |
| Apple, small, Kashmir | 13.99 | Chillies green-all varieties | 5.86 |
| Jack fruit, ripe | 14.01 | Mango ginger | 6.93 |
| Phalsa | 15.09 | Ginger, fresh | 8.97 |
| Grapes, seeded, round, black | 16.23 | Onion, big | 9.59 |
| Fig | 16.28 | Onion, small | 11.58 |
| Rambutan | 16.84 | Garlic, small clove | 21.84 |

--- **Author** ---
Dr. Prajakta J. Nande

# Clinical and Therapeutic Nutrition Practical Manual 1
For M.Sc. Food Science and Nutrition (Semester-III)

| | | | |
|---|---|---|---|
| Garlic, big clove | 21.93 | Linseeds | 10.99 |
| Garlic, single clove, Kashmir | 23.46 | Pistachio nut | 15.82 |
| **CONDIMENTS AND SPICES - DRY** | | Mustard seeds | 16.8 |
| Fenugreek seeds | 10.57 | Groundnut | 17.27 |
| Poppy seeds | 12.32 | Niger seeds, gray | 20.59 |
| Coriander seeds | 12.98 | Niger seeds, black | 22.98 |
| Cumin seeds | 22.62 | Cashew nut | 25.46 |
| Omum | 24.53 | Pine seeds | 26.77 |
| Mace | 26.51 | Safflower seeds | 30.18 |
| Nutmeg | 27.64 | Garden cress, seeds | 33.66 |
| Chillies, red | 29.46 | Arecanut, fresh | 45 |
| Pippali | 35.7 | Arecanut, dried, red color | 70.27 |
| Pepper, black | 36.22 | Arecanut, dried, brown | 70.42 |
| Turmeric powder | 47.22 | **SUGAR** | |
| Cardamom, green | 47.76 | Sugarcane, juice | 13.11 |
| Cardamom, black | 52.53 | Jaggery, cane | 84.87 |
| Cloves | 64 | **MUSHROOMS** | |
| Asafoetida | 71.95 | Button mushroom, fresh | 1.98 |
| **NUTS AND OIL SEEDS** | | Chicken mushroom, fresh | 2.76 |
| Almond | 3.04 | Shiitake mushroom, fresh | 8.98 |
| Coconut kernel, fresh | 6.3 | **MISCELLANEOUS FOODS** | |
| Sunflower seeds | 6.85 | Coconut water | 3.16 |
| Coconut kernel, dry | 8.01 | **MILK AND MILK PRODUCTS** | |
| Gingelly seeds, brown | 9.76 | Milk, whole, cow | 4.94 |
| Walnut | 10.14 | Milk, whole, buffalo | 8.39 |
| Gingelly seeds, black | 10.29 | Paneer | 12.41 |
| Gingelly seeds, white | 10.83 | Khoa | 16.53 |

*(Source: T. Longvah, R. Ananthan, K. Bhaskaracharya, K. Venkaiah. Indian Food Composition Tables, National Institute of Nutrition (Indian Council of Medical Research), 3-30, 2017)*

---

## ANNEXURE - 3

## PROTEIN CONTENT OF FOODS

| FOOD STUFFS | Protein (g/100 g) | Rice,raw, milled | 7.94 |
|---|---|---|---|
| | | Maize, dry | 8.8 |
| | | Varagu | 8.92 |
| **CEREALS AND MILLETS** | | Rice, raw,brown | 9.16 |
| Maize, tender, local | 3.57 | Wheat, vermicelli | 9.7 |
| Maize, tender, sweet | 4.16 | Jowar | 9.97 |
| Ragi | 7.16 | Samai | 10.13 |
| Rice flakes | 7.44 | Wheat flour, refined | 10.36 |
| Rice puffed | 7.47 | Wheat, vermicelli, roasted | 10.37 |
| Rice, parboiled, milled | 7.81 | Wheat flour | 10.57 |

--- **Author** ---
Dr. Prajakta J. Nande

# Clinical and Therapeutic Nutrition Practical Manual 1
### For M.Sc. Food Science and Nutrition (Semester-III)

| | | | | |
|---|---|---|---|---|
| Wheat, whole | 10.59 | Beet greens | 2.38 |
| Wheat , bulgur | 10.84 | Bathua leaves | 2.5 |
| Barley | 10.94 | Betel leaves, big (Kolkata) | 2.51 |
| Bajra | 10.96 | Betel leaves, small | 2.62 |
| Wheat, semolina | 11.38 | Amaranth spinosus, leaves, red and green mix | 2.8 |
| Quinoa | 13.11 | Amaranth leaves, red and green mix | 3.09 |
| Amaranth seeds, pale brown | 13.27 | Knol-khol, leaves | 3.12 |
| Amaranth seeds, black | 14.59 | Amaranth leaves, green | 3.29 |
| **GRAIN LEGUMES** | | Colocasia leaves, green | 3.42 |
| Bengal gram, whole | 18.77 | Mustard leaves | 3.52 |
| Rajmah, black | 19.01 | Amaranth spinosus, leaves, green | 3.54 |
| Rajmah, brown | 19.5 | Cabbage, collard greens | 3.63 |
| Moth bean | 19.75 | Fenugreek leaves | 3.68 |
| Field bean, white | 19.84 | Cauliflower leaves | 3.9 |
| Field bean, brown | 19.9 | Amaranth leaves, red | 3.93 |
| Rajmah, red | 19.91 | Pumpkin leaves, tender | 4.21 |
| Field bean, black | 19.93 | Brussels sprouts | 4.26 |
| Ricebean | 19.97 | Ponnaganni | 5.29 |
| Cowpea, brown | 20.36 | Parsley | 5.55 |
| Peas, dry | 20.43 | Garden cress | 5.62 |
| Red gram, whole | 20.47 | Tamarind leaves | 5.84 |
| Cowpea, white | 21.25 | Drumstick leaves | 6.41 |
| Bengal gram, dal | 21.55 | Agathi leaves | 8.01 |
| Red gram, dal | 21.7 | **OTHER VEGETABLES** | |
| Horse gram, whole | 21.73 | Plantain, stem | 0.35 |
| Black gram, whole | 21.97 | Bottle gourd, round, pale green | 0.42 |
| Lentil whole, brown | 22.49 | Bottle gourd, elongate, dark green | 0.49 |
| Green gram, whole | 22.53 | Papaya, raw | 0.5 |
| Lentil whole, yellowish | 22.87 | Bottle gourd, elongate, pale green | 0.53 |
| Black gram, dal | 23.06 | Snake gourd, short | 0.54 |
| Green gram, dal | 23.88 | Cho-cho-marrow | 0.66 |
| Lentil dal | 24.35 | Mango, green, raw | 0.69 |
| Soya bean, brown | 35.58 | Cucumber, green, elongate | 0.71 |
| Soya bean, white | 37.8 | Colocasia, stem, black | 0.76 |
| **GREEN LEAFY VEGETABLES** | | Tomato, ripe, hybrid | 0.76 |
| Cabbage, green | 1.36 | Ash gourd | 0.79 |
| Cabbage, violet | 1.39 | Cucumber, green, short | 0.83 |
| Pak choi leaves | 1.41 | Pumpkin, orange, round | 0.84 |
| Lettuce | 1.54 | Pumpkin, green, cylindrical | 0.87 |
| Basella leaves | 1.57 | Snake gourd, long, dark green | 0.89 |
| Cabbage, Chinese | 1.58 | Tomato, ripe, local | 0.9 |
| Rumex leaves | 1.62 | Colocasia, stem, green | 0.91 |
| Gogu leaves, red | 1.85 | Ridge gourd | 0.91 |
| Gogu leaves, green | 1.86 | Celery stalk | 0.98 |
| Spinach | 2.14 | Cucumber, round | 0.98 |
| Radish leaves | 2.22 | | |

--- **Author** ---
Dr. Prajakta J. Nande

# Clinical and Therapeutic Nutrition Practical Manual 1
For M.Sc. Food Science and Nutrition (Semester-III)

| | | | | |
|---|---|---|---|---|
| Ridge gourd, smooth skin | 0.98 | Mango, ripe, totapari | 0.41 |
| Snake gourd, long, pale green | 0.98 | Musk melon, orange flesh | 0.42 |
| Tinda, tender | 1.02 | Papaya, ripe | 0.42 |
| Zucchini, green | 1.1 | Apple, green | 0.46 |
| Capsicum, green | 1.11 | Mango, ripe, himsagar | 0.46 |
| Tomato, green | 1.12 | Palm fruit, tender | 0.5 |
| Plantain, green | 1.18 | Mango, ripe, gulabkhas | 0.52 |
| Kovai, small | 1.22 | Pineapple | 0.52 |
| Zucchini, yellow | 1.31 | Musk melon, yellow flesh | 0.53 |
| Bamboo shoot, tender | 1.33 | Mango, ripe, banganapalli | 0.54 |
| Bitter gourd, jagged, teeth ridges, short | 1.34 | Mango, ripe, kesar | 0.54 |
| | | Water melon, pale green | 0.59 |
| Capsicum, yellow | 1.35 | Water melon, dark green | 0.6 |
| Kovai, big | 1.39 | Grapes, seedless, round, green | 0.62 |
| Parwar | 1.4 | Mangosteen | 0.63 |
| Bitter gourd, jagged, teeth ridges, elongate | 1.44 | Plum | 0.64 |
| | | Mango, ripe, neelam | 0.68 |
| Capsicum, red | 1.47 | Mango, ripe, paheri | 0.68 |
| Plantain, flower | 1.47 | Pummelo | 0.68 |
| Brinjal-all varieties | 1.48 | Rambutan | 0.68 |
| Knol-khol | 1.58 | Orange, pulp | 0.7 |
| Bitter gourd, jagged, smooth ridges, elongate | 1.61 | Soursop | 0.74 |
| | | Grapes, seeded, round, black | 0.76 |
| Jack fruit, raw | 1.98 | Lime, sweet, pulp | 0.76 |
| Onion, stalk | 2.07 | Grapes, seeded, round, green | 0.77 |
| Ladies finger | 2.08 | Star fruit | 0.79 |
| French beans, hybrid | 2.12 | Jambu fruit, ripe | 0.82 |
| Cauliflower | 2.15 | Peach | 0.86 |
| French beans, country | 2.49 | Black berry | 0.92 |
| Drumstick | 2.62 | Sapota | 0.92 |
| Corn, baby | 2.69 | Grapes, seeded, round, red | 0.95 |
| Bean scarlet, tender | 2.86 | Strawberry | 0.97 |
| Field beans, tender, broad | 3.06 | Litchi | 0.99 |
| Cluster beans | 3.55 | Karonda fruit | 1.15 |
| Field beans, tender, lean | 3.71 | Dates, processed | 1.18 |
| Broad beans | 3.85 | Guava, pink flesh | 1.19 |
| Jack fruit, seed, mature | 5.79 | Banana, ripe, robusta | 1.23 |
| Peas, fresh | 7.25 | Grapes, seedless, round, black | 1.24 |
| Red gram, tender, fresh | 8.09 | Banana, ripe, montham | 1.25 |
| **FRUITS** | | Banana, ripe, red | 1.29 |
| Apple, small, Kashmir | 0.27 | Pomegranate, maroon seeds | 1.33 |
| Apple, big | 0.29 | Zizyphus | 1.34 |
| Apple, small | 0.31 | Grapes, seedless, oval, black | 1.41 |
| Gooseberry | 0.34 | Guava, white flesh | 1.44 |
| Pear | 0.36 | Apricot, processed | 1.47 |
| Lemon, juice | 0.41 | Banana, ripe, poovam | 1.49 |

--- **Author** ---
Dr. Prajakta J. Nande

# Clinical and Therapeutic Nutrition Practical Manual 1
## For M.Sc. Food Science and Nutrition (Semester-III)

| | | | |
|---|---|---|---|
| Cherries, red | 1.49 | Garlic, big clove | 6.92 |
| Currants, black | 1.51 | Curry leaves | 7.41 |
| Custard apple | 1.62 | **CONDIMENTS AND SPICES - DRY** | |
| Phalsa | 1.66 | Cloves | 5.86 |
| Fig | 2.03 | Mace | 6.24 |
| Dates, dry, dark brown | 2.38 | Nutmeg | 6.3 |
| Dates, dry, pale brown | 2.45 | Asafoetida | 6.34 |
| Raisins, dried, black | 2.57 | Cardamom, black | 6.69 |
| Bael fruit | 2.63 | Turmeric powder | 7.66 |
| Jack fruit, ripe | 2.74 | Cardamom, green | 8.1 |
| Raisins, dried, golden | 2.76 | Pepper, black | 10.12 |
| Tamarind, pulp | 2.92 | Pippali | 10.53 |
| Avocado fruit | 2.95 | Coriander seeds | 10.66 |
| Wood apple | 3.14 | Chillies, red | 12.69 |
| Apricot, dried | 3.17 | Cumin seeds | 13.91 |
| Manila tamarind | 3.56 | Omum | 15.89 |
| **ROOTS AND TUBERS** | | Poppy seeds | 20.31 |
| Radish, elongate, red skin | 0.67 | Fenugreek seeds | 25.41 |
| Radish, elongate, white skin | 0.77 | **NUTS AND OIL SEEDS** | |
| Radish, round, white skin | 0.8 | Arecanut fresh | 2.73 |
| Water chestnut | 0.86 | Coconut kernel, fresh | 3.84 |
| Radish, round, red skin | 0.89 | Arecanut, dried, brown | 5.78 |
| Carrot, orange | 0.95 | Arecanut, dried, red color | 6.64 |
| Tapioca | 1.03 | Coconut kernel, dry | 7.27 |
| Carrot, red | 1.04 | Pine seeds | 12.55 |
| Sweet potato, pink skin | 1.27 | Walnut | 14.92 |
| Sweet potato, brown skin | 1.33 | Safflower seeds | 17.66 |
| Potato, brown skin, small | 1.35 | Niger seeds, gray | 18.34 |
| Potato, brown skin, big | 1.54 | Almond | 18.41 |
| Potato, red skin | 1.83 | Linseeds | 18.55 |
| Lotus root | 1.94 | Cashew nut | 18.78 |
| Beet root | 1.95 | Niger seeds, black | 18.92 |
| Yam, ordinary | 2.18 | Gingelly seeds, black | 19.17 |
| Yam, elephant | 2.56 | Mustard seeds | 19.51 |
| Yam, wild | 3.07 | Gingelly seeds, brown | 21.61 |
| Colocasia | 3.31 | Gingelly seeds, white | 21.7 |
| **CONDIMENTS AND SPICES- FRESH** | | Pistachio nut | 23.35 |
| Mango ginger | 1.45 | Garden cress, seeds | 23.36 |
| Onion, big | 1.5 | Sunflower seeds | 23.53 |
| Onion, small | 1.82 | Groundnut | 23.65 |
| Ginger, fresh | 2.22 | **SUGARS** | |
| Chillies, green-all varieties | 2.36 | Sugarcane, juice | 0.16 |
| Coriander leaves | 3.52 | Jaggery, cane | 1.85 |
| Mint leaves | 4.66 | **MUSHROOMS** | |
| Garlic, single clove, Kashmir | 6.12 | Chicken mushroom, fresh | 1.84 |
| Garlic, small clove | 6.75 | Shiitake mushroom, fresh | 3.19 |

--- **Author** ---
Dr. Prajakta J. Nande

# Clinical and Therapeutic Nutrition Practical Manual 1
For M.Sc. Food Science and Nutrition (Semester-III)

| | | | |
|---|---|---|---|
| Button mushroom, fresh | 3.68 | Goat, heart | 19.38 |
| **MISCELLANEOUS FOODS** | | Pork, chops | 19.41 |
| Coconut water | 0.26 | Beef, chops | 19.82 |
| **MILK AND MILK PRODUCTS** | | Pork, liver | 19.89 |
| Milk,whole, cow | 3.26 | Goat, liver | 20.32 |
| Milk,whole, buffalo | 3.68 | Goat, shoulder | 20.33 |
| Khoa | 16.34 | Goat, chops | 20.39 |
| Paneer | 18.86 | Beef, shoulder | 20.56 |
| **EGG AND EGG PRODUCTS** | | Beef, liver | 20.73 |
| Eggs, poultry, white, raw | 10.84 | Goat, legs | 22.07 |
| Eggs, poultry, whole, raw | 13.28 | Beef, round (leg) | 22.64 |
| Egg, country hen, whole, raw | 13.43 | **MARINE FISH** | |
| Egg, poultry, yolk, raw | 15.74 | Bombay duck | 13.53 |
| **POULTRY** | | Sardine | 17.91 |
| Chicken, poultry, wing, skinless | 17.42 | Pomfret,black | 18.91 |
| Chicken, poultry, thigh, skinless | 18.18 | Pomfret, white | 19.02 |
| Chicken, poultry, legs, skinless | 19.44 | Mural | 19.04 |
| Poultry, chicken, liver | 21.57 | Salmon | 20.97 |
| Chicken, poultry, breast, skinless | 21.81 | Tuna | 24.5 |
| **ANIMAL MEAT** | | **MARINE SHELLFISH** | |
| Beef, brain | 10.55 | Crab | 10.23 |
| Goat, brain | 13.82 | Tiger prawns, orange | 14.25 |
| Pork, kidneys | 14.35 | Crab, sea | 15.36 |
| Pork, lungs | 15.13 | Lobster, brown | 15.96 |
| Pork, stomach | 15.36 | Lobster, king size | 18.54 |
| Goat, kidneys | 15.6 | **FRESH WATER FISH AND SHELLFISH** | |
| Beef, lungs | 15.66 | Prawns, small | 13.07 |
| Pork, heart | 16.31 | Crab | 13.23 |
| Goat, lungs | 16.86 | Catla | 17.94 |
| Beef, kidneys | 17.09 | Prawns, big | 19.24 |
| Pork, shoulder | 17.41 | Rohu | 19.71 |
| Beef, spleen | 17.42 | **FATTY FISH** | |
| Beef, heart | 17.68 | Hilsa | 21.8 |
| Goat, spleen | 18.45 | | |

*(Source: T. Longvah, R. Ananthan, K. Bhaskaracharya, K. Venkaiah. Indian Food Composition Tables, National Institute of Nutrition (Indian Council of Medical Research), 3-30, 2017)*

# Clinical and Therapeutic Nutrition Practical Manual 1
For M.Sc. Food Science and Nutrition (Semester-III)

## ANNEXURE - 4

## TOTAL FAT CONTENT OF FOODS

| FOOD STUFFS | Total Fat (g/100 g) |
| --- | --- |
| **CEREALS AND MILLETS** | |
| Wheat, vermicelli | 0.45 |
| Wheat, vermicelli, roasted | 0.49 |
| Rice, raw, milled | 0.52 |
| Rice, parboiled, milled | 0.55 |
| Wheat, semolina | 0.74 |
| Wheat flour, refined | 0.76 |
| Rice flakes | 1.14 |
| Rice, raw, brown | 1.24 |
| Barley | 1.3 |
| Maize, tender, sweet | 1.35 |
| Maize, tender, local | 1.4 |
| Wheat, bulgur | 1.45 |
| Wheat, whole | 1.47 |
| Wheat flour | 1.53 |
| Rice puffed | 1.62 |
| Jowar | 1.73 |
| Ragi | 1.92 |
| Varagu | 2.55 |
| Maize, dry | 3.77 |
| Samai | 3.89 |
| Bajra | 5.43 |
| Quinoa | 5.5 |
| Amaranth seeds, pale brown | 5.56 |
| Amaranth seeds, black | 5.74 |
| **GRAIN LEGUMES** | |
| Lentil whole, yellowish | 0.61 |
| Horse gram, whole | 0.62 |
| Lentil whole, brown | 0.64 |
| Rice bean | 0.74 |
| Lentil dal | 0.75 |
| Field bean, black | 0.92 |
| Field bean, white | 0.94 |
| Field bean, brown | 0.98 |
| Cowpea, white | 1.14 |
| Green gram, whole | 1.14 |
| Cowpea, brown | 1.15 |

| Green gram, dal | 1.35 |
| --- | --- |
| Red gram, whole | 1.38 |
| Red gram, dal | 1.56 |
| Black gram, whole | 1.58 |
| Rajmah, black | 1.62 |
| Rajmah, brown | 1.68 |
| Black gram, dal | 1.69 |
| Moth bean | 1.76 |
| Rajmah, red | 1.77 |
| Peas, dry | 1.89 |
| Bengal gram, whole | 5.11 |
| Bengal gram, dal | 5.31 |
| Soya bean, white | 19.42 |
| Soya bean, brown | 19.82 |
| **GREEN LEAFY VEGETABLES** | |
| Cabbage, green | 0.12 |
| Cabbage, Chinese | 0.13 |
| Cabbage, violet | 0.21 |
| Pak choi leaves | 0.25 |
| Cabbage, collard greens | 0.27 |
| Lettuce | 0.27 |
| Rumex leaves | 0.33 |
| Amaranth spinosus, leaves, red and green mix | 0.34 |
| Knol-khol, leaves | 0.35 |
| Amaranth spinosus, leaves, green | 0.36 |
| Cauliflower leaves | 0.42 |
| Bathua leaves | 0.44 |
| Basella leaves | 0.45 |
| Tamarind leaves, tender | 0.49 |
| Brussels sprouts | 0.5 |
| Mustard leaves | 0.51 |
| Radish leaves | 0.51 |
| Amaranth leaves, red and green mix | 0.53 |
| Amaranth leaves, red | 0.63 |
| Spinach | 0.64 |
| Amaranth leaves, green | 0.65 |
| Ponnaganni | 0.71 |
| Pumpkin leaves, tender | 0.74 |
| Beet greens | 0.75 |
| Betel leaves, big (Kolkata) | 0.75 |

--- Author ---
Dr. Prajakta J. Nande

# Clinical and Therapeutic Nutrition Practical Manual 1
## For M.Sc. Food Science and Nutrition (Semester-III)

| | | | | |
|---|---|---|---|---|
| Betel leaves, small | 0.75 | French beans, country | 0.26 |
| Garden cress | 0.8 | Onion, stalk | 0.26 |
| Fenugreek leaves | 0.83 | Snake gourd, short | 0.26 |
| Gogu leaves, red | 1.07 | Tomato, green | 0.27 |
| Gogu leaves, green | 1.09 | Parwar | 0.3 |
| Parsley | 1.14 | Brinjal-all varieties | 0.32 |
| Agathi leaves | 1.35 | Capsicum, green | 0.34 |
| Colocasia leaves, green | 1.38 | Colocasia, stem, black | 0.34 |
| Drumstick leaves | 1.64 | Bamboo shoot, tender | 0.35 |
| **OTHER VEGETABLES** | | Jack fruit, raw | 0.35 |
| Mango, green, raw | 0.08 | Knol-khol | 0.35 |
| Bottle gourd, round, pale green | 0.12 | Cluster beans | 0.37 |
| Drumstick | 0.12 | Capsicum, yellow | 0.41 |
| Bottle gourd, elongate, pale green | 0.13 | Cauliflower | 0.44 |
| Bottle gourd, elongate, dark green | 0.13 | Jack fruit, seed, mature | 0.44 |
| Peas, fresh | 0.13 | Capsicum, red | 0.47 |
| Ridge gourd, smooth skin | 0.13 | Zucchini, green | 0.47 |
| Ash gourd | 0.14 | Zucchini, yellow | 0.51 |
| Ridge gourd | 0.14 | Field beans, tender, lean | 0.6 |
| Broad beans | 0.15 | Plantain, flower | 0.63 |
| Cho-cho-marrow | 0.15 | Field beans, tender, broad | 0.64 |
| Cucumber, green, elongate | 0.16 | Red gram, tender, fresh | 0.92 |
| Plantain, stem | 0.16 | Bean scarlet, tender | 0.99 |
| Pumpkin, orange, round | 0.16 | Corn, baby | 1.33 |
| Tinda, tender | 0.17 | **FRUITS** | |
| Cucumber, green, short | 0.18 | Palm fruit, tender | 0.12 |
| Pumpkin, green, cylindrical | 0.18 | Orange, pulp | 0.13 |
| French beans, hybrid | 0.19 | Phalsa | 0.14 |
| Colocasia, stem, green | 0.22 | Jack fruit, ripe | 0.15 |
| Ladies finger | 0.22 | Pomegranate, maroon seeds | 0.15 |
| Papaya, raw | 0.23 | Tamarind, pulp | 0.15 |
| Plantain, green | 0.23 | Gooseberry | 0.16 |
| Bitter gourd, jagged, teeth ridges, elongate | 0.24 | Papaya, ripe | 0.16 |
| | | Pineapple | 0.16 |
| Bitter gourd, jagged, teeth ridges, short | 0.24 | Rambutan | 0.16 |
| | | Water melon, dark green | 0.16 |
| Celery stalk | 0.24 | Water melon, pale green | 0.16 |
| Cucumber, round | 0.24 | Jambu fruit, ripe | 0.17 |
| Kovai, big | 0.24 | Lime, sweet, pulp | 0.2 |
| Kovai, small | 0.24 | Mangosteen | 0.24 |
| Snake gourd, long, pale green | 0.25 | Guava, pink flesh | 0.25 |
| Snake gourd, long, dark green | 0.25 | Grapes, seedless, round, green | 0.26 |
| Tomato, ripe, hybrid | 0.25 | Litchi | 0.26 |
| Tomato, ripe, local | 0.25 | Musk melon, yellow flesh | 0.26 |
| Bitter gourd, jagged, smooth ridges, elongate | 0.26 | Pear | 0.27 |
| | | Banana, ripe, red | 0.29 |

--- **Author** ---
Dr. Prajakta J. Nande

# Clinical and Therapeutic Nutrition Practical Manual 1
For M.Sc. Food Science and Nutrition (Semester-III)

| | | | |
|---|---|---|---|
| Grapes, seeded, round, green | 0.29 | Avocado fruit | 13.86 |
| Grapes, seeded, round, red | 0.29 | **ROOTS AND TUBERS** | |
| Banana, ripe, montham | 0.32 | Radish, elongate, red skin | 0.13 |
| Grapes, seeded, round, black | 0.32 | Beet root | 0.14 |
| Guava, white flesh | 0.32 | Radish, round, white skin | 0.14 |
| Banana, ripe, robusta | 0.33 | Yam, elephant | 0.14 |
| Raisins, dried, black | 0.34 | Radish, elongate, white skin | 0.15 |
| Banana, ripe, poovam | 0.35 | Radish, round, red skin | 0.16 |
| Dates, dry, pale brown | 0.35 | Colocasia | 0.17 |
| Dates, dry, dark brown | 0.35 | Yam, ordinary | 0.17 |
| Grapes, seedless, round, black | 0.35 | Tapioca | 0.2 |
| Musk melon, orange flesh | 0.35 | Potato, brown skin, small | 0.22 |
| Raisins, dried, golden | 0.35 | Potato, red skin | 0.22 |
| Zizyphus | 0.35 | Potato, brown skin, big | 0.23 |
| Fig | 0.37 | Sweet potato, brown skin | 0.26 |
| Peach | 0.37 | Yam, wild | 0.3 |
| Star fruit | 0.39 | Sweet potato, pink skin | 0.33 |
| Plum | 0.4 | Water chestnut | 0.37 |
| Dates, processed | 0.41 | Carrot, orange | 0.47 |
| Pummelo | 0.42 | Carrot, red | 0.47 |
| Cherries, red | 0.46 | Lotus root | 0.93 |
| Grapes, seedless, oval, black | 0.46 | **CONDIMENTS AND SPICES - FRESH** | |
| Mango, ripe, totapari | 0.49 | Garlic, small clove | 0.14 |
| Apple, green | 0.5 | Garlic, big clove | 0.16 |
| Apple, small | 0.53 | Garlic, single clove, Kashmir | 0.16 |
| Currants, black | 0.53 | Onion, small | 0.16 |
| Mango, ripe, gulabkhas | 0.53 | Onion, big | 0.24 |
| Mango, ripe, himsagar | 0.54 | Mint leaves | 0.65 |
| Mango, ripe, banganapalli | 0.55 | Coriander leaves | 0.7 |
| Mango, ripe, neelam | 0.55 | Mango ginger | 0.7 |
| Strawberry | 0.56 | Chillies green-all varieties | 0.72 |
| Bael fruit | 0.57 | Ginger, fresh | 0.85 |
| Mango, ripe, kesar | 0.57 | Curry leaves | 1.06 |
| Mango, ripe, paheri | 0.58 | **CONDIMENTS AND SPICES - DRY** | |
| Apple, small, Kashmir | 0.6 | Asafoetida | 1.26 |
| Black berry | 0.63 | Pippali | 2.27 |
| Apple, big | 0.64 | Cardamom, green | 2.60 |
| Apricot, processed | 0.64 | Pepper, black | 2.74 |
| Custard apple | 0.67 | Cardamom, black | 2.80 |
| Apricot, dried | 0.74 | Turmeric powder | 5.03 |
| Lemon, juice | 0.75 | Fenugreek seeds | 5.72 |
| Soursop | 0.94 | Chillies, red | 6.4 |
| Manila tamarind | 1.14 | Cloves | 8.41 |
| Sapota | 1.26 | Cumin seeds | 16.64 |
| Karonda fruit | 1.67 | Coriander seeds | 17.47 |
| Wood apple | 3.62 | Omum | 21.11 |

--- **Author** ---
Dr. Prajakta J. Nande

# Clinical and Therapeutic Nutrition Practical Manual 1
## For M.Sc. Food Science and Nutrition (Semester-III)

| | | | | |
|---|---|---|---|---|
| Mace | 24.41 | Chicken, poultry, breast, skinless | 9 |
| Poppy seeds | 30.38 | Chicken, poultry, legs, skinless | 12.64 |
| Nutmeg | 36.52 | Chicken, poultry, wing, skinless | 13.81 |
| **NUTS AND OIL SEEDS** | | Chicken, poultry, thigh, skinless | 14.23 |
| Arecanut, dried, brown | 4.35 | **ANIMAL MEAT** | |
| Arecanut, dried, red color | 4.46 | Beef, spleen | 2.22 |
| Arecanut, fresh | 5.51 | Beef, lungs | 2.28 |
| Garden cress, seeds | 23.74 | Goat, spleen | 2.37 |
| Safflower seeds | 30.87 | Pork, lungs | 2.47 |
| Linseeds | 35.67 | Pork, spleen | 2.71 |
| Niger seeds, black | 38.61 | Goat, kidneys | 2.93 |
| Niger seeds, gray | 39.53 | Goat, lungs | 3.09 |
| Ground nut | 39.63 | Beef, heart | 3.57 |
| Mustard seeds | 40.19 | Pork, kidneys | 3.65 |
| Coconut kernel, fresh | 41.38 | Beef, liver | 3.96 |
| Pistachio nut | 42.49 | Beef, kidney | 4.01 |
| Gingelly seeds, white | 43.05 | Goat, heart | 4.4 |
| Gingelly seeds, black | 43.1 | Pork, heart | 4.87 |
| Gingelly seeds, brown | 43.22 | Goat, liver | 4.88 |
| Cashew nut | 45.2 | Goat, chops | 5.98 |
| Pine seeds | 48.79 | Beef, chops | 6.71 |
| Sunflower seeds | 51.85 | Beef, round (leg) | 7.38 |
| Almond | 58.49 | Pork, stomach | 7.81 |
| Coconut kernel, dry | 63.26 | Goat, legs | 7.94 |
| Walnut | 64.27 | Goat, brain | 8.06 |
| **SUGAR** | | Beef, brain | 9.28 |
| Jaggery, cane | 0.16 | Pork, chops | 11.3 |
| Sugarcane, juice | 0.4 | Goat, shoulder | 11.94 |
| **MUSHROOMS** | | Beef, shoulder | 14.59 |
| Chicken mushroom, fresh | 0.25 | Pork, shoulder | 18.83 |
| Button mushroom, fresh | 0.42 | **MARINE FISH** | |
| Shiitake mushroom, fresh | 0.76 | Mural | 0.58 |
| **MISCELLANEOUS FOODS** | | Bombay duck | 1.03 |
| Coconut water | 0.16 | Tuna | 1.44 |
| **MILK AND MILK PRODUCTS** | | Pomfret, black | 4.83 |
| Milk, whole, cow | 4.48 | Pomfret, white | 5.12 |
| Milk, whole, Buffalo | 6.58 | Sardine | 8.99 |
| Paneer | 14.78 | Salmon | 9.86 |
| Khoa | 20.62 | **MARINE SHELLFISH** | |
| **EGG AND EGG PRODUCTS** | | Lobster, brown | 0.56 |
| Eggs, poultry, white, raw | 0.06 | Crab, sea | 0.6 |
| Eggs, poultry, whole, raw | 9.15 | Tiger prawns, orange | 0.74 |
| Egg, country hen, whole, raw | 13 | Lobster, king size | 0.78 |
| Egg, poultry, yolk, raw | 26.34 | Crab | 1.41 |
| **POULTRY** | | **FRESH WATER FISH AND SHELLFISH** | |
| Poultry, chicken, liver | 4.08 | Prawns, big | 0.52 |

--- **Author** ---
Dr. Prajakta J. Nande

# Clinical and Therapeutic Nutrition Practical Manual 1
For M.Sc. Food Science and Nutrition (Semester-III)

| | | | |
|---|---|---|---|
| Prawns, small | 0.78 | Rohu | 2.39 |
| Crab | 0.89 | **FATTY FISH** | |
| Catla | 2.15 | Hilsa | 18.49 |

*(Source: T. Longvah, R. Ananthan, K. Bhaskaracharya, K. Venkaiah. Indian Food Composition Tables, National Institute of Nutrition (Indian Council of Medical Research), 3-30, 2017)*

## ANNEXURE - 5

## FIBER CONTENT OF FOODS

## SOLUBLE DIETARY FIBER (SDF)

| FOOD STUFFS | SDF (g/100 g) | | |
|---|---|---|---|
| **CEREALS AND MILLETS** | | Field bean, brown | 5.08 |
| Barley | 5.66 | Soya bean, brown | 5 |
| Quinoa | 4.46 | Black gram, whole | 4.94 |
| Bajra | 2.34 | Black gram, dal | 4.35 |
| Samai | 2.27 | Rice bean | 3.33 |
| Wheat, bulgur | 2.25 | Red gram, whole | 3.15 |
| Varagu | 2.11 | Cowpea, brown | 2.8 |
| Wheat, vermicelli, roasted | 1.76 | Cowpea, white | 2.79 |
| Wheat, vermicelli | 1.75 | Rajmah, red | 2.7 |
| Jowar | 1.73 | Lentil whole, brown | 2.66 |
| Ragi | 1.67 | Rajmah, brown | 2.62 |
| Amaranth seed, pale brown | 1.67 | Rajmah, black | 2.58 |
| Wheat flour | 1.63 | Bengal gram, whole | 2.52 |
| Wheat, whole | 1.6 | Lentil whole, yellowish | 2.51 |
| Wheat, semolina | 1.55 | Bengal gram, dal | 2.48 |
| Amaranth seed, black | 1.26 | Peas, dry | 2.47 |
| Maize, dry | 0.94 | Green gram, whole | 2.44 |
| Rice, raw, brown | 0.82 | Red gram, dal | 2.39 |
| Rice, raw, milled | 0.82 | Lentil dal | 1.83 |
| Rice flakes | 0.81 | Horse gram, whole | 1.83 |
| Rice puffed | 0.8 | Green gram, dal | 1.62 |
| Rice, parboiled, milled | 0.76 | Moth beans | 0.62 |
| Wheat flour, refined | 0.62 | **GREEN LEAFY VEGETABLES** | |
| Maize, tender, sweet | 0.59 | Garden cress | 83 |
| Maize, tender, local | 0.43 | Agathi leaves | 2.6 |
| **GRAINS AND LEGUMES** | | Drumstick leaves | 2.1 |
| Soya bean, white | 5.59 | Amaranth spinosus, leaves, green | 1.75 |
| Field bean, white | 5.54 | Fenugreek leaves | 1.7 |
| Field bean, black | 5.41 | Bathua leaves | 1.68 |
| | | Beet greens | 1.43 |
| | | Amaranth leaves, red and green | 1.37 |

--- Author ---
Dr. Prajakta J. Nande

# Clinical and Therapeutic Nutrition Practical Manual 1
## For M.Sc. Food Science and Nutrition (Semester-III)

| | | | |
|---|---|---|---|
| mix | | Cauliflower | 1.04 |
| Tamarind leaves, tender | 1.36 | Papaya, raw | 0.96 |
| Gogu leaves, green | 1.35 | Zucchini, green | 0.88 |
| Colocasia leaves, green | 1.29 | Ash gourd | 0.85 |
| Gogu leaves,red | 1.23 | Field beans, tender, lean | 0.82 |
| Amaranth leaves, green | 1.2 | Kovai, big | 0.81 |
| Amaranth spinosus, leaves, red and green | 1.2 | Plantain, green | 0.81 |
| Amaranth leaves, red | 1.19 | Capsicum, yellow | 0.8 |
| Ponnoganni | 1.11 | Jack fruit, seed, mature | 0.8 |
| Parsley | 1.09 | Plantain, stem | 0.8 |
| Knol-khol, leaves | 0.95 | Field beans, tender, broad | 0.79 |
| Brussels sprouts | 0.94 | Parwar | 0.79 |
| Cabbage, collard greens | 0.94 | Bean scarlet, tender | 0.74 |
| Mustard leaves | 0.87 | Capsicum, green | 0.73 |
| Spinach | 0.86 | Bitter gourd, jagged, teeth ridges | 0.68 |
| Cabbage, green | 0.85 | Cucumber, orange, round | 0.68 |
| Betel leaves, small | 0.8 | Snake gourd, short | 0.68 |
| Betel leaves, big (Kolkata) | 0.8 | Bitter gourd, jagged, smooth ridges, elongate | 0.67 |
| Pumpkin leaves, tender | 0.69 | French beans, hybrid | 0.65 |
| Radish leaves | 0.63 | Cucumber, green, elongate | 0.63 |
| Cabbage, violet | 0.62 | Capsicum, red | 0.61 |
| Cauliflower leaves | 0.62 | Ridge gourd | 0.61 |
| Basella leaves | 0.57 | Snake gourd, long, dark green | 0.58 |
| Lettuce | 0.47 | Snake gourd, long, pale green | 0.58 |
| Pak choi leaves | 0.47 | Tomato, green | 0.57 |
| Cabbage, Chinese | 0.45 | Cucumber, green, short | 0.54 |
| Rumex leaves | 0.34 | Jack fruit, raw | 0.54 |
| **OTHER VEGETABLES** | | Bitter gourd, jagged, teeth ridges, short | 0.53 |
| Red gram, tender, fresh | 2.25 | Celery stalk | 0.52 |
| Broad beans | 2.03 | Plantain, flower | 0.52 |
| Corn, baby | 1.62 | French beans, country | 0.51 |
| Onion, stalk | 1.45 | Ridge gourd, smooth skin | 0.51 |
| Mango, green, raw | 1.34 | Bamboo Shoot, tender | 0.49 |
| Cluster beans | 1.28 | Bottle gourd, elongate, pale green | 0.48 |
| Ladies finger | 1.28 | Zucchini, yellow | 0.47 |
| Peas, fresh | 1.28 | Knol-khol | 0.44 |
| Pumpkin, green | 1.25 | Bottle gourd, round, pale green | 0.38 |
| Drumstick | 1.23 | Bottle gourd, elongate, dark green | 0.37 |
| Colocasia, stem, black | 1.2 | Cho-cho-marrow | 0.36 |
| Brinjal-all varieties | 1.14 | Tomato, ripe, local | 0.33 |
| Kovai, small | 1.12 | Tinda, tender | 0.32 |
| Pumpkin, orange, round | 1.12 | Tomato, ripe, hybrid | 0.3 |
| Colocasia, stem, green | 1.07 | | |

--- Author ---
Dr. Prajakta J. Nande

# Clinical and Therapeutic Nutrition Practical Manual 1
For M.Sc. Food Science and Nutrition (Semester-III)

| FRUITS | |
|---|---|
| Bael fruit | 3 |
| Fig | 2.05 |
| Custard apple | 1.93 |
| Currants, black | 1.64 |
| Pear | 1.64 |
| Tamarind, pulp | 1.58 |
| Gooseberry | 1.55 |
| Dates, dry, dark brown | 1.53 |
| Raisins, dried, golden | 1.53 |
| Guava, white flesh | 1.45 |
| Wood apple | 1.44 |
| Avocado fruit | 1.42 |
| Dates, dry, pale brown | 1.42 |
| Jack fruit, ripe | 1.41 |
| Karonda fruit | 1.38 |
| Raisins, dried, black | 1.37 |
| Guava, pink flesh | 1.28 |
| Apple, big | 1.16 |
| Soursop | 1.16 |
| Sapota | 1.14 |
| Manila tamarind | 1.1 |
| Phalsa | 1.09 |
| Papaya, ripe | 1.08 |
| Banana, ripe, poovam | 1.04 |
| Zizyphus | 1.02 |
| Strawberry | 0.99 |
| Mango, ripe, paheri | 0.98 |
| Mango, ripe, kesar | 0.93 |
| Black berry | 0.91 |
| Peach | 0.91 |
| Mango, ripe, banganapalli | 0.87 |
| Dates, processed | 0.84 |
| Plum | 0.84 |
| Apple, green | 0.81 |
| Mango, ripe, neelam | 0.79 |
| Banana, ripe, montham | 0.78 |
| Cherries, red | 0.78 |
| Mango, ripe, totapari | 0.78 |
| Lime, sweet, pulp | 0.74 |
| Mango, ripe, himsagar | 0.73 |
| Banana, ripe, red | 0.72 |
| Banana, ripe, robusta | 0.71 |
| Musk melon, yellow flesh | 0.7 |

| | |
|---|---|
| Jambu fruit, ripe | 0.67 |
| Musk melon, orange flesh | 0.67 |
| Grapes, seedless, oval, black | 0.66 |
| Mango, ripe, gulabkhas | 0.64 |
| Mangosteen | 0.64 |
| Star fruit | 0.64 |
| Apple, small | 0.62 |
| Apricot, dried | 0.6 |
| Pineapple | 0.59 |
| Pomegranate, maroon seeds | 0.57 |
| Orange, pulp | 0.56 |
| Apple, small, Kashmir | 0.54 |
| Palm fruit, tender | 0.53 |
| Litchi | 0.53 |
| Grapes, seeded, round, black | 0.52 |
| Grapes, seeded, round, green | 0.44 |
| Grapes, seedless, round, green | 0.44 |
| Grapes, seeded, round, red | 0.43 |
| Water melon, pale green | 0.38 |
| Water melon, dark green (sugar baby) | 0.34 |
| Grapes, seedless, round, black | 0.32 |
| Pummelo | 0.31 |
| Rambutan | 0.3 |
| Apricot, processed | 0.16 |
| **ROOTS AND TUBERS** | |
| Lotus root | 1.84 |
| Sweet potato, brown skin | 1.43 |
| Sweet potato, pink skin | 1.41 |
| Carrot, red | 1.4 |
| Carrot, orange | 1.37 |
| Yam, wild | 1.29 |
| Yam, elephant | 0.92 |
| Water chestnut | 0.87 |
| Tapioca | 0.76 |
| Yam, ordinary | 0.76 |
| Radish, round, white skin | 0.74 |
| Radish, round, red skin | 0.73 |
| Beet root | 0.71 |
| Colocasia | 0.68 |
| Radish, elongate, white skin | 0.67 |
| Potato, brown skin, big | 0.58 |
| Potato, red skin | 0.57 |
| Potato, brown skin (small) | 0.54 |

--- **Author** ---
Dr. Prajakta J. Nande

# Clinical and Therapeutic Nutrition Practical Manual 1
For M.Sc. Food Science and Nutrition (Semester-III)

| | | | |
|---|---|---|---|
| Radish, elongate, red skin | 0.49 | **NUTS AND OIL SEEDS** | |
| **CONDIMENTS AND SPICES - FRESH** | | Linseeds | 4.33 |
| Curry leaves | 3.2 | Gingelly seeds, brown | 3.63 |
| Garlic, small clove | 2.86 | Gingelly seeds, black | 3.56 |
| Garlic, big clove | 2.66 | Gingelly seeds, white | 3.51 |
| Garlic, single clove, Kashmir | 1.81 | Mustard seeds | 3.47 |
| Chillies, green | 1.55 | Safflower seeds | 3.25 |
| Coriander leaves | 1.42 | Almond | 2.52 |
| Mint leaves | 1.4 | Pistachio nut | 2.41 |
| Ginger, fresh | 1.08 | Sunflower seeds | 2.29 |
| Mango ginger | 0.95 | Ground nut | 1.79 |
| Onion, big | 0.53 | Cashew nut | 1.63 |
| Onion, small | 0.46 | Garden cress, seeds | 1.59 |
| **CONDIMENT AND SPICES - DRY** | | Pine seeds | 1.57 |
| Fenugreek seeds | 19.92 | Coconut, kernel, dry | 1.33 |
| Poppy seeds | 11.06 | Arecanut, dried, brown | 1.3 |
| Coriander seeds | 9.54 | Arecanut, dried red color | 1.3 |
| Cloves | 6.46 | Arecanut, fresh | 1.03 |
| Cumin seeds | 4.62 | Coconut, kernel, fresh | 0.99 |
| Chillies, red | 4.6 | Walnut | 0.65 |
| Pippali | 4.57 | Niger seeds, black | 0.43 |
| Mace | 3.54 | Niger seeds, grey | 0.41 |
| Omum | 3.38 | **SUGAR** | |
| Cardamom, black | 2.74 | Sugarcane juice | 0.16 |
| Cardamom, green | 2.64 | **MUSHROOMS** | |
| Turmeric powder | 2.59 | Shiitake mushroom, fresh | 0.99 |
| Pepper, black | 2.54 | Button mushroom, fresh | 0.35 |
| Nutmeg | 1.46 | Chicken mushroom, fresh | 0.18 |
| Asafoetida | 1.23 | | |

*(Source: T. Longvah, R. Ananthan, K. Bhaskaracharya, K. Venkaiah. Indian Food Composition Tables, National Institute of Nutrition (Indian Council of Medical Research), 3-30, 2017)*

# INSOLUBLE DIETARY FIBER (IDF)

| FOOD STUFFS | IDF (g/100 g) | | |
|---|---|---|---|
| **CEREALS AND MILLETS** | | Bajra | 9.14 |
| Maize, dry | 11.29 | Wheat, semolina | 8.9 |
| Quinoa | 10.21 | Jowar | 8.49 |
| Barley | 9.98 | Wheat, vermicelli, roasted | 7.79 |
| Wheat flour | 9.73 | Wheat, vermicelli | 7.53 |
| wheat, whole | 9.63 | Wheat, bulgur | 6.56 |
| Ragi | 9.51 | Amaranth seeds, pale brown | 5.8 |
| | | Amaranth seeds, black | 5.76 |
| | | Samai | 5.45 |

--- **Author** ---
Dr. Prajakta J. Nande

| | | | | |
|---|---|---|---|---|
| Varagu | 4.29 | | Gogu leaves, green | 3.24 |
| Rice raw, brown | 3.6 | | Amaranth leaves, red and green mix | 3.23 |
| Maize, tender local | 3.29 | | Amaranth leaves, green | 3.21 |
| Rice, parboiled, milled | 2.98 | | Fenugreek leaves | 3.2 |
| Wheat flour, refined | 2.94 | | Mustard leaves | 3.04 |
| Maize, tender sweet | 2.71 | | Parsley | 2.79 |
| Rice flakes | 2.65 | | Gogu leaves, red | 2.66 |
| Rice raw, milled | 1.99 | | Cauliflower leaves | 2.37 |
| Rice puffed | 1.76 | | Bathua leaves | 2.32 |
| **GRAINS AND LEGUMES** | | | Beet green | 2.2 |
| Bengal gram,whole | 22.7 | | Cabbage, collard green | 2.04 |
| red gram whole | 19.69 | | Cabbage, green | 1.91 |
| Field bean, black | 17.99 | | Knol-khol leaves | 1.81 |
| Field bean, white | 17.45 | | Garden cress | 1.77 |
| Field bean, brown | 17.32 | | Basella leaves | 1.64 |
| Soyabean, white | 17.04 | | Cabbage, violet | 1.58 |
| Soyabean, brown | 16.56 | | Pumpkin leaves, tender | 1.56 |
| Black gram, whole | 15.47 | | Cabbage, Chinese | 1.55 |
| Rajmah, black | 15.16 | | Spinach | 1.52 |
| Green gram, whole | 14.59 | | Pak choi leaves | 1.44 |
| Peas, dry | 14.55 | | Betel leaves, green | 1.32 |
| Moth bean | 14.5 | | Lettuce | 1.32 |
| Rajmah, brown | 14.33 | | Radish leaves | 1.18 |
| Lentil whole, brown | 14.16 | | Betel leaves, small | 1.17 |
| Lentil whole, yellowish | 14.15 | | Rumex leaves | 0.93 |
| Rajmah, red | 13.86 | | **OTHER VEGETABLES** | |
| Rice bean | 10.04 | | Jackfruit seeds, mature | 7.83 |
| Cowpea, white | 8.91 | | Jackfruit, raw | 7.15 |
| Cowpea, brown | 8.75 | | Broad beans | 6.61 |
| Bengal gram dal | 8.67 | | Drumstick | 5.6 |
| Lentil dal | 8.6 | | Field beans, tender, lean | 5.37 |
| Green gram dal | 7.75 | | Peas, fresh | 5.04 |
| Black gram dal | 7.58 | | Field beans, tender, broad | 4.84 |
| Red gram dal | 6.67 | | Plantain flower | 4.72 |
| Horse gram, whole | 6.22 | | Corn, baby | 4.47 |
| **GREEN LEAFY VEGETABLES** | | | French beans, country | 3.88 |
| Tamarind leaves, tender | 9.32 | | Beans scarlet, tender | 3.76 |
| Drumstick leaves | 6.12 | | Onion stalk | 3.76 |
| Agathi, leaves | 6 | | Red gram, tender, fresh | 3.66 |
| Ponnoganni | 5.63 | | Cluster beans | 3.55 |
| Colocasia leaves, green | 4.32 | | French beans, hybrid | 3.53 |
| Amaranth spinousus leaves, green | 3.89 | | Bitter gourd, jagged, teeth ridges, elongate | 3.1 |
| Amaranth spinousus leaves, red and green mix | 3.82 | | Bitter gourd, jagged, smooth ridges, elongate | 3.05 |
| Amaranth leaves, red | 3.72 | | | |
| Brussels sprouts | 3.32 | | | |

# Clinical and Therapeutic Nutrition Practical Manual 1
For M.Sc. Food Science and Nutrition (Semester-III)

| | | | |
|---|---|---|---|
| Bitter gourd, jagged, teeth ridges, short | 2.96 | Guava, white flesh | 7.14 |
| Brinjal-all varieties | 2.84 | Gooseberry | 6.2 |
| Ladies finger | 2.8 | Guava, pink flesh | 6.12 |
| Plantain green | 2.79 | Karonda fruit | 5.87 |
| Cauliflower | 2.66 | Dates,processed | 5.68 |
| Ash gourd | 2.52 | Avocado fruit | 5.26 |
| Knol-khol | 2.31 | Pear | 4.02 |
| Kovai, big | 2.19 | Soursop | 3.79 |
| Kovai, small | 2.14 | Wood apple | 3.77 |
| Parwar | 1.82 | Tamarind pulp | 3.73 |
| Colocasia, stem, black | 1.81 | Black berry | 3.44 |
| Cucumber, orange, round | 1.78 | Phalsa | 3.44 |
| Bottle gourd, elongate, dark green | 1.74 | Bael fruit | 3.31 |
| | | Manila tamarind | 3.3 |
| Bottle gourd, round, pale green | 1.72 | Custard apple | 3.17 |
| Snake gourd long, pale green | 1.69 | Raisins, dried, golden | 3.04 |
| Snake gourd long, dark green | 1.69 | Pineapple | 2.88 |
| Mango green, raw | 1.68 | Apricot, dried | 2.72 |
| Tinda, tender | 1.68 | Zizyphus | 2.71 |
| Bottle gourd, elongate, pale green | 1.65 | Fig | 2.59 |
| Snake gourd, short | 1.61 | Raisins, dried, black | 2.55 |
| Cucumber, green, short | 1.6 | Currants black | 2.43 |
| Capsicum, red | 1.58 | Jambu fruit, ripe | 2.4 |
| Celery stalk | 1.57 | Pomegranate maroon seeds | 2.26 |
| Cucumber, green, elongate | 1.52 | Jackfruit, ripe | 2.21 |
| Pumpkin, orange, round | 1.44 | Star fruit | 2.17 |
| Tomato, ripe, local | 1.44 | Palm fruit, tender | 1.87 |
| Zucchini, green | 1.42 | Papaya, ripe | 1.75 |
| Capsicum, yellow | 1.39 | Apple green | 1.72 |
| Zucchini, yellow | 1.37 | Apple, small, Kashmir | 1.53 |
| Capsicum, green | 1.33 | Strawberry | 1.51 |
| Plantain, stem | 1.33 | Apple, small | 1.44 |
| Papaya, raw | 1.32 | Apple, big | 1.43 |
| Ridge gourd, smooth skin | 1.31 | Banana ripe, montham | 1.43 |
| Pumpkin, green, cylindrical | 1.28 | Cherries red | 1.35 |
| Tomato, ripe, hybrid | 1.27 | Lime, sweet, pulp | 1.33 |
| Colocasia, stem, green | 1.26 | Banana, ripe, poovam | 1.29 |
| Ridge gourd | 1.2 | Banana, ripe, red | 1.26 |
| Cho-cho-marrow | 1.19 | Banana, ripe, robusta | 1.23 |
| Bamboo shoot, tender | 1.06 | Mangosteen | 1.23 |
| Tomato, green | 1.05 | Plum | 1.23 |
| **FRUITS** | | Peach | 1.22 |
| Sapota | 8.46 | Mango, ripe, kesar | 1.09 |
| Dates, dry, dark brown | 7.57 | Mango, ripe, gulabkhas | 1.03 |
| Dates, dry, pale brown | 7.53 | Mango, ripe, banganapalli | 1.01 |
| | | Mango, ripe, peheri | 0.99 |

# Clinical and Therapeutic Nutrition Practical Manual 1
## For M.Sc. Food Science and Nutrition (Semester-III)

| | | | |
|---|---|---|---|
| Grapes, seedless, oval, black | 0.98 | Cumin seeds | 25.73 |
| Mango, ripe, neelam | 0.97 | Cardamom, black | 20.73 |
| Mango, ripe, totapari | 0.95 | Cardamom, green | 20.46 |
| Grapes, seeded, round, red | 0.85 | Turmeric powder | 18.79 |
| Grapes, seedless, round, green | 0.85 | Omum | 17.2 |
| Muskmelon, orange flesh | 0.84 | Mace | 16.78 |
| Grapes, seedless, round, black | 0.83 | Poppy seeds | 15.62 |
| Grapes, seeded, round, black | 0.82 | Curry leaves | 13.81 |
| Mango, ripe, himsagar | 0.82 | Nutmeg | 10.54 |
| Grapes, seeded, round, green | 0.81 | Mint leaves | 4.49 |
| Litchi | 0.81 | Ginger, fresh | 4.28 |
| Muskmelon, yellow flesh | 0.79 | Asafoetida | 3.9 |
| Orange, pulp | 0.73 | Mango ginger | 3.79 |
| Rambutan | 0.71 | Chillies green-all varieties | 3.41 |
| Pummelo | 0.49 | Coriander leaves | 3.24 |
| Apricot, processed | 0.43 | Garlic, small clove | 2.61 |
| Watermelon, pale green | 0.4 | Garlic, big clove | 2.56 |
| Watermelon, dark green (sugar baby) | 0.35 | Garlic, single clove | 2.2 |
| | | Onion, big | 1.92 |
| **ROOTS AND TUBERS** | | Onion, small | 0.7 |
| Tapioca | 3.85 | **NUTS AND OIL SEEDS** | |
| Yam,ordinary | 3.32 | Linseeds | 21.83 |
| Yam, wild | 3.29 | Coconut,kernel, dry | 14.55 |
| Yam, elephant | 3.25 | Gingelly seeds, brown | 13.58 |
| Carrot, red | 3.09 | Gingelly seeds, black | 13.51 |
| Lotus root | 2.86 | Gingelly seeds, white | 13.49 |
| Carrot, orange | 2.81 | Mustard seeds | 10.63 |
| Beetroot | 2.6 | Almond | 10.55 |
| Sweet potato, brown skin | 2.57 | Niger seeds, grey | 10.54 |
| Colocasia | 2.54 | Niger seeds, black | 10.5 |
| Sweet potato, pink skin | 2.53 | Safflower seeds | 10.24 |
| Waterchestnut | 2.15 | Arecanut, dried, brown | 10.14 |
| Radish, elongate, white skin | 1.98 | Arecanut, dried, red | 10.09 |
| Radish, elongate, red skin | 1.96 | Coconut, kernel, fresh | 9.43 |
| Radish, round, white skin | 1.63 | Groundnut | 8.58 |
| Radish, round, red skin | 1.56 | Sunflower seeds | 8.51 |
| Potato, brown skin, small | 1.15 | Pistachio nuts | 8.23 |
| Potato, brown skin, big | 1.13 | Arecanut, fresh | 6.59 |
| Potato, red skin | 1.11 | Garden cress seeds | 6.33 |
| **CONDIMENTS AND SPICES - DRY** | | Walnut | 4.74 |
| Coriander seeds | 35.27 | Cashew nut | 2.23 |
| Pepper black | 30.61 | Pineseeds | 2.23 |
| Pippali | 29.57 | **SUGARS** | |
| Cloves | 28.07 | Sugarcane juice | 0.4 |
| Fenugreek seeds | 27.63 | **MUSHROOMS** | |
| Chillies, red | 26.55 | Button mushroom, fresh | 2.76 |

**Clinical and Therapeutic Nutrition Practical Manual 1**
For M.Sc. Food Science and Nutrition (Semester-III)

| | |
|---|---|
| Shitake mushroom | 2.03 |
| Chicken mushroom, fresh | 1.82 |

*(Source: T. Longvah, R. Ananthan, K. Bhaskaracharya, K. Venkaiah. Indian Food Composition Tables, National Institute of Nutrition (Indian Council of Medical Research), 3-30, 2017)*

# TOTAL DIETARY FIBER (TDF)

| FOOD STUFFS | TDF (g/100 g) | | FOOD STUFFS | TDF (g/100 g) |
|---|---|---|---|---|
| **CEREALS AND MILLETS** | | | Peas, dry | 17.01 |
| Barley | 15.64 | | Rajmah, brown | 16.95 |
| Quinoa | 14.66 | | Lentil whole, brown | 16.82 |
| Maize, dry | 12.24 | | Lentil whole, yellowish | 16.66 |
| Bajra | 11.49 | | Rajmah, red | 16.57 |
| Wheat flour | 11.36 | | Bengal gram, dal | 15.15 |
| Wheat, whole | 11.23 | | Moth bean | 15.12 |
| Ragi | 11.18 | | Rice bean | 13.37 |
| Jowar | 10.22 | | Black gram, dal | 11.93 |
| Wheat, semolina | 9.72 | | Cowpea, white | 11.7 |
| Wheat, vermicelli, roasted | 9.55 | | Cowpea, brown | 11.54 |
| Wheat, vermicelli | 9.28 | | Lentil dal | 10.43 |
| Wheat, bulgur | 8.81 | | Green gram, dal | 9.37 |
| Samai | 7.72 | | Red gram, dal | 9.06 |
| Amaranth seed, pale brown | 7.47 | | Horse gram, whole | 7.88 |
| Amaranth seed, black | 7.02 | | **GREEN LEAFY VEGETABLES** | |
| Varagu | 6.39 | | Tamarind leaves, tender | 10.7 |
| Rice, raw, brown | 4.43 | | Agathi leaves | 8.6 |
| Rice, parboiled, milled | 3.74 | | Drumstick leaves | 8.21 |
| Maize, tender, local | 3.67 | | Ponnoganni | 6.74 |
| Rice flakes | 3.46 | | Colocasia leaves, green | 5.6 |
| Maize, tender, sweet | 3.3 | | Amaranth spinosus, leaves, red and green mix | 5.57 |
| Rice, raw, milled | 2.81 | | Amaranth spinosus, leaves green | 5.1 |
| Wheat flour, refined | 2.76 | | Amaranth leaves, red | 4.91 |
| Rice puffed | 2.56 | | Fenugreek leaves | 4.9 |
| **GRAIN LEGUMES** | | | Amaranth leaves, red and green mix | 4.6 |
| Bengal gram, whole | 25.22 | | Gogu leaves, green | 4.59 |
| Field bean, black | 23.4 | | Amaranth leaves, green | 4.41 |
| Field bean, white | 22.99 | | Brussels sprouts | 4.29 |
| Red gram, whole | 22.84 | | Bathua leaves | 4.01 |
| Soya bean, white | 22.63 | | Mustard leaves | 3.92 |
| Field bean, brown | 22.4 | | Gogu leaves, red | 3.89 |
| Soyabean, brown | 21.55 | | Parsley | 3.87 |
| Black gram, whole | 20.41 | | Beet greens | 3.64 |
| Rajmah, black | 17.74 | | Cauliflower leaves | 3.43 |
| Green gram, whole | 17.04 | | Cabbage, collard greens | 2.98 |

**--- Author ---**
Dr. Prajakta J. Nande

# Clinical and Therapeutic Nutrition Practical Manual 1
For M.Sc. Food Science and Nutrition (Semester-III)

| | | | |
|---|---|---|---|
| Cabbage, green | 2.76 | Parwar | 2.61 |
| Knol-khol leaves | 2.76 | Pumpkin orange, round, | 2.56 |
| Garden cress | 2.62 | Pumpkin, green, cylindrical | 2.53 |
| Spinach | 2.38 | Cucumber, orange, round | 2.46 |
| Pumpkin leaves, tender | 2.25 | Colocasia, stem, green | 2.33 |
| Basella leaves | 2.21 | Zucchini, green | 2.3 |
| Cabbage, violet | 2.21 | Snake gourd, short | 2.29 |
| Betel leaves, big | 2.12 | Papaya, raw | 2.28 |
| Cabbage, Chinese | 2.01 | Snake gourd, long, dark green | 2.27 |
| Betel leaves, small | 1.97 | Snake gourd, long, pale green | 2.27 |
| Pak choi leaves | 1.91 | Capsicum, red | 2.19 |
| Radish leaves | 1.82 | Capsicum, yellow | 2.19 |
| Lettuce | 1.79 | Cucumber, green, elongate | 2.14 |
| Rumex leaves | 1.27 | Cucumber, green,short | 2.13 |
| **OTHER VEGETABLES** | | Bottle gourd, elongate, pale green | 2.12 |
| Broad beans | 8.63 | Plantain stem | 2.12 |
| Jack fruit, seed, mature | 8.63 | Bottle gourd, elongate, dark green | 2.11 |
| Jack fruit, raw | 7.69 | Bottle gourd, round pale green | 2.1 |
| Drumstick | 6.83 | Celery stalk | 2.09 |
| Peas, fresh | 6.32 | Capsicum, green | 2.06 |
| Field beans, tender, lean | 6.19 | Tinda, tender | 2 |
| Corn, baby | 6.09 | Ridge gourd, smooth skin | 1.85 |
| Red gram, tender, fresh | 5.9 | Zucchini, yellow | 1.84 |
| Field beans, tender, broad | 5.64 | Ridge gourd | 1.81 |
| Plantain, flower | 5.25 | Tomato, ripe, local | 1.77 |
| Onion stalk | 5.21 | Tomato, green | 1.62 |
| Cluster beans | 4.83 | Tomato, ripe, hybrid | 1.58 |
| Bean scarlet, tender | 4.5 | Bamboo shoot, tender | 1.55 |
| French beans, country | 4.38 | Cho-cho-marrow | 1.55 |
| French beans, hybrid | 4.18 | **FRUITS** | |
| Ladies finger | 4.08 | Sapota | 9.6 |
| Brinjal-all varieties | 3.98 | Dates, dry dark brown | 9.1 |
| Bitter gourd, jagged, smooth ridges, elongate | 3.78 | Dates, dry pale, brown | 8.95 |
| | | Guava, white flesh | 8.59 |
| Bitter gourd, jagged, teeth ridges, elongate | 3.72 | Gooseberry | 7.75 |
| | | Guava, pink flesh | 7.39 |
| Cauliflower | 3.71 | Karonda fruit | 7.25 |
| Plantain green | 3.6 | Avocado fruit | 6.69 |
| Bitter gourd, jagged, teeth ridges, short | 3.49 | Dates, processed | 6.52 |
| | | Bael fruit | 6.31 |
| Ash ground | 3.37 | Tamarind, pulp | 5.31 |
| Kovai, small | 3.25 | Wood apple | 5.21 |
| Colocasia, stem, black | 3.01 | Custard apple | 5.1 |
| Mango, green, raw | 3.01 | Soursop | 4.95 |
| Kovai, big | 3 | Fig | 4.64 |
| Knol-khol | 2.75 | Raisins, dried, golden | 4.56 |

--- **Author** ---
Dr. Prajakta J. Nande

# Clinical and Therapeutic Nutrition Practical Manual 1
## For M.Sc. Food Science and Nutrition (Semester-III)

| | | | |
|---|---|---|---|
| Phalsa | 4.54 | Rambutan | 1.02 |
| Pear | 4.48 | Pummelo | 0.8 |
| Manila tamarind | 4.4 | Water melon, pale green | 0.7 |
| Black berry | 4.35 | Water melon, dark green (sugar baby) | 0.7 |
| Currants, black | 4.07 | Apricot, processed | 0.59 |
| Raisins, dried, black | 3.92 | **ROOTS AND TUBERS** | |
| Zizyphus | 3.73 | Lotus root | 4.7 |
| Jack fruit, ripe | 3.62 | Tapioca | 4.61 |
| Pineapple | 3.46 | Yam, wild | 4.57 |
| Apricot, dried | 3.32 | Carrot, red | 4.49 |
| Jambu fruit, ripe | 3.07 | Carrot, orange | 4.18 |
| Papaya, ripe | 2.83 | Yam elephant | 4.17 |
| Pomegranate, maroon seeds | 2.83 | Yam, ordinary | 4.08 |
| Star fruit | 2.81 | Sweet potato, brown skin | 3.99 |
| Apple, big | 2.59 | Sweet potato, pink skin | 3.94 |
| Apple, green | 2.54 | Beet root | 3.31 |
| Strawberry | 2.5 | Colocasia | 3.22 |
| Palm fruit, tender | 2.4 | Water chestnut | 3.02 |
| Banana ripe, poovam | 2.33 | Radish, elongate, white skin | 2.65 |
| Banana ripe, montham | 2.21 | Radish, elongate, red skin | 2.46 |
| Peach | 2.13 | Radish, round, white skin | 2.37 |
| Cherries, red | 2.12 | Radish, round, red skin | 2.29 |
| Apple, small, Kashmir | 2.07 | Potato, brown skin, big | 1.71 |
| Lime, sweet, pulp | 2.07 | Potato, brown skin, small | 1.69 |
| Plum | 2.07 | Potato, red skin | 1.68 |
| Apple, small | 2.06 | **CONDIMENTS AND SPICES - FRESH** | |
| Mango, ripe, kesar | 2.02 | Curry leaves | 16.83 |
| Banana, ripe, red | 1.98 | Mint leaves | 5.89 |
| Mango, ripe, paheri | 1.97 | Garlic, small clove | 5.47 |
| Banana, ripe, robusta | 1.94 | Ginger fresh | 5.36 |
| Mango, ripe, banganpalli | 1.88 | Garlic, big clove | 5.22 |
| Mangosteen | 1.87 | Chillies green-all varieties | 4.77 |
| Mango, ripe, neelam | 1.77 | Mango ginger | 4.74 |
| Mango, ripe, totapari | 1.73 | Coriander leaves | 4.66 |
| Mango, ripe, gulabkhas | 1.67 | Garlic, single clove, Kashmir | 4.01 |
| Grapes, seedless, oval, black | 1.64 | Onion, big | 2.45 |
| Mango, ripe, himsagar | 1.55 | Onion, small | 1.16 |
| Musk melon, orange flesh | 1.51 | **CONDIMENTS AND SPICES - DRY** | |
| Musk melon, yellow flesh | 1.49 | Fenugreek seeds | 47.55 |
| Grapes, seeded, round , black | 1.35 | Coriander seeds | 44.81 |
| Litchi | 1.34 | Cloves | 34.52 |
| Orange, pulp | 1.29 | Pippali | 34.14 |
| Grapes, seeded, round, red | 1.28 | Pepper, black | 33.16 |
| Grapes, seedless, round green | 1.28 | Chillies, red | 31.15 |
| Grapes, seeded, round, green | 1.25 | Cumin seeds | 30.35 |
| Grapes, seedless, round, black | 1.15 | | |

--- **Author** ---
Dr. Prajakta J. Nande

## Clinical and Therapeutic Nutrition Practical Manual 1
### For M.Sc. Food Science and Nutrition (Semester-III)

| | | | |
|---|---|---|---|
| Poppy seeds | 26.68 | Arecanut, dried, red colour | 11.11 |
| Cardamom, black | 23.46 | Niger seeds, gray | 10.96 |
| Cardamom, green | 23.1 | Niger seeds, black | 10.93 |
| Turmeric powder | 21.38 | Sunflower seeds | 10.8 |
| Omum | 20.58 | Pistachio nut | 10.64 |
| Mace | 20.31 | Coconut, kernel, fresh | 10.42 |
| Nutmeg | 11.99 | Ground nut | 10.38 |
| Asafoetida | 5.13 | Garden cress, seeds | 8.27 |
| **NUTS AND OIL SEEDS** | | Arecanut fresh | 7.63 |
| Linseeds | 26.17 | Walnut | 5.39 |
| Gingelly seeds, brown | 17.21 | Cashew nut | 3.86 |
| Gingelly seeds,black | 17.16 | Pine seeds | 3.79 |
| Gingelly seeds, white | 16.99 | **SUGARS** | |
| Coconut, kernel, dry | 15.88 | Sugarcane, juice | 0.56 |
| Mustard seeds | 14.1 | **MUSHROOMS** | |
| Safflower seeds | 13.49 | Button mushroom, fresh | 3.11 |
| Almond | 13.06 | Shitake mushroom, fresh | 3.02 |
| Areca nut, dried, brown | 11.44 | Chicken mushroom, fresh | 1.99 |

*(Source: T. Longvah, R. Ananthan, K. Bhaskaracharya, K. Venkaiah. Indian Food Composition Tables, National Institute of Nutrition (Indian Council of Medical Research), 3-30, 2017)*

## ANNEXURE - 6

## BRANCHED CHAIN AMINO ACID CONTENT OF FOODS

### ISOLEUCINE

| FOOD STUFFS | Isoleu--cine (g/100 g of Protein) | | |
|---|---|---|---|
| | | Barley | 3.63 |
| | | Maize, dry | 3.67 |
| | | Rice puffed | 3.68 |
| | | Ragi | 3.7 |
| | | Quinoa | 3.75 |
| **CEREALS AND MILLETS** | | Wheat flour | 3.78 |
| Wheat, vermicelli, roasted | 1.46 | Wheat, whole | 3.83 |
| Wheat, vermicelli | 1.56 | Rice, raw, brown | 4.08 |
| Amaranth seed, black | 2.82 | Samai | 4.14 |
| Amaranth seed, pale brown | 2.85 | Rice, parboiled, milled | 4.14 |
| Wheat flour, refined | 3.19 | Rice, raw, milled | 4.29 |
| Bajra | 3.45 | Varagu | 4.55 |
| Jowar | 3.45 | **GRAIN LEGUMES** | |
| Maize, tender, sweet | 3.45 | Red gram, whole | 3.38 |
| Wheat, semolina | 3.45 | Black gram, whole | 3.42 |
| Wheat, bulgur | 3.48 | Red gram, dal | 3.42 |
| Maize, tender, local | 3.55 | Horse gram, whole | 3.72 |
| Rice flakes | 3.62 | Lentil dal | 3.74 |

--- **Author** ---
Dr. Prajakta J. Nande

# Clinical and Therapeutic Nutrition Practical Manual 1
For M.Sc. Food Science and Nutrition (Semester-III)

| | | | |
|---|---|---|---|
| Black gram, dal | 3.75 | Tamarind leaves, tender | 4.2 |
| Rice bean | 3.80 | Amaranth leaves, red | 4.31 |
| Peas, dry | 3.87 | Spinach | 4.31 |
| Rajmah, black | 3.91 | Amaranth leaves, red and green | 4.33 |
| Green gram, dal | 4.07 | Gogu leaves, red | 4.34 |
| Cowpea, brown | 4.10 | Amaranth leaves, green | 4.39 |
| Lentil whole, yellowish | 4.12 | Fenugreek leaves | 4.47 |
| Green gram, whole | 4.17 | Garden cress | 4.51 |
| Lentil whole, brown | 4.17 | Parsley | 4.78 |
| Moth bean | 4.17 | Bathua leaves | 4.83 |
| Rajmah, red | 4.23 | Ponnoganni | 4.89 |
| Bengal gram, dal | 4.25 | Pumpkin leaves, tender | 5.27 |
| Rajmah, brown | 4.27 | Cabbage, Chinese | 5.72 |
| Bengal gram, whole | 4.34 | **OTHER VEGETABLES** | |
| Cowpea, white | 4.40 | Papaya, raw | 1.57 |
| Field bean, white | 4.41 | Bamboo shoot, tender | 2.19 |
| Soya bean, brown | 4.57 | Tomato, ripe, hybrid | 2.29 |
| Field bean, black | 4.57 | Plantain green | 2.59 |
| Soya bean, white | 4.59 | Cluster beans | 2.68 |
| Field bean, brown | 4.59 | Tomato green | 2.69 |
| **GREEN LEAFY VEGETABLES** | | Tomato, ripe, local | 2.69 |
| Betel leaves, big | 2.05 | Celery stalk | 2.93 |
| Betel leaves, small | 2.59 | Drumstick | 3.08 |
| Beet greens | 2.62 | Ladies finger | 3.26 |
| Agathi leaves | 2.8 | Red gram, tender, fresh | 3.31 |
| Amaranth spinosus, leaves, red and green | 3.03 | Peas, fresh | 3.33 |
| | | Knol-khol | 3.4 |
| Drumstick leaves | 3.1 | Capsicum red | 3.61 |
| Mustard leaves | 3.22 | Plantain, flower | 3.63 |
| Basella leaves | 3.3 | Brinjal-all varieties | 3.63 |
| Cauliflower leaves | 3.37 | Cucumber, green, short | 3.77 |
| Lettuce | 3.49 | French beans, country | 3.79 |
| Colocasia leaves, green | 3.51 | Capsicum, green | 3.79 |
| Cabbage, green | 3.56 | Cauliflower | 3.84 |
| Cabbage, violet | 3.56 | Kovai, small | 3.88 |
| Rumex leaves | 3.57 | Capsicum, yellow | 3.92 |
| Brussels sprouts | 3.58 | Bean scarlet, tender | 3.96 |
| Radish leaves | 3.59 | Field beans, tender, broad | 4.05 |
| Gogu leaves, green | 3.64 | Snake gourd, short | 4.06 |
| Pak choi leaves | 3.78 | Kovai, big | 4.1 |
| Cabbage, collard greens | 3.81 | Colocasia, stem, black | 4.1 |
| Amaranth spinosus, leaves green | 4.05 | Snake gourd, long, pale green | 4.11 |

**--- Author ---**
Dr. Prajakta J. Nande

# Clinical and Therapeutic Nutrition Practical Manual 1
For M.Sc. Food Science and Nutrition (Semester-III)

| | | | | |
|---|---|---|---|---|
| Tinda, tender | 4.11 | Grapes, seeded, round , black | 1.98 |
| Cucumber, green, elongate | 4.14 | Lime, sweet, pulp | 2.12 |
| Zucchini, green | 4.24 | Grapes, seeded, round, green | 2.2 |
| Zucchini, yellow | 4.25 | Plum | 2.2 |
| Colocasia, stem, green | 4.26 | Apricot, processed | 2.22 |
| Broad beans | 4.28 | Apricot, dried | 2.25 |
| Field beans, tender, lean | 4.3 | Custard apple | 2.26 |
| Ash gourd | 4.31 | Papaya, ripe | 2.27 |
| French beans, hybrid | 4.35 | Dates, process | 2.29 |
| Corn, baby | 4.35 | Peach | 2.54 |
| Parwar | 4.41 | Grapes, seedless, oval, black | 2.58 |
| Mango, green, raw | 4.44 | Pineapple | 2.61 |
| Pumpkin, green, cylindrical | 4.54 | Musk melon, yellow flesh | 2.72 |
| Ridge gourd | 4.6 | Lemon, juice | 2.72 |
| Bitter gourd, jagged, teeth ridges, short | 4.71 | Grapes, seedless, round, black | 2.74 |
| | | Star fruit | 2.8 |
| Cho-cho-marrow | 4.72 | Pummelo | 2.81 |
| Bitter gourd, jagged, teeth ridges elongate | 4.74 | Karonda fruit | 2.86 |
| | | Dates, dry | 3.05 |
| Cucumber, orange, round | 4.74 | Tamarind, pulp | 3.28 |
| Bitter gourd, jagged, smooth ridges, elongate | 4.85 | Bael fruit | 3.29 |
| | | Water melon, dark green (sugar baby) | 3.34 |
| Snake gourd, long, dark green | 4.85 | |
| Onion stalk | 4.88 | Avocado fruit | 3.45 |
| Jack fruit, raw | 4.9 | Cherries, red | 3.46 |
| Plantain stem | 4.92 | Water melon, pale | 3.49 |
| Ridge gourd, smooth skin | 4.92 | Grapes, seeded, round, red | 3.49 |
| Bottle gourd, elongate, pale green | 4.98 | Jack fruit, ripe | 3.49 |
| Pumpkin orange, round, | 5 | Sapota | 3.52 |
| Bottle gourd, elongate, dark green | 5.19 | Apple, big | 3.56 |
| Bottle gourd, round, pale green | 5.2 | Pear | 3.56 |
| Jack fruit, seed, mature | 5.5 | Strawberry | 3.61 |
| **FRUITS** | | Manila tamarind | 3.64 |
| Orange, pulp | 1.39 | Banana, ripe, robusta | 3.69 |
| Pomegranate, maroon seeds | 1.67 | Mango, ripe, banganapalli | 3.73 |
| Musk melon, orange flesh | 1.75 | Mango, ripe, gulabkhas | 3.79 |
| Raisins, dried, golden | 1.88 | Banana, ripe, poovam | 3.79 |
| Rambutan | 1.9 | Mango, ripe, himsagar | 3.8 |
| Dates, dry pale, brown | 1.92 | Apple, small | 3.86 |
| Gooseberry | 1.94 | Wood apple | 3.93 |
| Raisins, dried, black | 1.97 | Guava, pink, flesh | 3.94 |
| Grapes, seedless, round  green | 1.98 | Mango, ripe, kesar | 4.05 |

--- **Author** ---
Dr. Prajakta J. Nande

# Clinical and Therapeutic Nutrition Practical Manual 1
For M.Sc. Food Science and Nutrition (Semester-III)

| | |
|---|---|
| Guava, white, flesh | 4.08 |
| Zizyphus | 4.09 |
| Apple, small, Kashmir | 4.11 |
| Palm fruit, tender | 4.16 |
| Mango, ripe, totapari | 4.2 |
| Banana, ripe, red | 4.25 |
| Mango, ripe, neelam | 4.3 |
| Currants ,black | 4.35 |
| Mango, ripe, paheri | 4.36 |
| Soursop | 4.45 |
| Mangosteen | 4.54 |
| Litchi | 4.73 |
| Fig | 4.84 |
| Apple green | 4.85 |
| Black berry | 4.86 |
| Banana ripe, montham | 4.94 |
| Jambu fruit, ripe | 5.21 |

## ROOTS AND TUBERS

| | |
|---|---|
| Tapioca | 2.32 |
| Carrot, red | 3.04 |
| Colocasia | 3.06 |
| Radish, round, white skin | 3.16 |
| Potato, red skin | 3.19 |
| Water chestnut | 3.27 |
| Yam, wild | 3.27 |
| Radish, elongate, white skin | 3.33 |
| Potato, brown skin, big | 3.34 |
| Yam, elephant | 3.36 |
| Lotus root | 3.38 |
| Radish, elongate, red skin | 3.49 |
| Radish, round, red skin | 3.55 |
| Carrot, orange | 3.56 |
| Potato, brown skin, small | 3.77 |
| Yam, ordinary | 3.82 |
| Beet root | 3.9 |
| Sweet potato, pink skin | 4.42 |
| Sweet potato, brown skin | 4.56 |

## CONDIMENTS AND SPICES - FRESH

| | |
|---|---|
| Onion, big | 2.08 |
| Garlic, small clove | 2.24 |
| Garlic, big clove | 2.25 |
| Chillies, green-all varieties | 3.14 |
| Garlic, single clove, Kashmir | 3.44 |
| Curry leaves | 3.75 |
| Onion, small | 3.91 |
| Ginger | 3.98 |
| Mango ginger | 4.3 |
| Mint leaves | 4.34 |
| Coriander leaves | 4.37 |

## CONDIMENTS AND SPICES - DRY

| | |
|---|---|
| Omum | 1.7 |
| Cardamom, black | 1.8 |
| Cloves | 2.13 |
| Cardamom, green | 2.15 |
| Nutmeg | 2.23 |
| Mace | 2.35 |
| Pippali | 2.44 |
| Asafoetida | 2.49 |
| Poppy seeds | 3.64 |
| Chillies, red | 3.75 |
| Pepper, black | 3.85 |
| Cumin seeds | 4.43 |
| Coriander seeds | 4.52 |
| Turmeric powder | 4.54 |
| Fenugreek seeds | 4.57 |

## NUTS AND OIL SEEDS

| | |
|---|---|
| Arecanut, dried, red colour | 1.56 |
| Areca nut, dried, brown | 1.74 |
| Almond | 2.38 |
| Coconut, kernel, dry | 3.02 |
| Safflower seeds | 3.69 |
| Garden cress, seeds | 3.75 |
| Mustard seeds | 3.8 |
| Cashew nut | 3.86 |
| Pine seeds | 4 |
| Sunflower seeds | 4.21 |
| Coconut, kernel, fresh | 4.37 |
| Linseed | 4.47 |
| Niger seeds, black | 4.57 |
| Ground nut | 4.67 |
| Niger seeds, gray | 4.69 |
| Walnut | 4.74 |
| Gingelly seeds, brown | 5.01 |
| Pistachio nut | 5.22 |

--- Author ---
Dr. Prajakta J. Nande

# Clinical and Therapeutic Nutrition Practical Manual 1
For M.Sc. Food Science and Nutrition (Semester-III)

| | | | | |
|---|---|---|---|---|
| Gingelly seeds, black | 5.69 | | Goat, lungs | 2.54 |
| Gingelly seeds, white | 6.02 | | Goat, lungs | 2.58 |
| **SUGARS** | | | Goat, spleen | 2.7 |
| Jaggery, cane | 2.27 | | Sheep, liver | 2.83 |
| Sugarcane, | 3.81 | | Sheep, spleen | 2.89 |
| **MUSHROOMS** | | | Goat, brain | 2.98 |
| Button mushroom, fresh | 4.36 | | Goat, liver | 3.04 |
| Chicken mushroom, fresh | 4.42 | | Goat, heart | 3.08 |
| Shitake mushroom, fresh | 4.5 | | Sheep, heart | 3.18 |
| **MISCELLANEOUS FOODS** | | | Sheep, chops | 3.31 |
| Coconut water | 1.58 | | Goat, shoulder | 3.33 |
| **MILK AND MILK PRODUCTS** | | | Goat, kidney | 3.41 |
| Panner | 4.79 | | Goat, chops | 3.53 |
| Khoa | 4.93 | | Goat, legs | 3.63 |
| Milk, whole, buffalo | 5.3 | | Sheep, shoulder | 3.73 |
| Milk, whole, cow | 6.2 | | Sheep, kidney | 3.78 |
| **EGG AND EGG PRODUCTS** | | | Sheep, legs | 3.88 |
| Egg, duck, whole, raw | 1.83 | | **MARINE SHELLFISH** | |
| Egg, poultry, whole, raw | 2.15 | | Mud crab | 4.12 |
| Egg, poultry, yolk, raw | 2.19 | | Lobster, king size | 4.37 |
| Egg, poultry, white, raw | 2.25 | | Crab, sea | 4.48 |
| Egg, country hen, whole, raw | 2.25 | | Crab | 4.54 |
| **POULTRY** | | | Oyster | 4.56 |
| Country, hen, leg, with skin | 2.2 | | Tiger prawns, orange | 4.67 |
| Chicken, poultry, thigh, skinless | 2.54 | | Lobster, brown | 4.98 |
| Chicken, poultry, wing, skinless | 2.62 | | **FRESH WATER FISH AND SHELLFISH** | |
| Chicken, poultry, leg, skinless | 2.76 | | Tiger prawns | 2.96 |
| Country, hen, thigh, with skin | 2.87 | | Prawns, big | 2.99 |
| Poultry, chicken, liver | 3.2 | | Crab | 3.73 |
| Country, hen, wing, with skin | 3.5 | | Rohu | 4.09 |
| Chicken, poultry, breast, skinless | 3.57 | | Prawns, small | 4.11 |
| Country, hen, breast, with skin | 4.04 | | Cat fish | 4.46 |
| | | | Fresh water eel | 4.46 |
| **ANIMAL MEAT** | | | Gold fish | 4.47 |
| Sheep, brain | 2.47 | | | |

*(Source: T. Longvah, R. Ananthan, K. Bhaskaracharya, K. Venkaiah. Indian Food Composition Tables, National Institute of Nutrition (Indian Council of Medical Research), 259-312, 2017)*

# Clinical and Therapeutic Nutrition Practical Manual 1

For M.Sc. Food Science and Nutrition (Semester-III)

## LEUCINE

| FOOD STUFFS | Leucine (g/100 g of Protein) |
|---|---|
| **CEREALS AND MILLETS** | |
| Amaranth seed, black | 4.83 |
| Amaranth seed, pale brown | 4.94 |
| Wheat, vermicelli | 5.23 |
| Wheat, vermicelli, roasted | 5.63 |
| Quinoa | 6.08 |
| Wheat, flour | 6.13 |
| Wheat, flour, refined | 6.22 |
| Barley | 6.49 |
| Wheat, bulgur | 6.61 |
| Wheat, semolina | 6.71 |
| Wheat, whole | 6.81 |
| Rice puffed | 7.75 |
| Rice flakes | 8.05 |
| Rice, parboiled, milled | 8.08 |
| Samai | 8.08 |
| Rice, raw, milled | 8.09 |
| Rice, raw, brown | 8.4 |
| Bajra | 8.52 |
| Ragi | 8.86 |
| Maize, tender, local | 10.09 |
| Maize, tender, sweet | 10.61 |
| Varagu | 11.96 |
| Jowar | 12.03 |
| Maize, dry | 12.24 |
| **GRAIN LEGUMES** | |
| Red gram, dal | 6.73 |
| Horse gram, whole | 6.79 |
| Rajmah, black | 6.84 |
| Red gram, whole | 6.88 |
| Bengal gram, dal | 6.91 |
| Peas, dry | 7.02 |
| Lentil dal | 7.1 |
| Lentil whole, brown | 7.36 |
| Bengal gram, whole | 7.4 |
| Green gram, whole | 7.45 |

| | |
|---|---|
| Lentil whole, yellowish | 7.47 |
| Cowpea, brown | 7.49 |
| Black gram, whole | 7.58 |
| Rajmah, red | 7.78 |
| Moth bean | 7.85 |
| Rice bean | 7.86 |
| Green gram, dal | 7.9 |
| Black gram, dal | 7.93 |
| Rajmah, brown | 7.93 |
| Cowpea, white | 7.96 |
| Soya bean, white | 8.14 |
| Soya bean, brown | 8.27 |
| Field bean, white | 8.48 |
| Field bean, brown | 8.88 |
| Field bean, black | 8.91 |
| **GREEN LEAFY VEGETABLES** | |
| Brussels sprouts | 5.04 |
| Beet greens | 5.17 |
| Cabbage, green | 5.31 |
| Cabbage, violet | 5.31 |
| Cauliflower leaves | 5.36 |
| Cabbage, Chinese | 5.69 |
| Mustard leaves | 6.57 |
| Cabbage, collard leaves | 6.67 |
| Drumstick leaves | 6.7 |
| Rumex leaves | 6.82 |
| Radish leaves | 6.89 |
| Lettuce | 6.9 |
| Knol-khol, leaves | 7.2 |
| Colocasia leaves, green | 7.45 |
| Fenugreek leaves | 7.5 |
| Amaranth spinosus, leaves red and green | 7.57 |
| Agathi leaves | 7.58 |
| Gogu leaves, green | 7.6 |
| Amaranth spinosus, leaves green | 7.66 |
| Basella leaves | 7.68 |
| Parsley | 7.82 |
| Betel leaves, small | 7.86 |
| Betel leaves, big | 7.87 |

--- Author ---
Dr. Prajakta J. Nande

# Clinical and Therapeutic Nutrition Practical Manual 1
For M.Sc. Food Science and Nutrition (Semester-III)

| | | | |
|---|---|---|---|
| Pak choi leaves | 7.98 | Cucumber, orange, round | 6.43 |
| Amaranth leaves, green | 8.04 | Jack fruit, raw | 6.6 |
| Amaranth leaves, red | 8.2 | Tinda, tender | 6.7 |
| Amaranth leaves, red and green | 8.4 | French beans, hybrid | 6.71 |
| Gogu leaves, red | 8.6 | Cucumber, green, elongate | 6.94 |
| Tamarind leaves, tender | 8.7 | Plantain, flower | 7.06 |
| Spinach | 8.7 | Kovai, small | 7.14 |
| Ponnaganni | 8.77 | Jack fruit, seed, mature | 7.19 |
| Pumpkin leaves, tender | 8.85 | Bitter gourd, jagged, teeth ridges, short | 7.19 |
| Bathua leaves | 8.99 | Colocasia, stem, green | 7.2 |
| Garden Cress | 9.23 | Parwar | 7.22 |
| **OTHER VEGETABLES** | | French beans, country | 7.29 |
| Papaya, raw | 3.22 | Kovai, big | 7.32 |
| Tomato, green | 3.62 | Bitter gourd, jagged, teeth ridges, elongate | 7.4 |
| Knol-khol | 4.04 | Bitter gourd, jagged, teeth smooth, elongate | 7.4 |
| Tomato, ripe, hybrid | 4.18 | | |
| Celery stalk | 4.44 | Colocasia, stem, black | 7.53 |
| Plantain, stem | 4.59 | Broad beans | 7.63 |
| Cluster beans | 4.68 | Peas, fresh | 7.63 |
| Tomato, ripe, local | 4.71 | Bottle gourd, elongated pale green | 7.74 |
| Red gram, tender, fresh | 4.89 | Bottle gourd, round, pale green | 7.8 |
| Plantain, green | 4.98 | Bottle gourd, elongated dark green | 7.88 |
| Ladies finger | 5.04 | Mango, green, raw | 7.9 |
| Snake gourd, long, pale green | 5.22 | Corn, baby | 8.03 |
| Capsicum, yellow | 5.29 | Onion, stalk | 8.05 |
| Pumpkin, orange, round | 5.32 | Field beans, tender, broad | 8.19 |
| Ridge gourd | 5.34 | Field beans, tender, lean | 8.2 |
| Capsicum, red | 5.4 | Bean scarlet, tender | 8.31 |
| Pumpkin, green, cylindrical | 5.41 | Cho-cho-marrow | 8.64 |
| Brinjal-all varieties | 5.49 | **FRUITS** | |
| Zucchini, yellow | 5.5 | Orange, pulp | 2.11 |
| Brinjal-all varieties | 5.61 | Lemon juice | 2.51 |
| Snake gourd, short | 5.66 | Lime sweet, pulp | 2.66 |
| Ash gourd | 5.67 | Watermelon, dark green (sugar baby) | 2.87 |
| Capsicum, green | 5.68 | | |
| Zucchini, green | 5.68 | Watermelon, pale green | 3.1 |
| Snake gourd, long, dark green | 5.71 | Wood apple | 3.17 |
| Ridge gourd, smooth skin | 5.79 | Zizyphus | 3.59 |
| Drumstick | 5.98 | Muskmelon, yellow flesh | 3.67 |
| Cauliflower | 6.01 | Palm fruit, tender | 3.74 |
| Cucumber, green, short | 6.11 | Plum | 3.82 |
| Bamboo shoot, tender | 6.24 | | |

--- Author ---
Dr. Prajakta J. Nande

# Clinical and Therapeutic Nutrition Practical Manual 1
For M.Sc. Food Science and Nutrition (Semester-III)

| | | | |
|---|---|---|---|
| Pineapple | 3.97 | Mango, ripe, himsagar | 7.55 |
| Muskmelon, orange flesh | 4.09 | Blackberry | 7.82 |
| Pomegranate, maroon, seeds | 4.09 | Litchi | 8.08 |
| Apricot, processed | 4.12 | Mango, ripe, banganapalli | 8.18 |
| Apricot, dried | 4.22 | Banana, ripe, robusta | 8.23 |
| Gooseberry | 4.25 | Mango, ripe, paheri | 8.25 |
| Raisins, dried, golden | 4.26 | Mango, ripe, kesar | 8.26 |
| Papaya, ripe | 4.43 | Currant, black | 8.33 |
| Rambutan | 4.66 | Jambu fruit, ripe | 8.52 |
| Pummelo | 4.69 | Banana, ripe, red | 8.72 |
| Raisins, dried, black | 4.8 | Mango, ripe, totapari | 8.85 |
| Karonda fruit | 4.85 | Mangosteen | 9.1 |
| Custard apple | 4.88 | Mango, ripe, neelam | 9.19 |
| Pear | 4.95 | Mango, ripe, gulabkhas | 9.21 |
| Dates, processed | 4.98 | Banana, ripe | 9.22 |
| Apple, big | 5.17 | Banana, ripe, poovam | 9.41 |
| Dates, dry, pale brown | 5.17 | **ROOTS AND TUBERS** | |
| Dates, dry, dark brown | 5.23 | Carrot, red | 4.14 |
| Peach | 5.49 | Carrot, orange | 4.84 |
| Tamarind, pulp | 5.58 | Beetroot | 5.08 |
| Manila tamarind | 5.6 | Radish, elongate, red skin | 5.47 |
| Strawberry | 5.61 | Lotus root | 5.47 |
| Star fruit | 5.67 | Radish, round, white skin | 5.5 |
| Apple, small | 5.71 | Potato, red skin | 5.64 |
| Apple, green | 5.75 | Water chestnut | 5.85 |
| Fig | 5.8 | Yam, elephant | 6 |
| Grapes, seeded, round, red | 5.86 | Yam, wild | 6.09 |
| Bael fruit | 5.86 | Radish, elongate, white skin | 6.14 |
| Cherries, red | 5.88 | Radish, round, red skin | 6.19 |
| Grapes, seeded, rounded, black | 5.92 | Colocasia | 6.36 |
| Guava, pink, flesh | 6.01 | Potato, brown skin, big | 6.44 |
| Sapota | 6.1 | Yam, ordinary | 6.71 |
| Avocado fruit | 6.27 | Sweet potato, pink skin | 7.23 |
| Grapes, seedless, round, green | 6.31 | Potato, brown skin, small | 7.36 |
| Grapes, seedless, round, black | 6.44 | Tapioca | 7.51 |
| Soursop | 6.62 | Sweet potato, brown skin | 7.66 |
| Apple, small, Kashmir | 6.69 | **CONDIMENTS AND SPICES - FRESH** | |
| Jack fruit, ripe | 6.76 | Onion, big | 3.25 |
| Guava, white, flesh | 6.77 | Garlic big, clove | 3.79 |
| Grapes, seedless, round,  green | 7.15 | Garlic, small, clove | 4.07 |
| Phalsa | 7.19 | Onion small | 5.02 |
| Grapes, seedless, oval, black | 7.21 | Chillies green-all varieties | 5.05 |

--- Author ---
Dr. Prajakta J. Nande

# Clinical and Therapeutic Nutrition Practical Manual 1
For M.Sc. Food Science and Nutrition (Semester-III)

| | | | |
|---|---|---|---|
| Garlic, single, clove, Kashmir | 5.68 | Cashew nut | 7.02 |
| Coriander leaves | 6.08 | Pistachio nut | 7.55 |
| Ginger fresh | 6.49 | **SUGARS** | |
| Curry leaves | 6.51 | Jaggery, cane | 2.97 |
| Mint leaves | 8.22 | Sugarcane, juice | 3.55 |
| Mango ginger | 9.8 | **MUSHROOMS** | |
| **CONDIMENTS AND SPICES - DRY** | | Button mushroom, fresh | 6.88 |
| Nutmeg | 5.2 | Chicken mushroom, fresh | 7.03 |
| Omum | 5.26 | Shiitake mushroom, fresh | 7.14 |
| Asafoetida | 5.61 | **MISCELLANEOUS FOODS** | |
| Mace | 5.78 | Coconut water | 2.35 |
| Clove | 5.82 | **MILK AND MILK PRODUCTS** | |
| Poppy seeds | 5.98 | Paneer | 9.76 |
| Fenugreek seeds | 6 | Milk, whole, buffalo | 9.83 |
| Cardamom, black | 6.02 | Khoa | 10.34 |
| Cumin seeds | 6.23 | Milk, whole, cow | 10.66 |
| Chillies, red | 6.38 | **EGG AND EGG PRODUCTS** | |
| Coriander seeds | 6.73 | Egg, poultry, yolk, raw | 7.24 |
| Cardamom, green | 7.24 | Egg, country hen, whole, raw | 7.53 |
| Pepper, black | 8.25 | Egg, poultry, white, raw | 7.94 |
| Turmeric powder | 8.28 | Egg, poultry, whole, raw | 7.95 |
| Pippali | 8.49 | **POULTRY** | |
| **NUTS AND OIL SEEDS** | | Country hen, leg, with skin | 7.52 |
| Almond | 4.02 | Country hen, thigh, with skin | 7.65 |
| Arecanut, dried, red color | 4.26 | Chicken, poultry, leg, skinless | 7.84 |
| Arecanut, dried, brown | 4.43 | Chicken, poultry, thigh, skinless | 7.87 |
| Arecanut, fresh | 4.51 | Chicken, poultry, breast, skinless | 7.89 |
| Niger seeds, black | 4.71 | Country hen, wing, with skin | 7.9 |
| Niger seeds, gray | 5.22 | Country hen, breast, with skin | 7.96 |
| Gingerly seeds, white | 5.4 | Poultry, chicken, liver | 8.2 |
| Gingerly seeds black | 5.91 | Chicken, poultry, wing, skinless | 8.51 |
| Gingerly seeds, brown | 6.18 | **ANIMAL MEAT** | |
| Pine seeds | 6.23 | Sheep, lungs | 5.02 |
| Safflower seeds | 6.32 | Sheep, brain | 5.21 |
| Sunflower seeds | 6.38 | Goat, brain | 5.21 |
| Ground nut | 6.4 | Goat, spleen | 5.5 |
| Garden cress, seeds | 6.58 | Goat, lungs | 5.82 |
| Coconut, kernel, dry | 6.74 | Sheep, spleen | 5.9 |
| Linseeds | 6.81 | Goat, liver | 6.02 |
| Walnut | 6.87 | Sheep, liver | 6.2 |
| Coconut, kernel, fresh | 6.93 | Goat, chops | 6.24 |
| Mustard seeds | 6.96 | Sheep, kidneys | 6.34 |

--- Author ---
Dr. Prajakta J. Nande

# Clinical and Therapeutic Nutrition Practical Manual 1

For M.Sc. Food Science and Nutrition (Semester-III)

| | | | |
|---|---|---|---|
| Goat, heart | 6.35 | Tiger prawns, orange | 7.39 |
| Goat, kidneys | 6.46 | Tiger prawns, brown | 7.72 |
| Sheep, heart | 6.77 | Lobster, brown | 8.62 |
| Goat, legs | 6.81 | **FRESH WATER FISH AND SHELLFISH** | |
| Sheep, leg | 7.07 | Freshwater eel | 3.41 |
| Sheep, chops | 7.36 | Tiger prawns | 4.85 |
| Goat, shoulder | 7.66 | Crab | 5.19 |
| Sheep, shoulder | 7.68 | Rohu | 6.27 |
| **MARINE SHELLFISH** | | Gold fish | 6.31 |
| Crab | 6.35 | Prawns, big | 6.72 |
| Lobster, king size | 6.45 | Prawns, small | 6.76 |
| Mud crab | 6.9 | Cat fish | 7.29 |
| Oyster | 7.08 | Catla | 7.53 |
| Crab, sea | 7.3 | | |

*(Source: T. Longvah, R. Ananthan, K. Bhaskaracharya, K. Venkaiah. Indian Food Composition Tables, National Institute of Nutrition (Indian Council of Medical Research), 259-312, 2017)*

# VALINE

| FOOD STUFFS | Valine (g/100 g of Protein) | | |
|---|---|---|---|
| | | Varagu | 5.49 |
| | | Ragi | 5.65 |
| | | Rice, milled | 6.06 |
| | | Rice, parboiled, milled | 6.26 |
| | | Rice, brown | 6.72 |
| **CEREALS AND MILLETS** | | **GRAIN LEGUMES** | |
| Maize | 3.54 | Bengal gram, dal | 4.09 |
| Wheat, vermicelli | 3.54 | Black gram, whole | 4.11 |
| Wheat, vermicelli, roasted | 3.71 | Horse gram, whole | 4.16 |
| Maize, tender, sweet | 3.88 | Red gram, whole | 4.17 |
| Wheat four, refined | 4.01 | Red gram, dal | 4.38 |
| Wheat, bulgur | 4.28 | Bengal gram, whole | 4.58 |
| Amaranth seed, pale brown | 4.3 | Black gram, dal | 4.61 |
| Amaranth seed, black | 4.34 | Peas, dry | 4.67 |
| Wheat, semolina | 4.47 | Lentil whole, yellowish | 4.75 |
| Jowar | 4.51 | Rajmah, black | 4.83 |
| Quinoa | 4.55 | Lentil whole, brown | 4.85 |
| Barley | 4.78 | Cowpea, brown | 4.87 |
| Bajra | 4.79 | Moth bean | 4.9 |
| Wheat, whole | 5.11 | Field bean, white | 4.96 |
| Wheat four | 5.12 | Lentil dal | 5.02 |
| Samai | 5.31 | Soybean, brown | 5.04 |
| Rice puffed | 5.37 | Rajmah, red | 5.07 |
| Rice flakes | 5.4 | | |
| Maize | 5.41 | | |

--- Author ---
Dr. Prajakta J. Nande

# Clinical and Therapeutic Nutrition Practical Manual 1
For M.Sc. Food Science and Nutrition (Semester-III)

| | | | |
|---|---|---|---|
| Field bean, brown | 5.16 | Parsley | 6.19 |
| Green gram, dal | 5.21 | Fenugreek leaves | 6.27 |
| Rajmah, | 5.21 | **OTHER VEGETABLES** | |
| Rice bean | 5.23 | Tomato, ripe, hybrid | 2.74 |
| Field bean, black | 5.24 | Tomato, green | 3.09 |
| Cowpea, white | 5.31 | Papaya, raw | 3.16 |
| Green gram, whole | 5.45 | Tomato, ripe, local | 3.26 |
| Soybean, white | 5.53 | Bamboo shoot, tender | 3.69 |
| **GREEN LEAFY VEGETABLES** | | Cluster beans | 3.96 |
| Betel leaves, big (Kolkata) | 3.46 | Peas, fresh | 4.23 |
| Mustard leaves | 3.52 | Red gram, tender, fresh | 4.3 |
| Basella leaves | 3.88 | Ladies finger | 4.46 |
| Betel leaves, small | 3.93 | Bean scarlet ,tender | 4.54 |
| Rumex leaves | 3.97 | Brinjal-all varieties | 4.6 |
| Amaranth spined, leaves, red and green | 4.12 | Celery stalk | 4.64 |
| | | Plantain, flower | 4.75 |
| Amaranth spined, leaves, green | 4.18 | Corn, baby | 4.87 |
| Radish | 4.26 | Kovai, big | 4.97 |
| Beet greens | 4.27 | Drumstick | 5.02 |
| Drumstick leaves | 4.38 | Kovai, small | 5.05 |
| Gogu leaves, green | 4.55 | Field beans, tender, broad | 5.1 |
| Colocasia leaves, green | 4.64 | Ash gourd | 5.11 |
| Brussels sprouts | 4.74 | Capsicum, green | 5.17 |
| Cabbage, green | 4.83 | Capsicum, red | 5.17 |
| Cauliflower leaves | 4.93 | Field beans, tender, lean | 5.21 |
| Lettuce | 4.95 | Cucumber, green, short | 5.22 |
| Amaranth leaves, red and green | 4.98 | Capsicum, yellow | 5.24 |
| Amaranth leaves, green | 5.03 | Snake gourd, long, dark green | 5.27 |
| Amaranth leaves, red | 5.24 | Knol-khol | 5.31 |
| Cabbage, Chinese | 5.4 | French beans, country | 5.38 |
| Cabbage, violet | 5.47 | Snake gourd, short | 5.4 |
| Cabbage, collard greens | 5.64 | Broad beans | 5.41 |
| Tamarind leaves, tender | 5.65 | Plantain, green | 5.51 |
| Pak choi | 5.67 | Jack fruit, | 5.65 |
| Knol-khol, leaves | 5.7 | Snake gourd, long, pale green | 5.66 |
| Pumpkin leaves, tender | 5.82 | Zucchini, yellow | 5.71 |
| Spinach | 5.83 | Mango, green, | 5.79 |
| Ponnoganni | 5.95 | Tinda, tender | 5.79 |
| Agathi leaves | 5.99 | Cauliflower | 5.81 |
| Gogu leaves, red | 6.02 | Plantain, Stem | 5.84 |
| Bathua leaves | 6.07 | Zucchini, green | 5.87 |
| Garden cress | 6.17 | Onion, stalk | 5.9 |

--- Author ---
Dr. Prajakta J. Nande

# Clinical and Therapeutic Nutrition Practical Manual 1
For M.Sc. Food Science and Nutrition (Semester-III)

| | | | |
|---|---|---|---|
| Parwar | 5.95 | Musk melon, orange flesh | 3.33 |
| Ridge gourd | 5.95 | Guava, pink flesh | 3.36 |
| Colocasia, stem, black | 5.96 | Apple, big | 3.5 |
| Colocasia, stem, green | 5.96 | Water melon, dark green (sugar baby) | 3.54 |
| Pumpkin, green, cylindrical | 5.97 | Plum | 3.63 |
| French beans, hybrid | 5.98 | Water melon, pale green | 3.64 |
| Ridge gourd, smooth skin | 5.99 | Apple, green | 3.66 |
| Pumpkin, orange, round | 6.05 | Wood apple | 3.72 |
| Cucumber, green, elongate | 6.09 | Papaya, ripe | 3.93 |
| Cucumber, orange, round | 6.13 | Tamarind, pulp | 4.02 |
| Bitter gourd, jagged, teeth ridges, elongate | 6.49 | Pineapple | 4.07 |
| Bitter gourd, jagged, teeth ridges, short | 6.51 | Apple small, Kashmir | 4.18 |
| | | Star fruit | 4.21 |
| Bottle gourd, elongate, pale green | 6.58 | Pummelo | 4.23 |
| Bottle gourd, round, pale green | 6.64 | Palm fruit, tender | 4.31 |
| Cho-cho-marrow | 6.71 | Apple, small | 4.38 |
| Bitter gourd, jagged, smooth ridges, elongate | 6.76 | Avocado fruit | 4.48 |
| | | Strawberry | 4.51 |
| Jack fruit, seed, mature | 6.86 | Bael fruit | 4.62 |
| Bottle gourd, elongate, dark green | 6.98 | Karonda fruit | 4.62 |
| **FRUITS** | | Zizyphus | 4.67 |
| Lime, sweet, pulp | 1.73 | Rambutan | 4.77 |
| Apricot, processed | 2.12 | Cherries, red | 4.78 |
| Orange, pulp | 2.12 | Custard apple | 4.86 |
| Apricot, dried | 2.31 | Mango, ripe, himsagar | 4.87 |
| Pomegranate, maroon seeds | 2.4 | Manila tamarind | 4.92 |
| Grapes, seeded, round | 2.46 | Sapota | 5.03 |
| Grapes, seeded, round, black | 2.6 | Pear | 5.1 |
| Grapes, seedless, round, green | 2.7 | Currants, black | 5.11 |
| Grapes, seedless, round, black | 2.7 | Jack fruit, ripe | 5.18 |
| Grapes, seedless, oval, black | 2.73 | Mango, ripe, kesar | 5.23 |
| Grapes, seeded, round, red | 2.83 | Fig | 5.34 |
| Raisins, dried, golden | 2.84 | Mangosteen | 5.36 |
| Dates, dry, pale brown | 2.85 | Peach | 5.43 |
| Dates, processed | 2.85 | Phalsa | 5.76 |
| Raisins, dried, black | 2.87 | Banana, montham | 5.82 |
| Lemon, juice | 2.9 | Soursop | 5.91 |
| Gooseberry | 2.99 | Mango, ripe, banganapalli | 5.92 |
| Musk melon, yellow flesh | 3.06 | Mango, ripe, totapari | 5.92 |
| Guava, white flesh | 3.27 | Banana, robusta | 6.05 |
| Dates, dry, dark brown | 3.3 | Litchi | 6.05 |

--- Author ---
Dr. Prajakta J. Nande

# Clinical and Therapeutic Nutrition Practical Manual 1
For M.Sc. Food Science and Nutrition (Semester-III)

| | | | | |
|---|---|---|---|---|
| Banana, ripe, poovam | 6.11 | Cardamom, green | 2.85 |
| Mango, ripe, paheri | 6.13 | Mace | 3.09 |
| Mango, ripe, neelam | 6.29 | Nutmeg | 3.12 |
| Mango, ripe, gulabkhas | 6.32 | Pepper, black | 3.62 |
| Banana, red | 6.56 | Pippali | 3.82 |
| Black berry | 6.57 | Cloves | 4.31 |
| Jambu fruit, ripe | 6.99 | Poppy seeds | 4.33 |
| **ROOTS AND TUBERS** | | Fenugreek seeds | 4.43 |
| Potato, red skin | 3.26 | Omum | 4.7 |
| Water chestnut | 3.8 | Chillies, red | 4.82 |
| Potato, brown skin, small | 4.23 | Cumin seeds | 5.13 |
| Potato, brown skin, big | 4.29 | Turmeric powder | 5.81 |
| Carrot, red | 4.47 | Coriander seeds | 6.24 |
| Lotus root | 4.57 | **NUTS AND OIL SEEDS** | |
| Carrot, orange | 4.58 | Cashew nut | 3.23 |
| Yam, ordinary | 4.62 | Arecanut, dried, brown | 3.25 |
| Tapioca | 4.72 | Arecanut, dried, red color | 3.33 |
| Radish, elongate, red skin | 5.15 | Niger seeds, black | 3.69 |
| Radish, round, white skin | 5.18 | Ground nut | 3.92 |
| Radish, round, red skin | 5.27 | Safflower seeds | 4.35 |
| Colocasia | 5.37 | Almond | 4.45 |
| Radish, elongate, white skin | 5.57 | Niger seeds, gray | 4.5 |
| Sweet potato, brown skin | 5.57 | Gingelly seeds, white | 4.64 |
| Beet root | 5.6 | Garden cress, seeds | 4.69 |
| Sweet potato, pink skin | 5.72 | Pine seeds | 4.73 |
| Yam, elephant | 5.84 | Gingelly seeds, black | 4.78 |
| Yam, wild | 5.98 | Gingelly seeds, brown | 4.79 |
| **CONDIMENTS AND SPICES - FRESH** | | Coconut, kernel, dry | 4.81 |
| Onion, big | 2.75 | Arecanut, fresh | 4.89 |
| Garlic, big clove | 3.17 | Sunflower seeds | 4.99 |
| Garlic, single clove, Kashmir | 3.58 | Mustard seeds | 5 |
| Garlic, small clove | 3.79 | Pistachio nut | 5.27 |
| Curry leaves | 3.92 | Linseed | 5.31 |
| Onion, small | 3.93 | Walnut | 5.78 |
| Chillies, green-all varieties | 4.02 | Coconut, kernel, fresh | 5.83 |
| Ginger, fresh | 4.35 | **SUGARS** | |
| Mango ginger | 4.79 | Jaggery, cane | 3.45 |
| Mint leaves | 5.73 | Sugarcane, juice | 4.19 |
| Coriander leaves | 6.44 | **MUSHROOMS** | |
| **CONDIMENTS AND SPICES - DRY** | | Chicken mushroom, fresh | 5.36 |
| Asafoetida | 1.84 | Button mushroom, fresh | 5.48 |
| Cardamom, black | 2.64 | Shiitake mushroom, fresh | 6.08 |

**--- Author ---**
Dr. Prajakta J. Nande

# Clinical and Therapeutic Nutrition Practical Manual 1
For M.Sc. Food Science and Nutrition (Semester-III)

| MISCELLANEOUS FOODS | | Sheep, leg | 4.58 |
|---|---|---|---|
| Coconut water | 3.02 | Sheep, liver | 4.68 |
| **MILK AND MILK PRODUCTS** | | Goat, brain | 4.7 |
| Paneer | 5.68 | Goat, shoulder | 4.71 |
| Milk, whole, buffalo | 5.86 | Sheep, heart | 4.86 |
| Khoa | 6.1 | Goat, heart | 5.08 |
| Milk, whole, cow | 6.4 | Sheep, kidneys | 5.11 |
| **EGG AND EGG PRODUCTS** | | Goat, lungs | 5.15 |
| Egg, poultry, yolk | 5.66 | Goat, spleen | 5.27 |
| Egg, country hen, whole | 5.72 | Goat, kidneys | 5.44 |
| Egg, poultry, whole, | 5.82 | Sheep, spleen | 5.5 |
| Egg, poultry, white | 6.89 | **MARINE SHELLFISH** | |
| **POULTRY** | | Mud crab | 4.67 |
| Country hen, leg, with skin | 4.32 | Carb | 4.79 |
| Chicken, poultry, wing, skinless | 4.55 | Carb, sea | 4.91 |
| Chicken, poultry, thigh, skinless | 4.63 | Tiger prawns, brown | 5.06 |
| Chicken, poultry, leg, skinless | 4.92 | Tiger prawns, orange | 5.13 |
| Chicken, poultry, breast, skinless | 4.97 | Oyster | 5.31 |
| Country hen, thigh, with skin | 5.01 | Lobster, king size | 5.38 |
| Country hen, wing, with skin | 5.7 | Lobster, brown | 5.87 |
| Country hen, breast, with skin | 5.77 | **FRESHWATER FISH AND SHELLFISH** | |
| Poultry, chicken, liver | 5.82 | Crab | 3.96 |
| **ANIMAL MEAT** | | Freshwater eel | 4.56 |
| Goat, liver | 4 | Prawns, big | 4.72 |
| Sheep, shoulder | 4 | Tiger prawns | 4.75 |
| Sheep, brain | 4.19 | Cat fish | 5.15 |
| Sheep, chops | 4.23 | Prawns, small | 5.17 |
| Goat, chops | 4.45 | Catla | 5.18 |
| Goat, legs | 4.51 | Gold fish | 5.23 |
| Sheep, lungs | 4.53 | Rohu | 5.39 |

*(Source: T. Longvah, R. Ananthan, K. Bhaskaracharya, K. Venkaiah. Indian Food Composition Tables, National Institute of Nutrition (Indian Council of Medical Research), 259-312, 2017)*

--- Author ---
Dr. Prajakta J. Nande

**Clinical and Therapeutic Nutrition Practical Manual 1**
For M.Sc. Food Science and Nutrition (Semester-III)

## ANNEXURE - 7

## AROMATIC AMINO ACID CONTENT OF FOODS

## PHENYLALANINE

| FOOD STUFFS | Phenyl--alanine (g/100 g of Protein) |
|---|---|
| **CEREALS AND MILLETS** | |
| Maize, tender, sweet | 3.05 |
| Maize, tender, local | 3.95 |
| Amaranth seed, black | 3.98 |
| Wheat flour, refined | 4.29 |
| Quinoa | 4.35 |
| Wheat, bulgur | 4.46 |
| Amaranth seed, pale brown | 4.75 |
| Wheat, whole | 4.75 |
| Wheat, semolina | 4.77 |
| Bajra | 4.82 |
| Barley | 4.88 |
| Wheat, vermicelli | 4.9 |
| Wheat vermicelli, roasted | 4.96 |
| Wheat flour | 5.03 |
| Jowar | 5.1 |
| Maize, dry | 5.14 |
| Rice, parboiled, milled | 5.14 |
| Rice flakes | 5.22 |
| Rice puffed | 5.33 |
| Rice, raw, milled | 5.36 |
| Rice, raw, brown | 5.5 |
| Ragi | 5.7 |
| Samai | 6.14 |
| Varagu | 6.27 |
| **GRAIN LEGUMES** | |
| Lentil whole, brown | 4.61 |
| Lentil whole, yellowish | 4.67 |
| Peas, dry | 4.76 |
| Soya bean, brown | 5.01 |
| Soya bean, whole | 5.01 |
| Lentil dal | 5.1 |

| | |
|---|---|
| Rajmah, black | 5.32 |
| Cowpea, brown | 5.47 |
| Cowpea, white | 5.63 |
| Black gram, dal | 5.68 |
| Field bean, brown | 5.72 |
| Filed bean, white | 5.76 |
| Moth bean | 5.85 |
| Field bean, black | 5.88 |
| Black gram, whole | 5.9 |
| Rajmah, red | 5.9 |
| Rajmah, brown | 5.91 |
| Bengal gram, dal | 5.97 |
| Green gram, dal | 6.2 |
| Green gram, whole | 6.21 |
| Bengal gram, whole | 6.26 |
| Rice bean | 7.56 |
| Horse gram, whole | 8.08 |
| Red gram, whole | 8.71 |
| Red gram, dal | 8.76 |
| **GREEN LEAFY VEGETABLES** | |
| Cabbage, violet | 2.21 |
| Cabbage, green | 2.56 |
| Brussels sprouts | 3.23 |
| Cabbage, Chinese | 3.27 |
| Mustard leaves | 3.53 |
| Lettuce | 3.61 |
| Beet greens | 3.63 |
| Cauliflower leaves | 4.16 |
| Basella leaves | 4.17 |
| Amaranth spinosus, leaves, red and green | 4.34 |
| Colocasia leaves, green | 4.43 |
| Cabbage, collard greens | 4.56 |
| Betel leaves, big | 4.58 |
| Garden cress | 4.72 |
| Betel leaves, small | 4.73 |
| Amaranth leaves, red | 4.77 |

--- **Author** ---
Dr. Prajakta J. Nande

# Clinical and Therapeutic Nutrition Practical Manual 1
For M.Sc. Food Science and Nutrition (Semester-III)

| | | | | |
|---|---|---|---|---|
| Tamarind, tender | 4.86 | Broad beans | 3.86 |
| Knol- khol, leaves | 4.93 | Parwar | 3.86 |
| Amaranth spinosus, leaves, green | 5 | Kovai, big | 3.87 |
| Gogu leaves, green | 5.04 | Cauliflower | 3.88 |
| parsley | 5.31 | Papaya, raw | 3.91 |
| Spinach | 5.38 | Snake gourd, long, dark green | 3.95 |
| Ponnoganni | 5.41 | Jack fruit, raw | 3.96 |
| Fenugreek leaves | 5.52 | French beans, country | 4.04 |
| Gogu leaves, red | 5.65 | Colocasia, stem, black | 4.06 |
| Amaranth leaves, green | 5.68 | Onion, stalk | 4.09 |
| Bathua leaves | 5.73 | Snake gourd, long, pale green | 4.11 |
| Amaranth leaves, red and green | 5.88 | Cucumber, green, short | 4.14 |
| Pak choi leaves | 5.89 | Colocasia, stem, green | 4.14 |
| Radish leaves | 6 | Kovai, small | 4.16 |
| Agathi leaves | 6.03 | Ridge gourd | 4.21 |
| Pumpkin leaves, tender | 6.4 | French beans, hybrid | 4.22 |
| Drumstick leaves | 6.45 | Snake gourd, short | 4.25 |
| Rumex leaves | 7.92 | Brinjal-all varieties | 4.29 |
| **OTHER VEGETABLES** | | Tomato, ripe, local | 4.3 |
| Knol-khol | 1.9 | Cucumber, orange, round | 4.43 |
| Bitter gourd, jagged, teeth ridges, elongate | 2.6 | Ridge gourd, smooth skin | 4.45 |
| | | Plantain, stem | 4.5 |
| Pumpkin, green, cylindrical | 2.84 | Tomato, ripe, hybrid | 4.54 |
| Celery stalk | 2.92 | Field beans, tender, broad | 4.57 |
| Bitter gourd, jagged, smooth ridges, elongate | 2.98 | Cho-cho-marrow | 4.65 |
| | | Brinjal-all varieties | 4.7 |
| Capsicum, yellow | 2.98 | Zucchini, green | 4.73 |
| Cluster beans | 2.99 | Field beans, tender, lean | 4.73 |
| Bitter gourd, jagged, teeth ridges, short | 3.15 | Corn, baby | 4.85 |
| | | Pumpkin, orange, round | 4.91 |
| Capsicum, red | 3.16 | Peas, fresh | 5.02 |
| Cucumber, green, elongate | 3.17 | Bean scarlet, tender | 5.13 |
| Ash gourd | 3.22 | Plantain, green | 5.32 |
| Bottle gourd, round, pale green | 3.41 | Zucchini, yellow | 5.54 |
| Drumstick | 3.43 | Bamboo shoot, tender | 5.57 |
| Ladies finger | 3.44 | Jack fruit,seed, mature | 6.22 |
| Tomato, green | 3.47 | Red gram, tender, fresh | 8.56 |
| Capsicum, green | 3.49 | **FRUITS** | |
| Tinda, tender | 3.64 | Lime, sweet, pulp | 1.32 |
| Plantain, flower | 3.68 | Guava, white flesh | 1.34 |
| Bottle gourd, elongate, dark green | 3.71 | Guava, pink flesh | 1.55 |
| Bottle gourd, elongate, pale green | 3.73 | Musk melon, yellow flesh | 1.62 |
| Mango, green, raw | 3.75 | Orange, pulp | 1.77 |

--- **Author** ---
Dr. Prajakta J. Nande

# Clinical and Therapeutic Nutrition Practical Manual 1
For M.Sc. Food Science and Nutrition (Semester-III)

| | | | | |
|---|---|---|---|---|
| Musk melon, orange flesh | 1.82 | Custard apple | 4.16 |
| Papaya, ripe | 1.93 | Grapes, seedless, round, green | 4.17 |
| Rambutan | 2.41 | Avocado fruit | 4.24 |
| Raisins, dried, black | 2.44 | Banana, ripe, robusta | 4.28 |
| Pummelo | 2.45 | Manila tamarind | 4.35 |
| Strawberry | 2.5 | Currants, black | 4.42 |
| Raisins, dried, golden | 2.51 | Jack fruit, ripe | 4.49 |
| Water melon, dark green (sugar baby) | 2.58 | Grapes, seedless, round | 4.47 |
| | | Bael fruit | 4.81 |
| Dates, processed | 2.59 | Phalsa | 4.84 |
| Pineapple | 2.59 | Gooseberry | 4.85 |
| Apricot, processed | 2.69 | Soursop | 4.99 |
| Water melon, pale green | 2.69 | Blackberry | 5.18 |
| Apricot, dried | 2.73 | Banana, ripe, red | 5.28 |
| Plum | 2.75 | Banana, ripe, poovam | 5.32 |
| Palm fruit, tender | 2.76 | Lichi | 5.39 |
| Peach | 2.95 | Tamarind, pulp | 5.46 |
| Wood apple | 2.98 | Banana, ripe, montham | 5.52 |
| Pear | 3.04 | Jambu fruit, ripe | 5.63 |
| Grapes, seeded, round, green | 3.12 | Mangosteen | 6.21 |
| Pomegranate, maroon seeds | 3.18 | **ROOTS AND TUBERS** | |
| Mango, ripe, banganapalli | 3.2 | Carrot, red | 2.21 |
| Fig | 3.36 | Beet root | 2.31 |
| Mango, ripe, neelam | 3.38 | Carrot, orange | 2.84 |
| Apple, big | 3.39 | Radish, round, white skin | 3.12 |
| Dates, dry, dark brown | 3.46 | Radish, elongate, white skin | 3.26 |
| Zizyphus | 3.47 | Radish, elongate, red skin | 3.41 |
| Mango, ripe, kesar | 3.37 | Radish, round, red skin | 3.84 |
| Lemon, juice | 3.54 | Potato, brown skin, small | 4.11 |
| Dates, dry, pale brown | 3.55 | Lotus root | 4.32 |
| Grapes, seeded, round, black | 3.59 | Yam, ordinary | 4.54 |
| Apple, small | 3.74 | Potato, red skin | 4.59 |
| Mango, ripe, gulabkhas | 3.75 | Water chestnut | 4.64 |
| Grapes, seedless, oval, black | 3.85 | Colocasia | 5.22 |
| Karonda fruit | 3.86 | Tapioca | 5.29 |
| Apple, green | 3.86 | Sweet potato, pink skin | 5.35 |
| Mango, ripe, paheri | 3.94 | Potato, brown skin,big | 5.61 |
| Sapota | 3.95 | Yam,wild | 6.23 |
| Star fruit | 4.07 | Sweet potato, brown skin | 6.37 |
| Cherries, red | 4.1 | Yam, elephant | 6.46 |
| Grapes, seeded, round | 4.14 | **CONDIMENTS AND SPICES - FRESH** | |
| Mango, ripe, totapari | 4.15 | Onion, big | 2.77 |
| Apple, small , Kashmir | 4.16 | Garlic, small clove | 3.27 |

--- **Author** ---
Dr. Prajakta J. Nande

# Clinical and Therapeutic Nutrition Practical Manual 1
For M.Sc. Food Science and Nutrition (Semester-III)

| | | | |
|---|---|---|---|
| Garlic,single clove, Kashmir | 3.46 | Ground nut | 5.4 |
| Curry leaves | 3.5 | Pistachio nut | 5.52 |
| Garlic, big clove | 3.53 | Linseeds | 5.58 |
| Onion,small | 4.13 | Almond | 5.61 |
| Ginger, fresh | 4.36 | **SUGARS** | |
| Mango ginger | 4.52 | Jaggery, cane | 4.82 |
| Chillies green-all varieties | 4.69 | Sugarcane, juice | 5.11 |
| Mint leaves | 5.34 | **MUSHROOMS** | |
| Coriander leaves | 5.35 | Shiitake mushroom, fresh | 4.2 |
| **CONDIMENTS AND SPICES - DRY** | | Chicken mushroom, fresh | 4.5 |
| Omum | 3.23 | Button mushroom, fresh | 4.63 |
| Cardamom, black | 3.39 | **MISCELLANEOUS FOODS** | |
| Poppy seeds | 3.69 | Coconut water | 1.95 |
| Coriander seeds | 4.09 | **MILK AND MILK PRODUCTS** | |
| Cloves | 4.1 | Milk, whole, buffalo | 4.26 |
| Fenugreek seeds | 4.1 | Khoa | 5.08 |
| Pippali | 4.25 | Panner | 5.08 |
| Mace | 4.29 | Milk, whole, cow | 5.09 |
| Cardamom, green | 4.32 | **EGG AND EGG PRODUCTS** | |
| Asafoetida | 4.35 | Egg, poultry, whole, raw | 5.28 |
| Cumin seeds | 4.46 | Egg, poultry, whole, raw | 6.29 |
| Nutmeg | 4.86 | Egg, country, hen, whole, raw | 6.42 |
| Chillies, red | 5.09 | Egg, poultry, yolk, raw | 7.08 |
| Pepper, black | 5.15 | **POULTRY** | |
| Turmeric powder | 5.56 | Poultry, chicken, liver | 6.59 |
| **NUTS AND OIL SEEDS** | | Chicken, poultry, wing, skinless | 6.84 |
| Niger seeds, black | 3.14 | Chicken, poultry, thigh skinless | 7.01 |
| Arecanut, dried brown | 3.56 | Chicken, poultry leg, skinless | 7.07 |
| Arecanut, fresh | 3.65 | Chicken, poultry, breast, skinless | 7.23 |
| Pine seeds | 3.68 | Country, hen thigh, with skin | 7.32 |
| Niger seeds, gray | 3.72 | Country hen, leg, with skin | 7.42 |
| Arecanut, dried, red color | 3.83 | Country hen, breast, with skin | 7.67 |
| Gingelly seeds, brown | 3.83 | **ANIMAL MEAT** | |
| Garden cress, seeds | 3.89 | Sheep, kidney | 5.61 |
| Safflower seeds | 4.27 | Goat, liver | 5.64 |
| Gingelly seeds, white | 4.38 | Sheep, liver | 5.66 |
| Walnut | 4.41 | Goat, kidney | 5.74 |
| Mustard seeds | 4.47 | Goat, heart | 6.25 |
| Coconut, kernel, fresh | 4.51 | Sheep, heart | 6.45 |
| Gingelly seeds, black | 4.74 | Sheep, spleen | 6.55 |
| Cashew nut | 4.87 | Goat, spleen | 6.58 |
| Sunflower seeds | 4.97 | Goat, brain | 6.61 |
| Coconut, kernel, dry | 5.19 | Sheep, chops | 6.80 |

--- Author ---
Dr. Prajakta J. Nande

# Clinical and Therapeutic Nutrition Practical Manual 1
For M.Sc. Food Science and Nutrition (Semester-III)

| | | | |
|---|---|---|---|
| Sheep, brain | 6.83 | Tiger prawns, brown | 4.60 |
| Goat, chops | 7.06 | Crab | 4.72 |
| Goat, lungs | 7.16 | Lobster, king size | 4.83 |
| Goat, shoulder | 7.29 | **FRESH WATER FISH AND SHELLFISH** | |
| Sheep, lungs | 7.43 | Crab | 3.94 |
| Goat, leg | 7.76 | Fresh water eel | 4.07 |
| Sheep, legs | 7.78 | Prawns, big | 4.57 |
| Sheep, shoulder | 7.87 | Tiger prawns | 4.64 |
| **MARINE SHELLFISH** | | Gold fish | 5.14 |
| Tiger prawns, orange | 3.68 | Rohu | 5.26 |
| Lobster, brown | 3.70 | Cat fish | 5.30 |
| Oyster | 3.87 | Prawns, small | 5.37 |
| Mud crab | 4.07 | Catla | 5.49 |
| Crab, sea | 4.11 | | |

*(Source: T. Longvah, R. Ananthan, K. Bhaskaracharya, K. Venkaiah. Indian Food Composition Tables, National Institute of Nutrition (Indian Council of Medical Research), 259-312, 2017)*

# TRYPTOPHAN

| FOOD STUFFS | Trypto--phan (g/100 g of Protein) | | |
|---|---|---|---|
| | | Varagu | 1.32 |
| | | Bajra | 1.33 |
| | | Samai | 1.35 |
| | | Wheat, whole | 1.4 |
| | | Amaranth seed, black | 1.5 |
| | | Amaranth seed, pale brown | 1.69 |
| **CEREALS AND MILLETS** | | **GRAINS AND LEGUMES** | |
| Maize, dry | 0.57 | Rice bean | 0.62 |
| Maize, tender, local | 0.58 | Red gram, dal | 0.71 |
| Maize, tender, sweet | 0.7 | Field bean, black | 0.73 |
| Ragi | 0.91 | Red gram, whole | 0.75 |
| Wheatflour | 0.99 | Lentil whole, brown | 0.76 |
| Wheat, vermicelli, roasted | 0.99 | Field bean, brown | 0.78 |
| Rice, raw, brown | 1 | Lentil dal | 0.81 |
| Jowar | 1.03 | Peas, dry | 0.86 |
| Wheatflour, refined | 1.04 | Field bean, white | 0.89 |
| Wheat, semolina | 1.04 | Cowpea, white | 0.92 |
| Rice puffed | 1.07 | Mothbean | 0.92 |
| Wheat, vermicelli | 1.07 | Bengal gram, whole | 0.95 |
| Wheat, bulgur | 1.11 | Black gram, whole | 0.98 |
| Rice flakes | 1.11 | Green gram, whole | 1.02 |
| Rice, parboiled, milled | 1.15 | Rajmah, brown | 1.04 |
| Quinoa | 1.25 | Cowpea, brown | 1.05 |
| Rice, raw, milled | 1.27 | Rajmah, red | 1.05 |
| Barley | 1.28 | | |

--- Author ---
Dr. Prajakta J. Nande

# Clinical and Therapeutic Nutrition Practical Manual 1
For M.Sc. Food Science and Nutrition (Semester-III)

| | | | | |
|---|---|---|---|---|
| Black gram, dal | 1.07 | Basella leaves | 1.88 |
| Horse gram, whole | 1.08 | Beet greens | 3.76 |
| Bengal gram, dal | 1.09 | Bathua leaves | 4.16 |
| Rajmah, black | 1.22 | Agathi leaves | 4.44 |
| Green gram, dal | 1.24 | Amaranth leaves, red | 4.5 |
| Soyabean, brown | 1.59 | Basella leaves | 4.61 |
| Soyabean, white | 1.68 | Amaranth leaves, green | 4.62 |
| Lentil whole, yellowish | 0.75 | Amaranth leaves, red and green | 4.89 |
| **GREEN LEAFY VEGETABLES** | | Amaranth spinosus, leaves, red and green | 5.23 |
| Betel leaves, small | 0.69 | Amaranth, spinosus, leaves, green | 5.29 |
| Beet greens | 0.82 | **OTHER VEGETABLES** | |
| Cabbage,violet | 0.82 | Cucumber, green, elongate | 0.27 |
| Amaranth spinosus, leaves, green | 0.89 | Ladies finger | 0.49 |
| Brussels sprouts | 0.93 | Cucumber, orange, round | 0.52 |
| Cabbage, green | 0.93 | Tomato, ripe, hybrid | 0.52 |
| Fenugreek leaves | 0.99 | Drumstick | 0.53 |
| Betel leaves, big (Kolkata) | 1.00 | Jackfruit, raw | 0.53 |
| Amaranth leaves, green | 1.01 | Parwar | 0.59 |
| Colocasia leaves, green | 1.01 | Snake gourd, long, pale green | 0.6 |
| Gogu leaves, red | 1.04 | Tinda, tender | 0.62 |
| Knol-khol, leaves | 1.05 | Snake gourd, long, dark green | 0.63 |
| Gogu leaves, green | 1.07 | Snake gourd, short | 0.63 |
| Bathua leaves | 1.08 | Tomato, ripe, local | 0.64 |
| Amaranth leaves, red and green | 1.08 | Cucumber, green, short | 0.66 |
| Cauliflower leaves | 1.12 | Plantain, stem | 0.67 |
| Amaranth spinosus, leaves red and green | 1.17 | Plantain, green | 0.68 |
| Ponnoganni | 1.18 | Ridge gourd, smooth skin | 0.69 |
| Amaranth leaves, red | 1.2 | Ash gourd | 0.72 |
| Pak choi leaves | 1.23 | Ridge gourd | 0.72 |
| Lettuce | 1.23 | Colocasia, stem, green | 0.73 |
| Cabbage, collard greens | 1.24 | Pumpkin, green | 0.73 |
| Cabbage, Chinese | 1.24 | Tomato, green | 0.73 |
| Rumex leaves | 1.24 | Colocasia, stem, black | 0.75 |
| Garden cress | 1.26 | Field beans, tender, broad | 0.75 |
| Drumstick leaves | 1.27 | Pumpkin, orange, round | 0.77 |
| Mustard leaves | 1.31 | Knol-khol | 0.78 |
| Radish leaves | 1.39 | Brinjal-all varieties | 0.8 |
| Tamarind leaves, tender | 1.47 | Field beans, tender, lean | 0.8 |
| Spinach | 1.53 | French beans, hybrid | 0.8 |
| Parsley | 1.68 | Plantain, flower | 0.81 |
| Pumpkin leaves, tender | 1.76 | Peas, fresh | 0.84 |
| | | Kovai, small | 0.85 |

--- **Author** ---
Dr. Prajakta J. Nande

# Clinical and Therapeutic Nutrition Practical Manual 1
For M.Sc. Food Science and Nutrition (Semester-III)

| | | | |
|---|---|---|---|
| Zucchini, green | 0.85 | Phalsa | 0.66 |
| Cho-cho-marrow | 0.86 | Grapes, seeded, round, red | 0.69 |
| Zucchini, yellow | 0.86 | Grapes, seedless, oval, black | 0.69 |
| Beans scarlet, tender | 0.88 | Grapes, seedless, round, green | 0.69 |
| Broad beans | 0.88 | Apricot, dried | 0.7 |
| Cluster beans | 0.91 | Raisins, dried, golden | 0.7 |
| Capsicum, red | 0.92 | Litchi | 0.74 |
| Kovai, big | 0.93 | Gooseberry | 0.75 |
| Jackfruit, seed, mature | 0.94 | Sapota | 0.75 |
| Bamboo shoot, tender | 0.95 | Guava, pink flesh | 0.77 |
| Capsicum, green | 0.96 | Apple, green | 0.78 |
| Corn, baby | 0.96 | Grapes, seedless, round, black | 0.78 |
| French beans, country | 0.96 | Apricot, processed | 0.8 |
| Capsicum, yellow | 0.99 | Dates, processed | 0.8 |
| Red gram, tender, fresh | 0.99 | Banana, ripe, montham | 0.81 |
| Papaya, raw | 1 | Banana, ripe, red | 0.82 |
| Cauliflower | 1.06 | Blackberry | 0.83 |
| Mango, green, raw | 1.06 | Guava, white flesh | 0.83 |
| Onion, stalk | 1.07 | Jambu fruit, ripe | 0.83 |
| Celery stalk | 0.15 | Soursop | 0.84 |
| Bitter gourd, jagged, teeth ridges, elongate | 1.28 | Apple, small | 0.85 |
| | | Dates, dry, pale brown | 0.85 |
| Bitter gourd, jagged, smooth ridges, elongate | 1.32 | Fig | 0.85 |
| | | Karonda fruit | 0.85 |
| Bitter gourd, jagged, teeth ridges, short | 1.42 | Tamarind, pulp | 0.85 |
| | | Wood apple | 0.85 |
| Bottle gourd, elongate, dark green | 1.46 | Apple, big | 0.86 |
| Bottle gourd, elongate, pale green | 1.6 | Custardapple | 0.86 |
| Bottle gourd, round, pale green | 1.67 | Star fruit | 0.87 |
| **FRUITS** | | Zizyphus | 0.88 |
| Peach | 0.43 | Banana, ripe, poovam | 0.9 |
| Lemon, juice | 0.45 | Strawberry | 0.93 |
| Pomegranate, maroon seeds | 0.46 | Mango, ripe, banganapalli | 0.94 |
| Lime, sweet, pulp | 0.48 | Raisins, dried, black | 0.97 |
| Pummelo | 0.48 | Bael fruit | 0.98 |
| Grapes, seeded, round, black | 0.49 | Banana, ripe, robusta | 0.99 |
| Cherries, red | 0.5 | Avocado fruit | 1.04 |
| Musk melon, orange, flesh | 0.52 | Pineapple | 1.09 |
| Musk melon, yellow, flesh | 0.52 | Watermelon, pale green | 1.13 |
| Orange, pulp | 0.54 | Manila tamarind | 1.14 |
| Pear | 0.58 | Watermelon, dark green (sugar baby) | 1.15 |
| Jackfruit, ripe | 0.62 | | |
| Grapes, seeded, round, green | 0.66 | Mango, ripe, himsagar | 1.16 |

--- **Author** ---
Dr. Prajakta J. Nande

# Clinical and Therapeutic Nutrition Practical Manual 1
For M.Sc. Food Science and Nutrition (Semester-III)

| | | | | |
|---|---|---|---|---|
| Mango, ripe, totapari | 1.21 | Sweet potato, brown skin | 5.21 |
| Mangosteen | 1.21 | Sweet potato, pink skin | 5.26 |
| Plum | 1.21 | Tapioca | 5.76 |
| Rambutan | 1.25 | **CONDIMENTS AND SPICES - FRESH** | |
| Mango, ripe, kesar | 1.28 | Garlic, small clove | 0.73 |
| Mango, ripe, gulabkhas | 1.33 | Onion, small | 0.73 |
| Mango, ripe, neelam | 1.33 | Garlic, big clove | 0.83 |
| Currants, black | 1.47 | Garlic, single clove, Kashmir | 0.97 |
| Mango, ripe, paheri | 1.49 | Ginger, fresh | 0.99 |
| Papaya, ripe | 1.66 | Coriander leaves | 1.08 |
| Dates, dry, dark brown | 1.83 | Mint leaves | 1.23 |
| Apple, small, Kashmir | 85 | Onion, big | 1.23 |
| **ROOTS AND TUBERS** | | Mango ginger | 1.29 |
| Radish, elongate, white skin | 0.52 | Curry leaves | 1.64 |
| Radish, elongate, red skin | 0.56 | Garlic, small clove | 3.2 |
| Radish, round, red skin | 0.58 | Garlic, big clove | 3.65 |
| Radish, round, white skin | 0.6 | Radish elongated, red skin | 4.33 |
| Tapioca | 0.7 | Potato, brown skin, big | 4.39 |
| Beetroot | 0.86 | Chillies, green-all varieties | 4.42 |
| Yam, ordinary | 0.96 | Potato, red skin | 4.54 |
| Carrot, orange | 1.01 | Radish, elongated, white skin | 4.55 |
| Lotusroot | 1.02 | Sweet potato, brown skin | 5.21 |
| Potato, brown skin, big | 1.03 | Sweet potato, pink skin | 5.26 |
| Carrot, red | 1.13 | Tapioca | 5.76 |
| Yam, elephant | 1.13 | Curry leaves | 5.94 |
| Colocasia | 1.16 | **CONDIMENTS AND SPICES - DRY** | |
| Potato, brown skin, small | 1.17 | Pepper, black | 0.55 |
| Potato, brown skin, small | 1.19 | Poppy seeds | 0.82 |
| Potato, red skin | 1.2 | Cardamom, black | 0.86 |
| Yam, wild | 1.25 | Nutmeg | 0.88 |
| Sweet potato, pink skin | 1.46 | Cloves | 0.9 |
| Water chestnut | 1.6 | Chillies, red | 0.92 |
| Sweet potato, brown skin | 1.9 | Cumin seeds | 0.95 |
| Carrot, orange | 3.72 | Cardamom, green | 0.96 |
| Carrot, red | 3.97 | Coriander seeds | 1.18 |
| Radish, round, red skin | 4.01 | Fenugreek seeds | 1.19 |
| Radish, round, white skin | 4.12 | Asafoetida | 1.23 |
| Colocasia | 4.17 | Mace | 1.26 |
| Lotus root | 4.33 | Pippali | 1.31 |
| Radish, elongate, red skin | 4.33 | Omum | 1.38 |
| Potato, brown skin, big | 4.39 | Turmeric powder | 2.06 |
| Potato, red skin | 4.54 | **NUTS AND OIL SEEDS** | |
| Radish, elongate, white skin | 4.55 | Coconut, kernel, dry | 0.62 |

--- **Author** ---
Dr. Prajakta J. Nande

# Clinical and Therapeutic Nutrition Practical Manual 1
For M.Sc. Food Science and Nutrition (Semester-III)

| | | | | |
|---|---|---|---|---|
| Areca nut, fresh | 0.7 | Chicken poultry, leg, skinless | 1.16 |
| Areca nut, dried, red color | 0.76 | Chicken poultry, breast, skinless | 1.2 |
| Areca nut, dried, brown | 0.79 | Chicken poultry, thigh, skinless | 1.2 |
| Pine seeds | 0.83 | Chicken poultry, wing, skinless | 1.21 |
| Almond | 0.89 | Country hen, wing, with skin | 1.24 |
| Ground nut | 0.9 | Country hen, thigh, with skin | 1.26 |
| Walnut | 1.04 | Poultry, chicken, liver | 1.52 |
| Cashew nut | 1.05 | Country hen, breast, with skin | 1.8 |
| Gingelly seeds, black | 1.1 | **ANIMALMEAT** | |
| Niger seeds, grey | 1.11 | Sheep, liver | 1.19 |
| Sunflower seeds | 1.14 | Goat, liver | 1.22 |
| Gingelly seeds, white | 1.16 | Sheep, brain | 1.29 |
| Gingelly seeds, brown | 1.17 | Goat, heart | 1.31 |
| Coconut, kernel, fresh | 1.2 | Goat, shoulder | 1.34 |
| Mustard seeds | 1.23 | Goat, brain | 1.36 |
| Garden cress, seeds | 1.24 | Sheep, lungs | 1.36 |
| Niger seeds, black | 1.25 | Sheep, spleen | 1.38 |
| Pistachio nut | 1.42 | Sheep, heart | 1.4 |
| Safflower seeds | 1.43 | Sheep, shoulder | 1.42 |
| Linseeds | 1.57 | Goat, legs | 1.43 |
| **SUGARS** | | Goat, lungs | 1.45 |
| Jaggery, cane | 0.59 | Goat, spleen | 1.46 |
| Sugarcane juice | 0.75 | Sheep, leg | 1.47 |
| **MUSHROOMS** | | Sheep, chops | 1.5 |
| Button mushroom, fresh | 1.26 | Goat, kidneys | 1.5 |
| Chicken mushroom, fresh | 1.3 | Sheep, kidneys | 1.59 |
| Shitake mushroom, fresh | 1.32 | Goat, chops | 1.63 |
| **MISCELLANEOUS FOODS** | | **MARINE SHELLFISH** | |
| Coconut water | 0.78 | Crab,sea | 0.64 |
| **MILK AND MILK PRODUCTS** | | Tiger prawns, orange | 0.71 |
| Milk, whole, buffalo | 1.3 | Lobster, brown | 0.75 |
| Paneer | 1.42 | Tiger prawns, brown | 0.87 |
| Milk, whole, cow | 1.46 | Lobster, king size | 0.88 |
| Khoa | 1.59 | Oyster | 0.92 |
| **EGG AND EGG PRODUCTS** | | Mud crab | 1.15 |
| Egg poultry, whole | 1.38 | Crab | 1.41 |
| Egg country, hen, whole | 1.42 | **FRESH WATER FISH AND SHELLFISH** | |
| Egg country, hen, whole, raw | 1.42 | Catla | 0.74 |
| Egg poultry, yolk, raw | 1.47 | Crab | 0.93 |
| Egg poultry, white, raw | 1.5 | Tiger prawns | 0.94 |
| Egg poultry, whole, raw | 1.59 | Prawns, small | 1.02 |
| **POULTRY** | | Gold fish | 1.03 |
| Country hen, leg, with skin | 1.15 | Rohu | 1.04 |

--- Author ---
Dr. Prajakta J. Nande

# Clinical and Therapeutic Nutrition Practical Manual 1
For M.Sc. Food Science and Nutrition (Semester-III)

| | | | |
|---|---|---|---|
| Prawns,big | 1.11 | Cat fish | 1.18 |

*(Source: T. Longvah, R. Ananthan, K. Bhaskaracharya, K. Venkaiah. Indian Food Composition Tables, National Institute of Nutrition (Indian Council of Medical Research), 259-312, 2017)*

## TYROSINE

| FOOD STUFFS | Tyro-sine (g/100 g of Protein) |
|---|---|
| **CEREALS AND MILLETS** | |
| Wheat, vermicelli, roasted | 1.92 |
| Quinoa | 1.98 |
| Wheat flour | 2.1 |
| Wheat vermicelli | 2.18 |
| Wheat, bulgur | 2.46 |
| Wheat flour, refined | 2.62 |
| Bajra | 2.67 |
| Barley | 2.68 |
| Amaranth seeds, black | 2.85 |
| Wheat semolina | 3 |
| Amaranth seeds, pale brown | 3.1 |
| Wheat, whole | 3.12 |
| Maize, tender, local | 3.15 |
| Maize, tender, sweet | 3.26 |
| Ragi | 3.37 |
| Samai | 3.43 |
| Jowar | 3.61 |
| Maize, dry | 3.71 |
| Rise flakes | 3.75 |
| Varagu | 3.87 |
| Rice puffed | 4.13 |
| Rice, raw, brown | 4.36 |
| Rice, raw, milled | 4.36 |
| Rice, parboiled, milled | 4.43 |
| **GRAIN AND LEGUMES** | |
| Red gram, dal | 2.32 |
| Lentil whole, brown | 2.4 |
| Red gram, whole | 2.54 |
| Bengal gram, dal | 2.72 |
| Lentil whole, yellowish | 2.81 |
| Green gram, whole | 2.83 |

| | |
|---|---|
| Cowpea, brown | 2.83 |
| Bengal gram, whole | 2.88 |
| Moth bean | 2.93 |
| Green gram, dal | 2.95 |
| Lentil dal | 2.95 |
| Black gram, dal | 3.4 |
| Black gram, whole | 3.06 |
| Rajmah, black | 3.1 |
| Rajmah, red | 3.12 |
| Rice bean | 3.12 |
| Soy bean, brown | 3.21 |
| Rajmah, brown | 3.24 |
| Peas, dry | 3.25 |
| Cowpea, white | 3.25 |
| Soya bean, white | 3.32 |
| Field bean, white | 3.84 |
| Field bean, brown | 3.85 |
| Field bean, black | 4 |
| **GREEN LEAFY VEGETABLES** | |
| Cauliflower leaves | 0.77 |
| Cabbage, Chinese | 2.05 |
| Cabbage, green | 2.11 |
| Cabbage, violet | 2.29 |
| Brussels sprouts | 2.39 |
| Rumex leaves | 2.53 |
| Cabbage, collard greens | 2.78 |
| Drumstick leaves | 2.87 |
| Knol-khol, leaves | 2.9 |
| Beet green | 2.96 |
| Parsley | 3 |
| Lettuce | 3 |
| Amaranth leaves, red | 3.01 |
| Radish leaves | 3.05 |
| Mustard leaves | 3.21 |
| Ponnoganni | 3.25 |
| Betel leaves, small | 3.37 |
| Gogu leaves, green | 3.4 |

--- Author ---
Dr. Prajakta J. Nande

# Clinical and Therapeutic Nutrition Practical Manual 1
For M.Sc. Food Science and Nutrition (Semester-III)

| | | | | |
|---|---|---|---|---|
| Amaranth spinosus, leaves | 3.42 | Jack fruit, raw | 2.95 |
| Amaranth spinosus, green | 3.43 | French bean, hybrid | 2.95 |
| Basella leaves | 3.44 | Parwar | 2.96 |
| Pumpkin leaves, tender | 3.46 | Cucumber, green, elongate | 2.98 |
| Pak choi leaves | 3.48 | Snack gourd, long, dark green | 2.99 |
| Betel leaves, big | 3.48 | Kovai, big | 3.04 |
| Garden cress | 3.5 | Peas, fresh | 3.06 |
| Fenugreek leaves | 3.55 | Bottle gourd, elongate, pale green | 3.08 |
| Amaranth leaves, green | 3.69 | Colocasia, steam, green | 3.08 |
| Agathi leaves | 3.76 | Cucumber, orange, round | 3.11 |
| Amaranth leaves, red and green | 3.76 | Corn, Baby | 3.15 |
| Colocasia leaves, green | 3.78 | French bean, country | 3.15 |
| Gogu leaves, red | 3.8 | Ridge gourd, smooth skin | 3.24 |
| Tamarind leaves, tender | 3.93 | Ridge gourd | 3.27 |
| Spinach | 3.95 | Kovai, small | 3.31 |
| Bathua leaves | 3.98 | Ch-cho-marrow | 3.35 |
| **OTHER VEGETABLES** | | Field bean, tender, broad | 3.36 |
| Knol-khol | 2.01 | Mango, green, raw | 3.39 |
| Plantain, green | 2.09 | Bottle gourd, round, pale green | 3.56 |
| Drumstick | 2.16 | Colocasia, steam, black | 3.56 |
| Celery stalk | 2.21 | Field bean, tender, lean | 3.62 |
| Tomato, green | 2.27 | Bottle gourd, elongate, dark green | 3.65 |
| Ladies finger | 2.51 | Onion, stalk | 3.75 |
| Cucumber, green, short | 2.58 | Cluster bean | 4.17 |
| Snack gourd, long, pale green | 2.62 | Papaya raw | 4.38 |
| Red gram, tender, fresh | 2.63 | Pumpkin, green, cylindrical | 4.48 |
| Tomato, ripe, hybrid | 2.66 | Bitter gourd, jagged, teeth ridges, short | 4.61 |
| Tomato, ripe, local | 2.68 | | |
| Snack gourd, short | 2.79 | Bitter gourd, jagged, smooth ridge, elongate | 4.68 |
| Bean scarlet, tender | 2.83 | | |
| Plantain, steam | 2.83 | bitter gourd, jagged, teeth, elongate | 4.77 |
| Broad beans | 2.83 | Jack fruit, seeds, mature | 5.61 |
| Brinjal-all varieties | 2.85 | **FRUITS** | |
| Pumpkin, orange, round | 2.85 | Lime, sweet, pulp | 0.8 |
| Plantain, flower | 2.86 | Orange, pulp | 1.08 |
| Zucchini, green | 2.87 | Palm fruit, tender | 1.25 |
| Ash gourd | 2.88 | Lemon, juice | 1.35 |
| Capsicum, red | 2.89 | pear | 1.36 |
| Cauliflower | 2.89 | Raisins, dried, golden | 1.56 |
| Zucchini | 2.89 | Apple small, Kashmir | 1.58 |
| Capsicum, green | 2.91 | Plum | 1.61 |
| Capsicum, yellow | 2.93 | Musk melon, orange flesh | 1.65 |
| Tinda, tender | 2.94 | Musk melon, yellow flesh | 1.69 |

**--- Author ---**
Dr. Prajakta J. Nande

# Clinical and Therapeutic Nutrition Practical Manual 1
For M.Sc. Food Science and Nutrition (Semester-III)

| | | | |
|---|---|---|---|
| Peach | 1.76 | Papaya, ripe | 2.85 |
| Pomegranate, maroon seeds | 1.83 | Mangosteen | 2.86 |
| Pummelo | 1.83 | Strawberry | 2.88 |
| Manila, tamarind | 1.85 | Currants, black | 2.89 |
| Water melon, pale green | 1.87 | Litchi | 2.92 |
| Water melon, dark green (sugar baby) | 1.89 | Black berry | 3.03 |
| | | Pineapple | 3.1 |
| Apricot, processed | 1.96 | Karonda fruit | 3.12 |
| Banana, ripe, red | 1.97 | Jack fruit, ripe | 3.22 |
| Custard apple | 1.97 | Jambu fruit, ripe | 3.23 |
| Dates, dry, dark brown | 2 | Soursop | 3.31 |
| Grapes, seedless, oval, black | 2.01 | Sapota | 3.35 |
| Grapes, seedless, round black | 2.06 | Tamarind, pulp | 3.43 |
| Dates, processed | 2 | Apricot, dried | 3.43 |
| Apple, green | 2.1 | Ziziphus | 3.46 |
| Banana, ripe, robusta | 2.14 | Star fruit | 3.89 |
| Dates, dry, pale brown | 2.15 | **ROOTS AND TUBERS** | |
| Phalsa | 2.16 | Radish, round, red skin | 1.43 |
| Cherries, red | 2.2 | Radish, elongate, red skin | 1.62 |
| Raisins, dried, black | 2.2 | Carrot, orange | 1.71 |
| Mango, ripe, banganapalli | 2.21 | Radish, elongate, white skin | 1.73 |
| Banana, ripe, poovam | 2.22 | Carrot, red | 1.74 |
| Grapes, seeded, round, black | 2.24 | Radish, round, white skin | 1.78 |
| Mango, ripe, totapari | 2.27 | Tapioca | 1.92 |
| Banana, ripe, montham | 2.3 | Sweet potato, pink skin | 2.69 |
| Grapes, seeded, round, green | 2.34 | Lotus root | 2.7 |
| Apple, small | 2.39 | Beet root | 2.76 |
| Grapes, seedless, round, green | 2.4 | Potato, brown skin, small | 2.94 |
| Mango, ripe, gulabkhas | 2.41 | Yam, ordinary | 3.09 |
| Bael fruit | 2.43 | Yam, elephant | 3.17 |
| Mango, ripe, paheri | 2.45 | Potato, brown skin, big | 3.23 |
| Grapes, seeded, round,red | 2.49 | Sweet potato, brown skin | 3.26 |
| Wood Apple | 2.51 | Yam, wild | 3.34 |
| Mango, ripe, neelam | 2.54 | Water chestnut | 3.62 |
| Gooseberry | 2.6 | Colocasia | 3.89 |
| Guava, pink flesh | 2.63 | Potato, red skin | 3.92 |
| Avocado fruit | 2.64 | **CONDIMENTS AND SPICES - FRESH** | |
| Guava, white flesh | 2.66 | Onion, big | 1.92 |
| Apple, big | 2.67 | Onion, small | 2.24 |
| Mango, ripe, kesar | 2.7 | Chillies, green-all varieties | 2.64 |
| Rambutan | 2.7 | Curry leaves | 2.81 |
| Fig | 2.8 | Garlic, small clove, Kashmir | 3.07 |
| Mango, ripe, himsagar | 2.82 | Garlic, small clove | 3.27 |

# Clinical and Therapeutic Nutrition Practical Manual 1

For M.Sc. Food Science and Nutrition (Semester-III)

| | | | | |
|---|---|---|---|---|
| Mango ginger | 3.29 | **SUGARS** | | |
| Garlic, big clove | 3.31 | Jaggery, cane | 1 | |
| Mint leaves | 3.32 | Sugarcane, juice | 2.35 | |
| Coriander leaves | 3.42 | **MUSHROOMS** | | |
| Ginger, fresh | 3.78 | Shiitake mushroom, fresh | 3.1 | |
| **CONDIMENTS AND SPICES - DRY** | | Chicken mushroom | 3.18 | |
| Cardamom, black | 1.97 | Button mushroom, fresh | 3.2 | |
| Cardamom, green | 2.39 | **MISCELLANEOUS FOODS** | | |
| Asafoetida | 2.4 | Coconut water | 1.57 | |
| Nutmeg | 2.43 | **MILK AND MILK PRODUCTS** | | |
| Clove | 2.57 | Milk, whole, buffalo | 4.86 | |
| Fenugreek seeds | 2.57 | Khoa | 4.95 | |
| Omum | 2.74 | Paneer | 5.36 | |
| Coriander seeds | 3.05 | Milk, whole, cow | 5.48 | |
| Chillies, red | 3.09 | **EGG AND EGG PRODUCTS** | | |
| Turmeric powder | 3.12 | Egg, poultry, white, raw | 3.62 | |
| Cumin seeds | 3.27 | Egg, country hen, whole, raw | 3.7 | |
| Poppy seeds | 3.41 | Egg, poultry, whole, raw | 3.93 | |
| Mace | 3.78 | Egg, poultry, yolk, raw | 4.05 | |
| Pepper, black | 4.5 | **POULTRY** | | |
| Pippali | 4.97 | Chicken, poultry, wing skinless | 3.15 | |
| **NUTS AND OIL SEEDS** | | Chicken, poultry, thigh, skinless | 3.51 | |
| Sunflower seeds | 2.47 | Chicken, poultry, leg, skinless | 3.71 | |
| Coconut, kernel, dry | 2.69 | Poultry, chicken, liver | 3.81 | |
| Walnut | 2.73 | Country hen, wing, with skin | 3.86 | |
| Pine seeds | 2.74 | Chicken, poultry, breast skinless | 3.89 | |
| Cashew nut | 2.81 | Country hen, leg, with skin | 3.97 | |
| Arecanut, fresh | 2.84 | Country hen, thigh, with skin | 3.99 | |
| Arecanut, dried, red colour | 2.84 | Country hen, breast, with skin | 4.09 | |
| Niger seeds, grey | 2.87 | **ANIMAL MEAT** | | |
| Niger seeds, black | 3.02 | Sheep, spleen | 3.34 | |
| Mustard seeds | 3.03 | Sheep, lungs | 3.37 | |
| Pistachio nut | 3.18 | Goat, liver | 3.5 | |
| Arecanut, dried, brown | 3.18 | Sheep, chops | 3.59 | |
| Coconut, kernel, fresh | 3.2 | Sheep, liver | 3.67 | |
| Gingelly seeds, black | 3.22 | Sheep, liver | 3.67 | |
| Safflower seeds | 3.24 | Goat, chops | 3.71 | |
| Gingelly seeds, white | 3.3 | Goat, spleen | 3.74 | |
| Gingelly seeds, brown | 3.36 | Sheep, heart | 3.81 | |
| Almond | 3.38 | Goat, shoulder | 3.95 | |
| Garden cress, seeds | 3.47 | Goat, heart | 3.97 | |
| Linseeds | 3.48 | Sheep, leg | 4.1 | |
| Ground nut | 3.86 | Sheep, brain | 4.23 | |

## Clinical and Therapeutic Nutrition Practical Manual 1
For M.Sc. Food Science and Nutrition (Semester-III)

| | | | | |
|---|---|---|---|---|
| Sheep, kidney | 4.36 | Mud crab | 3.88 |
| Goat, lungs | 4.51 | Lobster, king | 4.53 |
| Goat, legs | 4.66 | **FRESH WATER FISH AND SHELLFISH** | |
| Goat, brain | 4.68 | Prawns, big | 2.66 |
| Goat, kidney | 4.77 | Catla | 2.88 |
| **MARINE SHELLFISH** | | Gold fish | 3.14 |
| Tiger prawns, orange | 3.4 | Rohu | 3.4 |
| Lobster, brown | 3.43 | Tiger prawns | 3.59 |
| Crab | 3.56 | Freshwater eel | 3.78 |
| Oyster | 3.61 | Cat fish | 3.82 |
| Tiger prawns, brown | 3.79 | Prawns, small | 3.86 |
| Crab, sea | 3.81 | Crabs | 5.17 |

*(Source: T. Longvah, R. Ananthan, K. Bhaskaracharya, K. Venkaiah. Indian Food Composition Tables, National Institute of Nutrition (Indian Council of Medical Research), 259-312, 2017)*

## ANNEXURE - 8

## FATTY ACID AND CHOLESTEROL CONTENT OF FOODS

## TOTAL SATURATED FATTY ACID (TSFA)

| FOOD STUFFS | TSFA (mg/ 100 g) | | |
|---|---|---|---|
| **CEREALS AND MILLETS** | | Ragi | 317 |
| Rice puffed | 46.84 | Rice, raw, brown | 346 |
| Wheat, vermicelli, roasted | 49.95 | Maize, dry | 413 |
| Wheat, vermicelli | 64.59 | Quinoa | 570 |
| Wheat, semolina | 88.87 | Samai | 589 |
| Wheat flour, refined | 98.55 | Bajra | 875 |
| Maize, tender, local | 109 | Amaranth seeds, pale brown | 1140 |
| Maize, tender, sweet | 123 | Amaranth seeds, black | 1280 |
| Rice, parboiled, milled | 150 | **GRAIN LEGUMES** | |
| Jowar | 163 | Lentil whole, yellowish | 76.17 |
| Rice, raw, milled | 184 | Lentil whole, brown | 81.22 |
| Wheat, whole | 191 | Lentil dal | 91.02 |
| Wheat, bulgur | 196 | Horse gram, whole | 135 |
| Wheat flour | 206 | Rice bean | 172 |
| Barley | 232 | Field bean, white | 186 |
| Varagu | 246 | Field bean, black | 188 |
| Rice flakes | 284 | Field bean, brown | 198 |
| | | Rajmah, black | 238 |
| | | Peas, dry | 242 |
| | | Rajmah, brown | 242 |

--- Author ---
Dr. Prajakta J. Nande

# Clinical and Therapeutic Nutrition Practical Manual 1
For M.Sc. Food Science and Nutrition (Semester-III)

| | | | | |
|---|---|---|---|---|
| Green gram, dal | 247 | Pumpkin leaves, tender | 267 |
| Rajmah, red | 256 | Parsley | 345 |
| Red gram, dal | 257 | Colocasia leaves, green | 426 |
| Black gram, whole | 258 | Agathi leaves | 490 |
| Green gram, whole | 274 | Drumstick leaves | 560 |
| Black gram, dal | 276 | **OTHER VEGETABLES** | |
| Red gram, whole | 277 | Peas, fresh | 19.01 |
| Cowpea, brown | 283 | Ash gourd | 25.26 |
| Cowpea, white | 285 | Mango, green, raw | 27.28 |
| Moth bean | 434 | Plantain, stem | 27.45 |
| Bengal gram, whole | 453 | Drumstick | 29.05 |
| Bengal gram, dal | 469 | Bottle gourd, round, pale green | 41.07 |
| Soya bean, white | 3002 | Bamboo shoot, tender | 41.09 |
| Soya bean, brown | 3092 | Bottle gourd, elongate, pale green | 41.44 |
| **GREEN LEAFY VEGETABLES** | | Bottle gourd, elongate, dark green | 42.04 |
| Garden cress | 28.68 | Broad beans | 42.62 |
| Cabbage, Chinese | 33.01 | Ridge gourd, smooth skin | 43.07 |
| Pak choi leaves | 38.98 | Pumpkin, orange, round | 44.58 |
| Cabbage, green | 46.54 | Tomato, green | 46.91 |
| Cabbage, violet | 58.42 | Jack fruit, raw | 47.36 |
| Rumex leaves | 60.92 | Tomato, ripe, hybrid | 47.65 |
| Cabbage, collard greens | 61.87 | Tinda, tender | 48.97 |
| Amaranth spinosus, leaves, green | 85.13 | Pumpkin, green, cylindrical | 53.32 |
| Amaranth spinosus, leaves, red and green mix | 85.96 | Ridge gourd | 54.49 |
| | | Zucchini, yellow | 56.92 |
| Basella leaves | 101 | Plantain, green | 57.13 |
| Knol-khol, leaves | 107 | Celery stalk | 62.79 |
| Beet greens | 108 | Cucumber, green, elongate | 64.17 |
| Cauliflower leaves | 115 | French beans, hybrid | 66.8 |
| Lettuce | 116 | Colocasia, stem, green | 67.53 |
| Bathua leaves | 120 | Cucumber, green, short | 67.77 |
| Mustard leaves | 142 | Kovai, big | 68.84 |
| Radish leaves | 147 | Papaya, raw | 69.15 |
| Tamarind leaves, tender | 176 | Ladies finger | 69.37 |
| Spinach | 183 | French beans, country | 71.07 |
| Amaranth leaves, green | 194 | Brinjal-all varieties | 71.15 |
| Amaranth leaves, red and green mix | 197 | Cucumber, round | 71.9 |
| | | Kovai, small | 75.33 |
| Fenugreek leaves | 199 | Cho-cho-marrow | 76.12 |
| Ponnaganni | 204 | Capsicum, green | 77.03 |
| Amaranth leaves, red | 210 | Tomato, ripe, local | 79.56 |
| Brussels sprouts | 226 | Capsicum, red | 86.39 |
| Betel leaves, small | 238 | Onion, stalk | 92.08 |
| Gogu leaves, red | 243 | Snake gourd, long, pale green | 94.9 |
| Gogu leaves, green | 245 | Snake gourd, long, dark green | 95.87 |
| Betel leaves, big (Kolkata) | 250 | Parwar | 95.93 |

**--- Author ---**
Dr. Prajakta J. Nande

# Clinical and Therapeutic Nutrition Practical Manual 1
## For M.Sc. Food Science and Nutrition (Semester-III)

| | | | | |
|---|---|---|---|---|
| Knol-khol | 97.4 | Grapes, seedless, round, green | 87.11 |
| Snake gourd, short | 100 | Fig | 89.44 |
| Capsicum, yellow | 102 | Litchi | 91.48 |
| Colocasia, stem, black | 103 | Grapes, seeded, round, red | 92.04 |
| Cluster beans | 107 | Grapes, seeded, round, green | 92.42 |
| Cauliflower | 117 | Musk melon, orange flesh | 92.94 |
| Zucchini, green | 119 | Dates, dry, pale brown | 97.03 |
| Bitter gourd, jagged, teeth ridges, short | 139 | Banana, ripe, red | 106 |
| | | Grapes, seeded, round, black | 106 |
| Bitter gourd, jagged, smooth ridges, elongate | 142 | Banana, ripe, montham | 110 |
| | | Banana, ripe, poovam | 113 |
| Bitter gourd, jagged, teeth ridges, elongate | 144 | Banana, ripe, robusta | 114 |
| | | Dates, dry, dark brown | 114 |
| Jack fruit, seed, mature | 146 | Pummelo | 115 |
| Field beans, tender, lean | 175 | Apple, green | 116 |
| Field beans, tender, broad | 182 | Zizyphus | 119 |
| Corn, baby | 211 | Raisins, dried, golden | 121 |
| Red gram, tender, fresh | 211 | Cherries, red | 125 |
| Bean scarlet, tender | 266 | Grapes, seedless, round, black | 129 |
| Plantain, flower | 273 | Soursop | 135 |
| **FRUITS** | | Custard apple | 138 |
| Plum | 20.05 | Rambutan | 144 |
| Star fruit | 20.77 | Apple, small | 149 |
| Peach | 23.9 | Dates, processed | 149 |
| Guava, pink flesh | 27.18 | Apple, big | 154 |
| Tamarind, pulp | 27.26 | Phalsa | 164 |
| Manila tamarind | 27.81 | Mango, ripe, banganapalli | 170 |
| Palm fruit, tender | 33.36 | Mango, ripe, kesar | 172 |
| Orange, pulp | 37.11 | Mango, ripe, himsagar | 174 |
| Jack fruit, ripe | 37.66 | Mango, ripe, totapari | 175 |
| Gooseberry | 38.48 | Apple, small, Kashmir | 176 |
| Water melon, dark green | 39.7 | Mangosteen | 176 |
| Pomegranate, maroon seeds | 42.5 | Mango, ripe, neelam | 178 |
| Grapes, seedless, oval, black | 45.63 | Mango, ripe, gulabkhas | 180 |
| Guava, white flesh | 49.3 | Apricot, processed | 185 |
| Water melon, pale green | 50.33 | Mango, ripe, paheri | 186 |
| Pineapple | 51.09 | Bael fruit | 190 |
| Papaya, ripe | 56.08 | Black berry | 195 |
| Raisins, dried, black | 62.47 | Apricot, dried | 200 |
| Strawberry | 66.21 | Lemon, juice | 202 |
| Jambu fruit, ripe | 66.49 | Sapota | 389 |
| Karonda fruit | 66.81 | Wood apple | 877 |
| Pear | 75.94 | Avocado fruit | 1237 |
| Lime, sweet, pulp | 76.4 | **ROOTS AND TUBERS** | |
| Musk melon, yellow flesh | 79 | Beet root | 31.17 |
| Currants, black | 83.33 | Yam, elephant | 35.72 |

**--- Author ---**
Dr. Prajakta J. Nande

# Clinical and Therapeutic Nutrition Practical Manual 1
## For M.Sc. Food Science and Nutrition (Semester-III)

| | |
|---|---|
| Potato, red skin | 39.87 |
| Radish, round, white skin | 41.15 |
| Colocasia | 41.84 |
| Yam, ordinary | 42.63 |
| Radish, elongate, red skin | 42.65 |
| Potato, brown skin, big | 43.56 |
| Radish, elongate, white skin | 43.88 |
| Potato, brown skin, small | 44.03 |
| Radish, round, red skin | 46.08 |
| Tapioca | 59.5 |
| Sweet potato, brown skin | 66.1 |
| Yam, wild | 79.51 |
| Water chestnut | 87.42 |
| Carrot, orange | 87.71 |
| Carrot, red | 88.91 |
| Sweet potato, pink skin | 101 |
| Lotus root | 249 |
| **CONDIMENTS AND SPICES- FRESH** | |
| Garlic, small clove | 32.63 |
| Garlic, big clove | 33.52 |
| Garlic, single clove, Kashmir | 34.76 |
| Onion, small | 41.01 |
| Onion, big | 60.81 |
| Mint leaves | 125 |
| Chillies green-all varieties | 129 |
| Mango ginger | 177 |
| Coriander leaves | 228 |
| Ginger, fresh | 231 |
| Curry leaves | 267 |
| **CONDIMENTS AND SPICES - DRY** | |
| Asafoetida | 242 |
| Cardamom, black | 493 |
| Pippali | 602 |
| Cumin seeds | 619 |
| Cardamom, green | 624 |
| Pepper, black | 654 |
| Fenugreek seeds | 770 |
| Coriander seeds | 952 |
| Omum | 1112 |
| Chillies, red | 1141 |
| Turmeric powder | 1634 |
| Poppy seeds | 2074 |
| Cloves | 2679 |
| Nutmeg | 3359 |
| Mace | 9309 |
| **NUTS AND OIL SEEDS** | |
| Arecanut, dried, red color | 1674 |
| Mustard seeds | 2112 |
| Safflower seeds | 2548 |
| Arecanut, dried, brown | 2605 |
| Linseeds | 2968 |
| Arecanut, fresh | 3389 |
| Pine seeds | 3801 |
| Pistachio nut | 4043 |
| Garden cress, seeds | 4101 |
| Almond | 4358 |
| Walnut | 5208 |
| Niger seeds, black | 5945 |
| Sunflower seeds | 6159 |
| Gingelly seeds, brown | 6250 |
| Gingelly seeds, black | 6317 |
| Gingelly seeds, white | 6430 |
| Cashew nut | 7816 |
| Groundnut | 8144 |
| Niger seeds, gray | 9737 |
| Coconut kernel, fresh | 28048 |
| Coconut kernel, dry | 43138 |
| **SUGAR** | |
| Jaggery, cane | 69.23 |
| Sugarcane, juice | 140 |
| **MUSHROOMS** | |
| Chicken mushroom, fresh | 59.6 |
| Button mushroom, fresh | 62.89 |
| Shiitake mushroom, fresh | 116 |
| **MISCELLANEOUS FOODS** | |
| Coconut water | 93.49 |
| **MILK AND MILK PRODUCTS** | |
| Milk,whole, cow | 2707 |
| Milk,whole, buffalo | 4630 |
| Paneer | 8851 |
| Khoa | 12936 |
| **EGG AND EGG PRODUCTS** | |
| Eggs, poultry, whole, raw | 2958 |
| Egg, country hen, whole, raw | 3792 |
| Egg, poultry, yolk, raw | 8580 |
| **POULTRY** | |
| Chicken, poultry, breast, skinless | 816 |
| Chicken, poultry, thigh, skinless | 1071 |
| Chicken, poultry, legs, skinless | 1157 |
| Chicken, poultry, wing, skinless | 1241 |
| Poultry, chicken, liver | 1328 |

--- **Author** ---
Dr. Prajakta J. Nande

# Clinical and Therapeutic Nutrition Practical Manual 1
For M.Sc. Food Science and Nutrition (Semester-III)

| ANIMAL MEAT | |
|---|---|
| Goat, legs | 816 |
| Goat, spleen | 816 |
| Goat, chops | 1071 |
| Goat, liver | 1071 |
| Goat, shoulder | 1157 |
| Goat, heart | 1157 |
| Beef, spleen | 1160 |
| Pork, kidneys | 1169 |
| Beef, lungs | 1198 |
| Goat, brain | 1241 |
| Goat, kidneys | 1241 |
| Pork, spleen | 1245 |
| Pork, lungs | 1247 |
| Goat, lungs | 1328 |
| Beef, shoulder | 1328 |
| Beef, heart | 1479 |
| Beef, liver | 1543 |
| Pork, heart | 1575 |
| Beef, kidney | 1743 |
| Beef, brain | 2490 |
| Beef, round (leg) | 2998 |
| Beef, chops | 3031 |
| Pork, stomach | 3327 |
| Pork, chops | 4803 |

| | |
|---|---|
| Pork, shoulder | 6887 |
| **MARINE FISH** | |
| Bombay duck | 398 |
| Mural | 495 |
| Tuna | 660 |
| Sardine | 1250 |
| Pomfret, black | 2229 |
| Pomfret, white | 2669 |
| Salmon | 4305 |
| **MARINE SHELLFISH** | |
| Lobster, brown | 106 |
| Crab, sea | 129 |
| Lobster, king size | 174 |
| Tiger prawns, orange | 177 |
| Crab | 214 |
| **FRESH WATER FISH AND SHELLFISH** | |
| Prawns, big | 86.86 |
| Prawns, small | 197 |
| Crab | 214 |
| Catla | 1670 |
| Rohu | 2047 |
| **FATTY FISH** | |
| Hilsa | 9286 |

*(Source: T. Longvah, R. Ananthan, K. Bhaskaracharya, K. Venkaiah. Indian Food Composition Tables, National Institute of Nutrition (Indian Council of Medical Research) 189-255, 2017)*

# TOTAL MONOUNSATURATED FATTY ACID (TMUFA)

| FOOD STUFFS | TMUFA (mg/ 100 g) |
|---|---|
| **CEREALS AND MILLETS** | |
| Wheat, vermicelli, roasted | 28.84 |
| Wheat, vermicelli | 36.06 |
| Rice puffed | 39.77 |
| Wheat flour, refined | 50.64 |
| Wheat, semolina | 67.34 |
| Rice, parboiled, milled | 86.66 |
| Barley | 90.79 |
| Rice, raw, milled | 117 |
| Wheat, whole | 141 |
| Maize, tender, local | 147 |

| | |
|---|---|
| Wheat flour | 149 |
| Wheat, bulgur | 152 |
| Maize tender, sweet | 176 |
| Rice, raw, brown | 203 |
| Varagu | 297 |
| Jowar | 314 |
| Rice flakes | 425 |
| Ragi | 585 |
| Maize, dry | 706 |
| Samai | 868 |
| Amaranth seeds, black | 1033 |
| Amaranth seeds, pale brown | 1043 |
| Bajra | 1047 |
| Quinoa | 1424 |

--- Author ---
Dr. Prajakta J. Nande

# Clinical and Therapeutic Nutrition Practical Manual 1
For M.Sc. Food Science and Nutrition (Semester-III)

| GRAIN LEGUMES | |
|---|---|
| Green gram, whole | 27.22 |
| Green gram, dal | 35.85 |
| Cowpea, brown | 60.58 |
| Field bean, white | 61.57 |
| Horse gram, whole | 68.89 |
| Cowpea, white | 70.12 |
| Moth bean | 72.25 |
| Red gram, whole | 78.55 |
| Field bean, black | 80.07 |
| Rajmah, red | 87.84 |
| Red gram, dal | 89.94 |
| Rajmah, brown | 91.76 |
| Lentil whole, yellowish | 92.18 |
| Lentil whole, brown | 102 |
| Rajmah, black | 105 |
| Lentil dal | 112 |
| Field bean, brown | 127 |
| Black gram, whole | 161 |
| Black gram, dal | 186 |
| Rice bean | 357 |
| Peas, dry | 398 |
| Bengal gram, dal | 876 |
| Bengal gram, whole | 890 |
| Soya bean, brown | 4558 |
| Soya bean, white | 4817 |
| **GREEN LEAFY VEGETABLES** | |
| Garden cress | 8.24 |
| Bathua leaves | 8.61 |
| Cabbage, Chinese | 15.97 |
| Amaranth spinosus, leaves, green | 16.46 |
| Pumpkin leaves, tender | 17.67 |
| Amaranth spinosus, leaves, red and green mix | 17.77 |
| Rumex leaves | 18.68 |
| Knol-khol leaves | 18.91 |
| Fenugreek leaves | 20.15 |
| Cauliflower leaves | 20.8 |
| Lettuce | 22.22 |
| Pak choi leaves | 23.03 |
| Radish leaves | 26.93 |
| Mustard leaves | 27.56 |
| Cabbage, green | 30.05 |
| Parsley | 32.94 |
| Ponnaganni | 33.38 |
| Cabbage, collard greens | 37.19 |

| | |
|---|---|
| Gogu leaves, green | 39.85 |
| Cabbage, violet | 41.14 |
| Tamarind leaves, tender | 42.3 |
| Spinach | 42.83 |
| Gogu leaves, red | 45.93 |
| Amaranth leaves, red and green mix | 46.59 |
| Amaranth leaves, red | 47.34 |
| Colocasia leaves, green | 47.63 |
| Amaranth leaves, green | 48.87 |
| Basella leaves | 51.28 |
| Agathi leaves | 57.67 |
| Beet greens | 79.51 |
| Betel leaves, small | 82.67 |
| Brussels sprouts | 88.69 |
| Betel leaves, big (Kolkata) | 93.43 |
| Drumstick leaves | 102 |
| **OTHER VEGETABLES** | |
| Ridge gourd | 2.57 |
| Plantain, stem | 2.71 |
| Ridge gourd, smooth skin | 2.95 |
| Snake gourd, short | 2.96 |
| Bottle gourd, round, pale green | 3.47 |
| Bottle gourd, elongate, pale green | 3.54 |
| Kovai, big | 4.35 |
| Kovai, small | 4.51 |
| Snake gourd, long, dark green | 4.77 |
| Snake gourd, long, pale green | 4.89 |
| Onion, stalk | 5.52 |
| Celery stalk | 5.94 |
| Tinda, tender | 6.28 |
| Bitter gourd, jagged, smooth ridges, elongate | 6.63 |
| Cucumber, round | 7.41 |
| Ash gourd | 7.43 |
| Bamboo shoot, tender | 7.45 |
| Bitter gourd, jagged, teeth ridges, short | 7.61 |
| Colocasia, stem, green | 7.78 |
| Bitter gourd, jagged, teeth ridges, elongate | 8.08 |
| Ladies finger | 8.1 |
| Cucumber, green, short | 8.4 |
| Broad beans | 8.53 |
| Bottle gourd, elongate, dark | 9.05 |

--- **Author** ---
Dr. Prajakta J. Nande

# Clinical and Therapeutic Nutrition Practical Manual 1
For M.Sc. Food Science and Nutrition (Semester-III)

| | | | |
|---|---|---|---|
| green | | Banana, ripe, robusta | 20.8 |
| Mango, green, raw | 9.25 | Dates, dry, dark brown | 21 |
| Cucumber, green, elongate | 10.57 | Musk melon, yellow flesh | 21.12 |
| French beans, country | 11.13 | Apricot, processed | 23.33 |
| French beans, hybrid | 11.85 | Gooseberry | 23.93 |
| Capsicum, green | 12.71 | Karonda fruit | 24.12 |
| Parwar | 13.19 | Pear | 24.26 |
| Cho-cho-marrow | 13.3 | Water melon, dark green | 24.84 |
| Colocasia, stem, black | 14.98 | Musk melon, orange flesh | 25.18 |
| Plantain, green | 16.21 | Papaya, ripe | 26.35 |
| Jack fruit, seed, mature | 16.28 | Dates, dry, pale brown | 30.43 |
| Zucchini, yellow | 21.32 | Pineapple | 31.15 |
| Brinjal-all varieties | 21.45 | Banana, ripe, poovam | 32.29 |
| Pumpkin, orange, round | 22.02 | Raisins, dried, golden | 32.64 |
| Cauliflower | 24.83 | Manila tamarind | 33.45 |
| Pumpkin, green, cylindrical | 25.17 | Star fruit | 33.62 |
| Field beans, tender, lean | 26.28 | Grapes, seedless, oval, black | 33.96 |
| Peas, fresh | 28.75 | Tamarind, pulp | 34.89 |
| Cluster beans | 30.24 | Lime, sweet,pulp | 35.18 |
| Tomato, ripe, hybrid | 30.5 | Guava, white flesh | 35.72 |
| Knol-khol | 31.62 | Palm fruit, tender | 38.32 |
| Plantain, flower | 31.69 | Soursop | 38.45 |
| Field beans, tender, broad | 33.91 | Pomegranate, maroon seeds | 38.51 |
| Tomato, green | 36.91 | Custard apple | 39.47 |
| Zucchini, green | 37.83 | Apple, green | 40.99 |
| Papaya, raw | 44.53 | Pummelo | 41 |
| Drumstick | 46.4 | Fig | 41.38 |
| Bean scarlet, tender | 46.81 | Jack fruit, ripe | 44.27 |
| Capsicum, red | 47.65 | Litchi | 45.63 |
| Red gram, tender, fresh | 51.13 | Raisins, dried, black | 46.53 |
| Capsicum, yellow | 55.55 | Dates, processed | 46.88 |
| Tomato, ripe, local | 58.66 | Apple, small | 46.96 |
| Jack fruit, raw | 115 | Lemon, juice | 47.4 |
| Corn, baby | 392 | Apple, small, Kashmir | 50.63 |
| **FRUITS** | | Apple, big | 51.13 |
| Grapes, seedless, round, green | 9.33 | Strawberry | 77.87 |
| Water melon, pale green | 10.96 | Black berry | 87.71 |
| Grapes, seeded, round, green | 11.1 | Cherries, red | 95.85 |
| Grapes, seeded, round, red | 12.18 | Bael fruit | 112 |
| Grapes, seeded, round, black | 12.73 | Apricot, dried | 118 |
| Grapes, seedless, round, black | 12.97 | Zizyphus | 126 |
| Guava, pink flesh | 13.97 | Mango, ripe, banganapalli | 134 |
| Banana, ripe, montham | 14.38 | Mango, ripe, himsagar | 134 |
| Banana, ripe, red | 17.78 | Mango, ripe, gulabkhas | 145 |
| Orange, pulp | 19.26 | Mango, ripe, neelam | 147 |
| Jambu fruit, ripe | 20.73 | Rambutan | 160 |

--- **Author** ---
Dr. Prajakta J. Nande

# Clinical and Therapeutic Nutrition Practical Manual 1
## For M.Sc. Food Science and Nutrition (Semester-III)

| | | | |
|---|---|---|---|
| Mangosteen | 165 | Turmeric powder | 448 |
| Phalsa | 167 | Pepper, black | 463 |
| Mango, ripe, totapari | 168 | Cloves | 605 |
| Mango, ripe, kesar | 169 | Fenugreek seeds | 675 |
| Plum | 170 | Chillies, red | 718 |
| Mango, ripe, paheri | 192 | Cardamom, green | 891 |
| Peach | 209 | Cardamom, black | 1083 |
| Sapota | 255 | Nutmeg | 1367 |
| Currants, black | 302 | Omum | 1387 |
| Wood Apple | 595 | Poppy seeds | 2353 |
| Avocado fruit | 8710 | Cumin seeds | 8379 |
| **ROOTS AND TUBERS** | | Mace | 9302 |
| Sweet potato, brown skin | 4.1 | Coriander seeds | 10769 |
| Radish, round, red skin | 6.08 | **NUTS AND OIL SEEDS** | |
| Yam, elephant | 6.75 | Arecanut, dried, brown | 466 |
| Radish, elongate, red skin | 7.29 | Arecanut, fresh | 599 |
| Radish, elongate, white skin | 9.14 | Arecanut, dried, red color | 897 |
| Tapioca | 9.2 | Coconut kernel, fresh | 2449 |
| Sweet potato, pink skin | 9.35 | Safflower seeds | 3589 |
| Potato, brown skin, small | 11.94 | Coconut kernel, dry | 3710 |
| Radish, round, white skin | 12.64 | Niger seeds, gray | 4452 |
| Yam, ordinary | 13.04 | Linseeds | 5112 |
| Potato, brown skin, big | 13.82 | Garden cress, seeds | 8131 |
| Potato, red skin | 14.91 | Niger seeds, black | 9033 |
| Carrot, red | 18.27 | Walnut | 11316 |
| Carrot, orange | 21.01 | Gingelly seeds, black | 15605 |
| Beet root | 21.26 | Gingelly seeds, brown | 15989 |
| Yam, wild | 22.66 | Gingelly seeds, white | 16124 |
| Colocasia | 22.92 | Sunflower seeds | 17803 |
| Lotus root | 84.12 | Ground nut | 18337 |
| Water chestnut | 105 | Pine seeds | 18624 |
| **CONDIMENTS AND SPICES - FRESH** | | Pistachio nut | 18922 |
| Coriander leaves | 9.06 | Mustard seeds | 21032 |
| Garlic, single clove, Kashmir | 10.83 | Cashew nut | 27907 |
| Mint leaves | 13.23 | Almond | 38336 |
| Garlic, small clove | 13.55 | **SUGAR** | |
| Garlic, big clove | 14.24 | Jaggery, cane | 21.67 |
| Onion, small | 15.83 | Sugarcane, juice | 29.7 |
| Chillies green-all varieties | 32.2 | **MUSHROOMS** | |
| Onion, big | 39.36 | Chicken mushroom, fresh | 3.02 |
| Curry leaves | 44.57 | Button mushroom, fresh | 6.82 |
| Mango ginger | 52.26 | Shiitake mushroom, fresh | 12.33 |
| Ginger, fresh | 67.97 | **MISCELLANEOUS FOODS** | |
| **CONDIMENTS AND SPICES - DRY** | | Coconut water | 24.11 |
| Asafoetida | 250 | **MILK AND MILK PRODUCTS** | |
| Pippali | 327 | Milk, whole, cow | 1214 |

--- Author ---
Dr. Prajakta J. Nande

# Clinical and Therapeutic Nutrition Practical Manual 1
For M.Sc. Food Science and Nutrition (Semester-III)

| | | | |
|---|---|---|---|
| Milk, whole, buffalo | 1919 | Beef, chops | 2680 |
| Paneer | 4300 | Goat, legs | 3038 |
| Khoa | 5664 | Beef, round (leg) | 3280 |
| **EGG AND EGG PRODUCTS** | | Goat, shoulder meat | 4902 |
| Eggs, poultry, whole, raw | 3481 | Pork, chops | 4972 |
| Egg, country hen, whole, raw | 5061 | Beef, shoulder | 6227 |
| Egg, poultry, yolk, raw | 10068 | Pork, shoulder | 8114 |
| **POULTRY** | | **MARINE FISH** | |
| Poultry, chicken, liver | 681 | Mural | 80.76 |
| Chicken, poultry, breast, skinless | 991 | Bombay duck | 171 |
| Chicken, poultry, thigh, skinless | 1461 | Tuna | 300 |
| Chicken, poultry, legs, skinless | 1506 | Sardine | 630 |
| Chicken, poultry, wing, skinless | 1777 | Pomfret, black | 972 |
| **ANIMAL MEAT** | | Pomfret, white | 1049 |
| Beef, spleen | 480 | Salmon | 2453 |
| Goat, kidneys | 566 | **MARINE SHELLFISH** | |
| Goat, spleen | 616 | Crab, sea | 64.32 |
| Beef, lungs | 647 | Lobster, brown | 72.73 |
| Pork, stomach | 700 | Tiger prawns, orange | 88.3 |
| Pork, spleen | 820 | Lobster, king size | 129 |
| Beef, liver | 826 | Crab | 140 |
| Beef, kidney | 835 | **FRESH WATER FISH AND SHELLFISH** | |
| Pork, kidneys | 846 | | |
| Beef, heart | 848 | Prawns, big | 56.77 |
| Pork, lungs | 867 | Crab | 140 |
| Goat, lungs | 894 | Prawns, small | 152 |
| Goat, liver | 921 | Catla | 1237 |
| Goat, heart | 1025 | Rohu | 2618 |
| Pork, heart | 1247 | **FATTY FISH** | |
| Goat, brain | 1447 | Hilsa | 6021 |
| Beef, brain | 1869 | | |
| Goat, chops | 2346 | | |

*(Source: T. Longvah, R. Ananthan, K. Bhaskaracharya, K. Venkaiah. Indian Food Composition Tables, National Institute of Nutrition (Indian Council of Medical Research) 189-255, 2017)*

# TOTAL POLYUNSATURATED FATTY ACID (TPUFA)

| FOOD STUFFS | TPUFA (mg/ 100 g) | | |
|---|---|---|---|
| **CEREALS AND MILLETS** | | Wheat, vermicelli | 220 |
| Rice puffed | 44.8 | Rice, raw, milled | 253 |
| Wheat, vermicelli, roasted | 170 | Maize, tender, sweet | 300 |
| Rice, parboiled, milled | 216 | Wheat, semolina | 325 |
| | | Wheat flour, refined | 343 |
| | | Maize, tender, local | 347 |
| | | Ragi | 431 |

# Clinical and Therapeutic Nutrition Practical Manual 1
For M.Sc. Food Science and Nutrition (Semester-III)

| | | | |
|---|---|---|---|
| Rice, raw, brown | 506 | Cabbage, collard greens | 117 |
| Jowar | 524 | Pak choi leaves | 138 |
| Barley | 575 | Knol-khol, leaves | 154 |
| Rice flakes | 577 | Amaranth spinosus, leaves, red and green mix | 168 |
| Varagu | 597 | Amaranth spinosus, leaves, green | 186 |
| Wheat, whole | 654 | Rumex leaves | 188 |
| Wheat, bulgur | 700 | Basella leaves | 203 |
| Wheat flour | 742 | Lettuce | 208 |
| Samai | 1277 | Bathua leaves | 219 |
| Maize, dry | 1606 | Cauliflower leaves | 224 |
| Bajra | 1984 | Radish leaves | 248 |
| Amaranth seeds, pale brown | 2266 | Ponnaganni | 250 |
| Amaranth seeds, black | 2279 | Betel leaves, big (Kolkata) | 256 |
| Quinoa | 2406 | Betel leaves, small | 277 |
| **GRAIN LEGUMES** | | Spinach | 295 |
| Rice bean | 62.93 | Tamarind leaves, tender | 306 |
| Horse gram, whole | 258 | Beet greens | 308 |
| Lentil whole, yellowish | 274 | Pumpkin leaves, tender | 313 |
| Lentil whole, brown | 277 | Mustard leaves | 323 |
| Lentil dal | 336 | Amaranth leaves, red | 326 |
| Field bean, brown | 460 | Amaranth leaves, red and green mix | 332 |
| Field bean, black | 468 | Amaranth leaves, green | 358 |
| Field bean, white | 503 | Fenugreek leaves | 445 |
| Green gram, dal | 534 | Parsley | 476 |
| Cowpea, brown | 550 | Agathi leaves | 532 |
| Cowpea, white | 557 | Gogu leaves, red | 567 |
| Green gram, whole | 611 | Gogu leaves, green | 584 |
| Red gram, whole | 637 | Drumstick leaves | 668 |
| Red gram, dal | 651 | Colocasia leaves, green | 689 |
| Black gram, whole | 718 | **OTHER VEGETABLES** | |
| Black gram, dal | 742 | Cho-cho-marrow | 22.58 |
| Rajmah, black | 827 | Drumstick | 27.21 |
| Moth bean | 848 | Plantain, stem | 28.5 |
| Peas, dry | 873 | Mango, green, raw | 30.13 |
| Rajmah, brown | 896 | Bitter gourd, jagged, teeth ridges, elongate | 40.78 |
| Rajmah, red | 931 | Bamboo shoot, tender | 51.46 |
| Bengal gram, whole | 2337 | Cucumber, green, short | 51.83 |
| Bengal gram, dal | 2476 | Bottle gourd, elongate, dark green | 52.92 |
| Soya bean, white | 11071 | Bitter gourd, jagged, teeth ridges, short | 55.2 |
| Soya bean, brown | 11279 | Peas, fresh | 56.24 |
| **GREEN LEAFY VEGETABLES** | | Ridge gourd, smooth skin | 57.98 |
| Cabbage, Chinese | 55.01 | Bitter gourd, jagged, smooth | 59.25 |
| Garden cress | 58.71 | | |
| Brussels sprouts | 84.92 | | |
| Cabbage, green | 91.4 | | |
| Cabbage, violet | 112 | | |

--- Author ---
Dr. Prajakta J. Nande

# Clinical and Therapeutic Nutrition Practical Manual 1
## For M.Sc. Food Science and Nutrition (Semester-III)

| | | | |
|---|---|---|---|
| ridges, elongate | | **FRUITS** | |
| Pumpkin, orange, round | 62.73 | Currants, black | 13.06 |
| Bottle gourd, round, pale green | 63.46 | Tamarind, pulp | 17.85 |
| Broad beans | 64.85 | Manila tamarind | 19.49 |
| Bottle gourd, elongate, pale green | 64.94 | Zizyphus | 35.25 |
| Pumpkin, green, cylindrical | 65.51 | Jack fruit, ripe | 38.07 |
| Cucumber, green, elongate | 67.93 | Orange, pulp | 47.63 |
| Cucumber, round | 68.7 | Papaya, ripe | 48.24 |
| Papaya, raw | 75.64 | Pineapple | 48.76 |
| Tinda, tender | 76.11 | Jambu fruit, ripe | 48.77 |
| Ash gourd | 76.47 | Pomegranate, maroon seeds | 49.99 |
| Snake gourd, long, pale green | 97.54 | Karonda fruit | 52.6 |
| Kovai, big | 98.82 | Plum | 59.08 |
| Onion, stalk | 98.98 | Peach | 62.61 |
| Snake gourd, long, dark green | 99 | Water melon, pale green | 65.38 |
| Snake gourd, short | 105 | Water melon, dark green | 67.46 |
| Jack fruit, raw | 107 | Gooseberry | 75.24 |
| Plantain, green | 107 | Palm fruit, tender | 76.42 |
| Ladies finger | 109 | Litchi | 78.89 |
| Tomato, green | 109 | Lime, sweet, pulp | 84.41 |
| Colocasia, stem, green | 110 | Mango, ripe, paheri | 86.32 |
| Kovai, small | 112 | Mangosteen | 88.6 |
| Parwar | 112 | Mango, ripe, totapari | 88.7 |
| Zucchini, yellow | 114 | Guava, pink flesh | 91.65 |
| Tomato, ripe, hybrid | 119 | Fig | 97.09 |
| French beans, country | 127 | Mango, ripe, gulabkhas | 99.3 |
| Knol-khol | 130 | Pear | 101 |
| Celery stalk | 131 | Banana, ripe, red | 108 |
| French beans, hybrid | 135 | Grapes, seedless, round, green | 113 |
| Cluster beans | 148 | Musk melon, yellow flesh | 114 |
| Brinjal-all varieties | 149 | Mango, ripe, kesar | 115 |
| Colocasia, stem, black | 154 | Mango, ripe, neelam | 116 |
| Capsicum, green | 172 | Grapes, seeded, round, green | 119 |
| Jack fruit, seed, mature | 181 | Raisins, dried, golden | 125 |
| Plantain, flower | 198 | Banana, ripe, robusta | 127 |
| Capsicum, yellow | 201 | Mango, ripe, himsagar | 127 |
| Tomato, ripe, local | 208 | Soursop | 130 |
| Cauliflower | 216 | Banana, ripe, montham | 132 |
| Capsicum, red | 217 | Custard apple | 132 |
| Zucchini, green | 251 | Grapes, seeded, round, red | 132 |
| Field beans, tender, lean | 281 | Mango, ripe, banganapalli | 132 |
| Field beans, tender, broad | 301 | Banana, ripe, poovam | 135 |
| Bean scarlet, tender | 429 | Dates, processed | 136 |
| Corn, baby | 459 | Grapes, seeded, round, black | 139 |
| Red gram, tender, fresh | 474 | Dates, dry, dark brown | 145 |
| Ridge gourd | 5508 | Bael fruit | 154 |

--- **Author** ---
Dr. Prajakta J. Nande

# Clinical and Therapeutic Nutrition Practical Manual 1
## For M.Sc. Food Science and Nutrition (Semester-III)

| | |
|---|---|
| Dates, dry, pale brown | 159 |
| Musk melon, orange flesh | 159 |
| Raisins, dried, black | 159 |
| Grapes, seedless, round, black | 162 |
| Guava, white flesh | 176 |
| Grapes, seedless, oval, black | 183 |
| Cherries, red | 187 |
| Pummelo | 187 |
| Star fruit | 191 |
| Apple, green | 223 |
| Apple, small | 224 |
| Black berry | 234 |
| Apple, small, Kashmir | 253 |
| Apple, big | 282 |
| Apricot, dried | 286 |
| Strawberry | 291 |
| Apricot, processed | 319 |
| Lemon, juice | 353 |
| Sapota | 358 |
| Rambutan | 362 |
| Phalsa | 381 |
| Avocado fruit | 1141 |
| Wood apple | 1435 |
| **ROOTS AND TUBERS** | |
| Radish, elongate, white skin | 53.64 |
| Radish, elongate, red skin | 56.73 |
| Radish, round, white skin | 62.26 |
| Beet root | 64.21 |
| Yam, ordinary | 72.34 |
| Yam, elephant | 73.52 |
| Radish, round, red skin | 75.85 |
| Colocasia | 77.41 |
| Tapioca | 91.29 |
| Water chestnut | 104 |
| Sweet potato, brown skin | 116 |
| Potato, red skin | 121 |
| Potato, brown skin, small | 128 |
| Potato, brown skin, big | 129 |
| Yam, wild | 142 |
| Sweet potato, pink skin | 180 |
| Carrot, orange | 266 |
| Carrot, red | 270 |
| Lotus root | 414 |
| **CONDIMENTS AND SPICES- FRESH** | |
| Garlic, small clove | 61.82 |
| Garlic, big clove | 66.9 |

| | |
|---|---|
| Onion, small | 71.16 |
| Garlic, single clove, Kashmir | 82.4 |
| Onion, big | 107 |
| Coriander leaves | 320 |
| Mango ginger | 334 |
| Mint leaves | 352 |
| Chillies green-all varieties | 413 |
| Curry leaves | 569 |
| Ginger, fresh | 831 |
| **CONDIMENTS AND SPICES - DRY** | |
| Nutmeg | 379 |
| Asafoetida | 514 |
| Cardamom, black | 517 |
| Cardamom, green | 583 |
| Pippali | 885 |
| Pepper, black | 1076 |
| Turmeric powder | 1940 |
| Coriander seeds | 2247 |
| Fenugreek seeds | 3133 |
| Chillies, red | 3263 |
| Cloves | 3428 |
| Cumin seeds | 4313 |
| Mace | 4731 |
| Omum | 5193 |
| Poppy seeds | 13847 |
| **NUTS AND OIL SEEDS** | |
| Arecanut, dried, brown | 403 |
| Arecanut, fresh | 522 |
| Coconut kernel, fresh | 639 |
| Arecanut, dried, red color | 918 |
| Coconut kernel, dry | 929 |
| Gingelly seeds, brown | 1907 |
| Cashew nut | 7482 |
| Mustard seeds | 8910 |
| Garden cress, seeds | 10464 |
| Ground nut | 11584 |
| Pistachio nut | 11946 |
| Almond | 13215 |
| Linseeds | 16147 |
| Gingelly seeds, white | 18597 |
| Safflower seeds | 18781 |
| Gingelly seeds, black | 19259 |
| Niger seeds, black | 21935 |
| Niger seeds, gray | 23564 |
| Pine seeds | 24202 |
| Sunflower seeds | 25580 |

--- **Author** ---
Dr. Prajakta J. Nande

# Clinical and Therapeutic Nutrition Practical Manual 1
For M.Sc. Food Science and Nutrition (Semester-III)

| | |
|---|---|
| Walnut | 44915 |
| **SUGAR** | |
| Jaggery, cane | 33.1 |
| Sugarcane, juice | 173 |
| **MUSHROOMS** | |
| Chicken mushroom, fresh | 137 |
| Button mushroom, fresh | 263 |
| Shiitake mushroom, fresh | 480 |
| **MISCELLANEOUS FOODS** | |
| Coconut water | 3.73 |
| **MILK AND MILK PRODUCTS** | |
| Milk, whole, cow | 138 |
| Milk, whole, buffalo | 200 |
| Paneer | 439 |
| Khoa | 790 |
| **EGG AND EGG PRODUCTS** | |
| Eggs, poultry, whole, raw | 1152 |
| Egg, country hen, whole, raw | 1936 |
| Egg, poultry, yolk, raw | 3238 |
| **POULTRY** | |
| Chicken, poultry, breast, skinless | 367 |
| Chicken, poultry, thigh, skinless | 520 |
| Chicken, poultry, wing, skinless | 658 |
| Chicken, poultry, legs, skinless | 661 |
| Poultry, chicken, liver | 1013 |
| **ANIMAL MEAT** | |
| Beef, lungs | 244 |
| Goat, chops | 259 |
| Beef, kidney | 291 |
| Goat, spleen | 352 |
| Goat, lungs | 374 |
| Beef, spleen | 393 |
| Pork, spleen | 397 |
| Goat, heart | 427 |
| Beef, chops | 437 |
| Pork, lungs | 469 |
| Goat, kidneys | 480 |

| | |
|---|---|
| Beef, round (leg) | 480 |
| Beef, heart | 490 |
| Beef, liver | 566 |
| Goat, legs | 567 |
| Goat, shoulder | 643 |
| Pork, chops | 660 |
| Pork, kidneys | 714 |
| Beef, brain | 848 |
| Goat, liver | 924 |
| Goat, brain | 939 |
| Beef, shoulder | 1008 |
| Pork, heart | 1019 |
| Pork, stomach | 1090 |
| Pork, shoulder | 2129 |
| **MARINE FISH** | |
| Bombay duck | 252 |
| Tuna | 306 |
| Mural | 354 |
| Sardine | 770 |
| Pomfret, white | 919 |
| Pomfret, black | 1161 |
| Salmon | 2297 |
| **MARINE SHELLFISH** | |
| Lobster, brown | 118 |
| Crab, sea | 146 |
| Tiger prawns, orange | 204 |
| Lobster, king size | 206 |
| Crab | 256 |
| **FRESH WATER FISH AND SHELLFISH** | |
| Prawns, big | 94.61 |
| Prawns, small | 166 |
| Crab | 256 |
| Rohu | 747 |
| Catla | 815 |
| **FATTY FISH** | |
| Hilsa | 1801 |

*(Source: T. Longvah, R. Ananthan, K. Bhaskaracharya, K. Venkaiah. Indian Food Composition Tables, National Institute of Nutrition (Indian Council of Medical Research) 189-255, 2017)*

# Clinical and Therapeutic Nutrition Practical Manual 1
For M.Sc. Food Science and Nutrition (Semester-III)

## LINOLEIC ACID (LA) (n6 FATTY ACID)

| FOOD STUFFS | n6 (mg/ 100 g) |
|---|---|
| **CEREALS AND MILLETS** | |
| Rice puffed | 43.42 |
| Wheat, vermicelli, roasted | 162 |
| Rice, parboiled, milled | 209 |
| Wheat, vermicelli | 209 |
| Rice, raw, milled | 234 |
| Maize tender, sweet | 292 |
| Wheat, semolina | 306 |
| Wheat flour, refined | 325 |
| Maize, tender, local | 337 |
| Ragi | 362 |
| Rice, raw, brown | 490 |
| Jowar | 508 |
| Barley | 549 |
| Rice flakes | 553 |
| Varagu | 576 |
| Wheat, whole | 616 |
| Wheat, bulgur | 657 |
| Wheat flour | 697 |
| Samai | 1230 |
| Maize, dry | 1565 |
| Bajra | 1844 |
| Quinoa | 2203 |
| Amaranth seeds, pale brown | 2223 |
| Amaranth seeds, black | 2259 |
| **GRAIN LEGUMES** | |
| Rice bean | 62.93 |
| Black gram, whole | 117 |
| Black gram, dal | 176 |
| Horse gram, whole | 207 |
| Lentil whole, yellowish | 217 |
| Lentil whole, brown | 221 |
| Lentil dal | 266 |
| Cowpea, brown | 343 |
| Rajmah, brown | 344 |
| Cowpea, white | 354 |
| Rajmah, red | 374 |
| Green gram, dal | 377 |
| Rajmah, black | 386 |
| Field bean, brown | 389 |
| Field bean, black | 398 |

| FOOD STUFFS | n6 (mg/ 100 g) |
|---|---|
| Field bean, white | 426 |
| Green gram, whole | 430 |
| Red gram, whole | 585 |
| Red gram, dal | 600 |
| Moth bean | 609 |
| Peas, dry | 728 |
| Bengal gram, whole | 2220 |
| Bengal gram, dal | 2360 |
| Soya bean, white | 9754 |
| Soya bean, brown | 9969 |
| **GREEN LEAFY VEGETABLES** | |
| Cabbage, Chinese | 11.68 |
| Pumpkin leaves, tender | 14.95 |
| Garden cress | 34.61 |
| Amaranth spinosus, leaves, red and green mix | 36.85 |
| Amaranth spinosus, leaves, green | 39 |
| Cabbage, green | 42.8 |
| Knol-khol leaves | 43 |
| Brussels sprouts | 43.82 |
| Radish leaves | 45.49 |
| Rumex leaves | 45.68 |
| Bathua leaves | 50.68 |
| Cabbage, violet | 52.26 |
| Cabbage, collard greens | 54.33 |
| Pak choi leaves | 60.03 |
| Lettuce | 74.85 |
| Spinach | 75.06 |
| Tamarind leaves, tender | 76.79 |
| Basella leaves | 80.67 |
| Fenugreek leaves | 82.83 |
| Mustard leaves | 83.12 |
| Cauliflower leaves | 84.83 |
| Beet greens | 101 |
| Betel leaves, small | 104 |
| Ponnaganni | 107 |
| Betel leaves, big (Kolkata) | 110 |
| Amaranth leaves, green | 111 |
| Amaranth leaves, red | 112 |
| Amaranth leaves, red and green mix | 118 |
| Agathi leaves | 125 |
| Gogu leaves, red | 132 |
| Gogu leaves, green | 150 |
| Parsley | 221 |

--- **Author** ---
Dr. Prajakta J. Nande

# Clinical and Therapeutic Nutrition Practical Manual 1
## For M.Sc. Food Science and Nutrition (Semester-III)

| | | | | |
|---|---|---|---|---|
| Drumstick leaves | 222 | Zucchini, green | 98.72 |
| Colocasia leaves, green | 353 | Cauliflower | 99 |
| **OTHER VEGETABLES** | | Celery stalk | 99 |
| Cho-cho-marrow | 12.6 | Tomato, ripe, hybrid | 104 |
| Plantain, stem | 14.12 | Colocasia, stem, black | 113 |
| Bitter gourd, jagged, teeth ridges, short | 17.5 | Brinjal-all varieties | 127 |
| | | Capsicum, green | 135 |
| Mango, green, raw | 17.53 | Jack fruit, seed, mature | 154 |
| Bitter gourd, jagged, teeth ridges, elongate | 17.74 | Plantain, flower | 154 |
| | | Capsicum, yellow | 161 |
| Drumstick | 19.14 | Capsicum, red | 180 |
| Bitter gourd, jagged, smooth ridges, elongate | 22.75 | Tomato, ripe, local | 185 |
| | | Field beans, tender, lean | 195 |
| Ridge gourd | 28.66 | Bean scarlet, tender | 203 |
| Ridge gourd, smooth skin | 29.79 | Field beans, tender, broad | 204 |
| Bottle gourd, elongate, dark green | 32.96 | Red gram, tender, fresh | 427 |
| Snake gourd, short | 34.56 | Corn, baby | 433 |
| Cucumber, green, short | 35.73 | **FRUITS** | |
| Pumpkin, orange, round | 36.17 | Tamarind, pulp | 4.99 |
| Pumpkin, green, cylindrical | 38.94 | Manila tamarind | 6.01 |
| Bottle gourd, elongate, pale green | 40.31 | Papaya, ripe | 10.33 |
| Bottle gourd, round, pale green | 40.53 | Mango, ripe, himsagar | 16 |
| Bamboo shoot, tender | 42.23 | Mango, ripe, neelam | 16.56 |
| Broad beans | 42.96 | Pineapple | 17.75 |
| Snake gourd, long, pale green | 42.96 | Mango, ripe, totapari | 18.64 |
| Zucchini, yellow | 43 | Mango, ripe, paheri | 20.4 |
| Snake gourd, long, dark green | 45.65 | Mangosteen | 20.48 |
| Cucumber, round | 45.94 | Jack fruit, ripe | 22.63 |
| Tinda, tender | 46.46 | Mango, ripe, kesar | 24.29 |
| Peas, fresh | 46.75 | Zizyphus | 27.18 |
| Onion, stalk | 55.43 | Mango, ripe, gulabkhas | 27.91 |
| Knol-khol | 59.04 | Currants, black | 30.58 |
| Kovai, big | 59.07 | Mango, ripe, banganapalli | 30.72 |
| French beans, country | 59.21 | Orange, pulp | 36.52 |
| Cucumber, green, elongate | 59.3 | Pomegranate, maroon seeds | 39.16 |
| French beans, hybrid | 62.83 | Jambu fruit, ripe | 42.4 |
| Papaya, raw | 66.04 | Karonda fruit | 45.12 |
| Jack fruit, raw | 68.67 | Gooseberry | 47.41 |
| Plantain, green | 72.89 | Fig | 50.57 |
| Ash gourd | 74.89 | Palm fruit, tender | 50.64 |
| Ladies finger | 76.82 | Water melon, dark green | 51.9 |
| Colocasia, stem, green | 82.53 | Litchi | 51.98 |
| Kovai, small | 83.07 | Banana, ripe, robusta | 53.5 |
| Cluster beans | 84.74 | Water melon, pale green | 54.86 |
| Parwar | 91.87 | Plum | 59.08 |
| Tomato, green | 95.45 | Banana, ripe, red | 61.66 |

--- **Author** ---
Dr. Prajakta J. Nande

# Clinical and Therapeutic Nutrition Practical Manual 1
For M.Sc. Food Science and Nutrition (Semester-III)

| | | | |
|---|---|---|---|
| Peach | 62.16 | Yam, ordinary | 56.32 |
| Banana, ripe, poovam | 65.5 | Yam, elephant | 57.08 |
| Lime, sweet, pulp | 67.81 | Beet root | 57.23 |
| Banana, ripe, montham | 68.33 | Colocasia | 69.01 |
| Musk melon, yellow flesh | 72.56 | Tapioca | 78.47 |
| Soursop | 77.98 | Potato, red skin | 92.44 |
| Custard apple | 78.56 | Sweet potato, brown skin | 96.29 |
| Grapes, seedless, round, green | 80.7 | Potato, brown skin, big | 97.45 |
| Grapes, seeded, round, green | 82.21 | Water chestnut | 97.81 |
| Grapes, seeded, round, red | 83.32 | Yam, wild | 111 |
| Guava, pink flesh | 84.36 | Sweet potato, pink skin | 154 |
| Pear | 84.54 | Carrot, orange | 241 |
| Bael fruit | 87.01 | Carrot, red | 246 |
| Raisins, dried, golden | 93.96 | Lotus root | 291 |
| Grapes, seeded, round, black | 94.88 | **CONDIMENTS AND SPICES - FRESH** | |
| Musk melon, orange flesh | 97.34 | Garlic, small clove | 56.95 |
| Grapes, seedless, round, black | 109 | Garlic, big clove | 60.62 |
| Cherries, red | 116 | Mint leaves | 65.09 |
| Dates, processed | 124 | Onion, small | 66.6 |
| Dates, dry, dark brown | 129 | Garlic, single clove, Kashmir | 73.1 |
| Pummelo | 134 | Onion, big | 100 |
| Dates, dry, pale brown | 140 | Coriander leaves | 151 |
| Raisins, dried, black | 147 | Curry leaves | 152 |
| Star fruit | 151 | Mango ginger | 256 |
| Black berry | 153 | Ginger, fresh | 302 |
| Rambutan | 160 | Chillies green-all varieties | 370 |
| Apricot, processed | 165 | **CONDIMENTS AND SPICES - DRY** | |
| Guava, white flesh | 165 | Nutmeg | 299 |
| Grapes, seedless, oval, black | 172 | Cardamom, black | 320 |
| Apple, green | 173 | Cardamom, green | 411 |
| Strawberry | 179 | Asafoetida | 470 |
| Apple, small | 195 | Pippali | 587 |
| Apricot, dried | 206 | Pepper, black | 818 |
| Apple, small, Kashmir | 211 | Turmeric powder | 1563 |
| Sapota | 233 | Fenugreek seeds | 2051 |
| Apple, big | 249 | Coriander seeds | 2203 |
| Lemon, juice | 270 | Cloves | 2737 |
| Phalsa | 362 | Chillies, red | 3081 |
| Wood apple | 799 | Cumin seeds | 4269 |
| Avocado fruit | 1078 | Mace | 4571 |
| **ROOTS AND TUBERS** | | Omum | 5116 |
| Radish, round, white skin | 15.71 | Poppy seeds | 13742 |
| Radish, round, red skin | 21.18 | **NUTS AND OIL SEEDS** | |
| Radish, elongate, white skin | 21.64 | Arecanut, dried, brown | 396 |
| Radish, elongate, red skin | 23.71 | Arecanut, fresh | 506 |
| Potato, brown skin, small | 54.34 | Coconut kernel, fresh | 639 |

**--- Author ---**
Dr. Prajakta J. Nande

# Clinical and Therapeutic Nutrition Practical Manual 1
For M.Sc. Food Science and Nutrition (Semester-III)

| | | | | |
|---|---|---|---|---|
| Arecanut, dried, red color | 901 | Beef, lungs | 92.04 |
| Coconut kernel, dry | 929 | Beef, spleen | 127 |
| Garden cress, seeds | 2839 | Goat, lungs | 135 |
| Linseeds | 3191 | Goat, spleen | 143 |
| Mustard seeds | 4932 | Beef, kidney | 148 |
| Cashew nut | 7427 | Goat, chops | 184 |
| Ground nut | 11584 | Beef, round (leg) | 201 |
| Pistachio nut | 11766 | Goat, kidneys | 236 |
| Almond | 13183 | Beef, liver | 236 |
| Gingelly seeds, white | 18477 | Pork, spleen | 237 |
| Safflower seeds | 18760 | Beef, chops | 249 |
| Gingelly seeds, brown | 18966 | Goat, heart | 292 |
| Gingelly seeds, black | 19123 | Pork, lungs | 326 |
| Niger seeds, black | 21871 | Beef, heart | 351 |
| Niger seeds, gray | 23300 | Goat, liver | 368 |
| Pine seeds | 23874 | Goat, legs | 374 |
| Sunflower seeds | 25545 | Goat, shoulder meat | 432 |
| Walnut | 36205 | Pork, kidneys | 474 |
| **SUGAR** | | Pork, chops | 521 |
| Jaggery, cane | 33.1 | Beef, shoulder | 575 |
| Sugarcane, juice | 145 | Pork, heart | 725 |
| **MUSHROOMS** | | Pork, stomach | 841 |
| Chicken mushroom, fresh | 111 | Pork, shoulder | 1839 |
| Button mushroom, fresh | 263 | **MARINE FISH** | |
| Shiitake mushroom, fresh | 417 | Mural | 5.88 |
| **MISCELLANEOUS FOODS** | | Bombay duck | 10.25 |
| Coconut water | 3.73 | Pomfret, white | 14.07 |
| **MILK AND MILK PRODUCTS** | | Tuna | 23.05 |
| Milk, whole, cow | 106 | Sardine | 42.33 |
| Milk, whole, buffalo | 132 | Pomfret, black | 51.5 |
| Paneer | 206 | Salmon | 119 |
| Khoa | 525 | **MARINE SHELLFISH** | |
| **EGG AND EGG PRODUCTS** | | Crab, sea | 5.83 |
| Eggs, poultry, whole, raw | 1022 | Lobster, king size | 15.75 |
| Egg, country hen, whole, raw | 1518 | Crab | 16.26 |
| Egg, poultry, yolk, raw | 2919 | Lobster, brown | 19.92 |
| Eggs, poultry, white, raw | | Tiger prawns, orange | 20.99 |
| **POULTRY** | | **FRESH WATER FISH AND SHELLFISH** | |
| Chicken, poultry, breast, skinless | 346 | | |
| Chicken, poultry, thigh, skinless | 490 | Crab | 16.26 |
| Chicken, poultry, wing, skinless | 623 | Prawns, big | 17.75 |
| Chicken, poultry, legs, skinless | 627 | Prawns, small | 41.37 |
| Poultry, chicken, liver | 680 | Catla | 214 |
| **ANIMAL MEAT** | | Rohu | 531 |
| Beef, brain | 39.04 | **FATTY FISH** | |
| Goat, brain | 43.2 | Hilsa | 136 |

**--- Author ---**
Dr. Prajakta J. Nande

# Clinical and Therapeutic Nutrition Practical Manual 1
For M.Sc. Food Science and Nutrition (Semester-III)

## ALPHA LINOLENIC ACID (ALA) (n3 FATTY ACID)

| FOOD STUFFS | n3 (mg/ 100 g) |
|---|---|
| **CEREALS AND MILLETS** | |
| Rice puffed | 1.39 |
| Rice, parboiled, milled | 7.18 |
| Maize, tender, sweet | 7.65 |
| Wheat, vermicelli, roasted | 8.55 |
| Rice, raw, milled | 9.51 |
| Maize, tender, local | 10.46 |
| Wheat, vermicelli | 11.26 |
| Rice, raw, brown | 16.1 |
| Jowar | 16.54 |
| Wheat flour, refined | 17.45 |
| Wheat, semolina | 19.21 |
| Amaranth seeds, black | 20.91 |
| Varagu | 21.02 |
| Rice flakes | 24.37 |
| Barley | 26.32 |
| Wheat, whole | 38.51 |
| Maize, dry | 40.76 |
| Wheat, bulgur | 42.69 |
| Amaranth seeds, pale brown | 43.03 |
| Wheat flour | 44.93 |
| Samai | 47.2 |
| Ragi | 68.58 |
| Bajra | 140 |
| Quinoa | 204 |
| **GRAIN LEGUMES** | |
| Red gram, dal | 51.44 |
| Red gram, whole | 51.67 |
| Horse gram, whole | 51.68 |
| Lentil whole, brown | 55.4 |
| Lentil whole, yellowish | 57.16 |
| Field bean, black | 69.82 |
| Field bean, brown | 70.06 |
| Lentil dal | 70.14 |
| Field bean, white | 76.61 |
| Bengal gram, dal | 116 |
| Bengal gram, whole | 117 |
| Peas, dry | 145 |
| Green gram, dal | 157 |
| Green gram, whole | 180 |
| Cowpea, white | 203 |

| | |
|---|---|
| Cowpea, brown | 207 |
| Moth bean | 240 |
| Rajmah, black | 541 |
| Rajmah, brown | 552 |
| Rajmah, red | 557 |
| Black gram, dal | 566 |
| Black gram, whole | 601 |
| Soya bean, brown | 1310 |
| Soya bean, white | 1318 |
| **GREEN LEAFY VEGETABLES** | |
| Garden cress | 24.1 |
| Brussels sprouts | 41.11 |
| Cabbage, Chinese | 43.33 |
| Cabbage, green | 48.61 |
| Cabbage, violet | 60.18 |
| Cabbage, collard greens | 62.6 |
| Pak choi leaves | 77.96 |
| Knol-khol leaves | 111 |
| Basella leaves | 123 |
| Amaranth spinosus, leaves, red and green mix | 131 |
| Lettuce | 134 |
| Cauliflower leaves | 139 |
| Ponnaganni | 143 |
| Rumex leaves | 143 |
| Betel leaves, big (Kolkata) | 146 |
| Amaranth spinosus, leaves, green | 147 |
| Bathua leaves | 169 |
| Betel leaves, small | 172 |
| Radish leaves | 203 |
| Beet greens | 207 |
| Amaranth leaves, red | 214 |
| Amaranth leaves, red and green mix | 214 |
| Spinach | 220 |
| Tamarind leaves, tender | 230 |
| Mustard leaves | 240 |
| Amaranth leaves, green | 247 |
| Parsley | 255 |
| Pumpkin leaves, tender | 298 |
| Colocasia leaves, green | 335 |
| Fenugreek leaves | 362 |
| Agathi leaves | 407 |
| Gogu leaves, green | 434 |
| Gogu leaves, red | 435 |

--- Author ---
Dr. Prajakta J. Nande

# Clinical and Therapeutic Nutrition Practical Manual 1
For M.Sc. Food Science and Nutrition (Semester-III)

| | | | | |
|---|---|---|---|---|
| Drumstick leaves | 446 | Onion, stalk | 43.55 |
| **OTHER VEGETABLES** | | Plantain, flower | 44.08 |
| Ash gourd | 1.58 | Red gram, tender, fresh | 47.24 |
| Drumstick | 8.07 | Snake gourd, long, dark green | 53.71 |
| Cucumber, green, elongate | 8.63 | Snake gourd, long, pale green | 54.59 |
| Bamboo shoot, tender | 9.24 | Cluster beans | 63.4 |
| Peas, fresh | 9.49 | French beans, country | 68.19 |
| Papaya, raw | 9.6 | Snake gourd, short | 70.55 |
| Cho-cho-marrow | 9.98 | Knol-khol | 71.39 |
| Mango, green, raw | 12.61 | Zucchini, yellow | 71.42 |
| Tomato, green | 13.57 | French beans, hybrid | 72.13 |
| Plantain, stem | 14.38 | Field beans, tender, lean | 86.04 |
| Tomato, ripe, hybrid | 14.7 | Field beans, tender, broad | 96.74 |
| Cucumber, green, short | 16.1 | Cauliflower | 117 |
| Bottle gourd, elongate, dark green | 19.35 | Zucchini, green | 152 |
| Parwar | 20.35 | Bean scarlet, tender | 227 |
| Broad beans | 21.88 | **FRUITS** | |
| Bottle gourd, round, pale green | 22.12 | Peach | 0.44 |
| Brinjal-all varieties | 22.65 | Pomegranate, maroon seeds | 1.82 |
| Cucumber, round | 22.76 | Jambu fruit, ripe | 6.37 |
| Bitter gourd, jagged, teeth ridges, elongate | 23.04 | Guava, pink flesh | 7.29 |
| | | Karonda fruit | 7.48 |
| Tomato, ripe, local | 23.59 | Zizyphus | 8.07 |
| Bottle gourd, elongate, pale green | 24.63 | Currants, black | 8.47 |
| Corn, baby | 25.69 | Water melon, pale green | 10.52 |
| Ridge gourd | 26.42 | Guava, white flesh | 11.08 |
| Jack fruit, seed, mature | 26.51 | Orange, pulp | 11.11 |
| Pumpkin, green, cylindrical | 26.57 | Grapes, seedless, oval, black | 11.29 |
| Pumpkin, orange, round | 26.57 | Dates, processed | 11.63 |
| Colocasia, stem, green | 27.75 | Raisins, dried, black | 11.91 |
| Ridge gourd, smooth skin | 28.19 | Tamarind, pulp | 12.86 |
| Kovai, small | 29.1 | Manila tamarind | 13.48 |
| Tinda, tender | 30.39 | Jack fruit, ripe | 15.44 |
| Celery stalk | 32.33 | Water melon, dark green | 15.55 |
| Ladies finger | 32.38 | Dates, dry, dark brown | 16.35 |
| Plantain, green | 33.77 | Pear | 16.58 |
| Bitter gourd, jagged, smooth ridges, elongate | 36.5 | Lime, sweet, pulp | 16.6 |
| | | Phalsa | 18.66 |
| Capsicum, green | 37.08 | Dates, dry, pale brown | 19.49 |
| Bitter gourd, jagged, teeth ridges, short | 37.7 | Palm fruit, tender | 25.78 |
| | | Litchi | 26.91 |
| Capsicum, red | 37.77 | Gooseberry | 27.83 |
| Jack fruit, raw | 38.57 | Apple, small | 29.52 |
| Capsicum, yellow | 39.49 | Pineapple | 30 |
| Kovai, big | 39.75 | Raisins, dried, golden | 30.87 |
| Colocasia, stem, black | 41.36 | Grapes, seedless, round, green | 32.12 |

**--- Author ---**
Dr. Prajakta J. Nande

# Clinical and Therapeutic Nutrition Practical Manual 1
## For M.Sc. Food Science and Nutrition (Semester-III)

| | | | | |
|---|---|---|---|---|
| Apple, big | 32.63 | Carrot, red | 24.1 |
| Grapes, seeded, round, green | 36.68 | Carrot, orange | 24.38 |
| Papaya, ripe | 37.91 | Sweet potato, pink skin | 25.92 |
| Grapes, seeded, round, red | 39.64 | Potato, red skin | 28.78 |
| Star fruit | 39.9 | Yam, wild | 30.93 |
| Musk melon, yellow flesh | 41.54 | Potato, brown skin, big | 31.84 |
| Apple, small, Kashmir | 41.61 | Radish, elongate, white skin | 32 |
| Grapes, seeded, round, black | 44.44 | Radish, elongate, red skin | 33.02 |
| Banana, ripe, red | 46.23 | Radish, round, white skin | 46.49 |
| Fig | 46.52 | Radish, round, red skin | 54.67 |
| Apple, green | 49.73 | Potato, brown skin, small | 73.68 |
| Grapes, seedless, round, black | 52.81 | Lotus root | 123 |
| Pummelo | 53.21 | **CONDIMENTS AND SPICES - FRESH** | |
| Custard apple | 53.47 | Onion, small | 4.55 |
| Soursop | 54.02 | Garlic, small clove | 4.86 |
| Musk melon, orange flesh | 61.33 | Garlic, big clove | 6.28 |
| Avocado fruit | 62.11 | Onion, big | 6.63 |
| Banana, ripe, montham | 63.24 | Garlic, single clove, Kashmir | 9.31 |
| Mango, ripe, paheri | 65.92 | Chillies green-all varieties | 43.14 |
| Bael fruit | 66.18 | Mango ginger | 78.26 |
| Mangosteen | 68.12 | Ginger, fresh | 78.99 |
| Banana, ripe, poovam | 69.67 | Coriander leaves | 169 |
| Mango, ripe, totapari | 70.06 | Mint leaves | 286 |
| Mango, ripe, gulabkhas | 71.39 | Curry leaves | 417 |
| Cherries, red | 71.55 | **CONDIMENTS AND SPICES - DRY** | |
| Banana, ripe, robusta | 73.44 | Asafoetida | 43.79 |
| Apricot, dried | 79.91 | Cumin seeds | 44 |
| Black berry | 80.24 | Coriander seeds | 44.01 |
| Lemon, juice | 83.53 | Omum | 76.71 |
| Mango, ripe, kesar | 90.87 | Nutmeg | 79.3 |
| Mango, ripe, neelam | 98.95 | Poppy seeds | 106 |
| Mango, ripe, banganapalli | 101 | Mace | 159 |
| Mango, ripe, himsagar | 111 | Cardamom, green | 172 |
| Strawberry | 112 | Chillies, red | 182 |
| Sapota | 125 | Cardamom, black | 197 |
| Apricot, processed | 154 | Pepper, black | 258 |
| Rambutan | 202 | Pippali | 299 |
| Wood apple | 636 | Turmeric powder | 377 |
| **ROOTS AND TUBERS** | | Cloves | 691 |
| Water chestnut | 6.16 | Fenugreek seeds | 1082 |
| Beet root | 6.98 | **NUTS AND OIL SEEDS** | |
| Colocasia | 8.4 | Ground nut | 0 |
| Tapioca | 12.83 | Arecanut, dried, brown | 7.42 |
| Yam, ordinary | 16.02 | Arecanut, fresh | 15.67 |
| Yam, elephant | 16.44 | Arecanut, dried, red color | 16.78 |
| Sweet potato, brown skin | 19.52 | Safflower seeds | 21.9 |

--- **Author** ---

Dr. Prajakta J. Nande

# Clinical and Therapeutic Nutrition Practical Manual 1
For M.Sc. Food Science and Nutrition (Semester-III)

| | | | | |
|---|---|---|---|---|
| Almond | 32.04 | Chicken, poultry, legs, skinless | 25.97 | |
| Sunflower seeds | 35.6 | Chicken, poultry, wing, skinless | 27.64 | |
| Cashew nut | 55.04 | Poultry, chicken, liver | 140 | |
| Niger seeds, black | 64.5 | **ANIMAL MEAT** | | |
| Gingelly seeds, brown | 112 | Beef, lungs | 6.14 | |
| Gingelly seeds, white | 120 | Beef, liver | 8.51 | |
| Gingelly seeds, black | 136 | Beef, kidney | 8.72 | |
| Pistachio nut | 171 | Goat, heart | 9.52 | |
| Pine seeds | 188 | Goat, kidneys | 10.37 | |
| Niger seeds, gray | 265 | Goat, spleen | 10.56 | |
| Mustard seeds | 3341 | Beef, heart | 11.43 | |
| Garden cress, seeds | 7484 | Beef, spleen | 12.22 | |
| Walnut | 8710 | Goat, lungs | 13.74 | |
| Linseeds | 12956 | Goat, chops | 16.12 | |
| **SUGAR** | | Goat, legs | 21.85 | |
| Sugarcane, juice | 28.34 | Pork, lungs | 21.91 | |
| **MUSHROOMS** | | Pork, spleen | 23.79 | |
| Chicken mushroom, fresh | 26.43 | Pork, kidneys | 26.28 | |
| **MILK AND MILK PRODUCTS** | | Goat, shoulder meat | 33.28 | |
| Milk, whole, cow | 20.52 | Pork, heart | 38.38 | |
| Milk, whole, buffalo | 34.76 | Beef, brain | 56.26 | |
| Paneer | 233 | Goat, liver | 56.53 | |
| Khoa | 265 | Beef, chops | 66.06 | |
| **EGG AND EGG PRODUCTS** | | Beef, round (leg) | 67.9 | |
| Eggs, poultry, whole, raw | 28.06 | Goat, brain | 80.48 | |
| Egg, country hen, whole, raw | 39.95 | Pork, stomach | 94.61 | |
| Egg, poultry, yolk, raw | 64.43 | Pork, chops | 112 | |
| **POULTRY** | | Beef, shoulder | 153 | |
| Chicken, poultry, breast, skinless | 12.63 | Pork, shoulder | 170 | |
| Chicken, poultry, thigh, skinless | 22.52 | | | |

*(Source: T. Longvah, R. Ananthan, K. Bhaskaracharya, K. Venkaiah. Indian Food Composition Tables, National Institute of Nutrition (Indian Council of Medical Research) 189-255, 2017)*

# CHOLESTEROL

| FOOD STUFFS | Chole-sterol (mg/100 g) | Chicken, poultry, wing, skinless | 54.52 |
|---|---|---|---|
| | | Chicken, poultry, breast, skinless | 61.55 |
| | | Chicken, poultry, legs, skinless | 84.25 |
| | | Chicken, poultry, thigh, skinless | 91.93 |
| **EGG AND EGG PRODUCTS** | | Poultry, chicken, liver | 268 |
| Egg, country hen, whole, raw | 355 | **ANIMAL MEAT** | |
| Eggs, poultry, whole, raw | 366 | Pork, shoulder | 44.38 |
| Egg, poultry, yolk, raw | 1076 | Beef, chops | 45.97 |
| **POULTRY** | | Pork, chops | 46.98 |

# Clinical and Therapeutic Nutrition Practical Manual 1
For M.Sc. Food Science and Nutrition (Semester-III)

| | | | | |
|---|---|---|---|---|
| Beef, round (leg) | 55.81 | **MARINE FISH** | | |
| Beef, shoulder | 66.36 | Mural | 17.43 |
| Goat, shoulder | 82.18 | Pomfret, white | 41.56 |
| Goat, legs | 82.52 | Tuna | 46.1 |
| Goat, chops | 88.37 | Bombay duck | 46.43 |
| Beef, heart | 92.73 | Pomfret, black | 48.16 |
| Goat, heart | 122 | Sardine | 49.12 |
| Pork, heart | 134 | Salmon | 61.27 |
| Pork, stomach | 187 | **MARINE SHELLFISH** | |
| Pork, spleen | 201 | Tiger prawns, orange | 19.47 |
| Pork, lungs | 232 | Crab, sea | 23.18 |
| Goat, spleen | 243 | Lobster, brown | 32.64 |
| Beef, liver | 261 | Lobster, king size | 41.13 |
| Pork, kidneys | 267 | Crab | 53.87 |
| Beef, lungs | 334 | **FRESH WATER FISH AND SHELLFISH** | |
| Beef, spleen | 353 | Rohu | 47.72 |
| Goat, liver | 415 | Crab | 52.91 |
| Goat, kidneys | 419 | Catla | 64.42 |
| Beef, kidney | 439 | Prawns, big | 87.28 |
| Goat, lungs | 448 | Prawns, small | 112 |
| Goat, brain | 1340 | **FATTY FISH** | |
| Beef, brain | 1668 | Hilsa | 19.26 |

*(Source: T. Longvah, R. Ananthan, K. Bhaskaracharya, K. Venkaiah. Indian Food Composition Tables, National Institute of Nutrition (Indian Council of Medical Research) 189-255, 2017)*

---

## ANNEXURE - 9

## SODIUM (Na) CONTENT OF FOODS

| FOOD STUFFS | Na (mg/ 100g) | Amaranth seeds, pale brown | 2.81 |
|---|---|---|---|
| **CEREALS AND MILLETS** | | Rice, parboiled, milled | 3.16 |
| Wheat flour, refined | 1.54 | Varagu | 3.35 |
| Wheat flour | 2.04 | Wheat, vermicelli, roasted | 3.43 |
| Wheat, bulgur | 2.09 | Rice, raw ,brown | 3.64 |
| Maize tender, sweet | 2.23 | Rice puffed | 3.69 |
| Maize, tender, local | 2.24 | Bajra | 4.11 |
| Wheat, semolina | 2.31 | Maize, dry | 4.44 |
| Rice, raw, milled | 2.34 | Quinoa | 4.5 |
| Wheat, whole | 2.5 | Ragi | 4.75 |
| Rice flakes | 2.58 | Samai | 4.77 |
| Amaranth seeds, black | 2.7 | Jowar | 5.42 |
| Wheat, vermicelli | 2.71 | Barley | 7.56 |
| | | **GRAIN LEGUMES** | |
| | | Field bean, black | 1.35 |

--- **Author** ---
Dr. Prajakta J. Nande

# Clinical and Therapeutic Nutrition Practical Manual 1
## For M.Sc. Food Science and Nutrition (Semester-III)

| | | | | |
|---|---|---|---|---|
| Field bean, brown | 1.41 | | Mustard leaves | 19.14 |
| Field bean, white | 1.7 | | Rumex leaves | 19.95 |
| Soya bean, brown | 2.07 | | Cabbage, Chinese | 20.28 |
| Soya bean, white | 2.83 | | Cabbage, collard greens | 22.98 |
| Rajmah, black | 9.4 | | Cabbage, violet | 24 |
| Green gram, dal | 10.14 | | Cauliflower leaves | 24.31 |
| Lentil dal | 10.27 | | Garden cress | 25.35 |
| Rajmah, red | 10.45 | | Knol-khol leaves | 26.08 |
| Rajmah, brown | 10.47 | | Pak choi leaves | 33.73 |
| Rice bean | 10.62 | | Ponnaganni | 39.36 |
| Lentil whole, yellowish | 10.87 | | Spinach | 42.55 |
| Lentil whole, brown | 11.2 | | Fenugreek leaves | 47.01 |
| Horse gram, whole | 12.14 | | Parsley | 53.08 |
| Green gram, whole | 12.48 | | Beet greens | 111 |
| Cowpea, white | 12.52 | | **OTHER VEGETABLES** | |
| Cowpea, brown | 13.63 | | Zucchini, yellow | 0.39 |
| Red gram, dal | 18.01 | | Zucchini, green | 0.4 |
| Black gram, dal | 18.88 | | Colocasia, stem, black | 0.45 |
| Red gram, whole | 19.03 | | Colocasia, stem, green | 0.6 |
| Bengal gram, dal | 20.83 | | Ash gourd | 0.77 |
| Peas, dry | 23.4 | | Bamboo shoot, tender | 1.12 |
| Moth bean | 26.34 | | Cho-cho-marrow | 1.28 |
| Bengal gram, whole | 26.56 | | Bottle gourd, elongate, dark green | 1.35 |
| Black gram, whole | 26.8 | | Corn, baby | 1.4 |
| **GREEN LEAFY VEGETABLES** | | | Bean scarlet, tender | 1.46 |
| Drumstick leaves | 9.34 | | Bottle gourd, elongate, pale green | 1.46 |
| Bathua leaves | 10.75 | | Bottle gourd, round, pale green | 1.52 |
| Colocasia leaves, green | 12.08 | | Kovai, big | 1.53 |
| Pumpkin leaves, tender | 12.2 | | Capsicum, yellow | 1.56 |
| Gogu leaves, green | 12.34 | | Capsicum, red | 1.7 |
| Tamarind leaves, tender | 13.43 | | Capsicum, green | 1.84 |
| Betel leaves, small | 14.04 | | Kovai, small | 2.2 |
| Gogu leaves, red | 14.08 | | Parwar | 2.29 |
| Amaranth leaves, red | 14.48 | | Snake gourd, short | 2.5 |
| Cabbage, green | 14.98 | | Red gram, tender, fresh | 2.54 |
| Amaranth spinosus, leaves, green | 15.66 | | Jack fruit, raw | 3.53 |
| Amaranth leaves, green | 16.08 | | Brinjal-all varieties | 3.55 |
| Amaranth spinosus, leaves, red and green mix | 16.27 | | Peas, fresh | 3.66 |
| | | | Jack fruit, seed, mature | 4 |
| Betel leaves, big (Kolkata) | 16.8 | | Cluster beans | 4.05 |
| Radish leaves | 17.39 | | Ridge gourd | 4.71 |
| Lettuce | 17.53 | | Snake gourd, long, dark green | 5.04 |
| Amaranth leaves, red and green mix | 17.55 | | Pumpkin, green, cylindrical | 5.21 |
| Agathi leaves | 18.12 | | Cucumber, green, short | 6.11 |
| Brussels sprouts | 18.51 | | Ridge gourd, smooth skin | 6.27 |
| Basella leaves | 18.74 | | Cucumber, green, elongate | 6.33 |

# Clinical and Therapeutic Nutrition Practical Manual 1
For M.Sc. Food Science and Nutrition (Semester-III)

| | | | |
|---|---|---|---|
| Snake gourd, long, pale green | 7.07 | Mango, ripe, banganapalli | 1.34 |
| Ladies finger | 7.37 | Manila tamarind | 1.35 |
| Plantain, flower | 7.51 | Gooseberry | 1.37 |
| Papaya, raw | 7.55 | Mango, ripe, gulabkhas | 1.39 |
| Cucumber, round | 8.16 | Apple, big | 1.43 |
| Pumpkin, orange, round | 8.81 | Mango, ripe, kesar | 1.43 |
| French beans, country | 8.84 | Pineapple | 1.43 |
| French beans, hybrid | 9.18 | Apple, small | 1.45 |
| Tomato, ripe, local | 9.73 | Currants, black | 1.45 |
| Celery stalk | 10.68 | Apple, green | 1.47 |
| Bitter gourd, jagged, smooth ridges, elongate | 11.16 | Orange, pulp | 1.47 |
| | | Wood apple | 1.48 |
| Tomato, ripe, hybrid | 11.86 | Zizyphus | 1.52 |
| Bitter gourd, jagged, teeth ridges, short | 12.59 | Plum | 1.55 |
| | | Bael fruit | 1.56 |
| Field beans, tender, lean | 12.76 | Star fruit | 1.56 |
| Bitter gourd, jagged, teeth ridges, elongate | 13.09 | Grapes, seeded, round, red | 1.59 |
| | | Apricot, processed | 1.6 |
| Tomato, green | 13.11 | Dates, processed | 1.6 |
| Field beans, tender, broad | 14.14 | Jack fruit, ripe | 1.62 |
| Onion, stalk | 15.52 | Water melon, pale green | 1.62 |
| Plantain, green | 18.57 | Mango, ripe, paheri | 1.63 |
| Tinda, tender | 20.61 | Cherries, red | 1.64 |
| Broad beans | 20.74 | Pear | 1.64 |
| Drumstick | 22.38 | Rambutan | 1.75 |
| Plantain, stem | 23.17 | Grapes, seedless, round, green | 1.81 |
| Knol-khol | 27.46 | Grapes, seedless, oval, black | 1.83 |
| Cauliflower | 30.72 | Grapes, seeded, round, green | 1.89 |
| Mango, green, raw | 33.15 | Guava, pink flesh | 1.89 |
| **FRUITS** | | Water melon, dark green | 1.89 |
| Litchi | 0.54 | Grapes, seedless, round, black | 1.92 |
| Banana, ripe, robusta | 0.85 | Grapes, seeded, round, black | 1.93 |
| Banana, ripe, poovam | 1 | Phalsa | 1.99 |
| Pummelo | 1.06 | Pomegranate, maroon seeds | 2.13 |
| Banana, ripe, red | 1.11 | Fig | 2.37 |
| Peach | 1.15 | Karonda fruit | 2.55 |
| Lime, sweet,pulp | 1.17 | Jambu fruit, ripe | 2.64 |
| Strawberry | 1.19 | Avocado fruit | 2.81 |
| Mango, ripe, neelam | 1.2 | Guava, white flesh | 2.87 |
| Black berry | 1.21 | Dates, dry, dark brown | 3.09 |
| Lemon, juice | 1.21 | Custard apple | 3.11 |
| Apple, small, Kashmir | 1.22 | Dates, dry, pale brown | 3.27 |
| Banana, ripe, montham | 1.25 | Mangosteen | 3.79 |
| Palm fruit, tender | 1.25 | Apricot, dried | 3.94 |
| Mango, ripe, himsagar | 1.31 | Sapota | 4.61 |
| Mango, ripe, totapari | 1.32 | Papaya, ripe | 6.68 |

267

--- **Author** ---
Dr. Prajakta J. Nande

# Clinical and Therapeutic Nutrition Practical Manual 1
For M.Sc. Food Science and Nutrition (Semester-III)

| | | | | |
|---|---|---|---|---|
| Soursop | 6.78 | | Turmeric powder | 24.41 |
| Raisins, dried, golden | 10.16 | | Poppy seeds | 25.35 |
| Raisins, dried, black | 10.99 | | Mace | 27.17 |
| Musk melon, orange flesh | 14.94 | | Omum | 28.58 |
| Musk melon, yellow flesh | 15.78 | | Coriander seeds | 34.41 |
| Tamarind, pulp | 24.92 | | Fenugreek seeds | 40.2 |
| **ROOTS AND TUBERS** | | | Cumin seeds | 125 |
| Potato, brown skin, small | 3.97 | | Cloves | 183 |
| Potato, brown skin, big | 4.11 | | **NUTS AND OIL SEEDS** | |
| Potato, red skin | 4.36 | | Pine seeds | 1.31 |
| Colocasia | 4.54 | | Walnut | 1.33 |
| Tapioca | 10.86 | | Almond | 1.5 |
| Yam, wild | 12.8 | | Sunflower seeds | 1.9 |
| Water chestnut | 13.08 | | Safflower seeds | 3.05 |
| Yam, elephant | 14.33 | | Mustard seeds | 3.97 |
| Yam, ordinary | 15.28 | | Arecanut, fresh | 5.53 |
| Lotus root | 20.63 | | Pistachio nuts | 6.93 |
| Radish, round, white skin | 24.14 | | Niger seeds, gray | 8.08 |
| Radish, elongate, red skin | 24.73 | | Coconut kernel, fresh | 8.12 |
| Radish, elongate, white skin | 28.2 | | Cashew nut | 9 |
| Sweet potato, pink skin | 29.04 | | Niger seeds, black | 10.7 |
| Sweet potato, brown skin | 29.6 | | Gingelly seeds, brown | 11.94 |
| Radish, round, red skin | 32.27 | | Arecanut, dried, brown | 12.06 |
| Carrot, orange | 52.33 | | Ground nut | 12.21 |
| Carrot, red | 60.69 | | Gingelly seeds, white | 15.43 |
| Beet root | 69.44 | | Gingelly seeds, black | 15.91 |
| **CONDIMENTS AND SPICES- FRESH** | | | Coconut kernel, dry | 16.68 |
| Chillies green-all varieties | 2.5 | | Arecanut, dried, red color | 17.13 |
| Onion, small | 4.06 | | Garden cress, seeds | 21.84 |
| Onion, big | 5.5 | | Linseeds | 32.93 |
| Mango ginger | 5.51 | | **SUGAR** | |
| Garlic, single clove, Kashmir | 8.87 | | Sugarcane, juice | 1.16 |
| Garlic, big clove | 9.42 | | Jaggery, cane | 25.38 |
| Ginger, fresh | 10.03 | | **MUSHROOMS** | |
| Garlic, small clove | 10.56 | | Button mushroom, fresh | 7.72 |
| Mint leaves | 16.87 | | Shiitake mushroom, fresh | 9.3 |
| Curry leaves | 18.66 | | Chicken mushroom, fresh | 10.22 |
| Coriander leaves | 37 | | **MISCELLANEOUS FOODS** | |
| **CONDIMENTS AND SPICES - DRY** | | | Coconut water | 28.09 |
| Nutmeg | 14.31 | | **MILK AND MILK PRODUCTS** | |
| Cardamom, green | 15.51 | | Paneer | 18.04 |
| Asafoetida | 16.04 | | Milk,whole, cow | 25.46 |
| Cardamom, black | 16.25 | | Milk,whole, buffalo | 30.1 |
| Pippali | 16.28 | | Khoa | 48.1 |
| Chillies, red | 19.45 | | **EGG AND EGG PRODUCTS** | |
| Pepper, black | 24.08 | | Egg, poultry, yolk, raw | 46.33 |

268

**--- Author ---**
Dr. Prajakta J. Nande

# Clinical and Therapeutic Nutrition Practical Manual 1
For M.Sc. Food Science and Nutrition (Semester-III)

| | | | | |
|---|---|---|---|---|
| Eggs, poultry, whole, raw | 123 | | Pork, stomach | 109 |
| Egg, country hen, whole, raw | 157 | | Beef, brain | 127 |
| Eggs, poultry, white, raw | 166 | | Goat, brain | 132 |
| **POULTRY** | | | Pork, kidneys | 138 |
| Chicken, poultry, breast, skinless | 36.7 | | Beef, kidney | 160 |
| Poultry, chicken, liver | 61.58 | | Goat, kidneys | 184 |
| Chicken, poultry, thigh, skinless | 64.59 | | **MARINE FISH** | |
| Chicken, poultry, legs, skinless | 65.07 | | Salmon | 20.25 |
| Chicken, poultry, wing, skinless | 72.78 | | Sardine | 38.49 |
| **ANIMAL MEAT** | | | Pomfret, white | 46.09 |
| Beef, chops | 32.47 | | Tuna | 52.89 |
| Beef, round (leg) | 38.96 | | Pomfret, black | 69 |
| Goat, legs | 42.77 | | Mural | 110 |
| Pork, chops | 43.7 | | Bombay duck | 223 |
| Beef, shoulder | 45.59 | | **MARINE SHELLFISH** | |
| Goat, chops | 45.72 | | Tiger prawns, orange | 61.05 |
| Goat, shoulder meat | 47.31 | | Lobster, brown | 140 |
| Pork, spleen | 49.14 | | Lobster, king size | 191 |
| Beef, liver | 50.14 | | Crab | 244 |
| Goat, spleen | 52.4 | | Crab, sea | 313 |
| Pork, shoulder | 54.47 | | **FRESH WATER FISH AND SHELLFISH** | |
| Goat, liver | 55.41 | | Rohu | 35.56 |
| Beef, spleen | 58.94 | | Catla | 36.56 |
| Pork, lungs | 61.41 | | Prawns, small | 77.71 |
| Beef, heart | 70.52 | | Crab | 280 |
| Pork, heart | 70.52 | | Prawns, big | 849 |
| Goat, heart | 73.21 | | **FATTY FISH** | |
| Goat, lungs | 85.72 | | Hilsa | 80.88 |
| Beef, lungs | 109 | | | |

*(Source: T. Longvah, R. Ananthan, K. Bhaskaracharya, K. Venkaiah. Indian Food Composition Tables, National Institute of Nutrition (Indian Council of Medical Research), 113-168, 2017)*

## ANNEXURE - 10

## POTASSIUM (K) CONTENT OF FOODS

| FOOD STUFFS | K (mg/ 100 g) | | Rice, parboiled, milled | 142 |
|---|---|---|---|---|
| **CEREALS AND MILLETS** | | | Rice flakes | 148 |
| Varagu | 94 | | Wheat flour, refined | 148 |
| Samai | 105 | | Wheat, vermicelli | 163 |
| Rice, raw, milled | 108 | | Maize, tender, local | 167 |
| Rice puffed | 140 | | Wheat, vermicelli, roasted | 177 |
| | | | Rice, raw, brown | 199 |
| | | | Barley | 268 |

--- Author ---
Dr. Prajakta J. Nande

# Clinical and Therapeutic Nutrition Practical Manual 1
For M.Sc. Food Science and Nutrition (Semester-III)

| Food | Value |
|---|---|
| Wheat, semolina | 284 |
| Maize, dry | 291 |
| Maize tender, sweet | 297 |
| Wheat flour | 311 |
| Jowar | 328 |
| Wheat, bulgur | 330 |
| Bajra | 365 |
| Wheat, whole | 366 |
| Amaranth seeds, pale brown | 413 |
| Amaranth seeds, black | 433 |
| Ragi | 443 |
| Quinoa | 474 |
| **GRAIN LEGUMES** | |
| Lentil whole, brown | 756 |
| Lentil whole, yellowish | 764 |
| Lentil dal | 786 |
| Peas, dry | 922 |
| Bengal gram, whole | 935 |
| Bengal gram, dal | 957 |
| Horse gram, whole | 1065 |
| Black gram, whole | 1093 |
| Black gram, dal | 1157 |
| Green gram, whole | 1177 |
| Rice bean | 1196 |
| Cowpea, brown | 1241 |
| Cowpea, white | 1243 |
| Field bean, brown | 1245 |
| Green gram, dal | 1268 |
| Field bean, black | 1272 |
| Red gram, whole | 1303 |
| Rajmah, red | 1324 |
| Moth bean | 1356 |
| Field bean, white | 1360 |
| Rajmah, black | 1362 |
| Rajmah, brown | 1366 |
| Red gram, dal | 1395 |
| Soya bean, brown | 1613 |
| Soya bean, white | 1634 |
| **GREEN LEAFY VEGETABLES** | |
| Gogu leaves, red | 161 |
| Cabbage, violet | 201 |
| Fenugreek leaves | 226 |
| Cabbage, green | 233 |
| Pak choi leaves | 250 |
| Cabbage, Chinese | 258 |
| Gogu leaves, green | 260 |

| Food | Value |
|---|---|
| Lettuce | 279 |
| Cabbage, collard greens | 292 |
| Radish leaves | 304 |
| Knol-khol leaves | 309 |
| Rumex leaves | 336 |
| Basella leaves | 337 |
| Cauliflower leaves | 374 |
| Garden cress | 379 |
| Drumstick leaves | 397 |
| Mustard leaves | 403 |
| Colocasia leaves, green | 404 |
| Pumpkin leaves, tender | 423 |
| Bathua leaves | 438 |
| Ponnaganni | 457 |
| Tamarind leaves, tender | 465 |
| Parsley | 466 |
| Beet greens | 530 |
| Amaranth leaves, red | 564 |
| Amaranth spinosus, leaves, green | 569 |
| Amaranth leaves, green | 572 |
| Amaranth spinosus, leaves, red and green mix | 588 |
| Amaranth leaves, red and green mix | 597 |
| Spinach | 625 |
| Brussels sprouts | 639 |
| Betel leaves, big (Kolkata) | 649 |
| Agathi leaves | 674 |
| Betel leaves, small | 678 |
| **OTHER VEGETABLES** | |
| Tinda, tender | 56 |
| Snake gourd, short | 84 |
| Snake gourd, long, pale green | 100 |
| Snake gourd, long, dark green | 104 |
| Bottle gourd, round, pale green | 116 |
| Parwar | 117 |
| Ridge gourd | 118 |
| Cho-cho-marrow | 120 |
| Bottle gourd, elongate, pale green | 124 |
| Ridge gourd, smooth skin | 125 |
| Zucchini, yellow | 131 |
| Mango, green, raw | 147 |
| Capsicum, green | 154 |
| Bean scarlet, tender | 164 |
| Kovai, small | 167 |
| Tomato, ripe, hybrid | 167 |
| Bottle gourd, elongate, dark green | 171 |

--- **Author** ---
Dr. Prajakta J. Nande

# Clinical and Therapeutic Nutrition Practical Manual 1
## For M.Sc. Food Science and Nutrition (Semester-III)

| | | | | |
|---|---|---|---|---|
| Papaya, raw | 173 | Apricot, processed | 95 |
| Zucchini, green | 178 | Apple, small | 100 |
| Cucumber, green, elongate | 183 | Jambu fruit, ripe | 103 |
| Cucumber, round | 185 | Apple, small, Kashmir | 106 |
| Pumpkin, green, cylindrical | 186 | Pear | 106 |
| Cucumber, green, short | 198 | Lemon, juice | 113 |
| Kovai, big | 198 | Mango, ripe, gulabkhas | 115 |
| Tomato, ripe, local | 204 | Apple, big | 116 |
| Capsicum, red | 224 | Water melon, dark green | 124 |
| Tomato, green | 225 | Water melon, pale green | 126 |
| Capsicum, yellow | 242 | Rambutan | 131 |
| Brinjal-all varieties | 247 | Mango, ripe, himsagar | 137 |
| Peas, fresh | 249 | Mango, ripe, neelam | 137 |
| Pumpkin, orange, round | 253 | Strawberry | 140 |
| Corn, baby | 260 | Mango, ripe, kesar | 143 |
| Ladies finger | 263 | Pineapple | 143 |
| Bitter gourd, jagged, teeth ridges, short | 282 | Mango, ripe, banganapalli | 144 |
| | | Mango, ripe, paheri | 153 |
| Celery stalk | 298 | Palm fruit, tender | 158 |
| Cluster beans | 301 | Star fruit | 159 |
| Onion, stalk | 312 | Mango, ripe, totapari | 160 |
| Field beans, tender, lean | 314 | Litchi | 161 |
| French beans, hybrid | 317 | Plum | 162 |
| French beans, country | 324 | Orange, pulp | 164 |
| Bitter gourd, jagged, teeth ridges, elongate | 326 | Cherries, red | 165 |
| | | Grapes, seeded, round, green | 166 |
| Jack fruit, raw | 327 | Grapes, seedless, round, green | 168 |
| Knol-khol | 327 | Grapes, seeded, round, black | 171 |
| Cauliflower | 329 | Papaya, ripe | 173 |
| Field beans, tender, broad | 345 | Lime, sweet, pulp | 182 |
| Bitter gourd, jagged, smooth ridges, elongate | 356 | Grapes, seeded, round, red | 188 |
| | | Pummelo | 189 |
| Broad beans | 362 | Musk melon, yellow flesh | 196 |
| Ash gourd | 372 | Black berry | 205 |
| Plantain, stem | 373 | Musk melon, orange flesh | 206 |
| Jack fruit, seed, mature | 376 | Pomegranate, maroon seeds | 206 |
| Colocasia, stem, black | 381 | Gooseberry | 223 |
| Plantain, green | 402 | Fig | 231 |
| Colocasia, stem, green | 414 | Grapes, seedless, round, black | 235 |
| Drumstick | 419 | Grapes, seedless, oval, black | 237 |
| Bamboo shoot, tender | 422 | Zizyphus | 237 |
| Plantain, flower | 488 | Soursop | 264 |
| Red gram, tender, fresh | 616 | Guava, pink flesh | 270 |
| **FRUITS** | | Custard apple | 278 |
| Mangosteen | 46 | Jack fruit, ripe | 279 |
| Apple, green | 94.55 | Sapota | 280 |

--- **Author** ---
Dr. Prajakta J. Nande

# Clinical and Therapeutic Nutrition Practical Manual 1
## For M.Sc. Food Science and Nutrition (Semester-III)

| | | | | |
|---|---|---|---|---|
| Peach | 281 | Garlic, big clove | 430 |
| Currants, black | 283 | Garlic, small clove | 453 |
| Guava, white flesh | 283 | Mint leaves | 539 |
| Apricot, dried | 285 | Coriander leaves | 546 |
| Dates, processed | 289 | Curry leaves | 584 |
| Banana, ripe, robusta | 306 | Garlic, single clove, Kashmir | 584 |
| Banana, ripe, red | 313 | **CONDIMENTS AND SPICES - DRY** | |
| Banana, ripe, poovam | 335 | Asafoetida | 245 |
| Wood apple | 347 | Nutmeg | 474 |
| Karonda fruit | 351 | Mace | 623 |
| Banana, ripe, montham | 362 | Poppy seeds | 646 |
| Phalsa | 362 | Fenugreek seeds | 891 |
| Manila tamarind | 376 | Cardamom, green | 1262 |
| Avocado fruit | 377 | Cardamom, black | 1331 |
| Bael fruit | 409 | Cloves | 1434 |
| Dates, dry, dark brown | 782 | Coriander seeds | 1473 |
| Dates, dry, pale brown | 804 | Pepper, black | 1487 |
| Tamarind, pulp | 836 | Omum | 1692 |
| Raisins, dried, golden | 913 | Pippali | 1852 |
| Raisins, dried, black | 1105 | Cumin seeds | 1886 |
| **ROOTS AND TUBERS** | | Chillies, red | 2245 |
| Radish, elongate, red skin | 255 | Turmeric powder | 2374 |
| Tapioca | 255 | **NUTS AND OIL SEEDS** | |
| Carrot, red | 267 | Coconut kernel, fresh | 246 |
| Carrot, orange | 273 | Arecanut, fresh | 329 |
| Radish, round, white skin | 287 | Walnut | 457 |
| Radish, elongate, white skin | 288 | Gingelly seeds, white | 460 |
| Beet root | 306 | Gingelly seeds, black | 480 |
| Radish, round, red skin | 308 | Gingelly seeds, brown | 491 |
| Sweet potato, pink skin | 329 | Arecanut, dried, brown | 524 |
| Sweet potato, brown skin | 345 | Safflower seeds | 550 |
| Water chestnut | 382 | Sunflower seeds | 559 |
| Yam, ordinary | 463 | Arecanut, dried, red color | 617 |
| Potato, brown skin, small | 474 | Cashew nut | 635 |
| Potato, red skin | 501 | Linseeds | 655 |
| Yam, elephant | 501 | Ground nut | 679 |
| Colocasia | 514 | Pine seeds | 686 |
| Potato, brown skin, big | 541 | Mustard seeds | 694 |
| Lotus root | 611 | Almond | 699 |
| Yam, wild | 654 | Niger seeds, black | 716 |
| **CONDIMENTS AND SPICES- FRESH** | | Coconut kernel, dry | 739 |
| Onion, small | 160 | Niger seeds, gray | 874 |
| Onion, big | 171 | Garden cress, seeds | 952 |
| Chillies green-all varieties | 341 | Pistachio nut | 1053 |
| Mango ginger | 384 | **SUGAR** | |
| Ginger, fresh | 407 | Sugarcane, juice | 150 |

272

**--- Author ---**
Dr. Prajakta J. Nande

# Clinical and Therapeutic Nutrition Practical Manual 1
## For M.Sc. Food Science and Nutrition (Semester-III)

| | | | | |
|---|---|---|---|---|
| Jaggery, cane | 488 | Pork, chops | 243 |
| **MUSHROOMS** | | Beef, heart | 258 |
| Button mushroom, fresh | 318 | Pork, heart | 268 |
| Shiitake mushroom, fresh | 323 | Goat, liver | 284 |
| Chicken mushroom, fresh | 340 | Beef, liver | 289 |
| **MISCELLANEOUS FOODS** | | Goat, brain | 296 |
| Coconut water | 215 | Beef, brain | 320 |
| **MILK AND MILK PRODUCTS** | | Pork, spleen | 325 |
| Paneer | 63.53 | Goat, shoulder meat | 332 |
| Milk, whole, buffalo | 109 | Goat, chops | 334 |
| Milk, whole, cow | 115 | Goat, legs | 339 |
| Khoa | 536 | Beef, spleen | 348 |
| **EGG AND EGG PRODUCTS** | | Goat, spleen | 368 |
| Egg,country hen,whole,raw | 62.33 | **MARINE FISH** | |
| Egg, poultry,yolk,raw | 118 | Bombay duck | 188 |
| Eggs, poultry,whole,raw | 138 | Sardine | 228 |
| Eggs, poultry,white,raw | 152 | Pomfret, white | 255 |
| **POULTRY** | | Pomfret, black | 295 |
| Chicken, poultry, wing, skinless | 185 | Mural | 330 |
| Poultry, chicken, liver | 241 | Salmon | 345 |
| Chicken, poultry, thigh, skinless | 263 | Tuna | 357 |
| Chicken, poultry, legs, skinless | 283 | **MARINE SHELLFISH** | |
| Chicken, poultry, breast, skinless | 295 | Tiger prawns, orange | 140 |
| **ANIMAL MEAT** | | Crab | 171 |
| Beef, chops | 11.54 | Lobster, brown | 212 |
| Beef, shoulder | 11.58 | Crab, sea | 252 |
| Beef, round (leg) | 18.14 | Lobster, king size | 315 |
| Goat, lungs | 180 | **FRESH WATER FISH AND SHELLFISH** | |
| Beef, kidney | 184 | Prawns, small | 224 |
| Goat, kidneys | 195 | Prawns, big | 269 |
| Pork, kidneys | 198 | Crab | 286 |
| Pork, lungs | 200 | Catla | 301 |
| Pork, stomach | 200 | Rohu | 303 |
| Beef, lungs | 216 | **FATTY FISH** | |
| Goat, heart | 224 | Hilsa | 341 |
| Pork, shoulder | 234 | | |

*(Source: T. Longvah, R. Ananthan, K. Bhaskaracharya, K. Venkaiah. Indian Food Composition Tables, National Institute of Nutrition (Indian Council of Medical Research), 113-168, 2017)*

**Clinical and Therapeutic Nutrition Practical Manual 1**
For M.Sc. Food Science and Nutrition (Semester-III)

## ANNEXURE - 11

## CALCIUM (Ca) CONTENT OF FOODS

| FOOD STUFFS | Ca (mg/ 100 g) | | |
|---|---|---|---|
| **CEREALS AND MILLETS** | | Cowpea, white | 84.1 |
| Maize, tender , local | 6.35 | Black gram, whole | 86.18 |
| Maize, tender, sweet | 6.37 | Green gram, whole | 92.43 |
| Rice, raw, milled | 7.49 | Rajmah, red | 126 |
| Rice, parboiled, milled | 8.11 | Rajmah, black | 134 |
| Maize, dry | 8.91 | Rajmah, brown | 134 |
| Rice flakes | 9.19 | Red gram, whole | 139 |
| Rice, raw, brown | 10.93 | Bengal gram, whole | 150 |
| Rice puffed | 15.09 | Moth bean | 154 |
| Varagu | 15.27 | Soya bean, white | 195 |
| Samai | 16.09 | Rice bean | 200 |
| Wheat, vermicelli | 19.42 | Soya bean, brown | 239 |
| Wheat flour, refined | 20.4 | Horse gram, whole | 269 |
| Wheat, vermicelli, roasted | 22.63 | **GREEN LEAFY VEGETABLES** | |
| Wheat, bulgur | 27.09 | Cabbage, violet | 48 |
| Bajra | 27.35 | Cabbage, green | 51.76 |
| Jowar | 27.6 | Brussels sprouts | 53.99 |
| Barley | 28.64 | Lettuce | 56.71 |
| Wheat, semolina | 29.38 | Cabbage, Chinese | 58.46 |
| Wheat flour | 30.94 | Tamarind leaves, tender | 66.93 |
| Wheat, whole | 39.36 | Spinach | 82.29 |
| Amaranth seeds, pale brown | 162 | Basella leaves | 93.89 |
| Amaranth seeds, black | 181 | Cauliflower leaves | 96.7 |
| Quinoa | 198 | Gogu leaves, red | 129 |
| Ragi | 364 | Rumex leaves | 131 |
| **GRAIN LEGUMES** | | Gogu leaves, green | 145 |
| Green gram, dal | 43.13 | Pak choi leaves | 150 |
| Lentil dal | 44.32 | Beet greens | 151 |
| Bengal gram, dal | 46.32 | Cabbage, collard greens | 170 |
| Black gram, dal | 55.67 | Mustard leaves | 191 |
| Red gram, dal | 71.73 | Betel leaves, small | 196 |
| Peas, dry | 75.11 | Betel leaves, big (Kolkata) | 207 |
| Field bean, brown | 75.2 | Bathua leaves | 211 |
| Lentil whole, brown | 76.13 | Colocasia leaves, green | 216 |
| Lentil whole, yellowish | 76.66 | Garden cress | 217 |
| Field bean, white | 77.24 | Radish leaves | 234 |
| Field bean, black | 78.16 | Amaranth leaves, red | 245 |
| Cowpea, brown | 81.73 | Amaranth leaves, red and green mix | 269 |
| | | Pumpkin leaves, tender | 271 |
| | | Fenugreek leaves | 274 |
| | | Parsley | 288 |

--- **Author** ---
Dr. Prajakta J. Nande

# Clinical and Therapeutic Nutrition Practical Manual 1
### For M.Sc. Food Science and Nutrition (Semester-III)

| | | | | |
|---|---|---|---|---|
| Drumstick leaves | 314 | Peas, fresh | 28.24 |
| Amaranth leaves, green | 330 | Colocasia, stem, black | 29.46 |
| Amaranth spinosus, leaves, green | 359 | Parwar | 30.76 |
| Knol-khol, leaves | 368 | Onion, stalk | 31.21 |
| Amaranth spinosus, leaves, red and green mix | 372 | Drumstick | 33.3 |
| | | Plantain, flower | 34.06 |
| Ponnaganni | 388 | Kovai, big | 34.39 |
| Agathi leaves | 901 | Knol-khol | 35.26 |
| **OTHER VEGETABLES** | | Kovai, small | 37.21 |
| Tomato, green | 8.49 | Jack fruit, seed, mature | 37.56 |
| Tomato, ripe, hybrid | 8.9 | Celery stalk | 38.73 |
| Bamboo shoot, tender | 10 | Colocasia, stem, green | 40.21 |
| Tomato, ripe, local | 10.17 | Bean scarlet, tender | 43.48 |
| Plantain, stem | 11.24 | Jack fruit, raw | 45.74 |
| Ridge gourd | 13.7 | French beans, hybrid | 49.9 |
| Plantain, green | 13.8 | French beans, country | 55.99 |
| Capsicum, green | 14.75 | Red gram, tender, fresh | 58.58 |
| Ridge gourd, smooth skin | 14.96 | Field beans, tender, lean | 58.59 |
| Bottle gourd, round, pale green | 15.05 | Broad beans | 64.37 |
| Bottle gourd, elongate, pale green | 15.42 | Field beans, tender, broad | 70.57 |
| Capsicum, red | 15.76 | Corn, baby | 76.51 |
| Bitter gourd, jagged, teeth ridges, short | 16.27 | Ladies finger | 86.12 |
| | | Cluster beans | 121 |
| Cucumber, green, elongate | 16.39 | **FRUITS** | |
| Brinjal-all varieties | 16.59 | Water melon, pale green | 4.35 |
| Bottle gourd, elongate, dark green | 16.64 | Mangosteen | 4.69 |
| Zucchini, green | 17.26 | Apple, small, Kashmir | 4.72 |
| Bitter gourd, jagged, smooth ridges, elongate | 17.62 | Star fruit | 4.97 |
| | | Banana, ripe, robusta | 5.07 |
| Snake gourd, short | 17.9 | Water melon, dark green | 5.29 |
| Cho-cho-marrow | 18.64 | Apple, small | 5.39 |
| Capsicum, yellow | 19.13 | Apricot, processed | 5.42 |
| Cucumber, green, short | 19.25 | Litchi | 5.77 |
| Ash gourd | 19.39 | Apple, green | 6.53 |
| Tinda, tender | 19.68 | Pear | 6.55 |
| Zucchini, yellow | 20.98 | Banana, ripe, montham | 6.77 |
| Bitter gourd, jagged, teeth ridges, elongate | 21.36 | Peach | 6.98 |
| | | Plum | 7.61 |
| Cucumber, round | 21.98 | Manila tamarind | 8.51 |
| Papaya, raw | 22.72 | Rambutan | 8.67 |
| Pumpkin, orange, round | 23.06 | Banana, ripe, poovam | 8.73 |
| Pumpkin, green, cylindrical | 24.1 | Musk melon, yellow flesh | 9.02 |
| Snake gourd, long, pale green | 24.6 | Banana, ripe, red | 9.56 |
| Cauliflower | 25.16 | Musk melon, orange flesh | 9.8 |
| Mango, green, raw | 27 | Soursop | 10.05 |
| Snake gourd, long, dark green | 27.11 | Grapes, seeded, round, black | 10.57 |

--- **Author** ---
Dr. Prajakta J. Nande

# Clinical and Therapeutic Nutrition Practical Manual 1
For M.Sc. Food Science and Nutrition (Semester-III)

| | | | | |
|---|---|---|---|---|
| Pomegranate, maroon seeds | 10.65 | Potato, brown skin, small | 8.53 |
| Karonda fruit | 10.81 | Potato, red skin | 8.62 |
| Pineapple | 10.88 | Potato, brown skin, big | 9.52 |
| Grapes, seeded, round, green | 11.16 | Yam, ordinary | 16.91 |
| Grapes, seeded, round, red | 11.27 | Beet root | 17.28 |
| Mango, ripe, neelam | 11.36 | Tapioca | 25.89 |
| Mango, ripe, totapari | 13.34 | Sweet potato, brown skin | 27.5 |
| Apple, big | 13.68 | Radish, elongate, red skin | 28.44 |
| Pummelo | 14.03 | Sweet potato, pink skin | 28.93 |
| Grapes, seedless, round, green | 14.22 | Colocasia | 30.18 |
| Guava, pink flesh | 14.22 | Radish, elongate, white skin | 30.2 |
| Papaya, ripe | 15.02 | Radish, round, white skin | 34.23 |
| Mango, ripe, paheri | 15.11 | Carrot, orange | 35.09 |
| Grapes, seedless, oval, black | 15.26 | Radish, round, red skin | 35.76 |
| Strawberry | 15.28 | Water chestnut | 37.15 |
| Mango, ripe, himsagar | 15.54 | Lotus root | 37.71 |
| Dates, processed | 15.73 | Carrot, red | 41.06 |
| Mango, ripe, kesar | 15.74 | Yam, wild | 44.13 |
| Mango, ripe, banganapalli | 15.77 | Yam, elephant | 46.91 |
| Sapota | 17.87 | **CONDIMENTS AND SPICES - FRESH** | |
| Guava, white flesh | 18.52 | Mango ginger | 13.74 |
| Grapes, seedless, round, black | 18.75 | Garlic, small clove | 17.63 |
| Mango, ripe, gulabkhas | 19.33 | Chillies green-all varieties | 18.45 |
| Orange, pulp | 19.52 | Ginger, fresh | 18.88 |
| Gooseberry | 20.14 | Garlic, single clove, Kashmir | 19 |
| Lemon, juice | 22.68 | Onion, small | 19.92 |
| Black berry | 23.81 | Garlic, big clove | 20.08 |
| Cherries, red | 23.88 | Onion, big | 21.03 |
| Jambu fruit, ripe | 25.36 | Coriander leaves | 146 |
| Lime, sweet, pulp | 25.79 | Mint leaves | 205 |
| Custard apple | 28.2 | Curry leaves | 659 |
| Avocado fruit | 28.48 | **CONDIMENTS AND SPICES - DRY** | |
| Apricot, dried | 28.57 | Chillies, red | 99.83 |
| Jack fruit, ripe | 35.03 | Turmeric powder | 122 |
| Currants, black | 40.32 | Fenugreek seeds | 135 |
| Zizyphus | 46.55 | Nutmeg | 148 |
| Bael fruit | 47.95 | Mace | 174 |
| Raisins, dried, golden | 51.83 | Asafoetida | 266 |
| Wood apple | 55.71 | Cardamom, black | 312 |
| Dates, dry, dark brown | 66.13 | Cardamom, green | 378 |
| Dates, dry, pale brown | 71.2 | Pepper, black | 405 |
| Raisins, dried, black | 73.24 | Pippali | 414 |
| Fig | 78.52 | Cloves | 567 |
| Tamarind, pulp | 149 | Coriander seeds | 718 |
| Phalsa | 153 | Cumin seeds | 878 |
| **ROOTS AND TUBERS** | | Omum | 1034 |

--- **Author** ---
Dr. Prajakta J. Nande

# Clinical and Therapeutic Nutrition Practical Manual 1
For M.Sc. Food Science and Nutrition (Semester-III)

| Food | Value |
|---|---|
| Poppy seeds | 1372 |
| **NUTS AND OIL SEEDS** | |
| Coconut, kernel, fresh | 8 |
| Pine seeds | 17 |
| Coconut, kernel, dry | 32 |
| Cashew nut | 34 |
| Arecanut, fresh | 34.03 |
| Arecanut, dried, red color | 51 |
| Ground nut | 54 |
| Arecanut, dried, brown | 61 |
| Walnut | 105 |
| Pistachio nut | 135 |
| Sunflower seeds | 176 |
| Safflower seeds | 211 |
| Almond | 228 |
| Linseeds | 257 |
| Garden cress, seeds | 318 |
| Niger seeds, gray | 375 |
| Mustard seeds | 402 |
| Niger seeds, black | 572 |
| Gingelly seeds, brown | 1174 |
| Gingelly seeds, white | 1283 |
| Gingelly seeds, black | 1664 |
| **SUGAR** | |
| Sugarcane, juice | 18 |
| Jaggery, cane | 107 |
| **MUSHROOMS** | |
| Chicken mushroom, fresh | 4.83 |
| Shiitake mushroom, fresh | 5.3 |
| Button mushroom, fresh | 18.38 |
| **MISCELLANEOUS FOODS** | |
| Coconut water | 27.47 |
| **MILK AND MILK PRODUCTS** | |
| Milk, whole, cow | 118 |
| Milk, whole, buffalo | 121 |
| Paneer | 476 |
| Khoa | 602 |
| **EGG AND EGG PRODUCTS** | |
| Eggs, poultry, white, raw | 5.64 |
| Eggs, poultry, whole, raw | 49.44 |
| Egg, country hen, whole, raw | 50.14 |
| Egg, poultry, yolk, raw | 116 |
| **POULTRY** | |
| Poultry, chicken, liver | 4.1 |
| Chicken, poultry, breast, skinless | 12.91 |
| Chicken, poultry, thigh, skinless | 18.37 |

| Food | Value |
|---|---|
| Chicken, poultry, legs, skinless | 20.52 |
| Chicken, poultry, wing, skinless | 28.13 |
| **ANIMAL MEAT** | |
| Beef, chops | 4.64 |
| Pork, heart | 4.74 |
| Beef, liver | 5.64 |
| Goat, heart | 5.71 |
| Goat, legs | 5.76 |
| Beef, round (leg) | 5.86 |
| Goat, liver | 6.09 |
| Beef, heart | 6.16 |
| Goat, shoulder | 6.18 |
| Beef, shoulder | 6.5 |
| Pork, kidneys | 6.71 |
| Pork, spleen | 6.98 |
| Goat, chops | 7.44 |
| Pork, chops | 8.12 |
| Goat, spleen | 8.35 |
| Beef, lungs | 9.31 |
| Beef, spleen | 9.4 |
| Pork, shoulder | 9.95 |
| Pork, lungs | 10.3 |
| Goat, lungs | 10.44 |
| Goat, brain | 10.61 |
| Beef, brain | 11.38 |
| Pork, stomach | 11.75 |
| Goat, kidneys | 12.37 |
| Beef, kidney | 15.31 |
| **MARINE FISH** | |
| Mural | 8.61 |
| Tuna | 9.28 |
| Pomfret, white | 13.64 |
| Pomfret, black | 18.1 |
| Salmon | 24.3 |
| Sardine | 42.26 |
| Bombay duck | 159 |
| **MARINE SHELLFISH** | |
| Lobster, king size | 66.44 |
| Tiger prawns, orange | 71.89 |
| Lobster, brown | 73.06 |
| Crab | 128 |
| Crab, sea | 333 |
| **FRESH WATER FISH AND SHELLFISH** | |
| Rohu | 39.37 |
| Catla | 43.53 |
| Prawns, big | 48.55 |

--- Author ---
Dr. Prajakta J. Nande

# Clinical and Therapeutic Nutrition Practical Manual 1
For M.Sc. Food Science and Nutrition (Semester-III)

| Prawns, small | 67.99 | FATTY FISH | |
|---|---|---|---|
| Crab | 199 | Hilsa | 19.82 |

*(Source: T. Longvah, R. Ananthan, K. Bhaskaracharya, K. Venkaiah. Indian Food Composition Tables, National Institute of Nutrition (Indian Council of Medical Research), 113-168, 2017)*

## ANNEXURE - 12

## MAGNESIUM (Mg) CONTENT OF FOODS

| FOOD STUFFS | Mg (mg/ 100 g) | | |
|---|---|---|---|
| **CEREALS AND MILLETS** | | Horse gram, whole | 152 |
| Rice, raw, milled | 19.3 | Green gram, dal | 155 |
| Rice, parboiled, milled | 26.72 | Red gram, whole | 155 |
| Wheat flour, refined | 30.69 | Bengal gram, whole | 160 |
| Wheat, vermicelli | 34.18 | Rajmah, black | 160 |
| Maize tender, sweet | 36.51 | Rajmah, brown | 164 |
| Wheat, semolina | 37.89 | Black gram, dal | 173 |
| Wheat, vermicelli, roasted | 39.03 | Field bean, brown | 173 |
| Maize, tender, local | 47.62 | Rajmah, red | 173 |
| Barley | 48.97 | Soya bean, white | 189 |
| Rice puffed | 64.59 | Black gram, whole | 190 |
| Rice flakes | 77.92 | Field bean, white | 190 |
| Samai | 91.41 | Field bean, black | 197 |
| Rice,raw ,brown | 93.91 | Green gram, whole | 198 |
| Wheat, bulgur | 116 | Rice bean | 201 |
| Quinoa | 119 | Moth bean | 205 |
| Varagu | 122 | Cowpea, brown | 213 |
| Bajra | 124 | Cowpea, white | 213 |
| Wheat flour | 125 | Soya bean, brown | 259 |
| Wheat, whole | 125 | **GREEN LEAFY VEGETABLES** | |
| Jowar | 133 | Cabbage, Chinese | 11.51 |
| Maize, dry | 145 | Cabbage, green | 17.99 |
| Ragi | 146 | Cabbage, violet | 26.87 |
| Amaranth seeds, pale brown | 270 | Brussels sprouts | 32.99 |
| Amaranth seeds, black | 325 | Cauliflower leaves | 41.5 |
| **GRAIN LEGUMES** | | Tamarind leaves, tender | 42.1 |
| Lentil dal | 74.69 | Lettuce | 43.22 |
| Lentil whole, yellowish | 86.38 | Pak choi leaves | 45.28 |
| Lentil whole, brown | 101 | Cabbage, collard greens | 45.9 |
| Bengal gram, dal | 118 | Rumex leaves | 48.33 |
| Red gram, dal | 119 | Bathua leaves | 48.41 |
| Peas, dry | 123 | Parsley | 49.18 |
| | | Mustard leaves | 51.63 |
| | | Radish leaves | 57.96 |
| | | Colocasia leaves, green | 59.44 |

--- Author ---
Dr. Prajakta J. Nande

# Clinical and Therapeutic Nutrition Practical Manual 1
## For M.Sc. Food Science and Nutrition (Semester-III)

| | | | | |
|---|---|---|---|---|
| Fenugreek leaves | 63.67 | | Knol-khol | 19.05 |
| Knol-khol leaves | 66 | | Colocasia, stem, green | 19.56 |
| Gogu leaves, red | 75.75 | | Capsicum, red | 19.57 |
| Garden cress | 79.24 | | Kovai, big | 19.6 |
| Ponnaganni | 80.39 | | Ash gourd | 19.95 |
| Gogu leaves, green | 83.09 | | Cucumber, round | 20.34 |
| Pumpkin leaves, tender | 84.21 | | Cucumber, green, elongate | 20.38 |
| Spinach | 86.97 | | Brinjal-all varieties | 21 |
| Betel leaves, small | 89.94 | | Snake gourd, long, dark green | 21.7 |
| Agathi leaves | 96.64 | | Cauliflower | 23.08 |
| Drumstick leaves | 97.09 | | Parwar | 24.59 |
| Betel leaves, big (Kolkata) | 107 | | Corn, baby | 25.47 |
| Beet greens | 120 | | Jack fruit, raw | 26.6 |
| Amaranth leaves, red and green mix | 146 | | Bitter gourd, jagged, teeth ridges, short | 31.58 |
| Basella leaves | 153 | | Bitter gourd, jagged, teeth ridges, elongate | 32.14 |
| Amaranth leaves, red | 177 | | Plantain, stem | 32.82 |
| Amaranth spinosus, leaves, red and green mix | 187 | | Bitter gourd, jagged, smooth ridges, elongate | 33.34 |
| Amaranth leaves, green | 194 | | French beans, hybrid | 34.98 |
| Amaranth spinosus, leaves, green | 202 | | Plantain, green | 35.64 |
| **OTHER VEGETABLES** | | | Jack fruit, seed, mature | 37.04 |
| Bamboo shoot, tender | 8.28 | | Drumstick | 38.1 |
| Pumpkin, orange, round | 10.43 | | Plantain, flower | 39.76 |
| Zucchini, yellow | 10.82 | | Peas, fresh | 40.11 |
| Bottle gourd, round, pale green | 10.89 | | Broad beans | 40.18 |
| Bottle gourd, elongate, pale green | 10.93 | | French beans, country | 43.01 |
| Colocasia, stem, black | 11.07 | | Bean scarlet, tender | 43.75 |
| Capsicum, green | 11.84 | | Field beans, tender, lean | 47.42 |
| Tomato, ripe, hybrid | 11.86 | | Field beans, tender, broad | 50.88 |
| Bottle gourd, elongate, dark green | 12.9 | | Red gram, tender, fresh | 56.95 |
| Cho-cho-marrow | 13.05 | | Ladies finger | 66.1 |
| Pumpkin, green, cylindrical | 13.27 | | Onion, stalk | 66.71 |
| Tomato, green | 13.57 | | Cluster beans | 81.74 |
| Tomato, ripe, local | 13.65 | | **FRUITS** | |
| Papaya, raw | 15.03 | | Apricot, processed | 4.29 |
| Snake gourd, short | 15.07 | | Apple, small, Kashmir | 5.19 |
| Zucchini, green | 15.41 | | Apple, green | 5.42 |
| Ridge gourd | 16.15 | | Apple, small | 5.48 |
| Celery stalk | 17.12 | | Gooseberry | 6.50 |
| Capsicum, yellow | 17.23 | | Pummelo | 6.83 |
| Mango, green, raw | 17.54 | | Grapes, seeded, round, green | 6.87 |
| Ridge gourd, smooth skin | 17.66 | | Grapes, seeded, round, red | 7.06 |
| Cucumber, green, short | 18.48 | | Water melon, pale green | 7.42 |
| Snake gourd, long, pale green | 18.7 | | Grapes, seeded, round, black | 7.47 |
| Kovai, small | 18.87 | | | |
| Tinda, tender | 18.96 | | | |

--- **Author** ---
Dr. Prajakta J. Nande

# Clinical and Therapeutic Nutrition Practical Manual 1
For M.Sc. Food Science and Nutrition (Semester-III)

| Food | Value | Food | Value |
|---|---|---|---|
| Pear | 7.61 | Manila tamarind | 32.98 |
| Plum | 7.79 | Raisins, dried, black | 33.76 |
| Peach | 8.06 | Bael fruit | 34.1 |
| Apple, big | 8.09 | Banana, ripe, robusta | 34.98 |
| Grapes, seedless, round, green | 8.43 | Custard apple | 38.47 |
| Lemon, juice | 8.9 | Banana, ripe, poovam | 43.79 |
| Musk melon, yellow flesh | 9.81 | Avocado fruit | 48.14 |
| Water melon, dark green | 9.91 | Dates, dry, pale brown | 73.79 |
| Mango, ripe, neelam | 10.1 | Dates, dry, dark brown | 75.23 |
| Grapes, seedless, round, black | 10.8 | Phalsa | 76.92 |
| Papaya, ripe | 10.97 | Tamarind, pulp | 82.73 |
| Orange, pulp | 11.05 | Palm fruit, tender | - |
| Pomegranate, maroon seeds | 11.07 | **ROOTS AND TUBERS** | |
| Grapes, seedless, oval, black | 11.29 | Radish, elongate, red skin | 13.34 |
| Mango, ripe, gulabkhas | 11.53 | Radish, round, white skin | 15.46 |
| Star fruit | 11.53 | Radish, elongate, white skin | 16.07 |
| Musk melon, orange flesh | 11.62 | Carrot, orange | 16.73 |
| Mangosteen | 12 | Sweet potato, brown skin | 17.37 |
| Mango, ripe, himsagar | 12.07 | Carrot, red | 18.83 |
| Mango, ripe, kesar | 12.53 | Sweet potato, pink skin | 21.05 |
| Mango, ripe, totapari | 12.55 | Radish, round, red skin | 22.25 |
| Pineapple | 12.68 | Potato, brown skin, small | 22.34 |
| Guava, pink flesh | 13.26 | Tapioca | 23.08 |
| Mango, ripe, banganapalli | 13.35 | Potato, brown skin, big | 24.07 |
| Apricot, dried | 14.04 | Potato, red skin | 25.54 |
| Mango, ripe, paheri | 14.28 | Lotus root | 26.58 |
| Dates, processed | 14.34 | Yam, ordinary | 30.4 |
| Cherries, red | 14.37 | Yam, wild | 31.75 |
| Litchi | 14.58 | Beet root | 33.21 |
| Guava, white flesh | 15.26 | Yam, elephant | 33.51 |
| Lime, sweet,pulp | 15.4 | Colocasia | 36.93 |
| Strawberry | 15.53 | Water chestnut | 57.43 |
| Sapota | 16.19 | **CONDIMENTS AND SPICES - FRESH** | |
| Currants, black | 16.66 | Onion, small | 15.16 |
| Zizyphus | 16.72 | Onion, big | 17.96 |
| Soursop | 17.7 | Garlic, small clove | 25.78 |
| Rambutan | 21.38 | Garlic, big clove | 27.08 |
| Wood apple | 23.7 | Chillies green-all varieties | 29.51 |
| Karonda fruit | 24.45 | Mango ginger | 36.86 |
| Fig | 26.18 | Garlic, single clove, Kashmir | 41.13 |
| Jambu fruit, ripe | 27.97 | Ginger, fresh | 54.66 |
| Raisins, dried, golden | 28.32 | Coriander leaves | 72.68 |
| Banana, ripe, montham | 30.22 | Mint leaves | 110 |
| Black berry | 30.90 | Curry leaves | 182 |
| Banana, ripe, red | 31.44 | **CONDIMENTS AND SPICES - DRY** | |
| Jack fruit, ripe | 31.84 | Asafoetida | 96.4 |

# Clinical and Therapeutic Nutrition Practical Manual 1
## For M.Sc. Food Science and Nutrition (Semester-III)

| | | | |
|---|---|---|---|
| Fenugreek seeds | 167 | Milk, whole, cow | 8.28 |
| Pippali | 189 | Milk, whole, buffalo | 10.05 |
| Pepper, black | 196 | Paneer | 26.62 |
| Mace | 207 | Khoa | 58.53 |
| Nutmeg | 212 | **EGG AND EGG PRODUCTS** | |
| Chillies, red | 231 | Egg, country hen, whole, raw | 11 |
| Turmeric powder | 260 | Eggs, poultry, white, raw | 11.42 |
| Omum | 273 | Eggs, poultry, whole, raw | 12.01 |
| Cardamom, black | 286 | Egg, poultry, yolk, raw | 13.17 |
| Cardamom, green | 330 | **POULTRY** | |
| Cloves | 334 | Poultry, chicken, liver | 16 |
| Coriander seeds | 343 | Chicken, poultry, breast, skinless | 20.2 |
| Poppy seeds | 393 | Chicken, poultry, thigh, skinless | 22.55 |
| Cumin seeds | 442 | Chicken, poultry, wing, skinless | 22.81 |
| **NUTS AND OIL SEEDS** | | Chicken, poultry, legs, skinless | 23.82 |
| Almond | 318 | **ANIMAL MEAT** | |
| Arecanut, dried, brown | 76.39 | Pork, chops | 9.82 |
| Arecanut, dried, red color | 91.01 | Goat, lungs | 11.48 |
| Arecanut, fresh | 47.6 | Beef, heart | 11.6 |
| Cashew nut | 307 | Pork, shoulder | 11.62 |
| Coconut kernel, dry | 97.21 | Goat, brain | 13.94 |
| Coconut kernel, fresh | 35 | Beef, liver | 14.7 |
| Garden cress, seeds | 307 | Beef, kidney | 15.01 |
| Gingelly seeds, black | 390 | Goat, spleen | 15.3 |
| Gingelly seeds, brown | 328 | Pork, spleen | 15.56 |
| Gingelly seeds, white | 372 | Beef, lungs | 15.66 |
| Ground nut | 197 | Beef, spleen | 15.8 |
| Mustard seeds | 266 | Beef, round (leg) | 15.84 |
| Linseeds | 349 | Pork, stomach | 16.08 |
| Niger seeds, black | 346 | Goat, heart | 18 |
| Niger seeds, gray | 379 | Goat, liver | 18 |
| Pine seeds | 268 | Pork, lungs | 18.23 |
| Pistachio nut | 149 | Beef, brain | 18.57 |
| Safflower seeds | 413 | Goat, kidneys | 18.6 |
| Sunflower seeds | 180 | Goat, chops | 21.13 |
| Walnut | 0.37 | Goat, shoulder meat | 21.39 |
| **SUGAR** | | Goat, legs | 21.71 |
| Sugarcane, juice | 13.03 | Beef, shoulder | 22.24 |
| Jaggery, cane | 115 | Pork, heart | 23.32 |
| **MUSHROOMS** | | Beef, chops | 26.59 |
| Chicken mushroom, fresh | 10.78 | **MARINE FISH** | |
| Button mushroom, fresh | 18.3 | Bombay duck | 24.27 |
| Shiitake mushroom, fresh | 24.47 | Sardine | 24.39 |
| **MISCELLANEOUS FOODS** | | Mural | 27.1 |
| Coconut water | 18.19 | Pomfret, black | 28.22 |
| **MILK AND MILK PRODUCTS** | | Salmon | 31.18 |

--- **Author** ---
Dr. Prajakta J. Nande

# Clinical and Therapeutic Nutrition Practical Manual 1
For M.Sc. Food Science and Nutrition (Semester-III)

| | | | | |
|---|---|---|---|---|
| Pomfret, white | 32.2 | **FRESH WATER FISH AND SHELLFISH** | |
| Tuna | 35.85 | Catla | 25.58 |
| **MARINE SHELLFISH** | | Rohu | 26.53 |
| Tiger prawns, orange | 30.5 | Prawns, small | 26.91 |
| Crab | 38.04 | Prawns, big | 39.25 |
| Lobster, brown | 45.34 | Crab | 66.77 |
| Lobster, king size | 50.16 | **FATTY FISH** | |
| Crab, sea | 80.04 | Hilsa | 30.62 |

*(Source: T. Longvah, R. Ananthan, K. Bhaskaracharya, K. Venkaiah. Indian Food Composition Tables, National Institute of Nutrition (Indian Council of Medical Research), 113-168, 2017)*

## ANNEXURE - 13

## IRON (Fe) CONTENT OF FOODS

| FOOD STUFFS | Iron (mg/ 100 g) | | |
|---|---|---|---|
| **CEREALS AND MILLETS** | | Red gram, dal | 3.9 |
| Maize tender, sweet | 0.54 | Green gram, dal | 3.93 |
| Rice, raw, milled | 0.65 | Field bean, black | 4.5 |
| Maize, tender, local | 0.71 | Black gram, dal | 4.67 |
| Rice, parboiled, milled | 0.72 | Rice bean | 4.76 |
| Rice, raw ,brown | 1.02 | Green gram, whole | 4.89 |
| Samai | 1.26 | Field bean, brown | 4.99 |
| Barley | 1.56 | Cowpea, white | 5.04 |
| Wheat flour, refined | 1.77 | Peas, dry | 5.09 |
| Wheat, vermicelli | 2.02 | Red gram, whole | 5.37 |
| Wheat, vermicelli, roasted | 2.09 | Field bean, white | 5.5 |
| Varagu | 2.34 | Cowpea, brown | 5.9 |
| Maize, dry | 2.49 | Black gram, whole | 5.97 |
| Wheat, semolina | 2.98 | Bengal gram, dal | 6.08 |
| Wheat, bulgur | 3.86 | Rajmah, red | 6.13 |
| Jowar | 3.95 | Rajmah, black | 6.17 |
| Wheat, whole | 3.97 | Rajmah, brown | 6.3 |
| Wheat flour | 4.1 | Bengal gram, whole | 6.78 |
| Rice flakes | 4.46 | Lentil dal | 7.06 |
| Rice puffed | 4.55 | Lentil whole, brown | 7.75 |
| Ragi | 4.62 | Moth bean | 7.9 |
| Bajra | 6.42 | Lentil whole, yellowish | 7.91 |
| Quinoa | 7.51 | Soya bean, white | 8.22 |
| Amaranth seeds, pale brown | 8.02 | Soya bean, brown | 8.29 |
| Amaranth seeds, black | 9.33 | Horse gram, whole | 8.76 |
| **GRAIN LEGUMES** | | **GREEN LEAFY VEGETABLES** | |
| | | Cabbage, violet | 0.24 |
| | | Cabbage, green | 0.35 |
| | | Cabbage, Chinese | 0.39 |

--- **Author** ---
Dr. Prajakta J. Nande

# Clinical and Therapeutic Nutrition Practical Manual 1
For M.Sc. Food Science and Nutrition (Semester-III)

| | | | | |
|---|---|---|---|---|
| Brussels sprouts | 1.54 | Bottle gourd, elongate, dark green | 0.34 |
| Cauliflower leaves | 2.42 | Plantain, green | 0.34 |
| Knol-khol leaves | 2.51 | Zucchini, yellow | 0.34 |
| Bathua leaves | 2.66 | Pumpkin, orange, round | 0.36 |
| Cabbage, collard greens | 2.67 | Brinjal-all varieties | 0.37 |
| Lettuce | 2.73 | Jack fruit, seed, mature | 0.37 |
| Mustard leaves | 2.84 | Capsicum, red | 0.38 |
| Tamarind leaves, tender | 2.84 | Kovai, big | 0.38 |
| Betel leaves, small | 2.87 | Mango, green, raw | 0.4 |
| Spinach | 2.95 | Plantain, flower | 0.4 |
| Betel leaves, big (Kolkata) | 3 | Tinda, tender | 0.41 |
| Colocasia leaves, green | 3.41 | Ridge gourd | 0.42 |
| Rumex leaves | 3.67 | Tomato, green | 0.42 |
| Pak choi leaves | 3.78 | Cucumber, round | 0.45 |
| Radish leaves | 3.82 | Cucumber, green, elongate | 0.46 |
| Ponnaganni | 3.88 | Ash gourd | 0.47 |
| Basella leaves | 4.2 | Snake gourd, long, dark green | 0.47 |
| Agathi leaves | 4.36 | Capsicum, green | 0.48 |
| Drumstick leaves | 4.56 | Cho-cho-marrow | 0.48 |
| Amaranth spinosus, leaves, red and green mix | 4.58 | Parwar | 0.5 |
| | | Ridge gourd, smooth skin | 0.5 |
| Amaranth leaves, green | 4.64 | Zucchini, green | 0.52 |
| Amaranth leaves, red and green mix | 5.28 | Colocasia, stem, green | 0.55 |
| Parsley | 5.51 | Cucumber, green, short | 0.59 |
| Pumpkin leaves, tender | 5.58 | Capsicum, yellow | 0.69 |
| Fenugreek leaves | 5.69 | Bean scarlet, tender | 0.73 |
| Beet greens | 5.8 | Drumstick | 0.73 |
| Garden cress | 6.19 | Colocasia, stem, black | 0.77 |
| Amaranth spinosus, leaves, green | 6.37 | Ladies finger | 0.84 |
| Amaranth leaves, red | 7.25 | Broad beans | 0.94 |
| Gogu leaves, green | 7.65 | Cauliflower | 0.96 |
| Gogu leaves, red | 9.56 | French beans, hybrid | 0.98 |
| **OTHER VEGETABLES** | | Bitter gourd, jagged, teeth ridges, short | 1.08 |
| Papaya, raw | 0.2 | | |
| Snake gourd, short | 0.2 | Bitter gourd, jagged, teeth ridges, elongate | 1.15 |
| Tomato, ripe, hybrid | 0.22 | | |
| Knol-khol | 0.24 | Red gram, tender, fresh | 1.18 |
| Bottle gourd, elongate, pale green | 0.26 | French beans, country | 1.25 |
| Plantain, stem | 0.26 | Bitter gourd, jagged, smooth ridges, elongate | 1.28 |
| Bottle gourd, round, pale green | 0.28 | | |
| Kovai, small | 0.29 | Celery stalk | 1.36 |
| Pumpkin, green, cylindrical | 0.29 | Corn, baby | 1.45 |
| Tomato, ripe, local | 0.3 | Field beans, tender, lean | 1.48 |
| Jack fruit, raw | 0.31 | Peas, fresh | 1.58 |
| Snake gourd, long, pale green | 0.32 | Field beans, tender, broad | 1.95 |
| Bamboo shoot, tender | 0.33 | Onion, stalk | 3.09 |

--- **Author** ---
Dr. Prajakta J. Nande

# Clinical and Therapeutic Nutrition Practical Manual 1
## For M.Sc. Food Science and Nutrition (Semester-III)

| | |
|---|---|
| Cluster beans | 3.9 |

| **FRUITS** | |
|---|---|
| Pummelo | 0.06 |
| Lime, sweet, pulp | 0.11 |
| Lemon, juice | 0.12 |
| Water melon, pale green | 0.16 |
| Musk melon, orange flesh | 0.18 |
| Apple, green | 0.2 |
| Apple, small, Kashmir | 0.21 |
| Musk melon, yellow flesh | 0.21 |
| Grapes, seeded, round, black | 0.22 |
| Water melon, dark green | 0.22 |
| Bael fruit | 0.23 |
| Papaya, ripe | 0.23 |
| Banana, ripe, red | 0.24 |
| Grapes, seeded, round, green | 0.24 |
| Grapes, seedless, round, green | 0.24 |
| Apple, small | 0.25 |
| Plum | 0.25 |
| Apple, big | 0.26 |
| Banana, ripe, robusta | 0.28 |
| Grapes, seedless, oval, black | 0.28 |
| Mango, ripe, totapari | 0.28 |
| Mangosteen | 0.28 |
| Pear | 0.28 |
| Pineapple | 0.28 |
| Mango, ripe, himsagar | 0.29 |
| Soursop | 0.29 |
| Pomegranate, maroon seeds | 0.31 |
| Guava, white flesh | 0.32 |
| Grapes, seeded, round, red | 0.33 |
| Jambu fruit, ripe | 0.33 |
| Banana, ripe, poovam | 0.35 |
| Peach | 0.35 |
| Cherries, red | 0.36 |
| Jack fruit, ripe | 0.36 |
| Mango, ripe, neelam | 0.36 |
| Strawberry | 0.36 |
| Rambutan | 0.37 |
| Mango, ripe, gulabkhas | 0.38 |
| Grapes, seedless, round, black | 0.39 |
| Banana, ripe, montham | 0.4 |
| Guava, pink flesh | 0.4 |
| Zizyphus | 0.4 |
| Custard apple | 0.42 |
| Mango, ripe, kesar | 0.43 |

| | |
|---|---|
| Star fruit | 0.45 |
| Wood apple | 0.45 |
| Sapota | 0.49 |
| Mango, ripe, banganapalli | 0.51 |
| Mango, ripe, paheri | 0.51 |
| Black berry | 0.63 |
| Fig | 0.69 |
| Manila tamarind | 0.71 |
| Litchi | 0.79 |
| Avocado fruit | 0.81 |
| Orange, pulp | 0.81 |
| Karonda fruit | 0.87 |
| Dates, processed | 0.89 |
| Apricot, processed | 1.12 |
| Gooseberry | 1.25 |
| Currants, black | 1.36 |
| Phalsa | 2.01 |
| Apricot, dried | 2.5 |
| Dates, dry, pale brown | 3.2 |
| Raisins, dried, golden | 4.26 |
| Dates, dry, dark brown | 4.79 |
| Raisins, dried, black | 6.81 |
| Tamarind, pulp | 9.16 |

| **ROOTS AND TUBERS** | |
|---|---|
| Sweet potato, brown skin | 0.35 |
| Radish, elongate, white skin | 0.36 |
| Radish, elongate, red skin | 0.37 |
| Radish, round, white skin | 0.41 |
| Radish, round, red skin | 0.42 |
| Sweet potato, pink skin | 0.51 |
| Potato, brown skin, small | 0.53 |
| Potato, brown skin, big | 0.57 |
| Carrot, orange | 0.6 |
| Colocasia | 0.66 |
| Potato, red skin | 0.66 |
| Carrot, red | 0.71 |
| Beet root | 0.76 |
| Water chestnut | 0.77 |
| Yam, ordinary | 0.77 |
| Tapioca | 0.81 |
| Yam, wild | 1.04 |
| Yam, elephant | 1.22 |
| Lotus root | 3.34 |

| **CONDIMENTS AND SPICES - FRESH** | |
|---|---|
| Onion, big | 0.43 |
| Onion, small | 0.53 |

--- Author ---

Dr. Prajakta J. Nande

# Clinical and Therapeutic Nutrition Practical Manual 1
For M.Sc. Food Science and Nutrition (Semester-III)

| | |
|---|---|
| Garlic, small clove | 0.88 |
| Garlic, single clove, Kashmir | 1.01 |
| Garlic, big clove | 1.05 |
| Chillies green-all varieties | 1.2 |
| Ginger, fresh | 1.9 |
| Mango ginger | 2.31 |
| Coriander leaves | 5.3 |
| Mint leaves | 8.56 |
| Curry leaves | 8.67 |
| **CONDIMENTS AND SPICES - DRY** | |
| Nutmeg | 2.33 |
| Chillies, red | 6.23 |
| Cardamom, black | 7.94 |
| Pippali | 7.99 |
| Cardamom, green | 8.33 |
| Fenugreek seeds | 8.47 |
| Cloves | 9.41 |
| Poppy seeds | 10.13 |
| Pepper, black | 11.91 |
| Omum | 13.65 |
| Asafoetida | 15.68 |
| Coriander seeds | 17.64 |
| Cumin seeds | 20.58 |
| Mace | 22.69 |
| Turmeric powder | 46.08 |
| **NUTS AND OIL SEEDS** | |
| Arecanut, fresh | 1.04 |
| Coconut kernel, fresh | 1.3 |
| Arecanut, dried, brown | 2.74 |
| Coconut kernel, dry | 3.13 |
| Walnut | 3.21 |
| Arecanut, dried, red color | 3.26 |
| Ground nut | 3.44 |
| Safflower seeds | 4.06 |
| Pine seeds | 4.5 |
| Pistachio nut | 4.5 |
| Almond | 4.59 |
| Linseeds | 5.44 |
| Sunflower seeds | 5.85 |
| Cashew nut | 5.95 |
| Mustard seeds | 13.49 |
| Gingelly seeds, black | 13.9 |
| Gingelly seeds, brown | 14.95 |
| Gingelly seeds, white | 15.04 |
| Garden cress, seeds | 17.2 |
| Niger seeds, black | 18.19 |

| | |
|---|---|
| Niger seeds, gray | 19.61 |
| **SUGAR** | |
| Sugarcane, juice | 1.12 |
| Jaggery, cane | 4.63 |
| **MUSHROOMS** | |
| Button mushroom, fresh | 0.29 |
| Chicken mushroom, fresh | 0.3 |
| Shiitake mushroom, fresh | 1.93 |
| **MISCELLANEOUS FOODS** | |
| Coconut water | 0.06 |
| **MILK AND MILK PRODUCTS** | |
| Milk, whole, cow | 0.15 |
| Milk, whole, buffalo | 0.16 |
| Paneer | 0.9 |
| Khoa | 2.23 |
| **EGG AND EGG PRODUCTS** | |
| Eggs, poultry, white, raw | 0.07 |
| Egg, country hen, whole, raw | 1.64 |
| Eggs, poultry, whole, raw | 1.82 |
| Egg, poultry, yolk, raw | 3.17 |
| **POULTRY** | |
| Chicken, poultry, breast, skinless | 0.83 |
| Chicken, poultry, thigh, skinless | 1.11 |
| Chicken, poultry, legs, skinless | 1.27 |
| Chicken, poultry, wing, skinless | 1.38 |
| Poultry, chicken, liver | 9.92 |
| **ANIMAL MEAT** | |
| Pork, shoulder | 0.91 |
| Pork, chops | 1 |
| Goat, shoulder meat | 1.48 |
| Goat, brain | 1.63 |
| Goat, legs | 1.77 |
| Goat, chops | 1.87 |
| Pork, stomach | 1.92 |
| Beef, chops | 1.95 |
| Beef, brain | 2.15 |
| Beef, shoulder | 2.22 |
| Beef, round (leg) | 2.3 |
| Goat, heart | 3.38 |
| Beef, heart | 3.62 |
| Pork, heart | 3.97 |
| Beef, kidney | 4.71 |
| Pork, kidneys | 6.26 |
| Goat, liver | 6.56 |
| Goat, kidneys | 6.73 |
| Pork, lungs | 6.76 |

--- **Author** ---
Dr. Prajakta J. Nande

# Clinical and Therapeutic Nutrition Practical Manual 1
For M.Sc. Food Science and Nutrition (Semester-III)

| | | | |
|---|---|---|---|
| Beef, lungs | 6.85 | **MARINE SHELLFISH** | |
| Goat, lungs | 7.1 | Lobster, king size | 0.35 |
| Beef, liver | 14.82 | Tiger prawns, orange | 0.39 |
| Pork, spleen | 27.21 | Lobster, brown | 0.77 |
| Beef, spleen | 31.68 | Crab, sea | 0.98 |
| Goat, spleen | 51.41 | Crab | 1.1 |
| **MARINE FISH** | | **FRESH WATER FISH AND SHELLFISH** | |
| Mural | 0.24 | Prawns, big | 0.78 |
| Pomfret, white | 0.31 | Prawns, small | 0.87 |
| Pomfret, black | 0.78 | Rohu | 1.04 |
| Bombay duck | 0.81 | Crab | 1.1 |
| Sardine | 0.83 | Catla | 1.14 |
| Salmon | 0.98 | **FATTY FISH** | |
| Tuna | 1.6 | Hilsa | 1.19 |

*(Source: T. Longvah, R. Ananthan, K. Bhaskaracharya, K. Venkaiah. Indian Food Composition Tables, National Institute of Nutrition (Indian Council of Medical Research), 113-168, 2017)*

## ANNEXURE - 14

## ZINC (Zn) CONTENT OF FOODS

| FOOD STUFFS | Zinc (mg/ 100 g) | | |
|---|---|---|---|
| | | Amaranth seeds, black | 2.66 |
| | | Bajra | 2.76 |
| | | Wheat flour | 2.85 |
| | | Wheat, whole | 2.85 |
| **CEREALS AND MILLETS** | | Quinoa | 3.31 |
| Maize, tender, sweet | 0.77 | **GRAIN LEGUMES** | |
| Wheat, vermicelli | 0.83 | Red gram, whole | 0.99 |
| Wheat flour, refined | 0.88 | Moth bean | 1.92 |
| Wheat, vermicelli, roasted | 0.88 | Rice bean | 2.29 |
| Maize, tender, local | 0.97 | Field bean, black | 2.42 |
| Rice, parboiled, milled | 1.08 | Field bean, brown | 2.44 |
| Rice, raw, milled | 1.21 | Green gram, dal | 2.49 |
| Rice puffed | 1.45 | Rajmah, brown | 2.6 |
| Rice flakes | 1.49 | Red gram, dal | 2.63 |
| Barley | 1.5 | Green gram, whole | 2.67 |
| Varagu | 1.65 | Rajmah, red | 2.69 |
| Rice, raw ,brown | 1.68 | Horse gram, whole | 2.71 |
| Samai | 1.82 | Field bean, white | 2.8 |
| Jowar | 1.96 | Black gram, dal | 3 |
| Wheat, bulgur | 1.97 | Black gram, whole | 3.05 |
| Wheat, semolina | 2.13 | Rajmah, black | 3.08 |
| Maize, dry | 2.27 | Peas, dry | 3.1 |
| Amaranth seeds, pale brown | 2.52 | Lentil whole, yellowish | 3.31 |
| Ragi | 2.53 | | |

--- **Author** ---
Dr. Prajakta J. Nande

# Clinical and Therapeutic Nutrition Practical Manual 1
## For M.Sc. Food Science and Nutrition (Semester-III)

| | | | | |
|---|---|---|---|---|
| Bengal gram, whole | 3.37 | Mango, green, raw | 0.09 |
| Cowpea, brown | 3.41 | Cho-cho-marrow | 0.1 |
| Soya bean, white | 3.47 | Pumpkin, orange, round | 0.11 |
| Cowpea, white | 3.57 | Snake gourd, short | 0.11 |
| Lentil whole, brown | 3.6 | Tomato, ripe, hybrid | 0.11 |
| Lentil dal | 3.61 | Tomato, ripe, local | 0.12 |
| Bengal gram, dal | 3.65 | Ash gourd | 0.13 |
| Soya bean, brown | 4.01 | Kovai, small | 0.13 |
| **GREEN LEAFY VEGETABLES** | | Plantain, stem | 0.14 |
| Cabbage, violet | 0.13 | Pumpkin, green, cylindrical | 0.14 |
| Beet greens | 0.16 | Snake gourd, long, pale green | 0.14 |
| Cabbage, green | 0.16 | Bottle gourd, elongate, pale green | 0.15 |
| Pak choi leaves | 0.16 | Bottle gourd, round, pale green | 0.15 |
| Cabbage, Chinese | 0.19 | Capsicum, green | 0.15 |
| Cauliflower leaves | 0.31 | Knol-khol | 0.15 |
| Cabbage, collard greens | 0.35 | Cucumber, round | 0.16 |
| Basella leaves | 0.39 | Tomato, green | 0.16 |
| Betel leaves, small | 0.39 | Cucumber, green, elongate | 0.17 |
| Knol-khol leaves | 0.42 | Jack fruit, raw | 0.17 |
| Rumex leaves | 0.46 | Bottle gourd, elongate, dark green | 0.18 |
| Spinach | 0.46 | Celery stalk | 0.18 |
| Betel leaves, big (Kolkata) | 0.47 | Kovai, big | 0.18 |
| Radish leaves | 0.49 | Cucumber, green, short | 0.19 |
| Lettuce | 0.51 | Colocasia, stem, green | 0.2 |
| Agathi leaves | 0.53 | Snake gourd, long, dark green | 0.2 |
| Fenugreek leaves | 0.54 | Tinda, tender | 0.2 |
| Brussels sprouts | 0.57 | Brinjal-all varieties | 0.21 |
| Gogu leaves, red | 0.63 | Ridge gourd | 0.22 |
| Gogu leaves, green | 0.65 | Parwar | 0.23 |
| Mustard leaves | 0.68 | Plantain, green | 0.23 |
| Drumstick leaves | 0.72 | Capsicum, yellow | 0.26 |
| Colocasia leaves, green | 0.82 | Ridge gourd, smooth skin | 0.26 |
| Amaranth leaves, green | 0.86 | Zucchini, yellow | 0.27 |
| Pumpkin leaves, tender | 0.9 | Jack fruit, seed, mature | 0.29 |
| Tamarind leaves, tender | 0.93 | Zucchini, green | 0.29 |
| Bathua leaves | 0.98 | Bitter gourd, jagged, teeth ridges, elongate | 0.31 |
| Ponnaganni | 0.99 | | |
| Amaranth leaves, red and green mix | 1.03 | Cauliflower | 0.31 |
| Amaranth spinosus, leaves, red and green mix | 1.11 | Drumstick | 0.31 |
| | | Capsicum, red | 0.34 |
| Parsley | 1.29 | Bitter gourd, jagged, teeth ridges, short | 0.36 |
| Amaranth leaves, red | 1.37 | | |
| Garden cress | 1.52 | Bamboo shoot, tender | 0.37 |
| Amaranth spinosus, leaves, green | 1.57 | French beans, hybrid | 0.37 |
| **OTHER VEGETABLES** | | Plantain, flower | 0.42 |
| Papaya, raw | 0.08 | Bitter gourd, jagged, smooth ridges, | 0.43 |

# Clinical and Therapeutic Nutrition Practical Manual 1
## For M.Sc. Food Science and Nutrition (Semester-III)

| | | | |
|---|---|---|---|
| elongate | | Black berry | 0.11 |
| Ladies finger | 0.45 | Cherries, red | 0.12 |
| French beans, country | 0.5 | Mango, ripe, banganapalli | 0.12 |
| Colocasia, stem, black | 0.54 | Mango, ripe, himsagar | 0.12 |
| Bean scarlet, tender | 0.57 | Soursop | 0.12 |
| Broad beans | 0.61 | Bael fruit | 0.14 |
| Cluster beans | 0.61 | Banana, ripe, robusta | 0.14 |
| Field beans, tender, lean | 0.63 | Strawberry | 0.14 |
| Field beans, tender, broad | 0.64 | Banana, ripe, montham | 0.15 |
| Onion, stalk | 0.99 | Banana, ripe, poovam | 0.17 |
| Peas, fresh | 1.09 | Jack fruit, ripe | 0.17 |
| Red gram, tender, fresh | 1.1 | Pomegranate, maroon seeds | 0.18 |
| Corn, baby | 1.13 | Sapota | 0.18 |
| **FRUITS** | | Mango, ripe, paheri | 0.2 |
| Orange, pulp | 0.04 | Currants, black | 0.21 |
| Apple, small | 0.05 | Guava, pink flesh | 0.21 |
| Gooseberry | 0.05 | Mangosteen | 0.21 |
| Grapes, seeded, round, black | 0.05 | Custard apple | 0.22 |
| Grapes, seeded, round, green | 0.05 | Fig | 0.22 |
| Grapes, seedless, round, green | 0.05 | Raisins, dried, black | 0.22 |
| Lime, sweet, pulp | 0.05 | Guava, white flesh | 0.23 |
| Palm fruit, tender | 0.05 | Litchi | 0.24 |
| Jambu fruit, ripe | 0.06 | Star fruit | 0.24 |
| Mango, ripe, gulabkhas | 0.06 | Karonda fruit | 0.25 |
| Pummelo | 0.06 | Raisins, dried, golden | 0.25 |
| Grapes, seeded, round, red | 0.07 | Apricot, processed | 0.26 |
| Mango, ripe, neelam | 0.07 | Wood apple | 0.31 |
| Pear | 0.07 | Apricot, dried | 0.41 |
| Water melon, pale green | 0.07 | Dates, processed | 0.42 |
| Apple, green | 0.08 | Phalsa | 0.48 |
| Apple, small, Kashmir | 0.08 | Rambutan | 0.53 |
| Lemon, juice | 0.08 | Manila tamarind | 0.56 |
| Mango, ripe, totapari | 0.08 | Dates, dry, dark brown | 0.58 |
| Papaya, ripe | 0.08 | Tamarind, pulp | 0.58 |
| Apple, big | 0.09 | Dates, dry, pale brown | 0.7 |
| Banana, ripe, red | 0.09 | Avocado fruit | 0.75 |
| Grapes, seedless, round, black | 0.09 | **ROOTS AND TUBERS** | |
| Musk melon, orange flesh | 0.09 | Sweet potato, pink skin | 0.14 |
| Musk melon, yellow flesh | 0.09 | Radish, elongate, red skin | 0.16 |
| Grapes, seedless, oval, black | 0.1 | Sweet potato, brown skin | 0.16 |
| Mango, ripe, kesar | 0.1 | Radish, round, white skin | 0.17 |
| Peach | 0.1 | Tapioca | 0.17 |
| Pineapple | 0.1 | Radish, round, red skin | 0.18 |
| Plum | 0.1 | Radish, elongate, white skin | 0.22 |
| Water melon, dark green | 0.1 | Carrot, orange | 0.25 |
| Zizyphus | 0.1 | Yam, elephant | 0.26 |

# Clinical and Therapeutic Nutrition Practical Manual 1
## For M.Sc. Food Science and Nutrition (Semester-III)

| | | | |
|---|---|---|---|
| Potato, brown skin, big | 0.28 | Ground nut | 3.18 |
| Beet root | 0.3 | Almond | 3.5 |
| Yam, wild | 0.31 | Niger seeds, gray | 3.62 |
| Yam, ordinary | 0.33 | Safflower seeds | 3.9 |
| Carrot, red | 0.34 | Mustard seeds | 4.03 |
| Potato, red skin | 0.34 | Pine seeds | 4.18 |
| Lotus root | 0.35 | Garden cress, seeds | 4.83 |
| Potato, brown skin, small | 0.38 | Linseeds | 4.86 |
| Colocasia | 0.41 | Niger seeds, black | 4.98 |
| Water chestnut | 0.67 | Cashew nut | 5.34 |
| **CONDIMENTS AND SPICES- FRESH** | | Sunflower seeds | 7.07 |
| Onion, small | 0.24 | Gingelly seeds, white | 7.77 |
| Chillies green-all varieties | 0.27 | Gingelly seeds, brown | 7.84 |
| Onion, big | 0.35 | Gingelly seeds, black | 8.59 |
| Ginger, fresh | 0.39 | **SUGAR** | |
| Mango ginger | 0.47 | Sugarcane, juice | 0.14 |
| Garlic, single clove, Kashmir | 0.66 | Jaggery, cane | 0.45 |
| Coriander leaves | 0.68 | **MUSHROOMS** | |
| Mint leaves | 0.75 | Button mushroom, fresh | 0.17 |
| Garlic, small clove | 0.81 | Chicken mushroom, fresh | 0.55 |
| Garlic, big clove | 0.89 | Shiitake mushroom, fresh | 1.21 |
| Curry leaves | 1.18 | **MISCELLANEOUS FOODS** | |
| **CONDIMENTS AND SPICES - DRY** | | Coconut water | 0.04 |
| Asafoetida | 0.98 | **MILK AND MILK PRODUCTS** | |
| Cloves | 1.13 | Milk, whole, buffalo | 0.3 |
| Mace | 1.16 | Milk, whole, cow | 0.33 |
| Pepper, black | 1.24 | Khoa | 2.34 |
| Nutmeg | 1.45 | Paneer | 2.74 |
| Pippali | 1.52 | **EGG AND EGG PRODUCTS** | |
| Chillies, red | 1.66 | Eggs, poultry, white, raw | 0.03 |
| Turmeric powder | 2.64 | Egg, country hen, whole, raw | 1.12 |
| Cardamom, green | 3.71 | Eggs, poultry, whole, raw | 1.23 |
| Fenugreek seeds | 3.8 | Egg, poultry, yolk, raw | 1.64 |
| Coriander seeds | 3.91 | **POULTRY** | |
| Cumin seeds | 4.29 | Chicken, poultry, breast, skinless | 0.78 |
| Cardamom, black | 4.75 | Chicken, poultry, thigh, skinless | 1.42 |
| Omum | 5.67 | Chicken, poultry, wing, skinless | 1.48 |
| Poppy seeds | 6.38 | Chicken, poultry, legs, skinless | 1.77 |
| **NUTS AND OIL SEEDS** | | Poultry, chicken, liver | 2.65 |
| Arecanut, fresh | 0.56 | **ANIMAL MEAT** | |
| Coconut kernel, fresh | 0.58 | Goat, brain | 1.08 |
| Arecanut, dried, brown | 0.89 | Beef, lungs | 1.18 |
| Arecanut, dried, red color | 1.02 | Pork, lungs | 1.18 |
| Coconut kernel, dry | 1.41 | Pork, shoulder | 1.4 |
| Pistachio nut | 2.42 | Goat, liver | 1.45 |
| Walnut | 2.94 | Beef, liver | 1.5 |

--- **Author** ---

Dr. Prajakta J. Nande

# Clinical and Therapeutic Nutrition Practical Manual 1
For M.Sc. Food Science and Nutrition (Semester-III)

| | | | |
|---|---|---|---|
| Beef, heart | 1.52 | Pomfret, black | 0.5 |
| Pork, heart | 1.6 | Salmon | 0.51 |
| Goat, heart | 1.7 | Pomfret, white | 0.53 |
| Beef, shoulder | 1.73 | Tuna | 0.69 |
| Pork, kidneys | 1.9 | Mural | 0.71 |
| Goat, kidneys | 1.95 | Sardine | 0.89 |
| Beef, kidney | 2.01 | **MARINE SHELLFISH** | |
| Pork, chops | 2.08 | Crab | 0.76 |
| Pork, spleen | 2.09 | Lobster, brown | 1.16 |
| Pork, stomach | 2.34 | Tiger prawns, orange | 1.16 |
| Goat, lungs | 2.44 | Lobster, king size | 1.92 |
| Beef, brain | 3.36 | Crab, sea | 3.07 |
| Goat, spleen | 3.48 | **FRESH WATER FISH AND SHELLFISH** | |
| Goat, legs | 3.52 | Catla | 0.68 |
| Beef, round (leg) | 3.77 | Rohu | 0.8 |
| Goat, shoulder meat | 4.19 | Prawns, small | 0.87 |
| Beef, spleen | 4.36 | Prawns, big | 1.44 |
| Goat, chops | 4.55 | Crab | 2.49 |
| Beef, chops | 4.64 | **FATTY FISH** | |
| **MARINE FISH** | | Hilsa | 0.64 |
| Bombay duck | 0.42 | | |

*(Source: T. Longvah, R. Ananthan, K. Bhaskaracharya, K. Venkaiah. Indian Food Composition Tables, National Institute of Nutrition (Indian Council of Medical Research), 113-168, 2017)*

---

## ANNEXURE - 15

## SELENIUM (Se) CONTENT OF FOODS

| FOOD STUFFS | Se(mg/ 100 g) | | |
|---|---|---|---|
| **CEREALS AND MILLETS** | | Amaranth seeds, black | 16.46 |
| | | Barley | 18.61 |
| Rice, raw, milled | 1.01 | Amaranth seeds, pale brown | 21.41 |
| Rice, parboiled, milled | 1.19 | Jowar | 26.29 |
| Maize, tender, sweet | 2.17 | Bajra | 30.4 |
| Rice, raw, brown | 2.26 | Samai | 40.41 |
| Maize, tender, local | 3.83 | Wheat, whole | 47.76 |
| Quinoa | 7.81 | Wheat flour | 53.12 |
| Maize, dry | 8.69 | **GRAIN LEGUMES** | |
| Wheat, bulgur | 10.54 | Rajmah, brown | 12.7 |
| Wheat, semolina | 10.93 | Red gram, dal | 14.36 |
| Varagu | 14.12 | Red gram, whole | 15.41 |
| Wheat, vermicelli, roasted | 14.29 | Soya bean, white | 16.85 |
| Ragi | 15.3 | Rajmah, black | 18.65 |
| Wheat, vermicelli | 15.33 | Moth bean | 18.82 |
| | | Soya bean, brown | 19 |

--- **Author** ---
Dr. Prajakta J. Nande

# Clinical and Therapeutic Nutrition Practical Manual 1
For M.Sc. Food Science and Nutrition (Semester-III)

| | |
|---|---|
| Field bean, white | 21.52 |
| Rajmah, red | 22.45 |
| Field bean, brown | 22.82 |
| Green gram, whole | 23.32 |
| Cowpea, brown | 23.95 |
| Black gram, dal | 23.99 |
| Cowpea, white | 26.55 |
| Black gram, whole | 27.98 |
| Horse gram, whole | 29.49 |
| Field bean, black | 32.55 |
| Lentil whole, brown | 33.14 |
| Bengal gram, whole | 41.23 |
| Lentil dal | 49.5 |
| Peas, dry | 50.07 |
| Green gram, dal | 50.14 |
| Bengal gram, dal | 50.97 |
| Lentil whole, yellowish | 56.28 |
| **GREEN LEAFY VEGETABLES** | |
| Pak choi leaves | 0.79 |
| Cauliflower leaves | 1.05 |
| Cabbage, green | 1.08 |
| Cabbage, violet | 1.08 |
| Fenugreek leaves | 1.29 |
| Pumpkin leaves, tender | 1.38 |
| Bathua leaves | 1.4 |
| Cabbage, Chinese | 1.85 |
| Brussels sprouts | 2.01 |
| Spinach | 2.09 |
| Cabbage, collard greens | 2.35 |
| Gogu leaves, green | 2.38 |
| Tamarind leaves, tender | 2.45 |
| Gogu leaves, red | 3.25 |
| Colocasia leaves, green | 4.3 |
| Rumex leaves | 5.37 |
| Betel leaves, small | 5.4 |
| Lettuce | 5.56 |
| Drumstick leaves | 5.95 |
| Basella leaves | 6.17 |
| Mustard leaves | 8.03 |
| Garden cress | 8.08 |
| Parsley | 10.24 |
| Knol-khol, leaves | 10.5 |
| Betel leaves, big (Kolkata) | 12.15 |
| Ponnaganni | 17.19 |
| Amaranth spinosus, leaves, red and green mix | 19.41 |

| | |
|---|---|
| Amaranth leaves, green | 20.97 |
| Amaranth leaves, red and green mix | 21.62 |
| Amaranth leaves, red | 22.55 |
| Amaranth spinosus, leaves, green | 28.97 |
| Agathi leaves | 30.7 |
| Radish leaves | 33.05 |
| Beet greens | 47.75 |
| **OTHER VEGETABLES** | |
| Bean scarlet, tender | 0.02 |
| Cucumber, round | 0.14 |
| Cho-cho-marrow | 0.16 |
| Cucumber, green, elongate | 0.17 |
| Capsicum, green | 0.18 |
| Cucumber, green, short | 0.19 |
| Corn, baby | 0.22 |
| Tinda, tender | 0.22 |
| Capsicum, yellow | 0.28 |
| Jack fruit, seed, mature | 0.33 |
| Capsicum, red | 0.34 |
| Pumpkin, green, cylindrical | 0.34 |
| Pumpkin, orange, round | 0.37 |
| Zucchini, yellow | 0.39 |
| Zucchini, green | 0.4 |
| Plantain, stem | 0.45 |
| Cauliflower | 0.47 |
| Ridge gourd | 0.59 |
| Colocasia, stem, black | 0.82 |
| Plantain, green | 0.82 |
| Ash gourd | 1.15 |
| Papaya, raw | 1.29 |
| Colocasia, stem, green | 1.48 |
| Cluster beans | 1.59 |
| Peas, fresh | 1.63 |
| Bottle gourd, elongate, pale green | 1.77 |
| Bottle gourd, round, pale green | 1.8 |
| Bottle gourd, elongate, dark green | 2.05 |
| Red gram, tender, fresh | 2.19 |
| Parwar | 2.32 |
| Bamboo shoot, tender | 2.58 |
| Plantain, flower | 2.82 |
| Drumstick | 3.12 |
| Celery stalk | 3.59 |
| Bitter gourd, jagged, teeth ridges, short | 3.72 |
| Bitter gourd, jagged, teeth ridges, elongate | 4.97 |

--- **Author** ---
Dr. Prajakta J. Nande

# Clinical and Therapeutic Nutrition Practical Manual 1
For M.Sc. Food Science and Nutrition (Semester-III)

| | | | |
|---|---|---|---|
| Bitter gourd, jagged, smooth ridges, elongate | 5.22 | Tapioca | 0.07 |
| Onion, stalk | 5.22 | Radish, elongate, white skin | 0.1 |
| Tomato, green | 8.25 | Radish, elongate, red skin | 0.13 |
| Broad beans | 9.03 | Radish, round, white skin | 0.13 |
| **FRUITS** | | Carrot, orange | 0.22 |
| Pineapple | 0.08 | Radish, round, red skin | 0.22 |
| Apple, small, Kashmir | 0.11 | Beet root | 0.25 |
| Orange, pulp | 0.19 | Potato, brown skin, small | 0.28 |
| Apple, small | 0.23 | Carrot, red | 0.29 |
| Apple, green | 0.25 | Colocasia | 0.3 |
| Strawberry | 0.3 | Potato, red skin | 0.32 |
| Sapota | 0.39 | Yam, wild | 0.56 |
| Dates, processed | 0.46 | Yam, ordinary | 0.57 |
| Litchi | 0.46 | Yam, elephant | 0.59 |
| Apple, big | 0.47 | Potato, brown skin, big | 0.75 |
| Pomegranate, maroon seeds | 0.55 | Water chestnut | 2.43 |
| Plum | 0.56 | Lotus root | 4.61 |
| Star fruit | 0.56 | **CONDIMENTS AND SPICES- FRESH** | |
| Peach | 0.67 | Onion, big | 0.35 |
| Bael fruit | 0.72 | Garlic, small clove | 0.37 |
| Lime, sweet, pulp | 0.72 | Garlic, single clove, Kashmir | 0.43 |
| Dates, dry, dark brown | 0.77 | Coriander leaves | 0.45 |
| Dates, dry, pale brown | 0.78 | Onion, small | 1.02 |
| Musk melon, orange flesh | 0.88 | Mint leaves | 10.79 |
| Apricot, processed | 1.03 | Curry leaves | 17.25 |
| Musk melon, yellow flesh | 1.35 | **CONDIMENTS AND SPICES - DRY** | |
| Mango, ripe, neelam | 1.36 | Cardamom, black | 3.99 |
| Zizyphus | 1.42 | Cumin seeds | 4.01 |
| Mango, ripe, paheri | 1.44 | Coriander seeds | 6.34 |
| Currants, black | 1.51 | Turmeric powder | 6.41 |
| Karonda fruit | 1.57 | Mace | 7.24 |
| Raisins, dried, golden | 1.72 | Nutmeg | 7.33 |
| Guava, white flesh | 1.84 | Poppy seeds | 7.68 |
| Mango, ripe, kesar | 1.85 | Cloves | 7.75 |
| Mango, ripe, totapari | 1.85 | Fenugreek seeds | 9.98 |
| Raisins, dried, black | 1.86 | Cardamom, green | 11.71 |
| Mango, ripe, himsagar | 1.9 | Pepper, black | 12.13 |
| Mango, ripe, banganapalli | 1.91 | Asafoetida | 13.42 |
| Apricot, dried | 2.05 | Chillies, red | 18.83 |
| Mango, ripe, gulabkhas | 2.05 | Pippali | 20.51 |
| Guava, pink flesh | 2.1 | Omum | 87.04 |
| Wood apple | 2.32 | **NUTS AND OIL SEEDS** | |
| Phalsa | 3.53 | Ground nut | 3.41 |
| Papaya, ripe | 12.78 | Almond | 3.61 |
| **ROOTS AND TUBERS** | | Safflower seeds | 6.33 |
| | | Walnut | 6.53 |

--- Author ---
Dr. Prajakta J. Nande

# Clinical and Therapeutic Nutrition Practical Manual 1
For M.Sc. Food Science and Nutrition (Semester-III)

| | | | | |
|---|---|---|---|---|
| Pistachio nut | 10.46 | Goat, legs | 17.76 |
| Pine seeds | 10.56 | Beef, round (leg) | 18.14 |
| Arecanut dried red color | 12.52 | Beef, liver | 20.2 |
| Cashew nut | 13.08 | Beef, heart | 20.66 |
| Arecanut dried brown | 15.21 | Pork, heart | 20.75 |
| Gingelly seeds black | 15.7 | Goat, brain | 21.7 |
| Coconut kernel dry | 25.25 | Goat, chops | 21.76 |
| Gingelly seeds white | 26.74 | Goat, lungs | 26 |
| Niger seeds black | 39.31 | Pork, stomach | 31.64 |
| Linseeds | 46.87 | Pork, spleen | 37.25 |
| Gingelly seeds brown | 52.64 | Beef, spleen | 37.55 |
| Garden cress seeds | 54.41 | Goat, liver | 48.12 |
| Mustard seeds | 71.47 | Goat, spleen | 48.55 |
| Niger seeds gray | 153.64 | Beef, kidney | 135 |
| **MILK AND MILK PRODUCTS** | | Goat, kidneys | 142 |
| Milk, whole, cow | 0.95 | Pork, kidneys | 206 |
| Milk, whole, buffalo | 1.45 | **MARINE FISH** | |
| Paneer | 23.14 | Tuna | 21.55 |
| Khoa | 44.97 | Bombay duck | 25.45 |
| **EGG AND EGG PRODUCTS** | | Mural | 26.36 |
| Eggs, poultry, white, raw | 21.23 | Pomfret, white | 29.33 |
| Eggs, poultry, whole, raw | 40.44 | Salmon | 36.34 |
| Egg, poultry, yolk, raw | 51.44 | Sardine | 50.21 |
| Egg,country hen, whole, raw | 62.33 | Pomfret, black | 50.25 |
| **POULTRY** | | **MARINE SHELLFISH** | |
| Chicken, poultry, breast, skinless | 18.56 | Lobster, brown | 33.82 |
| Chicken, poultry, thigh, skinless | 18.69 | Crab | 34.8 |
| Chicken, poultry, legs, skinless | 20.22 | Crab, sea | 37.69 |
| Chicken, poultry, wing, skinless | 20.52 | Tiger prawns, orange | 54.22 |
| Poultry, chicken, liver | 46.35 | Lobster, king size | 69.71 |
| **ANIMAL MEAT** | | **FRESH WATER FISH AND SHELLFISH** | |
| Beef, chops | 11.54 | Prawns, small | 19.92 |
| Beef, shoulder | 11.58 | Prawns, big | 28.59 |
| Goat, shoulder | 12.91 | Rohu | 51.5 |
| Pork, shoulder | 13.26 | Crab | 71.84 |
| Goat, heart | 15 | Catla | |
| Pork, chops | 15.06 | | |
| Beef, brain | 16.57 | | |
| Beef, lungs | 16.69 | | |
| Pork, lungs | 17.75 | | |

*(Source: T. Longvah, R. Ananthan, K. Bhaskaracharya, K. Venkaiah. Indian Food Composition Tables, National Institute of Nutrition (Indian Council of Medical Research), 113-168, 2017)*

**Clinical and Therapeutic Nutrition Practical Manual 1**
For M.Sc. Food Science and Nutrition (Semester-III)

## ANNEXURE - 16

## THIAMINE (VITAMIN B1) CONTENT OF FOODS

| FOOD STUFFS | B1(mg/ 100 g) | | |
|---|---|---|---|
| **CEREALS AND MILLETS** | | Bengal gram, whole | 0.37 |
| Amaranth seeds, black | 0.04 | Field bean, white | 0.37 |
| Amaranth seeds, pale brown | 0.04 | Lentil whole, brown | 0.4 |
| Rice, raw, milled | 0.05 | Lentil whole, yellowish | 0.42 |
| Maize, tender, sweet | 0.1 | Green gram, whole | 0.45 |
| Rice puffed | 0.11 | Moth bean | 0.45 |
| Rice flakes | 0.12 | Red gram, dal | 0.45 |
| Wheat, vermicelli, roasted | 0.12 | Rice bean | 0.46 |
| Wheat, vermicelli | 0.13 | Peas, dry | 0.56 |
| Wheat flour, refined | 0.15 | Soya bean, brown | 0.59 |
| Maize, tender, local | 0.17 | Soya bean, white | 0.61 |
| Rice, parboiled, milled | 0.17 | Red gram, whole | 0.74 |
| Wheat, bulgur | 0.24 | **GREEN LEAFY VEGETABLES** | |
| Bajra | 0.25 | Amaranth leaves, green | 0.01 |
| Samai | 0.26 | Amaranth leaves, red | 0.01 |
| Rice, raw, brown | 0.27 | Amaranth leaves, red and green mix | 0.01 |
| Varagu | 0.29 | Amaranth spinosus, leaves, green | 0.01 |
| Wheat, semolina | 0.29 | Amaranth spinosus, leaves, red and green mix | 0.01 |
| Maize, dry | 0.33 | Cabbage, Chinese | 0.01 |
| Jowar | 0.35 | Beet greens | 0.02 |
| Barley | 0.36 | Betel leaves, small | 0.02 |
| Ragi | 0.37 | Pak choi leaves | 0.02 |
| Wheat flour | 0.42 | Ponnaganni | 0.02 |
| Wheat, whole | 0.46 | Betel leaves, big (Kolkata) | 0.03 |
| Quinoa | 0.83 | Cabbage, collard greens | 0.03 |
| **GRAIN LEGUMES** | | Cabbage, green | 0.03 |
| Black gram, dal | 0.21 | Garden cress | 0.03 |
| Rajmah, black | 0.21 | Rumex leaves | 0.03 |
| Rajmah, brown | 0.26 | Cabbage, violet | 0.04 |
| Rajmah, red | 0.3 | Cauliflower leaves | 0.05 |
| Black gram, whole | 0.32 | Lettuce | 0.05 |
| Field bean, brown | 0.32 | Basella leaves | 0.06 |
| Horse gram, whole | 0.32 | Bathua leaves | 0.06 |
| Cowpea, brown | 0.33 | Brussels sprouts | 0.06 |
| Cowpea, white | 0.34 | Drumstick leaves | 0.06 |
| Lentil dal | 0.34 | Knol-khol, leaves | 0.06 |
| Bengal gram, dal | 0.35 | Radish leaves | 0.06 |
| Field bean, black | 0.35 | Pumpkin leaves, tender | 0.07 |
| Green gram, dal | 0.35 | Colocasia leaves, green | 0.08 |
| | | Mustard leaves | 0.08 |

--- **Author** ---
Dr. Prajakta J. Nande

# Clinical and Therapeutic Nutrition Practical Manual 1
For M.Sc. Food Science and Nutrition (Semester-III)

| | | | | |
|---|---|---|---|---|
| Fenugreek leaves | 0.11 | Cluster beans | 0.05 |
| Gogu leaves, red | 0.12 | French beans, hybrid | 0.05 |
| Tamarind leaves , tender | 0.12 | Jack fruit, raw | 0.05 |
| Gogu leaves, green | 0.13 | Parwar | 0.05 |
| Spinach | 0.16 | Zucchini, green | 0.05 |
| Parsley | 0.19 | Bamboo shoot, tender | 0.06 |
| Agathi leaves | 0.26 | Bitter gourd, jagged, teeth ridges, short | 0.06 |
| **OTHER VEGETABLES** | | Bitter gourd, jagged, smooth ridges, elongate | 0.06 |
| Cho-cho-marrow | 0.01 | | |
| Plantain, green | 0.01 | Brinjal-all varieties | 0.06 |
| Colocasia, stem, black | 0.02 | Jack fruit, seed, mature | 0.06 |
| Colocasia, stem, green | 0.02 | Field beans, tender, broad | 0.07 |
| Cucumber, green, elongate | 0.02 | Field beans, tender, lean | 0.08 |
| Cucumber, green, short | 0.02 | Tomato, green | 0.08 |
| Cucumber, round | 0.02 | Capsicum, red | 0.1 |
| Mango, green, raw | 0.02 | Broad beans | 0.12 |
| Papaya, raw | 0.02 | Bean scarlet, tender | 0.13 |
| Plantain, flower | 0.02 | Capsicum, yellow | 0.14 |
| Plantain, stem | 0.02 | Corn, baby | 0.15 |
| Ridge gourd | 0.02 | Red gram, tender, fresh | 0.23 |
| Ridge gourd, smooth skin | 0.02 | Peas, fresh | 0.27 |
| Tinda, tender | 0.02 | **FRUITS** | |
| Ash gourd | 0.03 | Apple, green | 0.01 |
| Bottle gourd, elongate, pale green | 0.03 | Apple, small | 0.01 |
| Bottle gourd, round, pale green | 0.03 | Apple, small, Kashmir | 0.01 |
| Bottle gourd, elongate, dark green | 0.03 | Banana, ripe, montham | 0.01 |
| Celery stalk | 0.03 | Banana, ripe, poovam | 0.01 |
| Onion, stalk | 0.03 | Banana, ripe, red | 0.01 |
| Pumpkin, green, cylindrical | 0.03 | Banana, ripe, robusta | 0.01 |
| Pumpkin, orange, round | 0.03 | Black berry | 0.01 |
| Snake gourd, long, pale green | 0.03 | Gooseberry | 0.01 |
| Snake gourd, long, dark green | 0.03 | Karonda fruit | 0.01 |
| Snake gourd, short | 0.03 | Mangosteen | 0.01 |
| Tomato, ripe, local | 0.03 | Musk melon, orange flesh | 0.01 |
| Zucchini, yellow | 0.03 | Musk melon, yellow flesh | 0.01 |
| Cauliflower | 0.04 | Palm fruit, tender | 0.01 |
| Drumstick | 0.04 | Sapota | 0.01 |
| French beans, country | 0.04 | Zizyphus | 0.01 |
| Knol-khol | 0.04 | Dates, dry, dark brown | 0.02 |
| Kovai, big | 0.04 | Jambu fruit, ripe | 0.02 |
| Kovai, small | 0.04 | Litchi | 0.02 |
| Ladies finger | 0.04 | Mango, ripe, totapari | 0.02 |
| Tomato, ripe, hybrid | 0.04 | Peach | 0.02 |
| Bitter gourd, jagged, teeth ridges, elongate | 0.05 | Pear | 0.02 |
| Capsicum, green | 0.05 | Plum | 0.02 |

--- **Author** ---
Dr. Prajakta J. Nande

# Clinical and Therapeutic Nutrition Practical Manual 1
For M.Sc. Food Science and Nutrition (Semester-III)

| | | | | |
|---|---|---|---|---|
| Water melon, dark green | 0.02 | Beet root | 0.01 |
| Water melon, pale green | 0.02 | Radish, elongate, white skin | 0.02 |
| Apple, big | 0.03 | Water chestnut | 0.02 |
| Bael fruit | 0.03 | Radish, elongate, red skin | 0.03 |
| Currants, black | 0.03 | Radish, round, red skin | 0.03 |
| Dates, dry, pale brown | 0.03 | Radish, round, white skin | 0.03 |
| Grapes, seeded, round, black | 0.03 | Carrot, orange | 0.04 |
| Grapes, seeded, round, green | 0.03 | Carrot, red | 0.04 |
| Grapes, seedless, oval, black | 0.03 | Yam, elephant | 0.04 |
| Grapes, seedless, round, black | 0.03 | Yam, ordinary | 0.04 |
| Guava, pink flesh | 0.03 | Potato, brown skin, small | 0.05 |
| Mango, ripe, banganapalli | 0.03 | Colocasia | 0.06 |
| Mango, ripe, gulabkhas | 0.03 | Potato, brown skin, big | 0.06 |
| Mango, ripe, himsagar | 0.03 | Potato, red skin | 0.06 |
| Mango, ripe, kesar | 0.03 | Sweet potato, pink skin | 0.06 |
| Mango, ripe, neelam | 0.03 | Lotus root | 0.07 |
| Mango, ripe, paheri | 0.03 | Sweet potato, brown skin | 0.07 |
| Papaya, ripe | 0.03 | Tapioca | 0.07 |
| Phalsa | 0.03 | Yam, wild | 0.12 |
| Soursop | 0.03 | **CONDIMENTS AND SPICES - FRESH** | |
| Apricot, dried | 0.04 | Mango ginger | 0.02 |
| Fig | 0.04 | Mint leaves | 0.02 |
| Grapes, seeded, round, red | 0.04 | Ginger, fresh | 0.04 |
| Grapes, seedless, round, green | 0.04 | Onion, big | 0.04 |
| Lemon, juice | 0.04 | Curry leaves | 0.07 |
| Wood apple | 0.04 | Onion, small | 0.07 |
| Dates, processed | 0.05 | Chillies, green all varieties | 0.09 |
| Guava, white flesh | 0.05 | Coriander leaves | 0.09 |
| Jack fruit, ripe | 0.05 | Garlic, big clove | 0.2 |
| Pineapple | 0.05 | Garlic, small clove | 0.2 |
| Lime, sweet, pulp | 0.06 | Garlic, single clove, Kashmir | 0.25 |
| Pomegranate, maroon seeds | 0.06 | **CONDIMENTS AND SPICES - DRY** | |
| Pummelo | 0.06 | Nutmeg | 0.04 |
| Strawberry | 0.06 | Cardamom, black | 0.05 |
| Avocado fruit | 0.07 | Pippali | 0.06 |
| Cherries, red | 0.07 | Pepper, black | 0.06 |
| Orange, pulp | 0.07 | Turmeric powder | 0.06 |
| Star fruit | 0.08 | Cardamom, green | 0.12 |
| Raisins, dried, black | 0.09 | Mace | 0.13 |
| Raisins, dried, golden | 0.09 | Coriander seeds | 0.19 |
| Rambutan | 0.11 | Fenugreek seeds | 0.28 |
| Custard apple | 0.13 | Omum | 0.3 |
| Manila tamarind | 0.18 | Chillies, red | 0.46 |
| Apricot, processed | 0.25 | Cumin seeds | 0.52 |
| Tamarind, pulp | 0.34 | Cloves | 0.53 |
| **ROOTS AND TUBERS** | | Asafoetida | 0.82 |

--- **Author** ---
Dr. Prajakta J. Nande

# Clinical and Therapeutic Nutrition Practical Manual 1
## For M.Sc. Food Science and Nutrition (Semester-III)

| | | | | |
|---|---|---|---|---|
| Poppy seeds | 0.87 | Chicken, poultry, legs, skinless | 0.17 |
| **NUTS AND OIL SEEDS** | | Poultry, chicken, liver | 0.28 |
| Arecanut, dried, red color | 0.03 | **ANIMAL MEAT** | |
| Coconut kernel, fresh | 0.03 | Beef, chops | 0.02 |
| Arecanut, fresh | 0.038 | Beef, shoulder | 0.03 |
| Arecanut, dried, brown | 0.04 | Beef, round (leg) | 0.04 |
| Coconut kernel, dry | 0.04 | Goat, chops | 0.05 |
| Almond | 0.15 | Goat, spleen | 0.06 |
| Gingelly seeds, brown | 0.27 | Goat, shoulder | 0.07 |
| Linseeds | 0.28 | Goat, legs | 0.07 |
| Gingelly seeds, black | 0.34 | Goat, lungs | 0.08 |
| Gingelly seeds, white | 0.36 | Pork, lungs | 0.08 |
| Pine seeds | 0.36 | Beef, lungs | 0.09 |
| Niger seeds, gray | 0.38 | Pork, stomach | 0.1 |
| Walnut | 0.4 | Beef, brain | 0.12 |
| Niger seeds, black | 0.46 | Goat, brain | 0.13 |
| Garden cress, seeds | 0.52 | Pork, spleen | 0.13 |
| Mustard seeds | 0.55 | Beef, liver | 0.17 |
| Groundnut | 0.57 | Pork, shoulder | 0.18 |
| Sunflower seeds | 0.59 | Goat, liver | 0.2 |
| Cashew nut | 0.61 | Beef, heart | 0.24 |
| Safflower seeds | 0.85 | Pork, kidneys | 0.24 |
| Pistachio nut | 0.98 | Beef, kidney | 0.26 |
| **SUGAR** | | Pork, heart | 0.28 |
| Sugarcane, juice | 0.03 | Pork, chops | 0.3 |
| Jaggery, cane | 0.04 | Beef, spleen | 0.31 |
| **MUSHROOMS** | | Goat, kidneys | 0.34 |
| Button mushroom, fresh | 0.01 | Goat, heart | 0.36 |
| Shiitake mushroom, fresh | 0.05 | **MARINE FISH** | |
| Chicken mushroom, fresh | 0.37 | Sardine | 0.01 |
| **MISCELLANEOUS FOODS** | | Bombay duck | 0.03 |
| Coconut water | 0.01 | Pomfret, white | 0.05 |
| **MILK AND MILK PRODUCTS** | | Mural | 0.06 |
| Paneer | 0.02 | Pomfret, black | 0.06 |
| Milk, whole, cow | 0.03 | Tuna | 0.06 |
| Milk, whole, buffalo | 0.05 | Salmon | 0.07 |
| Khoa | 0.11 | **MARINE SHELLFISH** | |
| **EGG AND EGG PRODUCTS** | | Crab | 0.01 |
| Eggs, poultry, white, raw | 0.02 | Lobster, brown | 0.01 |
| Eggs, poultry, whole, raw | 0.06 | Lobster, king size | 0.01 |
| Egg, poultry, yolk, raw | 0.11 | Tiger prawns, orange | 0.03 |
| Egg, country hen, whole, raw | 0.14 | Crab, sea | 0.05 |
| **POULTRY** | | **FRESH WATER FISH AND SHELLFISH** | |
| Chicken, poultry, wing, skinless | 0.08 | Catla | 0.01 |
| Chicken, poultry, breast, skinless | 0.1 | Crab | 0.01 |
| Chicken, poultry, thigh, skinless | 0.13 | Prawns, small | 0.01 |

--- **Author** ---
Dr. Prajakta J. Nande

## Clinical and Therapeutic Nutrition Practical Manual 1
### For M.Sc. Food Science and Nutrition (Semester-III)

| FATTY FISH | | Hilsa | 0.01 |
|---|---|---|---|

*(Source: T. Longvah, R. Ananthan, K. Bhaskaracharya, K. Venkaiah. Indian Food Composition Tables, National Institute of Nutrition (Indian Council of Medical Research), 33-60, 2017)*

# ANNEXURE - 17

# RIBOFLAVIN (VITAMIN B2) CONTENT OF FOODS

| FOOD STUFFS | B2 (mg/ 100 g) | | FOOD STUFFS | B2 (mg/ 100 g) |
|---|---|---|---|---|
| **CEREALS AND MILLETS** | | | Black gram, whole | 0.11 |
| Wheat, vermicelli | 0.01 | | Red gram, dal | 0.11 |
| Wheat, vermicelli , roasted | 0.01 | | Green gram, dal | 0.12 |
| Amaranth seeds, black | 0.04 | | Ricebean | 0.14 |
| Amaranth seeds, pale brown | 0.04 | | Bengal gram, dal | 0.15 |
| Rice flakes | 0.04 | | Red gram, whole | 0.15 |
| Rice puffed | 0.04 | | Lentil dal | 0.16 |
| Wheat, semolina | 0.04 | | Peas, dry | 0.16 |
| Rice, raw, milled | 0.05 | | Rajmah, black | 0.19 |
| Samai | 0.05 | | Rajmah, red | 0.19 |
| Rice, raw, brown | 0.06 | | Rajmah, brown | 0.21 |
| Rice, parboiled, milled | 0.06 | | Lentil whole, brown | 0.22 |
| Wheat flour, refined | 0.06 | | Lentil whole, yellowish | 0.22 |
| Maize, dry | 0.09 | | Soya bean, white | 0.23 |
| Maize, tender, local | 0.12 | | Bengal gram, whole | 0.24 |
| Wheat, bulgur | 0.12 | | Horse gram, whole | 0.24 |
| Jowar | 0.14 | | Soya bean, brown | 0.24 |
| Maize, tender, sweet | 0.14 | | Green gram, whole | 0.27 |
| Wheat flour | 0.15 | | **GREEN LEAFY VEGETABLES** | |
| Wheat, whole | 0.15 | | Tamarind leaves, tender | 0.03 |
| Ragi | 0.17 | | Cabbage, Chinese | 0.05 |
| Barley | 0.18 | | Cabbage, collard greens | 0.05 |
| Bajra | 0.2 | | Cabbage, green | 0.05 |
| Varagu | 0.2 | | Cabbage, violet | 0.05 |
| Quinoa | 0.22 | | Cauliflower leaves | 0.05 |
| **GRAIN LEGUMES** | | | Gogu leaves, red | 0.05 |
| Field bean, black | 0.07 | | Garden cress | 0.06 |
| Field bean, brown | 0.07 | | Gogu leaves, green | 0.06 |
| Field bean, white | 0.07 | | Betel leaves, small | 0.07 |
| Black gram, dal | 0.09 | | Colocasia leaves, green | 0.07 |
| Cowpea, brown | 0.09 | | Betel leaves, big (Kolkata) | 0.08 |
| Cowpea, white | 0.09 | | Lettuce | 0.09 |
| Moth bean | 0.09 | | Parsley | 0.1 |
| | | | Ponnaganni | 0.1 |
| | | | Spinach | 0.1 |
| | | | Amaranth spinosus, leaves, green | 0.13 |

--- **Author** ---
Dr. Prajakta J. Nande

# Clinical and Therapeutic Nutrition Practical Manual 1
## For M.Sc. Food Science and Nutrition (Semester-III)

| | | | | |
|---|---|---|---|---|
| Pumpkin leaves, tender | 0.13 | | Pumpkin, orange, round | 0.03 |
| Radish leaves | 0.13 | | Snake gourd, long, pale green | 0.03 |
| Rumex leaves | 0.14 | | Snake gourd, long, dark green | 0.03 |
| Amaranth spinosus, leaves, red and green mix | 0.15 | | Tinda, tender | 0.03 |
| | | | Tomato, ripe, local | 0.03 |
| Basella leaves | 0.15 | | Bitter gourd, jagged, teeth ridges, elongate | 0.04 |
| Knol-khol, leaves | 0.15 | | | |
| Brussels sprouts | 0.16 | | Bitter gourd, jagged, teeth ridges, short | 0.04 |
| Beet greens | 0.17 | | | |
| Mustard leaves | 0.18 | | Bitter gourd, jagged, smooth ridges, elongate | 0.04 |
| Amaranth leaves, green | 0.19 | | | |
| Amaranth leaves, red and green mix | 0.22 | | Celery stalk | 0.04 |
| Fenugreek leaves | 0.22 | | Colocasia, stem, black | 0.04 |
| Pak choi leaves | 0.22 | | French beans, hybrid | 0.05 |
| Amaranth leaves, red | 0.26 | | Jack fruit, raw | 0.05 |
| Agathi leaves | 0.33 | | Onion, stalk | 0.05 |
| Drumstick leaves | 0.45 | | Parwar | 0.05 |
| Bathua leaves | 0.51 | | Plantain, green | 0.05 |
| **OTHER VEGETABLES** | | | Tomato, green | 0.05 |
| Ash gourd | 0.01 | | Bamboo shoot, tender | 0.06 |
| Bottle gourd, elongate, pale green | 0.01 | | French beans, country | 0.06 |
| Bottle gourd, round, pale green | 0.01 | | Knol-khol | 0.06 |
| Bottle gourd, elongate, dark green | 0.01 | | Cauliflower | 0.07 |
| Cucumber, green, elongate | 0.01 | | Corn, baby | 0.07 |
| Cucumber, green, short | 0.01 | | Drumstick | 0.07 |
| Cucumber, round | 0.01 | | Field beans, tender, broad | 0.07 |
| Ridge gourd | 0.01 | | Field beans, tender, lean | 0.07 |
| Ridge gourd, smooth skin | 0.01 | | Ladies finger | 0.07 |
| Capsicum, yellow | 0.02 | | Red gram, tender, fresh | 0.09 |
| Kovai, big | 0.02 | | Zucchini, green | 0.09 |
| Kovai, small | 0.02 | | Broad beans | 0.1 |
| Mango, green, raw | 0.02 | | Brinjal-all varieties | 0.11 |
| Plantain, flower | 0.02 | | Bean scarlet, tender | 0.12 |
| Plantain, stem | 0.02 | | **FRUITS** | |
| Pumpkin, green, cylindrical | 0.02 | | Apple, big | 0.01 |
| Snake gourd, short | 0.02 | | Apple, small | 0.01 |
| Tomato, ripe, hybrid | 0.02 | | Apple, small, Kashmir | 0.01 |
| Zucchini, yellow | 0.02 | | Jack fruit, ripe | 0.01 |
| Capsicum, green | 0.03 | | Lemon, juice | 0.01 |
| Capsicum, red | 0.03 | | Lime, sweet, pulp | 0.01 |
| Cho-cho-marrow | 0.03 | | Mangosteen | 0.01 |
| Cluster beans | 0.03 | | Musk melon, orange flesh | 0.01 |
| Colocasia, stem, green | 0.03 | | Pomegranate, maroon seeds | 0.01 |
| Jack fruit, seed, mature | 0.03 | | Rambutan | 0.01 |
| Papaya, raw | 0.03 | | Strawberry | 0.01 |
| Peas, fresh | 0.03 | | Wood apple | 0.01 |

--- Author ---

Dr. Prajakta J. Nande

# Clinical and Therapeutic Nutrition Practical Manual 1
For M.Sc. Food Science and Nutrition (Semester-III)

| | | | | |
|---|---|---|---|---|
| Apple, green | 0.02 | Soursop | 0.04 |
| Banana, ripe, red | 0.02 | Mango, ripe, totapari | 0.05 |
| Black berry | 0.02 | Litchi | 0.06 |
| Cherries, red | 0.02 | Phalsa | 0.06 |
| Dates, processed | 0.02 | Tamarind, pulp | 0.07 |
| Fig | 0.02 | Avocado fruit | 0.08 |
| Grapes, seeded, round, green | 0.02 | Custard apple | 0.09 |
| Grapes, seedless, oval, black | 0.02 | Papaya, ripe | 0.11 |
| Jambu fruit, ripe | 0.02 | Manila tamarind | 0.14 |
| Karonda fruit | 0.02 | Palm fruit, tender | - |
| Musk melon, yellow flesh | 0.02 | **ROOTS AND TUBERS** | |
| Orange, pulp | 0.02 | Beet root | 0.01 |
| Peach | 0.02 | Potato, brown skin, big | 0.01 |
| Pear | 0.02 | Potato, brown skin, small | 0.01 |
| Plum | 0.02 | Potato, red skin | 0.01 |
| Pummelo | 0.02 | Yam, wild | 0.015 |
| Star fruit | 0.02 | Radish, elongate, red skin | 0.02 |
| Water melon, dark green | 0.02 | Radish, elongate, white skin | 0.02 |
| Water melon, pale green | 0.02 | Radish, round, red skin | 0.02 |
| Zizyphus | 0.02 | Radish, round, white skin | 0.02 |
| Banana, ripe, poovam | 0.03 | Tapioca | 0.02 |
| Banana, ripe, robusta | 0.03 | Water chestnut | 0.02 |
| Currants, black | 0.03 | Yam, ordinary | 0.02 |
| Dates, dry, pale brown | 0.03 | Carrot, orange | 0.03 |
| Dates, dry, dark brown | 0.03 | Carrot, red | 0.03 |
| Gooseberry | 0.03 | Colocasia | 0.03 |
| Grapes, seeded, round, black | 0.03 | Sweet potato, brown skin | 0.04 |
| Grapes, seeded, round, red | 0.03 | Sweet potato, pink skin | 0.04 |
| Grapes, seedless, round, green | 0.03 | Lotus root | 0.05 |
| Grapes, seedless, round, black | 0.03 | Yam, elephant | 0.05 |
| Guava, pink flesh | 0.03 | **CONDIMENTS AND SPICES - FRESH** | |
| Mango, ripe, himsagar | 0.03 | Onion, big | 0.01 |
| Pineapple | 0.03 | Onion, small | 0.02 |
| Sapota | 0.03 | Ginger, fresh | 0.04 |
| Apricot, dried | 0.04 | Coriander leaves | 0.05 |
| Apricot, processed | 0.04 | Mango ginger | 0.07 |
| Bael fruit | 0.04 | Chillies,green-all varieties | 0.11 |
| Banana, ripe, montham | 0.04 | Curry leaves | 0.13 |
| Guava, white flesh | 0.04 | Mint leaves | 0.19 |
| Mango, ripe, banganapalli | 0.04 | Garlic, single clove, Kashmir | 0.22 |
| Mango, ripe, gulabkhas | 0.04 | Garlic, small clove | 0.23 |
| Mango, ripe, kesar | 0.04 | Garlic, big clove | 0.25 |
| Mango, ripe, neelam | 0.04 | **CONDIMENTS AND SPICES - DRY** | |
| Mango, ripe, paheri | 0.04 | Asafoetida | 0.01 |
| Raisins, dried, black | 0.04 | Turmeric powder | 0.01 |
| Raisins, dried, golden | 0.04 | Nutmeg | 0.05 |

--- **Author** ---
Dr. Prajakta J. Nande

# Clinical and Therapeutic Nutrition Practical Manual 1
For M.Sc. Food Science and Nutrition (Semester-III)

| | | | |
|---|---|---|---|
| Cardamom, green | 0.07 | Khoa | 0.11 |
| Pepper, black | 0.09 | Milk, whole, buffalo | 0.13 |
| Poppy seeds | 0.1 | **EGG AND EGG PRODUCTS** | |
| Cardamom, black | 0.13 | Egg, country hen, whole, raw | 0.08 |
| Cumin seeds | 0.13 | Eggs, poultry, white, raw | 0.16 |
| Mace | 0.13 | Egg, poultry, yolk, raw | 0.16 |
| Fenugreek seeds | 0.14 | Eggs, poultry, whole, raw | 0.19 |
| Pippali | 0.14 | **POULTRY** | |
| Cloves | 0.22 | Chicken, poultry, breast, skinless | 0.06 |
| Coriander seeds | 0.23 | Chicken, poultry, wing, skinless | 0.07 |
| Omum | 0.23 | Chicken, poultry, thigh, skinless | 0.1 |
| Chillies, red | 0.83 | Chicken, poultry, legs, skinless | 0.13 |
| **NUTS AND OIL SEEDS** | | Poultry, chicken, liver | 0.2 |
| Arecanut, dried, brown | 0.03 | **ANIMAL MEAT** | |
| Cashew nut | 0.03 | Beef, chops | 0.06 |
| Arecanut, fresh | 0.031 | Beef, round (leg) | 0.06 |
| Coconut kernel, dry | 0.04 | Pork, stomach | 0.06 |
| Pistachio nut | 0.04 | Pork, shoulder | 0.1 |
| Linseeds | 0.05 | Pork, chops | 0.11 |
| Gingelly seeds, white | 0.07 | Beef, shoulder | 0.12 |
| Coconut kernel, fresh | 0.08 | Beef, lungs | 0.12 |
| Gingelly seeds, brown | 0.08 | Goat, chops | 0.13 |
| Pine seeds | 0.08 | Beef, brain | 0.13 |
| Gingelly seeds, black | 0.1 | Pork, lungs | 0.14 |
| Ground nut | 0.12 | Goat, legs | 0.15 |
| Walnut | 0.12 | Goat, spleen | 0.16 |
| Sunflower seeds | 0.13 | Goat, shoulder | 0.17 |
| Garden cress seeds | 0.15 | Goat, brain | 0.17 |
| Safflower seeds | 0.15 | Beef, spleen | 0.25 |
| Niger seeds, black | 0.23 | Beef, kidney | 0.27 |
| Arecanut, dried, red color | 0.24 | Pork, spleen | 0.27 |
| Almond | 0.26 | Beef, heart | 0.3 |
| Mustard seeds | 0.33 | Pork, heart | 0.3 |
| Niger seeds, gray | 0.35 | Goat, lungs | 0.32 |
| **SUGAR** | | Goat, heart | 0.33 |
| Jaggery, cane | 0.01 | Goat, kidneys | 0.34 |
| Sugarcane, juice | 0.04 | Beef, liver | 0.34 |
| **MUSHROOMS** | | Goat, liver | 0.37 |
| Button mushroom, fresh | 0.03 | Pork kidney | 0.37 |
| Chicken mushroom, fresh | 0.06 | **MARINE FISH** | |
| Shiitake mushroom, fresh | 0.16 | Bombay duck | 0.02 |
| **MISCELLANEOUS FOODS** | | Pomfret, black | 0.02 |
| Coconut water | 0.01 | Mural | 0.03 |
| **MILK AND MILK PRODUCTS** | | Pomfret, white | 0.03 |
| Paneer | 0.1 | Salmon | 0.06 |
| Milk, whole, cow | 0.11 | Sardine | 0.06 |

**--- Author ---**
Dr. Prajakta J. Nande

# Clinical and Therapeutic Nutrition Practical Manual 1
### For M.Sc. Food Science and Nutrition (Semester-III)

| | | | | |
|---|---|---|---|---|
| Tuna | 0.07 | | Prawns, big | 0.02 |
| **MARINE SHELLFISH** | | | Prawns, small | 0.03 |
| Lobster, brown | 0.01 | | Rohu | 0.04 |
| Lobster, king size | 0.02 | | Catla | 0.07 |
| Tiger prawns, orange | 0.03 | | Crab | 0.11 |
| Crab, sea | 0.06 | | **FATTY FISH** | |
| Crab | 0.1 | | Hilsa | 0.04 |
| **FRESH WATER FISH AND SHELLFISH** | | | | |

*(Source: T. Longvah, R. Ananthan, K. Bhaskaracharya, K. Venkaiah. Indian Food Composition Tables, National Institute of Nutrition (Indian Council of Medical Research), 33-60, 2017)*

## ANNEXURE - 18

## NIACIN (VITAMIN B3) CONTENT OF FOODS

| FOOD STUFFS | B3 (mg/ 100 g) | | | |
|---|---|---|---|---|
| **CEREALS AND MILLETS** | | | Cowpea, white | 1.51 |
| Amaranth seeds, black | 0.45 | | Cowpea, brown | 1.64 |
| Amaranth seeds, pale brown | 0.52 | | Black gram, dal | 1.76 |
| Wheat, vermicelli, roasted | 0.67 | | Lentil dal | 1.81 |
| Wheat flour, refined | 0.77 | | Horse gram, whole | 1.82 |
| Bajra | 0.86 | | Green gram, dal | 1.84 |
| Wheat, vermicelli | 0.86 | | Black gram, whole | 1.85 |
| Maize, tender, local | 1.13 | | Bengal gram, dal | 1.87 |
| Wheat, semolina | 1.13 | | Moth bean | 1.87 |
| Maize, tender, sweet | 1.14 | | Field bean, black | 1.88 |
| Samai | 1.29 | | Field bean, white | 1.96 |
| Ragi | 1.34 | | Field bean, brown | 2.04 |
| Varagu | 1.49 | | Red gram, dal | 2.09 |
| Rice flakes | 1.6 | | Bengal gram, whole | 2.1 |
| Rice, raw, milled | 1.69 | | Soya bean, brown | 2.12 |
| Quinoa | 1.7 | | Green gram, whole | 2.16 |
| Rice puffed | 1.87 | | Soya bean, white | 2.28 |
| Wheat, bulgur | 2.05 | | Rice bean | 2.32 |
| Jowar | 2.1 | | Rajmah, brown | 2.37 |
| Wheat flour | 2.37 | | Rajmah, red | 2.42 |
| Rice, parboiled, milled | 2.51 | | Red gram, whole | 2.42 |
| Wheat, whole | 2.68 | | Lentil whole, brown | 2.54 |
| Maize, dry | 2.69 | | Lentil whole, yellowish | 2.56 |
| Barley | 2.84 | | Rajmah, black | 2.61 |
| Rice, raw, brown | 3.4 | | Peas, dry | 2.69 |
| **GRAIN LEGUMES** | | | **GREEN LEAFY VEGETABLES** | |
| | | | Lettuce | 0.17 |
| | | | Cauliflower leaves | 0.21 |
| | | | Cabbage, green | 0.24 |

--- Author ---
Dr. Prajakta J. Nande

# Clinical and Therapeutic Nutrition Practical Manual 1
For M.Sc. Food Science and Nutrition (Semester-III)

| | | | |
|---|---|---|---|
| Cabbage, collard greens | 0.26 | Cho-cho-marrow | 0.23 |
| Cabbage, violet | 0.27 | Bamboo shoot, tender | 0.25 |
| Ponnaganni | 0.32 | Mango, green, raw | 0.26 |
| Rumex leaves | 0.33 | Bitter gourd, jagged, teeth ridges, elongate | 0.27 |
| Spinach | 0.33 | | |
| Parsley | 0.36 | Plantain, flower | 0.28 |
| Cabbage, Chinese | 0.38 | Bitter gourd, jagged, teeth ridges, short | 0.29 |
| Beet greens | 0.43 | | |
| Betel leaves, big (Kolkata) | 0.45 | Bitter gourd, jagged, smooth ridges, elongate | 0.3 |
| Basella leaves | 0.46 | | |
| Betel leaves, small | 0.47 | Cauliflower | 0.31 |
| Radish leaves | 0.47 | Field beans, tender, broad | 0.32 |
| Brussels sprouts | 0.5 | Field beans, tender, lean | 0.33 |
| Bathua leaves | 0.54 | Plantain, green | 0.33 |
| Gogu leaves, red | 0.56 | Snake gourd, long, dark green | 0.33 |
| Gogu leaves, green | 0.58 | Snake gourd, short | 0.33 |
| Mustard leaves | 0.58 | Snake gourd, long, pale green | 0.34 |
| Amaranth leaves, red | 0.62 | Cucumber, green, elongate | 0.35 |
| Amaranth spinosus, leaves, green | 0.63 | Cucumber, green, short | 0.35 |
| Pak choi leaves | 0.66 | Cucumber, round | 0.36 |
| Amaranth leaves, red and green mix | 0.69 | Knol-khol | 0.37 |
| Fenugreek leaves | 0.7 | Pumpkin, orange, round | 0.41 |
| Amaranth leaves, green | 0.71 | Zucchini, yellow | 0.42 |
| Amaranth spinosus, leaves, red and green mix | 0.72 | Pumpkin, green, cylindrical | 0.44 |
| | | Tomato, green | 0.46 |
| Tamarind leaves, tender | 0.79 | Celery stalk | 0.48 |
| Colocasia leaves, green | 0.8 | Kovai, small | 0.51 |
| Drumstick leaves | 0.82 | Tomato, ripe, hybrid | 0.51 |
| Knol-khol, leaves | 0.86 | Bean scarlet, tender | 0.52 |
| Agathi leaves | 1.18 | Tomato, ripe, local | 0.52 |
| Garden cress | 1.2 | Brinjal-all varieties | 0.53 |
| Pumpkin leaves, tender | 1.49 | Corn, baby | 0.53 |
| **OTHER VEGETABLES** | | Kovai, big | 0.55 |
| Ash gourd | 0.12 | Capsicum, green | 0.56 |
| Papaya, raw | 0.12 | Tinda, tender | 0.56 |
| Bottle gourd, elongate, pale green | 0.14 | Capsicum, yellow | 0.59 |
| Bottle gourd, round, pale green | 0.14 | Ladies finger | 0.61 |
| Bottle gourd, elongate, dark green | 0.14 | Drumstick | 0.62 |
| Onion, stalk | 0.14 | Capsicum, red | 0.66 |
| Colocasia, stem, black | 0.16 | Parwar | 0.67 |
| Plantain, stem | 0.18 | Cluster beans | 0.71 |
| Jack fruit, raw | 0.19 | Broad beans | 0.76 |
| Jack fruit, seed, mature | 0.19 | French beans, hybrid | 0.77 |
| Ridge gourd | 0.2 | French beans, country | 0.83 |
| Ridge gourd, smooth skin | 0.21 | Zucchini, green | 1.03 |
| Colocasia, stem, green | 0.22 | Peas, fresh | 1.28 |

--- **Author** ---
Dr. Prajakta J. Nande

# Clinical and Therapeutic Nutrition Practical Manual 1
For M.Sc. Food Science and Nutrition (Semester-III)

| | | | |
|---|---|---|---|
| Red gram, tender, fresh | 2.14 | Jack fruit, ripe | 0.42 |
| **FRUITS** | | Banana, ripe, poovam | 0.43 |
| Apple, small | 0.09 | Musk melon, yellow flesh | 0.43 |
| Apple, small, Kashmir | 0.09 | Plum | 0.44 |
| Grapes, seeded, round, red | 0.1 | Banana, ripe, red | 0.46 |
| Lemon, juice | 0.1 | Palm fruit, tender | 0.46 |
| Gooseberry | 0.12 | Banana, ripe, robusta | 0.47 |
| Grapes, seedless, round, green | 0.12 | Banana, ripe, montham | 0.48 |
| Pineapple | 0.12 | Raisins, dried, black | 0.48 |
| Grapes, seeded, round, green | 0.13 | Strawberry | 0.48 |
| Grapes, seedless, round, black | 0.13 | Dates, processed | 0.51 |
| Pear | 0.13 | Wood apple | 0.55 |
| Grapes, seeded, round, black | 0.14 | Mangosteen | 0.58 |
| Jambu fruit, ripe | 0.14 | Guava, pink flesh | 0.59 |
| Grapes, seedless, oval, black | 0.15 | Guava, white flesh | 0.6 |
| Lime, sweet, pulp | 0.17 | Raisins, dried, golden | 0.64 |
| Cherries, red | 0.19 | Custard apple | 0.69 |
| Pomegranate, maroon seeds | 0.2 | Soursop | 0.85 |
| Apple, green | 0.21 | Avocado fruit | 0.9 |
| Litchi | 0.23 | Apricot, processed | 1.07 |
| Mango, ripe, gulabkhas | 0.23 | Dates, dry, dark brown | 1.09 |
| Mango, ripe, neelam | 0.23 | Dates, dry, pale brown | 1.47 |
| Pummelo | 0.23 | Tamarind, pulp | 1.56 |
| Sapota | 0.24 | Apricot, dried | 1.66 |
| Apple, big | 0.25 | **ROOTS AND TUBERS** | |
| Bael fruit | 0.25 | Beet root | 0.21 |
| Karonda fruit | 0.25 | Carrot, orange | 0.22 |
| Mango, ripe, banganapalli | 0.26 | Radish, round, white skin | 0.24 |
| Mango, ripe, kesar | 0.26 | Carrot, red | 0.25 |
| Rambutan | 0.26 | Radish, elongate, white skin | 0.3 |
| Fig | 0.27 | Radish, round, red skin | 0.3 |
| Mango, ripe, himsagar | 0.27 | Radish, elongate, red skin | 0.31 |
| Mango, ripe, totapari | 0.27 | Lotus root | 0.43 |
| Mango, ripe, paheri | 0.28 | Tapioca | 0.45 |
| Orange, pulp | 0.28 | Colocasia | 0.51 |
| Water melon, dark green | 0.28 | Yam, ordinary | 0.56 |
| Peach | 0.29 | Yam, elephant | 0.61 |
| Water melon, pale green | 0.3 | Sweet potato, brown skin | 0.67 |
| Papaya, ripe | 0.33 | Sweet potato, pink skin | 0.69 |
| Zizyphus | 0.33 | Yam, wild | 0.7 |
| Star fruit | 0.34 | Water chestnut | 0.74 |
| Currants, black | 0.35 | Potato, brown skin, big | 1.04 |
| Black berry | 0.4 | Potato, red skin | 1.13 |
| Manila tamarind | 0.4 | Potato, brown skin, small | 1.36 |
| Phalsa | 0.4 | **CONDIMENTS AND SPICES - FRESH** | |
| Musk melon, orange flesh | 0.41 | Onion, small | 0.21 |

**--- Author ---**
Dr. Prajakta J. Nande

# Clinical and Therapeutic Nutrition Practical Manual 1

For M.Sc. Food Science and Nutrition (Semester-III)

| | | | | |
|---|---|---|---|---|
| Onion, big | 0.34 | Garden cress, seeds | 5.67 |
| Garlic, small clove | 0.36 | Ground nut | 11.35 |
| Garlic, single clove, Kashmir | 0.42 | **SUGAR** | |
| Ginger, fresh | 0.42 | Jaggery, cane | 0.02 |
| Mango ginger | 0.45 | Sugarcane, juice | 0.14 |
| Curry leaves | 0.73 | **MUSHROOMS** | |
| Mint leaves | 0.74 | Button mushroom, fresh | 0.68 |
| Garlic, big clove | 0.85 | Chicken mushroom, fresh | 1.45 |
| Chillies green-all varieties | 0.89 | Shiitake mushroom, fresh | 1.92 |
| Coriander leaves | 0.89 | **MISCELLANEOUS FOODS** | |
| **CONDIMENTS AND SPICES - DRY** | | Coconut water | 0.04 |
| Asafoetida | 0.43 | **MILK AND MILK PRODUCTS** | |
| Nutmeg | 0.51 | Milk, whole, buffalo | 0.07 |
| Cardamom, black | 0.52 | Milk, whole, cow | 0.08 |
| Poppy seeds | 0.77 | Paneer | 0.13 |
| Pepper, black | 0.85 | Khoa | 0.43 |
| Mace | 0.92 | **EGG AND EGG PRODUCTS** | |
| Pippali | 1.06 | Eggs, poultry, white, raw | 0.01 |
| Cardamom, green | 1.13 | Eggs, poultry, whole, raw | 0.11 |
| Cloves | 1.15 | Egg, country hen, whole, raw | 0.14 |
| Fenugreek seeds | 1.19 | Egg, poultry, yolk, raw | 0.69 |
| Coriander seeds | 1.2 | **POULTRY** | |
| Omum | 1.23 | Poultry, chicken, liver | 4.44 |
| Turmeric powder | 1.55 | Chicken, poultry, legs, skinless | 5.6 |
| Cumin seeds | 2.87 | Chicken, poultry, thigh, skinless | 5.62 |
| Chillies, red | 6.94 | Chicken, poultry, wing, skinless | 6.66 |
| **NUTS AND OIL SEEDS** | | Chicken, poultry, breast, skinless | 8.06 |
| Coconut kernel, fresh | 0.3 | **ANIMAL MEAT** | |
| Arecanut, dried, brown | 0.71 | Pork, stomach | 1.9 |
| Coconut kernel, dry | 0.71 | Beef, brain | 1.91 |
| Arecanut, fresh | 0.74 | Goat, brain | 2.04 |
| Arecanut, dried, red color | 0.8 | Goat, lungs | 2.79 |
| Pistachio nut | 0.86 | Pork, lungs | 3.11 |
| Walnut | 0.86 | Beef, lungs | 3.13 |
| Niger seeds gray | 0.88 | Pork, shoulder | 4.22 |
| Cashew nut | 1.03 | Beef, chops | 4.36 |
| Linseeds | 1.09 | Pork, chops | 4.49 |
| Safflower seed | 1.12 | Pork, heart | 5.13 |
| Niger seeds black | 1.14 | Goat, shoulder meat | 5.14 |
| Sunflower seeds | 1.6 | Goat, legs | 5.15 |
| Gingelly seeds, brown | 3.05 | Beef, shoulder | 5.18 |
| Gingelly seeds, black | 3.12 | Goat, spleen | 5.2 |
| Pine seeds | 3.52 | Beef, heart | 5.38 |
| Almond | 3.71 | Goat, kidneys | 5.5 |
| Mustard seeds | 3.8 | Goat, chops | 5.51 |
| Gingelly seeds, white | 3.94 | Goat, heart | 5.97 |

**--- Author ---**
Dr. Prajakta J. Nande

# Clinical and Therapeutic Nutrition Practical Manual 1
For M.Sc. Food Science and Nutrition (Semester-III)

| | | | | |
|---|---|---|---|---|
| Beef, round (leg) | 6.3 | Crab, sea | 0.97 |
| Pork, kidneys | 6.46 | Tiger prawns, orange | 1.18 |
| Beef, kidney | 6.52 | Crab | 1.66 |
| Beef, spleen | 7.45 | Lobster, king size | 1.87 |
| Pork, spleen | 7.8 | **FRESH WATER FISH AND SHELLFISH** | |
| Goat, liver | 12.88 | Prawns, small | 0.54 |
| Beef, liver | 14.01 | Prawns, big | 1.31 |
| **MARINE FISH** | | Crab | 1.54 |
| Bombay duck | 0.64 | Catla | 2.21 |
| Sardine | 0.91 | Rohu | 2.33 |
| Pomfret, white | 1.38 | **FATTY FISH** | |
| Pomfret, black | 2.61 | Hilsa | 1.19 |
| Mural | 2.65 | | |
| Salmon | 4.45 | | |
| Tuna | 4.73 | | |
| **MARINE SHELLFISH** | | | |
| Lobster, brown | 0.63 | | |

*(Source: T. Longvah, R. Ananthan, K. Bhaskaracharya, K. Venkaiah. Indian Food Composition Tables, National Institute of Nutrition (Indian Council of Medical Research), 33-60, 2017)*

## ANNEXURE - 19

## PYRIDOXINE (VITAMIN B6) CONTENT OF FOODS

| FOOD STUFFS | B6 (mg/ 100 g) | | |
|---|---|---|---|
| **CEREALS AND MILLETS** | | Wheat, whole | 0.26 |
| Amaranth seeds, black | 0.5 | Wheat, bulgur | 0.24 |
| Amaranth seeds, pale brown | 0.33 | Wheat, semolina | 0.11 |
| Bajra | 0.27 | Wheat, vermicelli | 0.03 |
| Barley | 0.31 | Wheat, vermicelli, roasted | 0.03 |
| Jowar | 0.28 | **GRAIN LEGUMES** | |
| Maize, dry | 0.34 | Bengal gram, dal | 0.19 |
| Maize, tender, local | 0.45 | Bengal gram, whole | 0.36 |
| Maize, tender, sweet | 0.38 | Black gram, dal | 0.22 |
| Quinoa | 0.21 | Black gram, whole | 0.53 |
| Ragi | 0.05 | Cowpea, brown | 0.3 |
| Rice flakes | 0.02 | Cowpea, white | 0.26 |
| Rice puffed | 0.07 | Field bean, black | 0.35 |
| Rice, raw ,brown | 0.37 | Field bean, brown | 0.37 |
| Rice, parboiled, milled | 0.22 | Field bean, white | 0.38 |
| Rice, raw, milled | 0.12 | Green gram, dal | 0.19 |
| Samai | 0.04 | Green gram, whole | 0.35 |
| Varagu | 0.07 | Horse gram, whole | 0.21 |
| Wheat flour, refined | 0.08 | Lentil dal | 0.18 |
| Wheat flour | 0.25 | Lentil whole, brown | 0.46 |
| | | Lentil whole, yellowish | 0.47 |
| | | Moth bean | 0.16 |

--- Author ---
Dr. Prajakta J. Nande

# Clinical and Therapeutic Nutrition Practical Manual 1
For M.Sc. Food Science and Nutrition (Semester-III)

| | | | | |
|---|---|---|---|---|
| Peas, dry | 0.26 | Ash gourd | 0.18 |
| Rajmah, black | 0.23 | Bamboo shoot, tender | 0.13 |
| Rajmah, brown | 0.21 | Bean scarlet, tender | 0.31 |
| Rajmah, red | 0.21 | Bitter gourd, jagged, teeth ridges, elongate | 0.05 |
| Red gram, dal | 0.24 | Bitter gourd, jagged, teeth ridges, short | 0.04 |
| Red gram, whole | 0.42 | Bitter gourd, jagged, teeth ridges, short | 0.04 |
| Rice bean | 0.13 | Bitter gourd, jagged, smooth ridges, elongate | 0.05 |
| Soya bean, brown | 0.43 | Bottle gourd, elongate, pale green | 0.02 |
| Soya bean, white | 0.45 | Bottle gourd, round, pale green | 0.02 |
| **GREEN LEAFY VEGETABLES** | | Bottle gourd, elongate, dark green | 0.01 |
| Agathi leaves | 0.22 | Brinjal-all varieties | 1.76 |
| Amaranth leaves, green | 0.21 | Broad beans | 10.03 |
| Amaranth leaves, red | 0.22 | Capsicum, green | 4.59 |
| Amaranth leaves, red and green mix | 0.19 | Capsicum, red | 5.47 |
| Amaranth spinosus, leaves, green | 0.22 | Capsicum, yellow | 0.25 |
| Amaranth spinosus, leaves, red and green mix | 0.2 | Cauliflower | 0.13 |
| Basella leaves | 0.18 | Celery stalk | 0.06 |
| Bathua leaves | 0.17 | Cho-cho-marrow | 0.07 |
| Beet greens | 0.13 | Cluster beans | 0.12 |
| Betel leaves, big (Kolkata) | 0.04 | Colocasia, stem, black | 0.06 |
| Betel leaves, small | 0.04 | Colocasia, stem, green | 0.07 |
| Brussels sprouts | 0.19 | Corn, baby | 0.16 |
| Cabbage, Chinese | 0.19 | Cucumber, green, elongate | 0.06 |
| Cabbage, collard greens | 0.24 | Cucumber, green, short | 0.07 |
| Cabbage, green | 0.13 | Cucumber, round | 0.04 |
| Cabbage, violet | 0.17 | Drumstick | 0.12 |
| Cauliflower leaves | 0.23 | Field beans, tender, broad | 0.42 |
| Colocasia leaves, green | 0.29 | Field beans, tender, lean | 0.38 |
| Drumstick leaves | 0.87 | French beans, country | 0.37 |
| Fenugreek leaves | 0.38 | French beans, hybrid | 0.44 |
| Garden cress | 0.2 | Jack fruit, raw | 0.04 |
| Gogu leaves, green | 0.33 | Jack fruit, seed, mature | 0.08 |
| Gogu leaves, red | 0.31 | Knol-khol | 0.19 |
| Knol-khol leaves | 0.28 | Kovai, big | 0.08 |
| Lettuce | 0.08 | Kovai, small | 0.05 |
| Mustard leaves | 0.16 | Ladies finger | 0.27 |
| Pak choi leaves | 0.96 | Mango, green, raw | 0.13 |
| Parsley | 0.19 | Onion, stalk | 0.17 |
| Ponnaganni | 0.19 | Papaya, raw | 0.03 |
| Pumpkin leaves, tender | 0.17 | Parwar | 0.2 |
| Radish leaves | 0.16 | Peas, fresh | 0.19 |
| Rumex leaves | 0.09 | Plantain, flower | 0.13 |
| Spinach | 0.15 | Plantain, green | 0.1 |
| Tamarind leaves, tender | 0.14 | Plantain, stem | 0.14 |
| **OTHER VEGETABLES** | | | |

--- **Author** ---
Dr. Prajakta J. Nande

# Clinical and Therapeutic Nutrition Practical Manual 1
For M.Sc. Food Science and Nutrition (Semester-III)

| | | | |
|---|---|---|---|
| Pumpkin, green, cylindrical | 0.05 | Karonda fruit | 0.08 |
| Pumpkin, orange, round | 0.08 | Lemon, juice | 0.03 |
| Red gram, tender, fresh | 0.3 | Lime, sweet, pulp | 0.05 |
| Ridge gourd | 0.07 | Litchi | 0.07 |
| Ridge gourd, smooth skin | 0.09 | Mango, ripe, banganapalli | 0.12 |
| Snake gourd, long, pale green | 0.1 | Mango, ripe, gulabkhas | 0.13 |
| Snake gourd, long, dark green | 0.07 | Mango, ripe, himsagar | 0.1 |
| Snake gourd, short | 0.06 | Mango, ripe, kesar | 0.1 |
| Tinda, tender | 0.06 | Mango, ripe, neelam | 0.12 |
| Tomato, green | 0.07 | Mango, ripe, paheri | 0.23 |
| Tomato, ripe, hybrid | 0.08 | Mango, ripe, totapari | 0.12 |
| Tomato, ripe, local | 0.09 | Mangosteen | 0.18 |
| Zucchini, green | 0.25 | Manila tamarind | 0.04 |
| Zucchini, yellow | 0.2 | Musk melon, orange flesh | 0.05 |
| **FRUITS** | | Musk melon, yellow flesh | 0.06 |
| Apple, big | 0.04 | Orange, pulp | 0.04 |
| Apple, green | 0.08 | Palm fruit, tender | 0.07 |
| Apple, small | 0.03 | Papaya, ripe | 0.04 |
| Apple, small, Kashmir | 0.04 | Peach | 0.1 |
| Apricot, dried | 0.1 | Pear | 0.09 |
| Apricot, processed | 0.17 | Phalsa | 0.03 |
| Avocado fruit | 0.18 | Pineapple | 0.13 |
| Bael fruit | 0.03 | Plum | 0.05 |
| Banana, ripe, montham | 0.51 | Pomegranate, maroon seeds | 0.29 |
| Banana, ripe, poovam | 0.5 | Pummelo | 0.04 |
| Banana, ripe, red | 0.45 | Raisins, dried, black | 0.17 |
| Banana, ripe, robusta | 0.44 | Raisins, dried, golden | 0.17 |
| Black berry | 0.05 | Rambutan | 0.04 |
| Cherries, red | 0.04 | Sapota | 0.12 |
| Currants, black | 0.09 | Soursop | 0.03 |
| Custard apple | 0.07 | Star fruit | 0.06 |
| Dates, dry, pale brown | 0.14 | Strawberry | 0.09 |
| Dates, dry, dark brown | 0.153 | Tamarind, pulp | 0.08 |
| Dates, processed | 0.06 | Water melon, dark green | 0.1 |
| Fig | 0.15 | Water melon, pale green | 0.07 |
| Gooseberry | 0.27 | Wood apple | 0.17 |
| Grapes, seeded, round, black | 0.11 | Zizyphus | 0.11 |
| Grapes, seeded, round, green | 0.09 | **ROOTS AND TUBERS** | |
| Grapes, seeded, round, red | 0.1 | Beet root | 0.07 |
| Grapes, seedless, oval, black | 0.11 | Carrot, orange | 0.11 |
| Grapes, seedless, round, green | 0.08 | Carrot, red | 0.07 |
| Grapes, seedless, round, black | 0.08 | Colocasia | 0.17 |
| Guava, white flesh | 0.11 | Lotus root | 0.19 |
| Guava, pink flesh | 0.16 | Potato, brown skin, big | 0.1 |
| Jack fruit, ripe | 0.22 | Potato, brown skin, small | 0.12 |
| Jambu fruit, ripe | 0.03 | Potato, red skin | 0.1 |

--- **Author** ---
Dr. Prajakta J. Nande

# Clinical and Therapeutic Nutrition Practical Manual 1
For M.Sc. Food Science and Nutrition (Semester-III)

| | | | | |
|---|---|---|---|---|
| Radish, elongate, red skin | 0.07 | Coconut kernel, fresh | 0.1 |
| Radish, elongate, white skin | 0.07 | Garden cress, seeds | 0.05 |
| Radish, round, red skin | 0.07 | Gingelly seeds, black | 0.64 |
| Radish, round, white skin | 0.07 | Gingelly seeds, brown | 0.49 |
| Sweet potato, brown skin | 0.12 | Gingelly seeds, white | 0.62 |
| Sweet potato, pink skin | 0.09 | Ground nut | 0.23 |
| Tapioca | 0.09 | Mustard seeds | 0.24 |
| Water chestnut | 0.13 | Linseeds | 0.35 |
| Yam, elephant | 0.22 | Niger seeds, black | 0.45 |
| Yam, ordinary | 0.17 | Niger seeds, gray | 0.34 |
| Yam, wild | 0.2 | Pine seeds | 0.11 |
| **CONDIMENTS AND SPICES - FRESH** | | Pistachio nut | 0.96 |
| Chillies green-all varieties | 0.28 | Safflower seeds | 0.93 |
| Coriander leaves | 0.19 | Sunflower seeds | 0.94 |
| Curry leaves | 0.57 | Walnut | 0.8 |
| Garlic, big clove | 0.56 | **SUGAR** | |
| Garlic, small clove | 0.77 | Jaggery, cane | 0.71 |
| Garlic, single clove, Kashmir | 0.97 | Sugarcane, juice | 0.4 |
| Ginger, fresh | 0.2 | **MUSHROOMS** | |
| Mango ginger | 0.18 | Button mushroom, fresh | 0.12 |
| Mint leaves | 0.17 | Chicken mushroom, fresh | 0.11 |
| Onion, big | 0.1 | Shiitake mushroom, fresh | 0.45 |
| Onion, small | 0.12 | **MISCELLANEOUS FOODS** | |
| **CONDIMENTS AND SPICES - DRY** | | Coconut water | 0.06 |
| Asafoetida | 0.02 | **MILK AND MILK PRODUCTS** | |
| Cardamom, green | 0.15 | Milk, whole, buffalo | 0.04 |
| Cardamom, black | 0.2 | Milk, whole, cow | 0.04 |
| Chillies, red | 0.42 | Paneer | 0.04 |
| Cloves | 0.03 | Khoa | 0.06 |
| Coriander seeds | 0.04 | **EGG AND EGG PRODUCTS** | |
| Cumin seeds | 0.39 | Eggs, poultry, whole, raw | 0.16 |
| Fenugreek seeds | 0.77 | Eggs, poultry, white, raw | 0.29 |
| Mace | 0.3 | Egg, poultry, yolk, raw | 0.14 |
| Nutmeg | 0.1 | Egg, country hen, whole, raw | 0.18 |
| Omum | 0.24 | **POULTRY** | |
| Pippali | 0.6 | Chicken, poultry, legs, skinless | 0.33 |
| Pepper, black | 0.27 | Chicken, poultry, thigh, skinless | 0.38 |
| Poppy seeds | 0.42 | Chicken, poultry, breast, skinless | 0.53 |
| Turmeric powder | 0.13 | Chicken, poultry, wing, skinless | 0.39 |
| **NUTS AND OIL SEEDS** | | Poultry, chicken, liver | 0.92 |
| Almond | 0.09 | **ANIMALMEAT** | |
| Arecanut, dried, brown | 0.32 | Goat, shoulder meat | 0.26 |
| Arecanut, dried, red color | 0.21 | Goat, chops | 0.3 |
| Arecanut, fresh | 0.25 | Goat, legs | 0.31 |
| Cashew nut | 0.16 | Goat, brain | 0.28 |
| Coconut kernel, dry | 0.15 | Goat, lungs | 0.14 |

--- **Author** ---
Dr. Prajakta J. Nande

# Clinical and Therapeutic Nutrition Practical Manual 1
For M.Sc. Food Science and Nutrition (Semester-III)

| | | | |
|---|---|---|---|
| Goat, heart | 0.23 | Bombay duck | 98 |
| Goat, liver | 0.65 | Mural | 67.24 |
| Goat, spleen | 0.33 | Pomfret, black | 76 |
| Goat, kidneys | 0.4 | Pomfret, white | 130 |
| Beef, shoulder | 0.48 | Salmon | 150 |
| Beef, chops | 0.34 | Sardine | 140 |
| Beef, round (leg) | 0.44 | Tuna | 68.24 |
| Beef, brain | 0.25 | **MARINE SHELLFISH** | |
| Beef, lungs | 0.23 | Crab | 120 |
| Beef, heart | 0.25 | Crab, sea | 117 |
| Beef, liver | 0.3 | Lobster, brown | 216 |
| Beef, spleen | 0.26 | Lobster, king size | 156 |
| Beef, kidney | 0.22 | Tiger prawns, orange | 112 |
| Pork, shoulder | 0.41 | **FRESH WATER FISH AND SHELLFISH** | |
| Pork, chops | 0.36 | Catla | 114 |
| Pork, lungs | 0.19 | Rohu | 240 |
| Pork, heart | 0.3 | Crab | 202 |
| Pork, stomach | 0.19 | Prawns, big | 186 |
| Pork, spleen | 0.3 | Prawns, small | 207 |
| Pork, kidneys | 0.37 | **FATTY FISH** | |
| **MARINE FISH** | | Hilsa | 120 |

*(Source: T. Longvah, R. Ananthan, K. Bhaskaracharya, K. Venkaiah. Indian Food Composition Tables, National Institute of Nutrition (Indian Council of Medical Research), 33-60, 2017)*

---

# ANNEXURE - 20

# TOTAL FOLATE (VITAMIN B9) CONTENT OF FOODS

| FOOD STUFFS | B9 (mg/ 100 g) | | |
|---|---|---|---|
| **CEREALS AND MILLETS** | | Wheat flour | 29.22 |
| Rice flakes | 8.46 | Wheat, whole | 30.09 |
| Rice, raw, milled | 9.32 | Barley | 31.58 |
| Rice, parboiled, milled | 9.75 | Ragi | 34.66 |
| Rice, raw, brown | 11.51 | Bajra | 36.11 |
| Wheat, vermicelli, roasted | 13.21 | Samai | 36.2 |
| Wheat, vermicelli | 14.35 | Jowar | 39.42 |
| Wheat flour, refined | 16.25 | Varagu | 39.49 |
| Amaranth seeds, pale brown | 24.65 | Maize tender, sweet | 59.71 |
| Wheat, semolina | 25.68 | Maize, tender, local | 62.96 |
| Maize, dry | 25.81 | Quinoa | 173 |
| Wheat, bulgur | 26.3 | **GRAIN LEGUMES** | |
| Amaranth seeds, black | 27.44 | Lentil dal | 49.99 |
| | | Black gram, dal | 88.75 |
| | | Green gram, dal | 92.11 |
| | | Red gram, dal | 108 |

--- Author ---
Dr. Prajakta J. Nande

# Clinical and Therapeutic Nutrition Practical Manual 1
For M.Sc. Food Science and Nutrition (Semester-III)

| | | | | |
|---|---|---|---|---|
| Peas, dry | 110 | Amaranth leaves, red | 81.95 |
| Lentil whole, yellowish | 121 | Brussels sprouts | 85.01 |
| Rice bean | 122 | Gogu leaves, red | 88.63 |
| Lentil whole, brown | 132 | Basella leaves | 90.31 |
| Black gram, whole | 134 | Tamarind leaves, tender | 91.82 |
| Green gram, whole | 145 | Pak choi leaves | 98.5 |
| Horse gram, whole | 163 | Mustard leaves | 110 |
| Bengal gram, dal | 182 | Agathi leaves | 120 |
| Red gram, whole | 229 | Spinach | 142 |
| Cowpea, brown | 231 | Colocasia leaves, green | 159 |
| Bengal gram, whole | 233 | Parsley | 197 |
| Cowpea, white | 249 | **OTHER VEGETABLES** | |
| Soya bean, white | 288 | Tomato, green | 12.51 |
| Field bean, white | 289 | Plantain, stem | 12.85 |
| Field bean, black | 291 | Ash gourd | 14.11 |
| Field bean, brown | 292 | Cucumber, green, short | 14.67 |
| Soya bean, brown | 297 | Knol-khol | 14.76 |
| Rajmah, red | 316 | Tomato, ripe, hybrid | 15.41 |
| Rajmah, brown | 330 | Snake gourd, long, dark green | 16.52 |
| Rajmah, black | 332 | Cucumber, green, elongate | 16.84 |
| Moth bean | 349 | Bamboo shoot, tender | 17.05 |
| **GREEN LEAFY VEGETABLES** | | Snake gourd, short | 17.74 |
| Beet greens | 11.52 | Snake gourd, long, pale green | 18.34 |
| Betel leaves, big (Kolkata) | 15.96 | Cucumber, round | 18.77 |
| Betel leaves, small | 16.56 | Zucchini, green | 18.85 |
| Lettuce | 30.69 | Plantain, green | 18.96 |
| Pumpkin leaves, tender | 33.82 | Tomato, ripe, local | 19.46 |
| Cabbage, violet | 34.81 | Parwar | 19.96 |
| Rumex leaves | 41.01 | Broad beans | 20.46 |
| Amaranth spinosus, leaves, green | 41.44 | Zucchini, yellow | 21.5 |
| Knol-khol leaves | 41.55 | Celery stalk | 22.48 |
| Bathua leaves | 42.55 | Pumpkin, orange, round | 24.14 |
| Drumstick leaves | 42.89 | Colocasia, stem, green | 25.32 |
| Cauliflower leaves | 42.99 | Mango, green, raw | 25.86 |
| Amaranth spinosus, leaves, red and green mix | 44.23 | Ridge gourd, smooth skin | 27.36 |
| | | Ridge gourd | 29.26 |
| Cabbage, green | 46.36 | Papaya, raw | 29.79 |
| Ponnaganni | 48.42 | Colocasia, stem, black | 30.88 |
| Radish leaves | 53.14 | Pumpkin, green, cylindrical | 31.6 |
| Cabbage, Chinese | 54.51 | Brinjal-all varieties | 33.93 |
| Garden cress | 58.1 | Jack fruit, raw | 35.73 |
| Cabbage, collard greens | 63.46 | Cluster beans | 41.24 |
| Amaranth leaves, red and green mix | 69.08 | Bottle gourd, elongate, pale green | 41.99 |
| Amaranth leaves, green | 70.33 | Tinda, tender | 43.23 |
| Gogu leaves, green | 74.94 | Bean scarlet, tender | 45.26 |
| Fenugreek leaves | 75.26 | Corn, baby | 45.53 |

--- **Author** ---
Dr. Prajakta J. Nande

# Clinical and Therapeutic Nutrition Practical Manual 1
## For M.Sc. Food Science and Nutrition (Semester-III)

| | | | |
|---|---|---|---|
| Cauliflower | 45.95 | Gooseberry | 7.86 |
| Bottle gourd, elongate, dark green | 46.31 | Grapes, seedless, round, green | 8.31 |
| French beans, country | 47.45 | Grapes, seeded, round, green | 8.35 |
| Kovai, big | 48.68 | Star fruit | 8.43 |
| Plantain, flower | 49.27 | Currants, black | 8.48 |
| Bottle gourd, round, pale green | 49.59 | Grapes, seeded, round, black | 8.69 |
| Kovai, small | 50.13 | Karonda fruit | 8.72 |
| Bitter gourd, jagged, teeth ridges, short | 51.45 | Grapes, seedless, round, black | 8.89 |
| | | Strawberry | 8.91 |
| Capsicum, green | 51.85 | Tamarind, pulp | 9.79 |
| Jack fruit, seed, mature | 54.58 | Apricot, dried | 10.5 |
| Peas, fresh | 54.77 | Sapota | 10.83 |
| Onion, stalk | 57.61 | Lemon, juice | 12.43 |
| Bitter gourd, jagged, smooth ridges, elongate | 60.03 | Dates, dry, dark brown | 12.8 |
| | | Pummelo | 13.44 |
| Bitter gourd, jagged, teeth ridges, elongate | 60.28 | Mangosteen | 13.52 |
| | | Fig | 13.67 |
| French beans, hybrid | 61.98 | Plum | 14.29 |
| Capsicum, red | 62.54 | Lime, sweet, pulp | 15.38 |
| Drumstick | 62.75 | Litchi | 15.69 |
| Cho-cho-marrow | 63.03 | Banana, ripe, robusta | 16.81 |
| Ladies finger | 63.68 | Banana, ripe, montham | 17.93 |
| Capsicum, yellow | 66.15 | Pineapple | 18.21 |
| Red gram, tender, fresh | 94.21 | Dates, dry, pale brown | 18.65 |
| Field beans, tender, broad | 123 | Banana, ripe, red | 18.92 |
| Field beans, tender, lean | 127 | Orange, pulp | 19.46 |
| **FRUITS** | | Banana, ripe, poovam | 19.95 |
| Apple, big | 3.04 | Musk melon, yellow flesh | 20.23 |
| Apple, green | 3.43 | Musk melon, orange flesh | 22.31 |
| Apple, small | 3.52 | Phalsa | 22.56 |
| Apple, small, Kashmir | 3.97 | Black berry | 22.95 |
| Manila tamarind | 4.24 | Palm fruit, tender | 24.4 |
| Cherries, red | 4.92 | Dates, processed | 24.53 |
| Pear | 5.28 | Guava, white flesh | 29.76 |
| Apricot, processed | 5.42 | Jack fruit, ripe | 32.15 |
| Water melon, pale green | 5.55 | Guava, pink flesh | 32.17 |
| Water melon, dark green | 5.88 | Raisins, dried, golden | 34.68 |
| Zizyphus | 5.99 | Raisins, dried, black | 38.3 |
| Soursop | 6.09 | Pomegranate, maroon seeds | 38.64 |
| Peach | 6.34 | Bael fruit | 55.22 |
| Wood apple | 6.51 | Papaya, ripe | 60.9 |
| Grapes, seedless, oval, black | 7.22 | Mango, ripe, paheri | 65.28 |
| Rambutan | 7.35 | Avocado fruit | 67.1 |
| Grapes, seeded, round, red | 7.49 | Mango, ripe, neelam | 68.7 |
| Custard apple | 7.6 | Mango, ripe, totapari | 77.69 |
| Jambu fruit, ripe | 7.63 | Mango, ripe, banganapalli | 82.05 |

--- **Author** ---
Dr. Prajakta J. Nande

# Clinical and Therapeutic Nutrition Practical Manual 1
For M.Sc. Food Science and Nutrition (Semester-III)

| | | | | |
|---|---|---|---|---|
| Mango, ripe, gulabkhas | 84.35 | Chillies, red | 51.5 |
| Mango, ripe, kesar | 90.43 | Omum | 51.79 |
| Mango, ripe, himsagar | 90.98 | Pippali | 66.45 |
| **ROOTS AND TUBERS** | | Nutmeg | 74.78 |
| Water chestnut | 9.8 | Poppy seeds | 78.73 |
| Potato, brown skin, small | 13.85 | **NUTS AND OIL SEEDS** | |
| Sweet potato, pink skin | 14.44 | Arecanut, dried, brown | 7.54 |
| Potato, brown skin, big | 15.51 | Arecanut, dried, red color | 8.57 |
| Sweet potato, brown skin | 15.62 | Coconut kernel, dry | 24.27 |
| Yam, ordinary | 15.68 | Cashew nut | 25.2 |
| Potato, red skin | 17.83 | Coconut kernel, fresh | 25.41 |
| Colocasia | 19.91 | Arecanut, fresh | 26.51 |
| Yam, elephant | 20.54 | Garden cress, seeds | 30.92 |
| Yam, wild | 21.01 | Pine seeds | 31.64 |
| Radish, round, white skin | 22.6 | Almond | 36.46 |
| Carrot, red | 23.67 | Walnut | 57.95 |
| Carrot, orange | 24.04 | Pistachio nut | 64.9 |
| Radish, round, red skin | 24.59 | Niger seeds, gray | 73.13 |
| Radish, elongate, red skin | 24.65 | Sunflower seeds | 81.79 |
| Tapioca | 25.64 | Safflower seeds | 82.41 |
| Lotus root | 26.49 | Linseeds | 86.5 |
| Radish, elongate, white skin | 29.75 | Ground nut | 90.87 |
| Beet root | 97.37 | Gingelly seeds, brown | 92.63 |
| **CONDIMENTS AND SPICES- FRESH** | | Mustard seeds | 94.88 |
| Ginger, fresh | 10.82 | Gingelly seeds, black | 127 |
| Chillies green-all varieties | 21.5 | Gingelly seeds, white | 131 |
| Mango ginger | 22.62 | Niger seeds, black | 140 |
| Onion, big | 28.88 | **SUGAR** | |
| Onion, small | 29.68 | Jaggery, cane | 14.4 |
| Coriander leaves | 51.01 | Sugarcane, juice | 44.53 |
| Garlic, small clove | 78.82 | **MUSHROOMS** | |
| Garlic, big clove | 85.77 | Button mushroom, fresh | 8.28 |
| Garlic, single clove, Kashmir | 92.25 | Shiitake mushroom, fresh | 10.92 |
| Mint leaves | 106 | Chicken mushroom, fresh | 11.13 |
| Curry leaves | 117 | **MISCELLANEOUS FOODS** | |
| **CONDIMENTS AND SPICES - DRY** | | Coconut water | 10.88 |
| Cardamom, green | 2.85 | **MILK AND MILK PRODUCTS** | |
| Cardamom, black | 4.96 | Milk, whole, cow | 7.03 |
| Turmeric powder | 13.86 | Milk, whole, buffalo | 8.57 |
| Pepper, black | 21.89 | Paneer | 93.31 |
| Coriander seeds | 22.07 | Khoa | 94.25 |
| Asafoetida | 26.28 | **EGG AND EGG PRODUCTS** | |
| Cumin seeds | 27.79 | Eggs, poultry, white, raw | 4.96 |
| Mace | 32.65 | Eggs, poultry, whole, raw | 49.32 |
| Cloves | 32.81 | Egg, country hen, whole, raw | 54.6 |
| Fenugreek seeds | 51.11 | Egg, poultry, yolk, raw | 112 |

--- **Author** ---
Dr. Prajakta J. Nande

# Clinical and Therapeutic Nutrition Practical Manual 1
For M.Sc. Food Science and Nutrition (Semester-III)

| POULTRY | | | Beef, kidney | 53.68 |
|---|---|---|---|---|
| Chicken, poultry, legs, skinless | 7.47 | | Pork, kidneys | 59.61 |
| Chicken, poultry, wing, skinless | 7.87 | | Goat, kidneys | 68.76 |
| Chicken, poultry, thigh, skinless | 9 | | Goat, liver | 178 |
| Chicken, poultry, breast, skinless | 10.44 | | Beef, liver | 1744 |
| Poultry, chicken, liver | 1032 | | **MARINE FISH** | |
| **ANIMAL MEAT** | | | Pomfret, white | 961 |
| Goat, brain | 1.3 | | Salmon | 1136 |
| Goat, chops | 1.53 | | Mural | 1146 |
| Goat, heart | 1.63 | | Tuna | 1374 |
| Goat, lungs | 1.8 | | Pomfret, black | 2056 |
| Goat, shoulder meat | 2.08 | | Sardine | 2266 |
| Beef, round (leg) | 2.11 | | Bombay duck | 2784 |
| Goat, legs | 2.25 | | **MARINE SHELLFISH** | |
| Goat, spleen | 3.3 | | Crab, sea | 774 |
| Beef, spleen | 3.4 | | Tiger prawns, orange | 807 |
| Pork, heart | 4.73 | | Lobster, brown | 1129 |
| Beef, brain | 5.39 | | Lobster, king size | 1997 |
| Beef, chops | 5.69 | | Crab | 2304 |
| Pork, spleen | 5.92 | | **FRESH WATER FISH AND SHELLFISH** | |
| Pork, lungs | 6.36 | | Rohu | 1263 |
| Pork, shoulder | 6.7 | | Prawns, small | 1306 |
| Pork, stomach | 6.87 | | Crab | 1783 |
| Beef, lungs | 6.98 | | Prawns, big | 1826 |
| Pork, chops | 7.74 | | Catla | 1926 |
| Beef, shoulder | 8.06 | | **FATTY FISH** | |
| Beef, heart | 8.5 | | Hilsa | 2875 |

*(Source: T. Longvah, R. Ananthan, K. Bhaskaracharya, K. Venkaiah. Indian Food Composition Tables, National Institute of Nutrition (Indian Council of Medical Research), 33-60, 2017)*

## ANNEXURE - 21

# TOTAL ASCORBIC ACID (VITAMIN C) CONTENT OF FOODS

| FOOD STUFFS | C (mg/ 100 g) | | Pumpkin leaves, tender | 12.33 |
|---|---|---|---|---|
| | | | Betel leaves, big (Kolkata) | 18.4 |
| | | | Cabbage, Chinese | 19.35 |
| **CEREALS AND MILLETS** | | | Betel leaves, small | 24.51 |
| Maize, tender, local | 4.26 | | Tamarind leaves, tender | 28.22 |
| Maize tender, sweet | 5.72 | | Gogu leaves, green | 29.65 |
| **GRAIN LEGUMES** | | | Spinach | 30.28 |
| Rice bean | 1.11 | | Cabbage, green | 33.25 |
| **GREEN LEAFY VEGETABLES** | | | Gogu leaves, red | 35.43 |
| Lettuce | 11.91 | | Beet greens | 35.83 |

--- Author ---
Dr. Prajakta J. Nande

# Clinical and Therapeutic Nutrition Practical Manual 1
For M.Sc. Food Science and Nutrition (Semester-III)

| | | | | |
|---|---|---|---|---|
| Colocasia leaves, green | 40.71 | Ridge gourd, smooth skin | 8.1 |
| Cabbage, collard greens | 40.76 | Corn, baby | 8.59 |
| Bathua leaves | 41.03 | Jack fruit, seed, mature | 9.68 |
| Garden cress | 42.75 | Broad beans | 10.98 |
| Cabbage, violet | 43.49 | Ash gourd | 11.41 |
| Cauliflower leaves | 52.84 | Celery stalk | 12.3 |
| Rumex leaves | 53.76 | Tinda, tender | 14.2 |
| Pak choi leaves | 55.6 | Red gram, tender, fresh | 15.13 |
| Fenugreek leaves | 58.25 | Bamboo shoot, tender | 15.74 |
| Mustard leaves | 60.32 | Zucchini, green | 15.78 |
| Basella leaves | 63.36 | French beans, country | 15.84 |
| Radish leaves | 65.76 | Tomato, green | 16.41 |
| Knol-khol leaves | 71.11 | Zucchini, yellow | 16.71 |
| Amaranth leaves, red and green mix | 77.24 | Jack fruit, raw | 17.51 |
| Amaranth spinosus, leaves, red and green mix | 77.3 | Kovai, big | 17.62 |
| | | Cluster beans | 17.96 |
| Amaranth spinosus, leaves, green | 82.56 | Parwar | 19.24 |
| Amaranth leaves, green | 83.54 | Cho-cho-marrow | 20.21 |
| Amaranth leaves, red | 86.21 | Papaya, raw | 20.73 |
| Brussels sprouts | 89.45 | Kovai, small | 21.06 |
| Ponnaganni | 103 | Ladies finger | 22.51 |
| Drumstick leaves | 108 | Plantain, green | 23.28 |
| Agathi leaves | 121 | Tomato, ripe, hybrid | 25.27 |
| Parsley | 133 | Onion, stalk | 27.23 |
| **OTHER VEGETABLES** | | Tomato, ripe, local | 27.47 |
| French beans, hybrid | 1.38 | Peas, fresh | 38.4 |
| Brinjal-all varieties | 2.09 | Bitter gourd, jagged, teeth ridges, elongate | 46.53 |
| Snake gourd, short | 2.3 | | |
| Snake gourd, long, pale green | 2.72 | Cauliflower | 47.14 |
| Snake gourd, long, dark green | 2.85 | Bitter gourd, jagged, teeth ridges, short | 50.87 |
| Plantain, stem | 3.77 | | |
| Bottle gourd, elongate, dark green | 3.8 | Bitter gourd, jagged, smooth ridges, elongate | 54.3 |
| Field beans, tender, lean | 3.84 | | |
| Bottle gourd, elongate, pale green | 4.33 | Knol-khol | 64.7 |
| Bottle gourd, round, pale green | 4.54 | Drumstick | 71.86 |
| Colocasia, stem, black | 5.15 | Mango, green, raw | 90.24 |
| Ridge gourd | 5.42 | Capsicum, red | 112 |
| Colocasia, stem, green | 5.83 | Capsicum, green | 123 |
| Field beans, tender, broad | 5.99 | Capsicum, yellow | 127 |
| Cucumber, green, elongate | 6.11 | **FRUITS** | |
| Cucumber, green, short | 6.21 | Apricot, dried | 0.24 |
| Cucumber, round | 6.24 | Palm fruit, tender | 0.25 |
| Plantain, flower | 6.49 | Raisins, dried, golden | 1.85 |
| Bean scarlet, tender | 6.61 | Raisins, dried, black | 2.05 |
| Pumpkin, green, cylindrical | 7.29 | Plum | 2.26 |
| Pumpkin, orange, round | 8.04 | Apple, green | 2.9 |

# Clinical and Therapeutic Nutrition Practical Manual 1
## For M.Sc. Food Science and Nutrition (Semester-III)

| | | | | |
|---|---|---|---|---|
| Pear | 3.31 | Orange, pulp | 42.72 |
| Apple, big | 3.57 | Papaya, ripe | 43.09 |
| Tamarind, pulp | 3.62 | Lime, sweet, pulp | 46.96 |
| Dates, dry, dark brown | 3.84 | Lemon, juice | 48.16 |
| Apple, small | 4 | Pummelo | 48.89 |
| Apple, small, Kashmir | 4.24 | Mango, ripe, himsagar | 49.09 |
| Dates, dry, pale brown | 4.42 | Strawberry | 50.2 |
| Banana, ripe, robusta | 4.76 | Manila tamarind | 55.78 |
| Phalsa | 5.11 | Soursop | 59.54 |
| Peach | 5.49 | Zizyphus | 60.93 |
| Jack fruit, ripe | 6.73 | Rambutan | 65 |
| Banana, ripe, poovam | 6.74 | Karonda fruit | 135 |
| Banana, ripe, red | 6.74 | Currants, black | 182 |
| Bael fruit | 7.5 | Guava, white flesh | 214 |
| Apricot, processed | 7.98 | Guava, pink flesh | 222 |
| Banana, ripe, montham | 8.06 | Gooseberry | 252 |
| Cherries, red | 8.82 | **ROOTS AND TUBERS** | |
| Avocado fruit | 9.36 | Colocasia | 1.83 |
| Water melon, pale green | 11.45 | Beet root | 5.26 |
| Pomegranate, maroon seeds | 12.69 | Water chestnut | 5.26 |
| Water melon, dark green | 13.26 | Carrot, orange | 6.22 |
| Dates, processed | 15.51 | Carrot, red | 6.76 |
| Grapes, seedless, round, green | 16.47 | Yam, ordinary | 13.88 |
| Jambu fruit, ripe | 16.47 | Radish, round, white skin | 14 |
| Fig | 16.92 | Yam, wild | 14.06 |
| Grapes, seeded, round, green | 17.1 | Yam, elephant | 15.22 |
| Grapes, seeded, round, black | 18.3 | Tapioca | 15.51 |
| Black berry | 19.45 | Radish, round, red skin | 15.69 |
| Grapes, seeded, round, red | 20.59 | Radish, elongate, red skin | 17.63 |
| Sapota | 20.96 | Sweet potato, brown skin | 17.94 |
| Musk melon, yellow flesh | 21.32 | Radish, elongate, white skin | 19.91 |
| Custard apple | 21.51 | Sweet potato, pink skin | 22.2 |
| Wood apple | 22.17 | Potato, brown skin, big | 23.15 |
| Musk melon, orange flesh | 22.76 | Potato, red skin | 25.04 |
| Grapes, seedless, round, black | 22.79 | Potato, brown skin, small | 26.41 |
| Mango, ripe, totapari | 25.26 | Lotus root | 26.63 |
| Mangosteen | 26.33 | **CONDIMENTS AND SPICES - FRESH** | |
| Grapes, seedless, oval, black | 27.32 | Mango ginger | 1.62 |
| Mango, ripe, gulabkhas | 27.65 | Ginger, fresh | 5.43 |
| Mango, ripe, kesar | 29.08 | Curry leaves | 6.04 |
| Mango, ripe, neelam | 29.93 | Onion, big | 6.69 |
| Mango, ripe, paheri | 30.75 | Onion, small | 10.96 |
| Star fruit | 33.55 | Garlic, big clove | 12.62 |
| Litchi | 33.82 | Garlic, small clove | 13.57 |
| Mango, ripe, banganapalli | 33.97 | Garlic, single clove, Kashmir | 15.38 |
| Pineapple | 36.37 | Mint leaves | 17.16 |

--- Author ---
Dr. Prajakta J. Nande

# Clinical and Therapeutic Nutrition Practical Manual 1
For M.Sc. Food Science and Nutrition (Semester-III)

| | | | | |
|---|---|---|---|---|
| Coriander leaves | 23.87 | **MUSHROOMS** | | |
| Chillies green-all varieties | 94.07 | Chicken mushroom, fresh | 0.45 | |
| **NUTS AND OIL SEEDS** | | **MISCELLANEOUS FOODS** | | |
| Almond | 0.74 | Coconut water | 0.64 | |
| Coconut kernel, fresh | 0.8 | **MILK AND MILK PRODUCTS** | | |
| Walnut | 0.88 | Milk, whole, cow | 2.01 | |
| **SUGAR** | | Milk, whole, buffalo | 2.37 | |
| Sugarcane, juice | 6.73 | | | |

*(Source: T. Longvah, R. Ananthan, K. Bhaskaracharya, K. Venkaiah. Indian Food Composition Tables, National Institute of Nutrition (Indian Council of Medical Research), 33-60, 2017)*

**--- Author ---**
Dr. Prajakta J. Nande

**Clinical and Therapeutic Nutrition Practical Manual 1**
For M.Sc. Food Science and Nutrition (Semester-III)

## ANNEXURE - 22

# LABORATORY REFERENCE VALUES: BLOOD, PLASMA AND SERUM

| Test | Specimen | Conventional Units | SI Units |
|---|---|---|---|
| Acetoacetate | Plasma | < 3 mg/L | < 0.3 mmol/L |
| Acetylcholinesterase (AChE), red blood cells | Blood | 26.7–49.2 U/g Hb | 1.72–3.17 x 106 U/mol Hb |
| Acid phosphatase (adults) | Serum | 0.5–5 U/L | 8–83 nkat/L |
| Activated partial thromboplastin time (aPTT) | Plasma | 30–40 seconds | — |
| Adrenocorticotropic hormone (ACTH) | Serum | 9–52 pg/mL (morning draw) | 2–11 pmol/L (morning draw) |
| Albumin | Serum | 3.5–5.4 g/dL | 35–54 g/L |
| Aldosterone: | | | |
| Standing | Serum | 7–20 ng/dL | 194–554 pmol/L |
| Supine | Serum | 2–5 ng/dL | 55–138 pmol/L |
| Alkaline phosphatase (ALP) | Serum | 36–150 U/L | 0.5–2.5 mckat/L |
| Alpha-1 antitrypsin (AAT) | Serum | 100–273 mg/dL | 18–50 mcmol/L |
| Alpha fetoprotein (AFP) | Serum | < 20 ng/mL | < 20 mcg/L |
| Aminolevulinic acid, Delta (ALA) | Serum | 15–23 mcg/L | 1.14–1.75 mcmol/L |
| Aminotransferase, alanine (ALT) | Serum | < 35 U/L | < 0.58 mckat/L |
| Aminotransferase, aspartate (AST) | Serum | < 35 U/L | < 0.58 mckat/L |
| Ammonia | Plasma | 40–80 mcg/dL | 23–47 mcmol/L |
| Amylase | Serum | < 110 U/L | < 1.8 mckat/L |
| Antibodies to extractable nuclear antigen (AENA) | Serum | < 20.0 units/mL | — |
| Anti–cyclic citrullinated peptide (anti-CCP) antibodies | Serum | ≤ 20 units/mL | — |
| Antidiuretic hormone (ADH; arginine vasopressin) | Plasma | < 1.7 pg/mL | < 1.57 pmol/L |
| Anti–double-stranded DNA (dsDNA) antibodies, IgG | Serum | < 25 IU | — |
| Antimitochondrial M2 antibodies | Serum | < 0.1 units | — |
| Antineutrophil cytoplasmic | Serum | Negative | — |

--- Author ---
Dr. Prajakta J. Nande

# Clinical and Therapeutic Nutrition Practical Manual 1
For M.Sc. Food Science and Nutrition (Semester-III)

| Test | Specimen | Conventional Units | SI Units |
|---|---|---|---|
| antibodies (cANCA) | | | |
| Antinuclear antibodies (ANA) | Serum | ≤ 1.0 units | — |
| Anti–smooth muscle antibodies (ASMA) titer | Serum | ≤ 1:80 | — |
| Antistreptolysin O titer | Serum | < 150 units | — |
| Antithyroid microsomal antibody titer | Serum | < 1:100 | — |
| +Antitrypsin, Alpha-1 (AAT) | Serum | 83–199 mg/dL | 15.3–36.6 mcmol/L |
| Apolipoproteins: | | | |
| A-I, females | Serum | 98–210 mg/dL | 0.98–2.1 g/L |
| A-I, males | Serum | 88–180 mg/dL | 0.88–1.8 g/L |
| B-100, females | Serum | 44–148 mg/dL | 0.44–1.48 g/L |
| B-100, males | Serum | 55–151 mg/dL | 0.55–1.51 g/L |
| Bicarbonate | Serum | 23–28 mEq/L | 23–28 mmol/L |
| Bilirubin: | | | |
| Direct | Serum | 0–0.3 mg/dL | 0–5.1 mcmol/L |
| Total | Serum | 0.3–1.2 mg/dL | 5.1–20.5 mcmol/L |
| Blood Volumes (Radioisotope Labeling): | | | |
| Plasma, females* | Blood | 28–43 mL/kg body wt | 0.028–0.043 L/kg body wt |
| Plasma, males* | Blood | 25–44 mL/kg body wt | 0.025–0.044 L/kg body wt |
| Red blood cells, females* | Blood | 20–30 mL/kg body wt | 0.02–0.03 L/kg body wt |
| Red blood cells, males* | Blood | 25–35 mL/kg body wt | 0.025–0.035 L/kg body wt |
| Brain (B-type) natriuretic peptide (BNP) | Plasma | < 100 pg/mL | < 100 ng/L |
| Calcitonin, age ≥ 16 years: | | | |
| Females | Serum | < 8 pg/mL | < 8ng/L |
| Males | Serum | < 16 pg/mL | < 16 ng/L |
| Calcium | Serum | 9–10.5 mg/dL | 2.2–2.6 mmol/L |
| Cancer antigen (CA): | | | |
| CA 125 | Serum | < 35 U/mL | < 35 kU/L |

# Clinical and Therapeutic Nutrition Practical Manual 1
For M.Sc. Food Science and Nutrition (Semester-III)

| Test | Specimen | Conventional Units | SI Units |
|---|---|---|---|
| CA 15-3 | Serum | < 30 U/mL | < 30 kU/L |
| Carbon dioxide (CO2) content | Serum | 23–28 mEq/L | 23–28 mmol/L |
| Carbon dioxide partial pressure (PCO2) | Blood | Arterial: 35–45 mm Hg<br>Venous: 38–50 mm Hg | Arterial: 4.7–6.0 kPa<br>Venous: 5.1–6.7 kPa |
| Carboxyhemoglobin | Plasma | 0.5–5% | — |
| Carcinoembryonic antigen (CEA) | Serum | < 3 ng/mL<br>Patients who smoke: < 5 ng/mL | < 3 mcg/L<br>Patients who smoke: < 5 mcg/L |
| Carotene | Serum | 75–300 mcg/dL | 1.4–5.6 mcmol/L |
| CD4:CD8 ratio | Blood | 1.0–4.0 | — |
| CD4+ T-cell count | Blood | 640–1175/mcL | 0.64–1.18 x 109/L |
| CD8+ T-cell count | Blood | 335–875/mcL | 0.34–0.88 x 109/L |
| Ceruloplasmin | Serum | 14–40 mg/dL | 0.93–2.65 mcmol/L |
| Chloride | Serum | 98–106 mEq/L | 98–106 mmol/L |
| Cholesterol, Desirable Level: | | | |
| High-density lipoprotein (HDL-C) | Plasma | ≥ 40 mg/dL | ≥ 1.04 mmol/L |
| Low-density lipoprotein (LDL-C) | Plasma | ≤ 130 mg/dL | ≤ 3.36 mmol/L |
| Total (TC) | Plasma | 150–199 mg/dL | 3.88–5.15 mmol/L |
| Coagulation factors: | | | |
| Factor I | Plasma | 150–300 mg/dL | 1.5–3.5 g/L |
| Factor II | Plasma | 60–150% of normal | — |
| Factor IX | Plasma | 60–150% of normal | — |
| Factor V | Plasma | 60–150% of normal | — |
| Factor VII | Plasma | 60–150% of normal | — |
| Factor VIII | Plasma | 60–150% of normal | — |
| Factor X | Plasma | 60–150% of normal | — |
| Factor XI | Plasma | 60–150% of normal | — |
| Factor XII | Plasma | 60–150% of normal | — |

Complement: (C3 and C4 are the most commonly measured complement components. A complement test may be used to monitor people with an autoimmune disorder. It is done to see if treatment for their condition is working. When the complement system is turned on during inflammation, levels of complement proteins may go down.)

# Clinical and Therapeutic Nutrition Practical Manual 1
For M.Sc. Food Science and Nutrition (Semester-III)

| Test | Specimen | Conventional Units | SI Units |
|------|----------|--------------------|----------|
| C3 | Serum | 90–180 mg/dL | 0.9–1.8 g/L |
| C4 | Serum | 10–40 mg/dL | 0.10–0.40 g/L |
| Total (CH50) | Serum | 30–75 U/mL | 30–75 kU/L |
| Copper | Serum | 70–155 mcg/dL | 11–24.3 mcmol/L |
| Cortisol: | | | |
| 1 hour after cosyntropin | Serum | > 18 mcg/dL and usually ≥ 8 mcg/dL above baseline | > 498 nmol/L and usually ≥ 221 nmol/L above baseline |
| At 5 PM | Serum | 3–13 mcg/dL | 83–359 nmol/L |
| At 8 AM | Serum | 8–20 mcg/dL | 251–552 nmol/L |
| After overnight suppression test | Serum | < 5 mcg/dL | < 138 nmol/L |
| C-peptide | Serum | 0.9–4.3 ng/mL | 297–1419 pmol/L |
| C-reactive protein (CRP) | Serum | < 0.8 mg/dL | < 8.0 mg/L |
| C-reactive protein, highly sensitive (hsCRP) | Serum | < 0.2 mg/dL | < 2.0 mg/L |
| Creatine kinase (CK) | Serum | 30–170 U/L | 0.5–2.83 mckat/L |
| Creatinine | Serum | Men: 0.7–1.2 mg/dL Women: 0.5–1.0 mg/dL | Men: 60–110 mcmol/L Women: 45–90 mcmol/L |
| D-dimer | Plasma | ≤ 500 ng/mL FEU (Fibrinogen Equivalent Units) | < 3 nmol/L FEU |
| Dehydroepiandrosterone Sulfate (DHEA-S): | | | |
| Females | Plasma | 0.6–3.3 mg/mL | 1.6–8.9 mcmol/L |
| Males | Plasma | 1.3–5.5 mg/mL | 3.5–14.9 mcmol/L |
| Delta-aminolevulinic acid (ALA) | Serum | 15–23 mcg/L | 1.14–1.75 mcmol/L |
| 11-Deoxycortisol (DOC): | | | |
| After metyrapone | Plasma | > 7 mcg/dL | > 203 nmol/L |
| Basal | Plasma | < 5 mcg/dL | < 145 nmol/L |
| D-Xylose level 2 hours after ingestion of 25 g of D-xylose | Serum | > 20 mg/dL | > 1.3 nmol/L |
| Epinephrine, supine | Plasma | < 75 ng/L | < 410 pmol/L |
| Erythrocyte Sedimentation Rate (ESR): | | | |
| Females | Blood | 0–20 mm/hour | 0–20 mm/hour |

# Clinical and Therapeutic Nutrition Practical Manual 1
For M.Sc. Food Science and Nutrition (Semester-III)

| Test | Specimen | Conventional Units | SI Units |
|---|---|---|---|
| Males | Blood | 0–15 mm/hour | 0–20 mm/hour |
| Erythropoietin | Serum | 2.6–18.5 mIU/mL | 2.6–18.5 IU/L |
| Estradiol, females: | | | |
| Day 1–10 of menstrual cycle | Serum | 14–27 pg/mL | 50–100 pmol/L |
| Day 11–20 of menstrual cycle | Serum | 14–54 pg/mL | 50–200 pmol/L |
| Day 21–30 of menstrual cycle | Serum | 19–40 pg/mL | 70–150 pmol/L |
| Estradiol, males | Serum | 10–30 pg/mL | 37–110 pmol/L |
| Ferritin: | | | |
| Females | Serum | 30–200 ng/mL | 30–200 mcg/L |
| Males | Serum | 30–300 ng/mL | 30–300 mcg/L |
| Fetoprotein, Alpha (AFP) | Serum | < 8.4 ng/mL | < 8.4 mcg/L |
| Fibrinogen | Plasma | 150–350 mg/dL | 1.5–3.5 g/L |
| Folate (Folic Acid): | | | |
| Red blood cells | Blood | 160–855 ng/mL | 362–1937 nmol/L |
| Serum | Serum | 2.5–20 ng/mL | 5.7–45.3 nmol/L |
| Follicle-Stimulating Hormone (FSH), females: | | | |
| Follicular or luteal phase | Serum | 5–20 mU/mL | 5–20 U/L |
| Midcycle peak | Serum | 30–50 mU/mL | 30–50 U/L |
| Postmenopausal | Serum | > 35 mU/mL | > 35 U/L |
| Follicle-stimulating hormone (FSH), adult males | Serum | 5–15 mU/mL | 5–15 U/L |
| Fructosamine (glycated protein) | Plasma | 200–285 mcmol/L | 200-285 mcmol/L |
| Gamma-glutamyl transpeptidase (GGT) | Serum | Adult male: 8–61 U/L Adult female: 5–36 U/L | Adult male: 0.14–1.03 mckat/L Adult female:0.09–0.61 mckat/L |
| Gastrin | Serum | 0–180 pg/mL | 0–180 ng/L |
| Globulins: | Serum | 2.5–3.5 g/dL | 25–35 g/L |
| Alpha-1 globulins | Serum | 0.2–0.4 g/dL | 2–4 g/L |
| Alpha-2 globulins | Serum | 0.5–0.9 g/dL | 5–9 g/L |
| Beta globulins | Serum | 0.6–1.1 g/dL | 6–11 g/L |
| Beta-2 microglobulin | Serum | 0.7–1.8 mcg/mL | 0.7–1.8 mg/L |
| Gamma globulins | Serum | 0.7–1.7 g/dL | 7–17 g/L |

--- Author ---
Dr. Prajakta J. Nande

# Clinical and Therapeutic Nutrition Practical Manual 1

For M.Sc. Food Science and Nutrition (Semester-III)

| Test | Specimen | Conventional Units | SI Units |
|---|---|---|---|
| Glucose: | | | |
| 2-hour postprandial | Plasma | < 140 mg/dL | < 7.8 mmol/L |
| Fasting | Plasma | 70–105 mg/dL | 3.9–5.8 mmol/L |
| Glucose-6-phosphate dehydrogenase (G6PD) | Blood | 5–15 U/g Hb | 0.32–0.97 mU/ mol Hb |
| Glutamyl transpeptidase, Gamma (GGT) | Serum | Adult male: 8–61 U/L Adult female: 5–36 U/L | Adult male: 0.14–1.03 mckat/L Adult female: 0.09–0.61 mckat/L |
| Growth Hormone: | | | |
| After oral glucose | Plasma | < 2 ng/mL | < 2 mcg/L |
| In response to provocative stimuli | Plasma | > 7 ng/mL | > 7 mcg/L |
| Haptoglobin | Serum | 30–200 mg/dL | 0.3–2 g/L |
| Hematocrit: | | | |
| Females | Blood | 36–47% | — |
| Males | Blood | 41–51% | — |
| Hemoglobin: | | | |
| Females | Blood | 12–16 g/dL | 120–160 g/L |
| Males | Blood | 14–17 g/dL | 140–170 g/L |
| Hemoglobin A1C | Blood | 4.7–8.5% | — |

Hemoglobin Electrophoresis, Adults

(It measures the different types of hemoglobin in blood and checks for hemoglobinopathy, which are disorders caused by abnormal types of hemoglobin. The test can help diagnose serious conditions like sickle cell anemia, and is also one of several tests that screen newborn babies for sickle cell anemia and other rare but serious illnesses. It can also be used to check treatment for diseases with abnormal hemoglobin, and to help couples find out how likely they are to have a child with certain inherited forms of anemia.)

| | | | |
|---|---|---|---|
| Hb A1 | Blood | 95–98% | — |
| Hb A2 | Blood | 2–3% | — |
| Hb C | Blood | 0% | — |
| Hb F | Blood | 0.8–2.0% | — |
| Hb S | Blood | 0% | — |
| Hemoglobin Electrophoresis, Hb F in Children: | | | |
| Neonate | Blood | 50–80% | — |
| 1–6 months | Blood | 8% | — |

# Clinical and Therapeutic Nutrition Practical Manual 1

For M.Sc. Food Science and Nutrition (Semester-III)

| Test | Specimen | Conventional Units | SI Units |
|------|----------|---------------------|----------|
| > 6 months | Blood | 1–2% | — |
| Homocysteine: | | | |
| Females | Plasma | 0.40–1.89 mg/L | 3–14 mcmol/L |
| Males | Plasma | 0.54–2.16 mg/L | 4–16 mcmol/L |
| Human chorionic gonadotropin (hCG), quantitative | Serum | < 5 mIU/mL | < 5 IU/L |
| Immunoglobulins: | | | |
| IgA | Serum | 70–300 mg/dL | 0.7–3.0 g/L |
| IgD | Serum | < 8 mg/dL | < 80 mg/L |
| IgE | Serum | 0.01–0.04 mg/dL | 0.1–0.4 mg/L |
| IgG | Serum | 640–1430 mg/dL | 6.4–14.3 g/L |
| IgG1 | Serum | 280–1020 mg/dL | 2.8–10.2 g/L |
| IgG2 | Serum | 60–790 mg/dL | 0.6–7.9 g/L |
| IgG3 | Serum | 14–240 mg/dL | 0.14–2.4 g/L |
| IgG4 | Serum | 11–330 mg/dL | 0.11–3.3 g/L |
| IgM | Serum | 20–140 mg/dL | 0.2–1.4 g/L |
| Insulin, fasting | Serum | 2.6–24.9 mcIU/mL | 15.6–149.4 pmol/L |

International Normalized Ratio (INR): It is the preferred test of choice for patients taking vitamin K antagonists (VKA). It can also be used to assess the risk of bleeding or the coagulation status of the patients. Patients taking oral anticoagulants are required to monitor INR to adjust the VKA doses because these vary between patients. The INR is derived from prothrombin time (PT) which is calculated as a ratio of the patient's PT to a control PT standardized for the potency of the thromboplastin reagent developed by the World Health Organization (WHO) using the formula: INR = Patient PT ÷ Control PT

PT, the time in seconds, is measured in plasma to form a clot in the presence of sufficient concentration of calcium and tissue thromboplastin by activating coagulation via the extrinsic pathway. INR monitoring is most commonly required for the patients who are on warfarin, a vitamin K antagonist. The dose of warfarin is adapted based on INR scores so that it remains in the therapeutic range to prevent thrombosis from subtherapeutic INR or hemorrhagic complications from supratherapeutic INR. The anticoagulant effect of warfarin indicated by an INR in the target range also guides when to discontinue heparin. A subtherapeutic international normalized ratio (INR) is an INR level that is below the target range. For example, an INR of less than 2.0 is considered subtherapeutic. A subtherapeutic INR can increase the risk of thrombosis, such as recurrent venous thromboembolism. In patients taking warfarin, a subtherapeutic INR can also increase the risk of symptomatic intracerebral hemorrhage after intravenous Thrombolysis. Supratherapeutic international normalized ratio (INR) is an INR level that is above the therapeutic range and can indicate a significant risk of bleeding. Bleeding can occur in the gastrointestinal tract, hematuria, or intracranial hemorrhage.)

--- Author ---

Dr. Prajakta J. Nande

# Clinical and Therapeutic Nutrition Practical Manual 1
For M.Sc. Food Science and Nutrition (Semester-III)

| Test | Specimen | Conventional Units | SI Units |
|---|---|---|---|
| Therapeutic range (standard intensity therapy) | Plasma | 2.0–3.0 | — |
| Therapeutic range in higher risk patients (eg, those with prosthetic heart valves) | Plasma | 2.5–3.5 | — |
| Therapeutic range in patients with lupus anticoagulant | Plasma | 3.0–3.5 | — |
| Iron | Serum | Males: 50–150 mcg/dL Females: 35–145 mcg/dL | Males: 9.2–27.5 mcmol/L Females: 6.4–26.5 mcmol/L |
| Iron-binding capacity, total (TIBC) | Serum | 250–460 mcg/dL | 45–82 mcmol/L |
| Lactate dehydrogenase (LDH) | Serum | 60–160 U/L | 1–1.67 mckat/L |
| Lactic acid, venous | Blood | 6–16 mg/dL | 0.67–1.8 mmol/L |
| Lactose tolerance test | Plasma | > 15 mg/dL increase in plasma glucose level | > 0.83 mmol/L increase in plasma glucose level |
| Lead | Blood | Pediatric patients: < 20 mcg/dL Adult patients: < 80 mcg/dL | Pediatric patients: < 0.97 mcmol/L Adult patients: < 3.86 mcmol/L |
| Leukocyte alkaline phosphatase (LAP) score | Peripheral blood smear | 13–130/100/ polymorphonuclear (PMN) leukocyte neutrophils and bands | — |
| Lipase | Serum | < 95 U/L | < 1.58 mckat/L |
| Lipoprotein (a) [Lp(a)] | Serum | ≤ 10 mg/dL | < 13nmol/L |
| Luteinizing hormone (LH), females: | | | |
| Follicular or luteal phase | Serum | 5–22 mU/mL | 5–22 U/L |
| Midcycle peak | Serum | 30–250 mU/mL | 30–250 U/L |
| Postmenopausal | Serum | > 30 mU/mL | > 30 U/L |
| Luteinizing hormone, males | Serum | 3–15 mU/mL | 3–15 U/L |
| Magnesium | Serum | 1.5–2.4 mg/dL | 0.62–0.99 mmol/L |
| Manganese | Serum | 0.3–0.9 ng/mL | 5.5–16.4 nmol/L |
| Mean corpuscular hemoglobin (MCH) | Blood | 28–32 pg | — |

--- Author ---
Dr. Prajakta J. Nande

# Clinical and Therapeutic Nutrition Practical Manual 1
For M.Sc. Food Science and Nutrition (Semester-III)

| Test | Specimen | Conventional Units | SI Units |
|------|----------|--------------------|----------|
| Mean corpuscular hemoglobin concentration (MCHC) | Blood | 32–36 g/dL | 320–360 g/L |
| Mean corpuscular volume (MCV) | Blood | 80–100 fL | — |
| Metanephrines, Fractionated: (A metanephrines test measures the amount of metanephrine and normetanephrine in a patient's blood or urine to help diagnose or rule out rare tumors of the adrenal gland or outside the adrenal glands. These tumors are called pheochromocytomas and paragangliomas, and they produce excess hormones called catecholamines that break down into metanephrines) | | | |
| Metanephrines, free | Plasma | < 0.50 nmol/L | — |
| Normetanephrines, free | Plasma | < 0.90 nmol/L | — |
| Methemoglobin | Blood | < 1.0% | — |
| Methylmalonic acid (MMA) | Serum | ≤ 400 nmol/L | 47.2 ng/L |
| Myoglobin: | | | |
| Females | Serum | 25–58 mcg/L | 1.4–3.5 nmol/L |
| Males | Serum | 28–72 mcg/L | 1.6–4.1 nmol/L |
| Norepinephrine, supine | Plasma | 50–440 pg/mL | 0.3–2.6 nmol/L |
| N-Terminal propeptide of BNP (NT-proBNP) | Plasma | < 75 years: < 125 pg/mL <br> ≥ 75 years: < 450 pg/mL | < 125 ng/L <br> < 450 ng/L |
| 5'-Nucleotidase (5'NT) | Serum | 4–11.5 U/L | — |
| Osmolality | Plasma | 275–295 mOsm/kg $H_2O$ | 275–295 mmol/ kg $H_2O$ |
| Osmotic fragility test | Blood | Increased fragility if hemolysis occurs in > 0.5% sodium chloride <br> Decreased fragility if hemolysis is incomplete in 0.3% sodium chloride | — |
| Oxygen partial pressure (PO2) | Blood | Arterial: 80–100 mm Hg | 10.7–13.3 kPa |
| Parathyroid hormone (PTH) | Serum | 10–65 pg/mL | 10–65 ng/L |
| Parathyroid hormone–related peptide (PTHrP) | Plasma | < 2.0 pmol/L | — |
| Partial thromboplastin time, activated (aPTT) | Plasma | 25–35 seconds | — |

--- Author ---
Dr. Prajakta J. Nande

# Clinical and Therapeutic Nutrition Practical Manual 1
For M.Sc. Food Science and Nutrition (Semester-III)

| Test | Specimen | Conventional Units | SI Units |
|---|---|---|---|
| pH | Blood | Arterial: 7.35–7.45 <br> Venous: 7.32–7.43 | — <br> — |
| Phosphorus, inorganic | Serum | 3.0–4.5 mg/dL | 0.97–1.45 mmol/L |
| Platelet count | Blood | 150–350 x 103/mcL | 150–350 x 109/L |
| Platelet life span, using chromium-51 (51Cr) | — | 8–12 days | — |
| Porphyrins | Plasma | ≤ 1.0 mcg/dL | ≤ 10 mcg/L |
| Potassium | Serum | 3.5–5 mEq/L | 3.5–5 mmol/L |
| Prealbumin (transthyretin) | Serum | 18–45 mg/dL | 180–450 mg/L |
| Progesterone: | | | |
| Follicular phase | Serum | < 1 ng/mL | < 0.03 nmol/L |
| Luteal phase | Serum | 3–30 ng/mL | 0.1–0.95 nmol/L |
| Prolactin: | | | |
| Females (nonpregnant) | Serum | < 20 mcg/L | < 870 pmol/L |
| Males | Serum | < 15 mcg/L | < 652 pmol/L |
| Prostate-specific antigen, total (PSA-T) | Serum | 0–4 ng/mL | 0–4 mcg/L |
| Prostate-specific antigen, ratio of free to total (PSA-F:PSA-T) | Serum | > 0.25 | — |
| Protein C activity | Plasma | 67–131% | — |
| Protein C resistance, activated ratio (APC-R) | Plasma | 2.2–2.6 | — |
| Protein S activity | Plasma | 82–144% | — |
| Protein, total | Serum | 6–7.8 g/dL | 60–78 g/L |
| Prothrombin time (PT) | Plasma | 11–13 seconds | — |
| Pyruvic acid | Blood | 0.08–0.16 mmol/L | — |
| Red blood cell count | Blood | 4.2–5.9 x 106 cells/mcL | 4.2–5.9 x 1012 cells/L |
| Red blood cell survival rate, using 51Cr | Blood | T1/2 = 28 days | — |

Renin Activity, Plasma (PRA), (Upright, in males and females aged 18–39 years): (Standing upright can cause a rise in plasma renin activity (PRA) that starts within 15 minutes and peaks between 60 and 120 minutes. This increase is due to changes in the amount of the enzyme, not other elements of the renin-angiotensin system. Upright posture can increase PRA regardless of sodium intake in the diet)

# Clinical and Therapeutic Nutrition Practical Manual 1
For M.Sc. Food Science and Nutrition (Semester-III)

| Test | Specimen | Conventional Units | SI Units |
|---|---|---|---|
| Sodium-depleted | Plasma | 2.9–24 ng/mL/hour | 2.9–24 mcg/L/hour |
| Sodium-repleted | Plasma | 0.6 (or lower)–4.3 ng/mL/hour | 0.6 (or lower)–4.3 mcg/L/hour |
| Reticulocyte Count: | | | |
| Percentage | Blood | 0.5–1.5% | — |
| Absolute | Blood | 23–90 x 103/mcL | 23–90 x 109/L |
| Rheumatoid factor (RF), by nephelometry | Serum | < 20 IU/mL | < 20 kIU/L |
| Sodium | Serum | 136–145 mEq/L | 136–145 mmol/L |
| Testosterone (Total), Adults: | | | |
| Females | Serum | 20–75 ng/dL | 0.7–2.6 nmol/L |
| Males | Serum | 300–1200 ng/dL | 10–42 nmol/L |
| Thrombin time | Plasma | 18.5–24 seconds | — |
| Thyroid iodine-123 (123I) uptake | — | 5–30% of administered dose at 24 hour | — |
| Thyroid-stimulating hormone (TSH) | Serum | 0.5–5.0 mcIU/mL | 0.5–5.0 mIU/L |
| Thyroxine (T4): | | | |
| Free | Serum | 0.9–2.4 ng/dL | 12–31 pmol/L |
| Free index | — | 4–11 | — |
| Total | Serum | 5–12 mcg/dL | 64–155 nmol/L |
| Transferrin | Serum | 200–360 mg/dL | 2.0–3.6 g/L |
| Transferrin saturation | Serum | 20–50% | — |
| Triglycerides (fasting) | Serum | Normal: < 150 mg/dL Borderline: 150–199 mg/dL High: 200–499 mg/dL Very high: ≥ 500 mg/dL | Normal: < 1.69 mmol/L Borderline: 1.69–2.25 mmol/L High: 2.26–5.64 mmol/L Very high: > 5.65 mmol/L |
| Triiodothyronine (T3): | | | |
| Uptake | Serum | 25–35% | — |
| Total | Serum | 70–195 ng/dL | 1.1–3.0 nmol/L |
| Troponin I (Contemporary assay) | Plasma | < 0.04 ng/mL | < 0.04 mcg/L |

--- Author ---
Dr. Prajakta J. Nande

# Clinical and Therapeutic Nutrition Practical Manual 1
For M.Sc. Food Science and Nutrition (Semester-III)

| Test | Specimen | Conventional Units | SI Units |
|------|----------|--------------------|----------|
| Troponin I, highly sensitive (hs-TnI) | Serum | Females: ≤ 10 ng/L <br> Males: ≤ 15 ng/L | <1.0 mcg/L <br> <1.5 mcg/L |
| Troponin T (Contemporary assay) | Serum | ≤ 0.03 ng/mL | ≤ 0.03 mcg/L |
| Troponin T, highly sensitive (hs-TnT) | Serum | Females: ≤ 10 ng/L <br> Males: ≤ 15 ng/L | <1.0 mcg/L <br> <1.5 mcg/L |
| Urea nitrogen (BUN) | Serum | 8–20 mg/dL | 2.9–7.1 mmol/L |
| Uric acid | Serum | 2.5–8 mg/dL | 0.15–0.47 mmol/L |
| Vitamin B12 | Serum | 200–800 pg/mL | 148–590 pmol/L |
| Vitamin C (Ascorbic Acid): | | | |
| Leukocyte | Blood | < 20 mg/dL | < 1136 mcmol/L |
| Total | Blood | 0.4–1.5 mg/dL | 23–85 mcmol/L |
| Vitamin D: | | | |
| 1,25-Dihydroxycholecalciferol (calcitriol) | Serum | 25–65 pg/mL | 65–169 pmol/L |
| 25-Hydroxycholecalciferol | Serum | 15–80 ng/mL | 37–200 nmol/L |
| White blood cell count | Blood | 4.5–11 x 103 cells/mcL | 4.5–11 x 109 cells/L |
| Segmented neutrophils | | 2.6–8.5 x 103 cells/mcL | 2.6–8.5 x 109 cells/L |
| Band neutrophils | | 0–1.2 x 103 cells/mcL | 0–1.2 x 109 cells/L |
| Lymphocytes | | 0.77–4.5 x 103 cells/mcL | 0.77–4.5 x 109 cells/L |
| Monocytes | | 0.14–1.3 x 103 cells/mcL | 0.14–1.3 x 109 cells/L |
| Eosinophils | | 0–0.55 x 103 cells/mcL | 0–0.55 x 109 cells/L |
| Basophils | | 0–0.22 x 103 cells/mcL | 0–0.22 x 109 cells/L |
| Zinc | Serum | 66–110 mcg/dL | 10.1–16.8 mcmol/L |

*American Board of Internal Medicine: ABIM Laboratory Test Reference Ranges−July 2021; Cited from https://www.msdmanuals.com/en-in/professional/multimedia/table/representative-laboratory-reference-values-blood-plasma-and-serum on 28-08-2024 at IST 10.48 pm.

mckat = microkatal; pkat = picokatal.

--- Author ---
Dr. Prajakta J. Nande

www.ingramcontent.com/pod-product-compliance
Ingram Content Group UK Ltd.
Pitfield, Milton Keynes, MK11 3LW, UK
UKHW060214240426
12048UKWH00031BB/1725